THE ENGLISH CHORISTER

The English Chorister

A History

Alan Mould

hambledon
continuum

Hambledon Continuum is an imprint of Continuum Books
Continuum UK, The Tower Building, 11 York Road, London SE1 7NX
Continuum US, 80 Maiden Lane, Suite 704, New York, NY 10038

www.continuumbooks.com

First published 2007
Reprinted 2007

British Library Cataloguing-in-Publication Data
A catalogue record for this book is available from the British Library.

ISBN 1 85285 513 4 (Hardback)
ISBN 1 8472 5058 0 (Paperback)

Typeset by Egan Reid Ltd, Auckland, New Zealand
Printed and bound by MPG Books Ltd, Cornwall, Great Britain

Contents

Illustrations

Plates

Between Pages 174 and 175

Text Illustrations

Tables

for
Chorister Grandson
Tom

Ex ore infantium
perfecisti laudem

Acknowledgements

I am deeply indebted to four people. Roger Bowers's published research underlies a great deal of the material in the early chapters. He not only responded to letters and e-mails on matters of detail with alacrity but undertook to read through the medieval material when it was complete. His notes on the text were of exceptional generosity and enabled the correction of very many errors. Michael Barcroft showed similar kindness in reading and commenting on everything prior to the eighteenth century. He courteously dealt with infelicities of style and presentation, encouraging me to reorder or to rewrite text when greater clarity was needed. Richard Osmond generously undertook the heavy labour of reading the proofs, bringing a fresh eye to a text over familiar to the author. Jane Capon read all but the final chapters and has been a constant source of encouragement. None of them bears responsibility for any mistakes that remain, which are wholly the responsibility of the author.

On particular matters, help has come from many friends, colleagues and local experts. Brian Crosby (Durham) and David Baldwin (the Chapel Royal), both authors of indispensable books, responded most helpfully to queries. David Gahan, with great generosity, sent to me his research notes on the early history of the choir of St John's College, Cambridge, and provided information on successive Canterbury choir schools. A photocopy of Maria Hackett's *Brief Account*, along with other materials, was made for me in the 1980s by the late Lydia Smallwood, when I was preparing a talk. To have Hackett's *Brief Account* complete on my desk, when working on the chapters on Victorian choristers, was invaluable. Andrew Dobbins put the choristers' common room at St Paul's at my disposal, thereby bringing to light unique material not only on former St Paul's choristers but also on the founding and early days of the Choir Schools' Association. Work on CSA was also aided by Tim Ham and John Morris, who opened the archives respectively of the Independent Schools' Association (ISA) and the Incorporated Association of Preparatory Schools (IAPS) to me. Michael Barry and David Horner provided material for the history of the Federation of Old Choristers' Associations, as did Michael Cook for the Friends of Cathedral Music. Tim Allerton wrote me a detailed eyewitness account of the closing months of the Eton Choir School. Robert Western shone a light into the mists that shrouded facets of the Lincoln choristers' education. Peter Preece sent me fascinating information about the London College of Choristers, having been a chorister there himself in the 1930s. Barry Ferguson, by way of encouragement, has kept slipping me bits of information. Michael Barcroft, Stephen Cleobury and the late Lionel Dakers made time to meet me and discuss matters concerning the training of the twentieth-century choristers. Many other friends and colleagues have also helped in expected and unexpected ways. I thank them all.

Books on individual foundations or photocopies of material were sent to me, often as gifts, by the late George Guest (Bangor), Kevin Riley (Bristol), Stephen Drew (Durham), Jennifer Rimer and Dennis Townhill (Edinburgh), Vivian Bairstow (Eton), Michael Barry (Guildford), Tim Lowe (Hereford), Andrew Corbett (King's College, Cambridge), Jonathon Edmunds (New College, Oxford), Paul Greenfield and Robert Woodcock (Norwich), Christopher Nickless (Rochester), Barry Lyndon and D.P. Symonds (Tenbury), Mrs Elizabeth Cairncross (Wells), Brian Rees (Winchester) and Tim Keyes (Worcester).

No matter how helpful individuals and the books on my shelves have been, the bulk of the research has been dependent on libraries. Over seven years I have failed to meet a single unhelpful librarian. Exeter Cathedral and the Education Faculty of Exeter University provided me with priceless materials on R.H. Couchman. The librarian of Westminster Abbey produced the final piece of the jigsaw puzzle that explained the founding of CSA. The staff of St John's College Library, Cambridge, made available the whole run of the *Gentleman's Magazine* in which Maria Hackett first appeared in print. Most of the materials on Maria Hackett, however, are in the Manuscript Room of the Guildhall Library and here, too, I have enjoyed the best of help. The British Library found materials for me not available elsewhere. But for the past six years two libraries have been central to my work. Along the Cambridge University Library's miles of open shelves, stacked with both books and journals, one is constantly led from the known to the unknown. Its lending privileges for alumni are of extraordinary generosity. To its librarians queries are not bothers but welcome challenges. Special thanks must be expressed to the staffs of the Anderson Room (music), the Rare Books Room and the Official Publications Room. My second home for five years has been the library of Sarum College in the Close at Salisbury. Welcomed by Tim Macquiban, the principal, and Linda Cooper and her staff, and sustained by its unfailingly good catering and guided by the smiling librarians Jenny Monds and Helen Tandy, much of the book has been written here, mostly in one of the library's satellite 'padded cells' where solitude and silence have made sustained writing possible.

Late in 1998 Jane Capon, information officer of the Choir Schools' Association, thought that the association should have its history written. The CSA committee agreed and early in 1999, recently retired, I undertook to investigate the archives.

A shock was in store: all the association's records for its first quarter century had been lost in the Second World War. The next step was to investigate the possibility of writing a history of the choir schools themselves. From this, but guided by my publisher, Martin Sheppard, who insisted that, whilst the choir schools risked being a dull subject, choristers themselves were full of interest, emerged the idea for this history. Jane Capon and successive members of the CSA committee, notably Howard Tomlinson, have subsequently given enthusiastic backing to the venture, voting generous contributions towards research expenses. In return, a proportion of royalties from the book will benefit the Choir Schools' Association Bursary Trust, which provides funds towards the fees of choristers from families less able to afford them.

That I have been able to research and write this book is thanks to my wife, Nesta, who not only agreed with me that the book should be written, patiently accepting the theft of five and more years of what were supposed to be our retirement together, but urged me to buy a laptop to make use of Sarum College's facilities. If Jane Capon was the book's originator in 1999, Nesta has been its facilitator and my sustainer ever since. She alone has borne the strain and ensured its completion.

When in June 2002 Martin Sheppard agreed to publish the book, we both thought that perhaps two years might see the work finished. His sympathetic acceptance of the fact that the writing and research has taken twice as long as expected, and that it has resulted in a book much longer than first agreed, is as remarkable as the sharpness of his eye and his tolerance in dealing with my drafts, along with his professional ability to imagine the book in print from the beginning. Subsequently, Ben Hayes, Lois Taylor and Anya Wilson of Continuum have brought both high professional skills and great kindness in seeing the book through its final pre-publication stages.

Final thanks must go to those who led me to value the English chorister as a cultural and spiritual treasure whose history called for celebration: the singing boys in the choir schools with whom I lived and worked and worshipped for more than two decades, the source of so much laughter alongside the beauty of holiness and the holiness of beauty. They are the *sine qua non* of all that follows.

Abbreviations

BL	British Library
CSP	*Calendar of State Papers*
DNB	*Dictionary of National Biography*
MS(S)	Manuscript(s)
NGD	*New Grove Dictionary of Music and Musicians*
ODNB	*Oxford Dictionary of National Biography*
PP	Parliamentary Papers
TNA	The National Archive (formerly Public Records Office)
VCH	Victoria County History

Introduction

Choristers have sung services in the choirs of England's cathedrals and other large churches for over fourteen hundred years and continue to do so today. The term is often loosely used to describe any group of singers, whatever their ages. The chorus members of English opera houses are often described as 'choristers'. Sometimes even solo singers are called choristers. Poets call birds choristers. This looseness has a long history. In the seventeenth century Lieutenant Hammond, who went on two long tours of the country keeping in his journal accounts of the various cathedral services he attended, wrote enthusiastically of 'snowy white choristers'. At times when describing 'choristers' he is clearly referring to the boys, at others he is equally clearly describing the whole choir of boys and men. On the other hand, the word can have a very precise and technical meaning. The word – or rather its Latin forebear – emerged in the second half of the thirteenth century as *chorista* or *querista* and it referred exclusively to a boy with unbroken voice singing in the choir of a secular (meaning non-monastic) cathedral. Prior to the thirteenth century they had simply been *pueri* – boys. (In the early middle ages the boys who sang in the choirs of monasteries and the girls who sang in nunneries were called oblates rather than choristers.) The boys who later in the middle ages sang in the Lady chapel choirs were called *pueri de capella* (chapel boys) or *clerici beate Marie* (clerks of the blessed Mary). Today there is a clear definition used by anyone who works in the world of cathedral music: a chorister is a boy or a girl who sings in the choir of a choral foundation. Boys and girls who sing in ordinary parish choirs are 'choirboys' and 'choirgirls'. It is this definition of 'chorister' – a boy or a girl who sings in the choir of a choral foundation – that has given this book its title and this is the sense in which it will be used throughout.

A 'choral foundation' refers to a church (or cathedral or monastery) in which a force of choral singers has been established, whether by statute, custom or endowment, to sing regularly. This book is a history of choristers singing in cathedrals, whether secular cathedrals like Chichester and Hereford or those that were originally monastic, like Ely and Winchester. It is also a history of choristers singing in collegiate foundations such as St George's, Windsor, and those such as Eton and King's College, Cambridge, which have combined the roles of education and prayer. Finally, it includes those few parish churches where daily services have been or are still required to be sung chorally.

These sung services fall into two main categories: the sacramental eucharist, or mass or holy communion, and the non-sacramental 'offices'. In the middle ages both the monastic and the secular choirs, in obedience to the Psalmist's 'seven times a day will I praise Thee', sang matins, prime, terce, sext, none, vespers and compline, spread out through the day and the night. At the Reformation Thomas Cranmer devised, from four of these offices, the Anglican services of matins (morning prayer) and evensong (evening prayer). The singing of the offices of matins and evensong has been the heart of the choristers' work in the Church of England since the sixteenth century. Choirs generally sing in 'quires', the semi-enclosed spaces traditionally found eastward of the nave. This distinction of spelling is useful in distinguishing the singers (the choir) from the part of the cathedral or church in which they sing (the quire).

The medieval secular cathedrals had singing boys as part of their community from their foundation. At the Reformation there was no break in these cathedrals: the boys and men of the choir remained in post and adjusted to the new vernacular liturgy. The Benedictine and Augustinian monasteries, including those that were also cathedrals, used singing boys – oblates – until about the middle of the twelfth century when they were deemed unsuitable for a monastery. Thereafter, it was not until about the late 1530s, after the Dissolution, that boys returned to sing in such quires as those of Durham and Canterbury. But even here there was a link with the monastic years, because generally from the late fourteenth century almonry boys had sung in their Lady chapels. We know for certain from Durham, and by probability from everywhere else, that these boys formed the nucleus of the post-Dissolution treble line. If a choral foundation clearly employed choristers in the sixteenth century, I have traced the history of that foundation both before the boys were strictly choristers (as in the monastic Lady chapels) and after that foundation ceased singing daily services (as the Chapel Royal did in the eighteenth century). In all the cathedrals the Commonwealth brought about a hiatus.

This is a history of the *English* chorister, because the choral foundations of the British Isles were overwhelmingly in England. But where choral foundations in Wales, Scotland or Ireland played a significant part, I have used them to provide evidence. It is fundamentally a history of the *office* of chorister, of choristerships, but individual boys, and more rarely girls, feature to lend colour and particularity, humour and pathos, to the story.

Any author trying to cover fourteen hundred years of developments in some fifty foundations inevitably has to rely on the work of others more than on primary research. Fortunately there are many excellent printed editions of documents essential to the story. There are also some fine local histories specifically of the choristers, such are Dora Robertson's moving *Sarum Close* and the histories of the Durham choristers by Brian Crosby and those of St George's, Windsor, by Neville Wridgway. Choristers are often found centre stage in the broader school histories that have been written for about half the choir schools. There is, of course, much literature about the cathedrals. Particularly helpful are the volumes published in recent years on Canterbury, Hereford, Lincoln, Norwich, St Paul's and York. Choristers also make frequent appearances in the huge literature on church music. What is disappointing is to note that the histories of education (a dying genre) have, after the medieval period, almost nothing to say about choir schools and chorister education. Finally, in the last two centuries, increasing numbers of choristers have put pen to paper and left record of what being a chorister was actually like. Constraints of space have made it impossible to include more than a modest selection from these records.

This first history of the English chorister ventures onto largely untilled ground. I hope it will not only be useful and enjoyable to the general reader, but that it will also stimulate research into some of the many areas where I have done little more than turn over the topsoil. Maria Hackett, in the introduction to her *Brief Account of the Cathedral and Collegiate Schools* (1827) wrote: 'The following pages, in their present imperfect state … are open to the liberal criticism which will correct an error without asperity, or supply an omission with courtesy and candour.' I can hope for no more.

1

Beginnings

The use of boy choristers in Christian worship reflects the practice of the Jewish Temple. Intermittently during the first millennium BC the Jews had maintained a song school in which not only men but also Levite boys were trained to sing the psalms, their unbroken voices adding sweetness to the deeper adult sound.[1] In the Christian gospels, Mark and Matthew describe Jesus and his disciples singing hymns, presumably the Jewish Passover Hallel psalms, at the close of the Last Supper. Paul urges the singing of hymns and psalms,[2] and several passages in his letters look like fragments of liturgical text that could be said or sung as appropriate. Clemens Romanus, pope in the final decade of the first century, a Roman of Jewish parentage, commends, in his *Epistle to the Corinthians*, the singing of psalms and hymns, provided they are sung in the context of acts of worship.[3] But this is not to claim direct continuity. Although Jewish practice, especially the practice of domestic worship, may have been a model for some in the early church, the links between Jewish and Christian liturgy in the early Christian centuries were probably slight.[4]

For three hundred years the Christians were a threatened, clandestine sect, their gatherings conducted behind closed doors. 'Churches' were congregations of worshippers, not buildings in which to worship. But that there was singing when circumstances permitted can hardly be in doubt. As George Herbert was to put it:

> The Church with psalms *must* shout,
> No door can keep them out.

Significant liturgical material has survived from these heroic first centuries of the church, such as the *Apology of Justin* from the mid-second century and the anonymous *Didache* from a similar period or earlier. It has been widely accepted that by the close of the second century the 'four-action shape' of the eucharist as we know it today had emerged.[5] This certainty is now challenged; indeed it has been said that the effect of recent liturgical scholarship has been to reduce rather than increase our corpus of knowledge.[6] Nevertheless, one thing must be certain: there can hardly have been scope for formal choral establishments during the first three Christian centuries.

Then in 313 AD the Emperor Constantine by the Edict of Milan lifted the ban on Christian worship. The whole picture was suddenly changed, as if dam gates had burst open. Under Pope Sylvester I (314–36) churches were built; for half a century there was a wave of widespread liturgical consolidation. Councils of the church were convened to encourage uniformity of doctrine, most notably the First Council of Nicaea (325 AD), which defined the fundamentals of Christian faith as articulated in its Nicene creed. And it was during Sylvester's papacy that the *Schola Cantorum*, a song school, was established at Rome for the training of both adult and boy singers.

Elsewhere communities could already be found developing primitive forms of monasticism, for whom a daily cycle of worship was their chief *raison d'être*. Here too bodies of custom that must have included song were being built up and taught to novices. It may or may not have been from one such that the earliest surviving Christian music derives: the fragmentary Oxyrhynchus papyrus. This contains, written on the back of a cereals bill, what appears to be a late third-century solo hymn in the Greek diatonic manner from an Egyptian Christian congregation.

Outside the monastic communities, it was in the bishops' households, their *familiae*, that boys were given a Christian education, central to which was the learning of music for worship and its expression in the liturgy. We know that the first of Sylvester's councils, the Council of Arles in 314, was attended by three British bishops, including Eborius of York. Can we assume that within their *familiae*, alongside priests and deacons, were some of the first English boy choristers? It is a reasonable possibility but with absolutely no evidence to substantiate it. In any case, the British church fell victim to the heathen Anglo-Saxon invaders, its surviving clergy driven to the Celtic fringes, where it continued, largely independent of Rome and unknown to the rest of Christendom, with liturgies increasingly idiosyncratic.

Reliable evidence begins to accumulate with the sending by Pope Gregory I of a mission to Britain in 596 led by Augustine. The following year the Kentish King Ethelbert, after meeting Augustine and his companions on the Isle of Thanet, invited them to Canterbury. Bede describes their arrival: 'Tradition says that as they approached the city, bearing the holy cross and the likeness of our great King and the Lord Jesus Christ as was their custom, they sang in unison a litany.'[7] Augustine had been a monk in Rome and most of his companions were also under monastic vows. They will have learnt Roman liturgical practice and almost certainly entered Canterbury singing plainsong after the Roman manner.

Augustine's first necessity at Canterbury was to establish, in property given to him by the king, a *familia*, a household committed to a routine of worship, from which would spring his missionary endeavour. There was a huge task of training and teaching to be done, even amongst his own missionary party. His forty young monks may well have included only one or a few in priest's orders. Some Frankish presbyters had joined him; and he had brought some slave boys from Rome, partly no doubt as domestics and perhaps because they spoke the vernacular.

Bede describes how at first their worship took place in the little church of St Martin, built during the Roman occupation, where Ethelbert's Christian queen, Bertha, used to go to pray. After Ethelbert had himself been converted and Augustine had been consecrated bishop, the king provided for the building of a new church on the site of another earlier building, St Saviour's. This, later known as Christ Church, together with its domestic buildings, is the original of today's cathedral and its precinct. It was endowed by the king with productive estates for the maintenance of the episcopal *familia*. In the early years Augustine released his monks from the strict monastic rule in order that they could concentrate on building and teaching and missionary work. Nevertheless, mass was regularly said and 'the psalms were sung'; that is to say, there was some form of choral 'office' with the psalms at their core. Five years after their arrival, an independent monastery of SS. Peter and Paul, later to be rededicated as St Augustine's, was founded and endowed by the king, with the intention that the kings of Kent and their archbishops would be buried there. It has been suggested that, in imitation of the Roman model familiar to Augustine, mass would have been celebrated and the office sung at Christ Church, with the secular clergy singing mass, lauds and vespers together with the monks, whilst leaving the monks alone to maintain the other day hours and the long night vigil.[8] From the first Augustine wished to attract to his household boys to become his clergy of the future. From the age of seven they were received, blessed, tonsured and admitted to the first three grades of the ministry: ostiarius, exorcist and lector. As soon as possible they would join with other members of the community in choir. Though not in name 'choristers', nor in the strict medieval sense of the later word in practice, they were boys who sang daily services in quire.[9]

Then in 531 the Council of Toledo made provision for young secular boys, who, 'immediately they have received the tonsure shall be handed over to the ministry of the lectors; they ought to be taught in the house of the church, in the bishop's presence, by his deputy.' This deputy was the senior presbyter of the bishop's household, the *capischola* or *magister scholarum*. His task was to teach the boys to learn, in Latin of course, the whole psalter and other parts of the liturgy by heart, and this was made easier by being chanted rather than spoken, the music being an aid to the memory. Liturgy was not an addition to, still less an interruption to, education: it was the very heart of education. The reading of Latin and the study of grammar and rhetoric were added, for at least some of the boys, as they grew older. As lectors boys would be required to read specified short lessons in the offices.

In addition to singing and reading there were, at mass, other roles for the boys to undertake. The next minor order above lector was that of acolyte. One could become an acolyte in one's teens. This would entail being a taperer or a bearer of holy water or a thurifer or immediate server to the celebrant, deacon and sub-deacon at the altar. Augustine's hope and expectation would have been that from among such boys the best would want to proceed in their twenties to the diaconate and later to the priesthood. Indeed, within a hundred years there was to be an indigenous Anglo-Saxon archbishop of Canterbury, one who undoubtedly began his vocation in just this way.

There would have been two chief sources for these young boys. First, families from the cathedral and monastic estates, themselves converted to Christianity, would appreciate the benefit of having sons accepted into the secure environment of Christ Church, brought up in a faith that promised eternal life and given the first steps of an education otherwise unobtainable. Only in Italy were there secular schools. For the low-born at least there would be no sort of commitment to a monastic life or any obligation to celibacy. Outside the monasteries, only the diaconate and priesthood at this time entailed celibacy. Such boys, once reaching adult years, whilst remaining in minor orders might work in the *familia* as domestic servants or in the cathedral as sacristans or help with the missionary work of the clergy. Gregory made it clear to Augustine that such men could marry, and should be waged and provided with accommodation in the precinct, whilst remaining under ecclesiastical rule and joining in the worship of the cathedral, that is if they did not simply opt to return to their villages. The sons of nobles and of other well-born families would also be welcomed into the community with an expectation that they would in due course be prepared for ordination into the diaconate and priesthood, younger sons not expected to inherit their father's estate for whom a career in the church offered the best hope of a worthy and fulfilling life.

A life-long expectation of commitment to the religious life would have been more implicit in the acceptance of children into monastic houses. Benedict's rule, which, in its late sixth-century Roman version, would have been the model for the life of Augustine's monks at SS. Peter and Paul, Canterbury, deals with the acceptance of children into the community.[10] The child was quite explicitly *given* to the community and, with no probationary period, the donation was absolute. Thus, about 670, Bede's parents, of whom nothing is known except that they lived on one of the estates of the abbey of Wearmouth, put him at the age of seven into the care of its abbot, Benedict Biscop, with just such an expectation, and one that was to be brilliantly fulfilled. Large elements of Bede's boyhood life would have been familiar to the later medieval choristers. It is no coincidence that Bede should have included in the proud catalogue of his own writings a hymnal and that his *Ecclesiastical History* shows a recurring interest in the development and teaching of Roman plainchant.

Not only sons were given to religious houses. Bede records a memorable instance of a father determining to place a daughter in a nunnery.[11] In 655 King Oswy of Northumbria was at war with the heathen Penda of Mercia. Battle was impending with the odds stacked heavily against Oswy. He put himself in God's hands and vowed that, if he should be given victory in battle, he would consecrate his recently-born daughter, Elfleda, to God. Not only did his men defeat an army three times more numerous than his own, but after the battle the Mercian survivors fled only to find the River Winwaed in spate and overflowing its banks. 'Many more were drowned while attempting to escape than perished by the sword.' Thus Oswy's prayer was answered and he and his kingdom were saved in a quasi-replication of God saving the Israelites from the Egyptians.

Oswy fulfilled his vow. He gave thanks to God 'and dedicated his daughter Elfleda, who was scarcely a year old, to His service in perpetual virginity'. If Bede's dates are correct, Elfleda was sent as an infant three year old to the saintly Abbess Hilda at Hartlepool. When, two years later, Hilda founded her famous double house of monks and nuns at Whitby, little Elfleda went with her.[12] Such early oblation was unusual but not unknown. Willibrord, the eighth-century missionary saint who was to convert the Frisians, was, according to Alcuin's biography of him, oblated to the monastery at Ripon as soon as he had been weaned in order that 'he would see nothing dishonourable nor would he hear anything that was not holy'.[13] And Hildemar, in his commentary on the Rule of Benedict, commends such infant oblation on the grounds that such boys grew up 'pure and not of the world'.[14] And indeed, in due course Elfleda became 'a mistress of the monastic life, until at sixty years of age', Bede concludes, 'this holy virgin departed to the wedding-feast and embrace of her heavenly Bridegroom'. So near-contemporary evidence confirms that the Anglo-Saxons had not only young boys singing in their monasteries but also young girls singing in nunnery quires, and that it was not unknown for children to join the religious houses as what would now be thought of as infant probationers.

At Canterbury Augustine's mission had proved hugely successful. 'Great numbers gathered each day to hear the word of God, forsaking their heathen rites, and entering the unity of Christ's holy Church as believers.'[15] Indeed, in 601 Gregory felt the need to write to Augustine warning him lest he shall fall into the sin of pride at his achievements. Augustine received a pallium from Rome, giving him metropolitan authority, and the mission began to expand from eastern Kent. Very early in the seventh century episcopal bases were established at London and Rochester. By the 630s bishops had been appointed to serve the East Angles from Dunwich and the West Saxons from Dorchester-on-Thames. Here too *familiae* were built up which will have included boys.[16]

Meanwhile, Paulinus had been sent in 625 to establish Christianity in Northumbria and, even after he returned to Kent in 633, James the Deacon remained in the north and taught the people chant 'after the Uses of Rome and Canterbury'.[17] In the following decade, under the Irishman Aidan, the great Christian revival in the north east began, with Lindisfarne, Wearmouth and Jarrow at its heart. But from 669 York became, under Wilfred, the hub; and it was York that was to become, as it has remained, the metropolitan see of northern England. James's tradition of musical excellence at York was maintained when Wilfred invited another expert in chant, Eddi, to come from Kent as singing master.[18] In the following decades York was to become famous as a centre of education.[19]

Very little is known about the way in which teaching developed in these early monastic and cathedral centres.[20] At first, as we have seen, it will have been essentially liturgical with the groundings of sung, spoken and ultimately read Latin. This was the seventh-century 'primary' syllabus. And indeed, in the eleventh century, Guido of Arrezzo was to write, perhaps a touch optimistically, that 'as soon as they have read the psalter attentively, small boys are able to understand the meaning of all books'.[21] But with astonishing rapidity these early teachers took their boys further, until 'grammar', that is the structure and some of the literature of Latin, provided a 'secondary' education and led on to a wide range of higher studies. Out of this revival grew a flourishing Christian culture, spreading through western Europe, perhaps unique in the rapidity of its development. Bede, an oblate from the age of seven, was one of the first fruits of this flowering; Aldhelm, Boniface and Willibrord three of its finest.

Even the liturgical regimen, the 'primary' syllabus, remains in any sort of detail obscure. There was by 600 AD a common, established framework. A great deal of the mass, however, would be the same as is found, for instance, in today's Roman Latin missal. And the pattern of the monastic hours, the divine office, was a following of the psalmist's undertakings: 'seven times a day do I praise thee' and 'at midnight I will rise to give thanks unto thee'. Then as now the heart of the office was the structured recitation of the psalter. But the detail varied: first as between the major streams of liturgy, the Roman, the Milanese Ambrosian, the Frankish Gallican and the Iberian Mozarabic uses, and, within these, lesser variations from region to region and house to house. Augustine, for instance, was not bound by the rule of Benedict, even though Pope Gregory had ensured its widespread use in late sixth-century Rome. Indeed, Gregory himself had specifically recommended that, in establishing a liturgy at Canterbury, Augustine should be selective: 'My brother', wrote Gregory, in a letter generally accepted by scholars as authentic:

> you are familiar with the usage of the Roman church in which you were brought up. But
> if you have found customs, whether in the Roman, Gallican or any other churches that

may be more acceptable to God, I wish you to make careful selection of them, and teach the church of the English, which is still young in the Faith, whatever you can profitably learn from the various churches.[22]

Still less can we hear the sounds of their chants.[23] Of course their singing was within the broad category that has come to be called 'Gregorian' plainchant. Throughout the seventh century the *Schola Cantorum* in Rome was the root from which this came. Bede tells how in 680 Benedict Biscop set up a brilliant choral workshop, bringing the world expert, John, archcantor of the apostolic see, to Wearmouth to teach his monks the chant for the liturgical year as it was sung at St Peter's:

> John taught the cantors of the monastery the theory and practice of singing and reading aloud, and he put in writing all that was necessary for the proper observance of festivals throughout the year [and] all who were proficient singers came from nearly all the monasteries of the province to hear him and he received many invitations to teach elsewhere.[24]

Bede was perhaps aged seven in 680. This may be an eye-witness account, or it could be that Bede heard of it a little later from monks still agog with the memory. Note the care with which Bede describes what John did and did not write down. He did not write down the music. All music at this time was taught and learned from memory to memory. In the total absence of any evidence to the contrary, it is best to assume that practical notation had not yet been formulated. The earliest surviving written Christian liturgical music almost certainly dates from the early ninth century.[25] Virtually certainly,[26] the earliest musical notation to have survived in Britain dates from the following century, that is to say the tenth. So when we read of the mid eighth-century Egbert, archbishop of York, having studied a chant book ('*liber antiphonarius*') in Rome,[27] and of the Council of Cloveshoe (747) referring to Roman books for the mass, baptism and festivals requiring the correct chants to be sung, this is not evidence that such books contained notated music. The earliest surviving liturgical books come from late eighth-century France and none contains musical notation.[28] Quite simply, no musical evidence exists.

Nor can we say of these hidden centuries, the seventh, eighth and ninth, whether the earliest boy oblates and choristers sang their plainsong all together, in monody, an octave above the men; or whether they were already beginning to be used to sing brief solo passages, short antiphons and responses; or to experiment with passages of 'discant' or 'organum', adding primitive touches of harmony, even if only in parallel to the main chant, splashes of brilliance to special moments such as alleluias on festal days. What can be said is that in the first half of the eighth century English monasticism stood at a high point. It was from these English monasteries that the famous conversion of mainland central Europe came under Boniface, Willibald and others. English monasticism around 750 was established, well ordered, widely respected and valued.

A roll-call of locations where the daily singing of the *opus Dei* must have been heard includes names familiar to modern ears: Canterbury and York, London and Winchester, Rochester and Hereford, Lichfield and Chester, Gloucester and Worcester and more beside. Some of these, London for example, were bishops' sees staffed by canons regular within an episcopal *familia*; some, like Chester and Gloucester, were monasteries, more or less Benedictine, not yet the sees of bishops; some, like Worcester, were early examples of that peculiarly English hybrid, the monastery whose abbot was also the diocesan bishop; others, including Canterbury, wobbled for some centuries between the secular and the monastic condition.

Then disaster struck. In the year 789 the Anglo-Saxon chronicler recorded the arrival of 'the first ships of the Danes to come to England'.[29] Five years later 'Northumbria was ravaged by the heathen' and over the next century Viking raids became endemic, ravishing swathes of East Anglia and Kent, and of Wessex as far as Cornwall. Most ominously, in 865 a large Viking army took winter quarters in East Anglia, extending their policy from mere destruction to extensive settlement. Appalling damage was suffered by the monasteries, whose buildings, albeit modest by later standards and mostly built of wood, were unmistakable landmarks. Their treasures of jewelled reliquaries, altarware and vestments acted like magnets. Already in the 790s Lindisfarne and Jarrow had been sacked. By 870 no monastery is said to have survived north of the Humber.

A vivid account of how boy oblates fared during the harrowing of East Anglia in September 870 comes from the Chronicle of Crowland.[30] News of the defeat of a Saxon army and sight of the smoke and flames from the pillage of neighbouring fenland settlements reached Crowland during matins, just before daybreak. The abbot Theodore ordered the chalices and plate to be thrown down the abbey well. Then thirty or so of the able-bodied brethren were instructed to gather up the most precious of the monastery's treasures and relics, including the body of their founder, St Guthlac, his scourge and his psalter, and to take them by boat across the fen so as to hide with them until the expected sacking of the monastery was over. The abbot vested himself and, with a few of the older monks and all the boys, resumed the regular round of the liturgy. As mass was ending

the Pagans bursting into the church, the venerable abbot was slain upon the holy altar, his assistants, standing around him, were all beheaded by the barbarians; while the old men and children, on attempting to fly from the choir, were seized and examined with most cruel torments, that they might disclose where the treasures of the church were concealed, and afterwards were put to death.

One ten-year-old boy, Turgar, had seen the sub-prior murdered in the refectory and begged to be killed alongside him. But the Danish Earl Sidroc, touched by the child, 'remarkable for the beauty of his face and person', stripped him of his cowl, and, throwing over him a Danish sleeved tunic, kept charge of him while the Danes sacked the place and set it on fire. The Danes then moved on the great abbey of Medeshamsted (the later Peterborough) and wrought similar destruction. Their next target was Huntingdon, but while crossing the Nene some of their loot-filled carts fell into the river. For a short while there was disarray while the recovery of the treasures was attempted. Turgar saw his chance and escaped, managing under cover of darkness to make his way back to Crowland. There he found that the able-bodied brethren had returned and were endeavouring to put out fires and recover bodies for burial. Turgar was able to tell the appalling tale of all that he had witnessed.

The traditional view has been that by the last quarter of the ninth century monasticism had been virtually eliminated from Anglo-Saxon England,[31] an opinion traceable back to King Alfred's own letter introducing his translation of Pope Gregory's *Pastoral Care* in which he asserts that at the time of his accession he knew of not a single person south of the Thames who could read any Latin. Asser's contemporary *Life of Alfred* paints a similar picture.[32] But recent research is less pessimistic. Both archaeological evidence and detailed study of grants and deeds suggest that the episcopal abbeys of Sherborne and Winchester, to take just two examples, survived the Viking troubles, though even here the full monastic life may well have been replaced by communities of secular clergy.[33]

Clothing an oblate.

2

Anglo-Saxon Choir Children

For Christian recovery, secure peace and a supportive monarchy were necessities. These conditions were first achieved in post-Viking England by King Alfred, who drove the Danes to the north and east of Watling Street and initiated an intellectual and cultural revival. The ninth century saw the founding or refounding of several West Saxon religious houses, notably a group of distinguished nunneries. But the really significant revival of English religious life had to wait for a further century, for the reign of the pious Edgar (959–75) and it came enriched with all the enthusiasm of the newly reformed monasticism of continental western Europe.

On mainland Europe, half a century before Alfred, Charlemagne had been the hero. King of the Franks from 771, and crowned emperor of the west by the pope in 800, he established episcopal and monastic schools for the training of an educated militia for the conversion of pagan lands. Uniformity of doctrine and practice mattered to him. Through successive synods convened at Aachen, Charlemagne imposed a model liturgy and a uniform plainchant throughout the churches of the empire, fundamentally that of Rome.[1] Not long after his death, a synod of 817 issued a revised and extended version of the eighth-century bishop Chrodegang of Metz's famous rule for the *familiae* of the Frankish bishops. In every episcopal *familia* the youngest of the canons were to be 'small children and youths', tonsured lectors or acolytes, trained in chant and liturgy, living with the older canons in the common hall under the charge of a senior canon of proven life.

The most illustrious of Charlemagne's establishments was his own imperial palace with its royal chapel and palace school. There, to the familiar primary 'chorister' syllabus of Latin, chant and liturgy, were added courses that for centuries were to form the curriculum of European grammar schools and universities. Charlemagne drew to his palace some of the most accomplished teachers of ninth-century Europe. Children of nobles and other lay boys, looking to secular careers, were also invited to his school to be trained for his civil service. In the following century a further impulse of reform spread from Cluny in Burgundy, and its famous daughter monastery at Fleury-sur-Loire, through northern France and Flanders, bringing to their churches an unprecedented richness of liturgical worship.

Under King Edgar this tide of enthusiasm and reform crossed the Channel. The leading figure was the monk Dunstan, appointed by King Edgar to be bishop successively of Worcester, London and Canterbury. He promoted his successor at Worcester, Oswald, to York where for twenty years he was archbishop. Abbot Ethelwold of Abingdon was appointed bishop of the royal seat at Winchester. All three were monks in the Benedictine tradition. All three had experience of the latest and best continental practice. All three turned their cathedrals into houses of clerks under monastic vows.[2] Further, they brought about a wave of refoundations of houses that had been destroyed and were now to survive and flourish for half a millennium, amongst the most notable being Ely and Evesham, Malmesbury and Peterborough, St Albans and the establishment of an important new foundation just outside London called the West Minster.

Hitherto English monasteries had been independent houses and little if any attempt had been made to ensure uniform custom and practice. That had facilitated their drift into secularisation in difficult times. In future this was not to be. In 970 Ethelwold, under the patronage of the king, summoned to Winchester all the heads of monastic houses, bishops, abbots and abbesses in England, together with representatives from Fleury and Ghent. There his persuasive chairmanship gained unanimous acceptance of a code of monastic life and liturgy, known as the *Regularis Concordia*, which all were to observe, based on the contemporary continental development of the Rule of Benedict.

Our knowledge of the life of children in Anglo-Saxon religious houses must take its foundations from such books of monastic regulations. Two things need to be said at the start. First, whatever the regulations might say, throughout the middle ages practice continued to vary from house to house and from time to time: there is, for example, no likelihood that the routine of eleventh-century Worcester exactly matched that of Ethelwold's tenth-century Winchester. Secondly, almost all early monastic regulations fail to state what was so obvious or so well known to contemporaries that they saw no need to record it. These regulations were an endeavour to 'get things right': to put in writing what was deemed proper practice, especially on matters novel or uncertain. So they often deal in small particulars. The broad sweep of the Rule of St Benedict was exceptional.

Nobody had been more anxious to regulate the particulars of life in his monastery than the anonymous early sixth-century Roman 'Master'. His lengthy and pedantic rule, the *Regula Magistri*, tackles such disagreeable minutiae as 'the disposal of filth extracted from the nose' while singing the psalms.[3] All such early attempts at establishing or recording monastic practice were local documents intended for an individual house or small clusters of houses. Even Benedict's Rule was equally local, written some time between 530 and 547 solely for his monks at Monte Cassino. It could very easily have been lost sight of or wholly lost had not Pope Gregory the Great acquired it, admired it and adapted it as the model for the monastic life which he encouraged at Rome during his pontificate. The fundamental reason why Benedict's Rule became the root of virtually all later monastic practice was its excellence. To read the 'Master's' Rule and then pass on to Benedict's is to go from choking marshland to pure mountain air. Benedict's brief manual is simple yet profound, firm yet flexible, practical yet deeply spiritual. It is one of the masterworks of the human spirit.[4] And it underlies all late Anglo-Saxon practice. Furthermore, some of its more puzzling gaps can be filled from the happy survival of an extensive commentary on the Rule of Benedict by the ninth-century French monk Hildemar.[5] Other details, especially on the everyday singing of the Office, or recent innovations from the Continent, appear in the *Regularis Concordia*.[6] Here we find some of the very earliest details of English liturgical practice.

The expectation was that there would be children in these communities, boys in monasteries and girls in nunneries, and that the boys, the *pueri nutriti*, would have a specific role to perform in the liturgy. There is one other source that particularly concerns these oblate children that is of prime value, the *Colloquy* of Aelfric,[7] written around the opening of the eleventh century. Aelfric was one of twelve monks taken from Abingdon to Winchester by Ethelwold on his appointment as bishop there in 963. Aelfric went on to be the first abbot of Cerne and then abbot of the more important abbey of Eynsham near Oxford. Above all he was a writer, earning the nickname *Grammaticus* on account of his writing the earliest Anglo-Saxon/Latin Grammar. His *Colloquy* is a charming Anglo-Saxon/Latin text-book for schoolboys, built round lively descriptions of the lives of different classes of people, not least monastic boy oblates. Where Benedict and Ethelwold tell us what should happen, Aelfric's fictional pupils tell us what actually did happen — by no means always the same thing. By collating those sections of Benedict's Rule, sometimes as glossed by Hildemar, and Ethelwold's *Regularis Concordia*, as they apply to monastic children, with passages from Aelfric's dialogues, and with a little help from other sources, it is possible to establish a remarkably detailed picture of the life and worship of boys in English monasteries and, by implication, girls in the nunneries, from about 970 to the Conquest. All these writers expressed themselves entirely in the masculine, although the *Regularis Concordia* was certainly written to apply to nuns as well as monks.

We are not talking of large numbers of children. Exact numbers are impossible to guess, as there are no records. Reliable lists of pupils do not appear in England before the fifteenth century. Few monasteries and fewer nunneries were large. Around the close of the tenth century there were about thirty houses of men and perhaps seven of women.[8] Canterbury may have housed as many as 150 monks;[9] Shaftesbury, with over a hundred nuns, became and remained the largest English nunnery. At the opposite extreme, rather over a century later, Cranborne had just a prior and two monks. Nevertheless, until the mid-twelfth century oblation was the chief route of entry to the monastic life. So a mixture of deduction and intuition suggests that in the larger houses boys and youths are likely to have accounted for at least a fifth of a large monastic community at any time.[10]

Young children were brought to abbots and abbesses, usually by upper-class fathers, but occasionally by widows, as *gifts*. They were to be oblates,[11] donated to God and to the monastic community. Both the parents and the child were to want this move to the cloister.[12] Seven was usually the youngest age, when infancy gave way to childhood, but sometimes younger children were accepted.[13] There was an expectation, not always fulfilled, that by seven children would have some grounding in reading and chant.[14] The objective was to have them participating in choir with the monks or nuns as soon as possible. There was no period of probation, as there was with adult novices.[15] Unlike adult novices, the child oblates came to the community untarnished by exposure to the world. Once given, they were there for life. Nor were they required on reaching maturity to confirm their father's vows on their own behalf. This practice offends deeply against modern preconceptions; indeed, it came to seem unapt by the late twelfth century, after which it withered and eventually was banned. Yet for at least six hundred years it was taken for granted as the best way, and the most usual way, of entering the religious life. The child left one caring family and joined another one. There are a few, but very few, records of young oblates kicking against the pricks and making their escape or being deemed unsuitable by their abbot. There are also records of surprisingly young children playing havoc until their families let them join a monastery or nunnery. There must have been misfits, but perhaps fewer of them than we might expect. There were more than a few famous successes and doubtless countless good souls who began worthy and fulfilled lives by being children of the quire.[16]

Prior to the formal ceremony the boy would be tonsured and clothed in a habit.[17] Then the parents would accompany their son into chapel for the principal mass of the day. The father, no doubt aided by his clerks, would have prepared a document, a *petitio*, by which the abbot was begged to accept the boy as a perpetual gift and, with him, a donation, usually of productive land, the scale of which would depend upon the wealth and piety of the donor. An assurance was given that the boy had been disinherited and a promise was also made that the boy would never in future be given anything by the family, so that his vow of poverty would not be at hazard.[18] At the offertory father and boy would come up to the altar, the father bearing the petition and the boy bearing the elements for consecration. The petition and the boy's hands were wrapped in the altar cloth and the offerings made.[19] The boy was now under vows of poverty, chastity and obedience and would never again leave the monastery unless as an adult on monastic business. Contact with the family was severely restricted. Even letters were to be opened first by the abbot who could pass them to whomsoever he wished, not necessarily the addressee. They were to receive no gifts.[20] But there were two kinds of continuing contact: the provision of visits by family members on special festivals and the work that the oblate would do for his family by prayer. It is not unusual to find the documents referring to these boys as 'monks' and to girls as 'nuns': they were already sharing the adults' work in choir, the *opus Dei*.

First it must be stressed that, notwithstanding recent views to the contrary,[21] the monastic oblates, unlike the novices, were brought up amongst the adult brethren, sleeping alongside them in the dormitory, working alongside them in the cloister, worshipping with them in the principal church. The rules of the Master and of Benedict, and the regulations of Ethelwold and of Lanfranc for Canterbury, make this clear. Before we turn to their choral work it is helpful to note the pastoral care that Benedict and others ensured for the monastic children. The Council of Toledo, in 531, had required the master of the boys to be the senior presbyter. By the tenth century delegation had occurred. The *pueri* were placed specifically under the charge of two masters, one for the *decani* boys and one for the *cantoris* boys,[22] no doubt senior monks. Indeed Hildemar makes the exceptional recommendation that each group of ten boys should be under the supervision of three or four experienced monks.[23] They were likely to be assisted in their teaching by some of the older boys. When Odilo, fifth abbot of Cluny, wrote of how, as a novice, he learnt 'not to disdain menial tasks, such as the cleaning of lanterns, the scouring of floors, the care of the children', he was writing of just such a role.[24] Indeed, caring for young tenth-century oblates must often have been a burden. It was hedged around by the most absolute rules to ensure the boys' moral safety: 'Youths are not to accompany monks on journeys. There is to be no embracing or kissing of children but only spiritual affection shown. No monk must ever take a boy with him alone. Not even on the excuse of some spiritual matter shall any monk presume to take with him a young boy alone for any private purpose', but, following Benedict's guidance, 'let the children always remain under the care of their master. Nor shall the master himself be allowed to be in company with a boy without a third person as witness; but let the master and *schola*[25] go together in the accustomed manner wherever reason and necessity demand.'[26]

There was concern for proper diet, more robust than that offered to today's chorister. They shared the monks' diet, which always included a choice of cooked food, but with smaller portions for the younger boys.[27] The 'Master' accorded his children the full adult diet from the age of twelve. Of children Benedict wrote, 'let there be constant consideration for their weakness, and on no account let the rigour of the Rule in regard to food [as in Lent and Advent] be applied to them'. They were to take their meals before the regular hours and not suffer the full rigours of fasts.[28] For drink they were to be served beer rather than wine; but there is a charming reference in the Abingdon Chronicle to Queen Edith making a grant of land in order to supply the cloister children with daily morning milk,[29] and in Hertfordshire there is a small manor called Childwick, a place-name which can and almost certainly did mean 'the children's dairy-farm', which is recorded in the *Gesta Abbatum Monasterii Sancti Albani* as having been given to St Alban's Abbey for the provision of milk for the abbey children.[30] Each morning, after changing into day shoes, the whole *schola* are to go with their masters to wash their faces 'as is customary' before singing the Office.[31] Hildemar provides the touching and surprising detail that the oblate master kept, in the washroom, the boys' towels, combs, soap and shoe-polish.[32] On Good Fridays, after the Veneration of the Cross, the ministers 'and children who can' are to shave (for the first time since mid-Lent) and then bathe themselves,[33] this being the only reference to bathing in the whole of *Regularis Concordia*. Indeed, Benedict's Rule provides for the sick to bathe as often as is expedient but permission for the young to take a bath 'should be granted seldom'.[34] Arrangements were made to enable the boys to attend to 'the necessities of nature' more frequently than the adults.[35] When not in choir Hildemar indicates that the boys assisted with some of the routine manual work of the monastery such as cleaning, food preparation and wood-cutting.[36]

Their lessons in reading and chant were taught in the cloister, where much of their time outside choir was spent. There seems to be no English evidence descriptive of how chant was taught. The great majority of teaching must have been simply oral. But there were aids to learning, perhaps most famously the 'monochord', said to have been invented by Pythagoras, and described in detail by Odo in his tenth-century *Enchiridion Musices*. The monochord was a wooden device, about three feet in length, with a string stretched from end to end, notes marked out by letter, G to a, along its two-octave length, with a movable bridge which enabled the string to sound each semitone precisely. Odo, writing about 935, urges that the monochord is preferable to a human teacher since, unlike a teacher, the monochord 'cannot mislead' and 'never deceives'. He makes remarkable claims that, with its use, he has taught boys several antiphons note-perfect within three, four or seven days, later teaching them 'to sing at sight, extempore without fault, anything'.[37] English texts, however, make no reference to this instrument. The oblates' day cannot have been all work and worship. It is clear that there were times when they could chatter because this is specifically forbidden on Sundays and the most solemn feasts.[38] Hildemar reports time for recreation, an hour's play in the meadows each week, at the discretion of the abbot. Half a century later than Hildemar, the *Vita sancti Maghorii* reports the oblates of St-Malo going out daily to play during the afternoon monastic rest period.[39] It is said that hollows in the cloisters at Canterbury cathedral are evidence of the playing of a form of bagatelle and hopscotch.

Discipline was characteristic of its time. The great threat to the adult monks was excommunication, a ban on receiving the consecrated bread and wine at mass. But Benedict recognised that for children this might seem an easy option: so the almost universal punishment for any fault beyond the trivial was to be 'severe fasts or sharp stripes in order that they may be cured'.[40] Aelfric's master asks his pupil whether he has been flogged today. 'No, I was very careful', replies the boy. 'And what of the others?' asks the master. But the boy keeps his counsel and says, 'You'd better ask them about that!' Mistakes in psalm singing were regarded as particularly serious if the culprit failed to own up 'because the culprit would not repair by humility the fault he committed through carelessness'.[41] (So the almost universal custom in today's choir practices of the confessional raising of a hand when a mistake has been made has a continuous history of some 1400 years.) But if there is no owning up: 'infantes autem pro tali culpa vapulent' (they should be whipped). Aelfric's pupil is something of a prig about this whipping business: 'We would rather be flogged than remain ignorant', he says, 'but we know you will be kind to us and not flog us unless obliged to do so.' Lest Benedict seems brutish with regard to discipline, bear in mind his chapter 70: 'Boys up to fifteen years of age shall be carefully controlled and watched by all, yet this too with all moderation and prudence. But if any venture without the abbot's instructions to treat the boys with immoderate severity, let him undergo the discipline of the Rule.' There was, furthermore, always available the promise of spiritual absolution: even though 'on the score of their tender age' they are 'as yet untroubled by temptation' still they should 'make their confession in the customary way as their elder brethren do'.[42]

For some four hours of the day and night every day throughout the year, the children were in choir. Here speaks Aelfric's pupil:

> At night, when I heard the bell, I got out of bed and went to church and sang the nocturne with the brethren. Then we sang the martyrology and lauds. After that, prime and the seven psalms with litanies and the first ['morrow'] mass; next tierce and the mass for the day; after that sext, then I ate and drank and slept [the pre-noon siesta]; then we got up again and sang nones and now here we are – ready to learn!

Several hours were set aside for teaching, while the older monks did their reading, writing or physical work. Apart from vespers, the day offices were relatively brief. Matins, sung at 6 a.m. in the winter and between 3 and 4 a.m. in the summer, was the longest of the 'hours'. It was expected that the pueri, who slept in the dormitory each in his own bed but amongst those of the monks,[43] would be the most difficult section of the community to wake for the night office. 'Sometimes I hear the bell and get up; sometimes my master wakes me with his ash-stick', explains Aelfric's pupil. Steps were taken to get them into choir in the dark together. The 'little bell is rung continually' until the last of the children is in church. Then, at their places before the two rows of monks on each side, they said their private *trina oratio*.[44] After compline, the last day office, the children said their *trina oratio* aloud, then the monastic brethren repeated it.

Once a boy was one of the *psalterati*, that is, he knew the chanted psalter by heart, then his liturgical teaching would concentrate on 'propers', items specific to particular days. Such less familiar material arose especially on festivals. The calendar had been steadily acquiring new festivals and the liturgy for special days had itself been expanding, particularly under the influence of Cluny, to add splendour to festal occasions and solemnity to grave ones. This growth of unfamiliar material was almost certainly the prime motive for the development of musical notation, which first appeared in England about this time. At last we can answer the question: what did they sing? Two copies of the *Winchester Troper*, with chants and tropes notated in neumes, have survived. The Bodleian Library copy, generally deemed to be the earlier, contains material probably from the late tenth century; the later, now at Corpus Christi College, Cambridge, comes from about 1050. The spectacular element in the Cambridge copy is that it contains the earliest known part-writing, *organum*.[45] Another eleventh-century notated manuscript comes from Exeter.[46] The singers clearly knew the music by heart, except for the innovative *Alleluia … Optimum Partem*, so the cantor has interlined the text with a scribble of neumes, the earliest form of western musical notation, to remind him of the chant he had to teach his community for the festival of St Mary Magdalene. It was for the cantor's memory only, not to be sung from in quire. Nobody could possibly sing from the scribbles up the right-hand margin. It was on such festivals that the boys, singing alone, provided significant elements, most particularly during the eight holy days from Palm Sunday to Easter, which included the especially solemn *triduum* of Maundy Thursday, Good Friday and Holy Saturday.

On Palm Sunday the principal mass was preceded by a procession, sometimes out of the monastery to a nearby church where cut palms were waiting for them. Here the boys began the antiphon *Pueri Hebraeorum*, following which the palms were distributed. The procession then returned to the monastery church and, at the west door, the boys went in first, leaving the monks outside. From within the church the boys sang the first verse of Theodulph of Orleans's great plainchant hymn, *Gloria Laus et Honor*, well known to modern English singers in John Mason Neale's fine translation:

> All glory, laud and honour
> To Thee, Redeemer, King;

xi. kł' aug̃. SC̄E MARIE MAGDALENE.

Gaudeamus oms in dn̄o diem festum celebrantes sub
honore marie magdalene de cuius conuersione gau
dent angeli & conlaudant filium di. p̄ Cr̄ stam.
Largire nobis clementissime pater. coll'.
quo sicut beata maria magdalene dn̄m dm̄
sup omnia diligendo. suorum ueniam obtinu
peccaminū. ita p nobis apud mīsc̄diam tuam.
sempiternam impetre& beatitudinē. p. epłā.
Mulierem fortem. V̄R Adiuuabit eam deꝰ.
Alleluia.   yꝯ Optimam partem
elegit sibi maria que non auferetur ab ea in eternum.
SEQ. Scalam ad celos. EVGL'. Rogabat ih̄m
quidam phariseus. usq̄: q̄n dilexit multum.
fferimus dn̄e preces & hostias ō Diffusa ꞅ gr̄a.
in honore sc̄e marie magdalene. gaudentes sc̄a.
presta q̄s. ut & conuenienter hec agere. & re-
medium sempiternum ualeamus ad quirere. p.

Sc̄ificet nos dn̄e &
muniat intercedente
beata magdalene di
uini muneris libano
& celestiū uirtutū
coheredes faciat. p.

D̄s qui nos p unigenitū cō Dilexisti iustitiam. pcōm
tuū. beate marie magdalene dilectione multa

> To whom the lips of children
> Made sweet Hosannas ring.[47]

Then the hymn was taken up by the brethren outside the west door.[48]

For the night of Maundy Thursday the *Regularis Concordia* specified a ritual which, to the boys involved, must have been utterly unforgettable: 'an outward representation of that which is spiritual'. After the post-gospel antiphon twenty-four candles were extinguished, one by one after each antiphon and respond. In this gathering darkness two children on the right of the choir sang *Kyrie Eleison* 'with a clear voice'; two on the left answered *Christe Eleison* and two stationed at the west of the choir said *Domine, Miserere nobis*; after which the whole choir responded, *Christus dominus factus est obediens usque ad mortem* (Christ the Lord was made obedient even unto death). This procedure was repeated three times, candles being extinguished progressively until, in darkness, the community said their silent prayers. For the three nights of the *triduum* this procedure was followed, 'thus setting forth clearly the terror of darkness at Our Lord's passion … and the consolation of apostolic preaching'.[49]

Ambiguity in the use of the word *schola* leaves it unclear whether the boys or the semi-chorus had special chants to sing on Easter Eve. But at Easter matins it was one of the children who sang the triumphant *Surrexit Dominus de Sepulchro* and at prime the chapter and verse, *Haec Dies*, was monotoned, and likewise for the whole of the Easter octave.[50]

The boys also had a role that stems from Maundy Thursday. Every day at the monastery *hospitium*, the department that from the thirteenth-century was to feature significantly in the boys' life as the almonry, food would be given to poor men who came asking for alms. But each day three men were to be chosen to receive not the usual dole but the superior food from the monks' table. On Saturdays this was to be distributed by the children of the right-hand choir with their master and on Sundays, likewise, by those of the left-hand choir.[51]

To the Christian of the early middle ages to give a son or daughter to a monastic community was to set him or her on the way to the best of all possible earthly lives. It was as accepted a procedure as infant baptism remains to many a Christian today. It was closely paralleled by the practice, at least in aristocratic families, of the binding betrothal of sons and daughters whilst still of tender years. We cannot ask the children of the cloister what they thought of it and can only guess at the authenticity of the words of Aelfric's pupils. Yet, a century after Aelfric's death, the passing bell for child oblation was already sounding. In part it was that the educational opportunities offered by oblation were becoming available in the song schools of the secular cathedrals and the more advanced town parishes with no obligation to life-long claustration. New vocations were also opening up for which the monasteries could not prepare. But there was also a growing unease about the very propriety of committing young children to the cloister for life. As early as Lanfranc's time, his Constitutions were to make clear that child oblates must be given the opportunity in their late teens to take life vows for themselves or to leave the monastery. Not long after this, in 1119, the reform movement of Cîteaux, the Cistercian white monks, were to be given a constitution that banned child oblation and child education from their order. All postulants must join no earlier than their late teens and serve at least a year's novitiate before taking vows. From the following century papal and conciliar pronouncements began to apply this rule to all monastic orders. But already, by the middle of the twelfth century, the English Benedictine houses had become free of children. Within their walls the unbroken voices of oblates were no longer heard.[52]

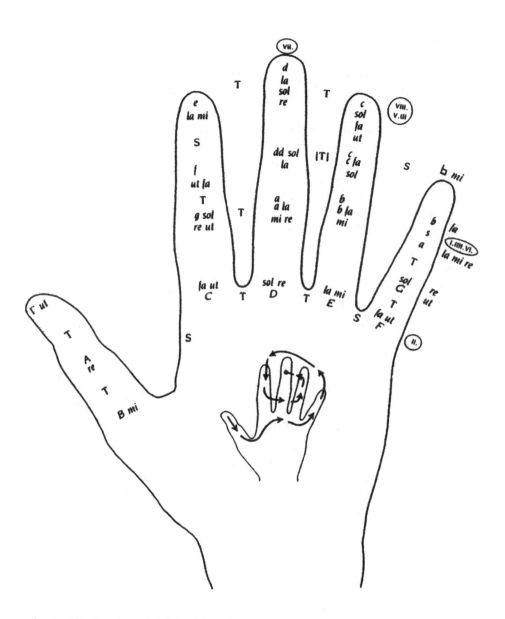

The Guidonian Hand. This aid to learning the Gamut, the medieval scales or modes, attributed to Guido d'Arezzo (probably erroneously), will have been known to all choristers at least until Tudor times.

3

Choristers of the High Middle Ages

The tenth-century movement to establish bishops in churches served by Benedictine monks had quickly foundered under the second great wave of Viking attacks between *c.* 980 and 1016. York reverted to being a community of secular canons. Canterbury, if Eadmer is to be believed, was in the hands of pseudo-monks delighting in coloured clothes and fine food, hunting with horses, hounds and hawks.[1] When the Conqueror set about reforming the English church he brought over from Normandy as church leaders a number of outstanding Benedictines. Two of them, Lanfranc and Anselm, Italians from the great Norman monastery of Bec, were to be successively archbishops of Canterbury. The expectation must have been that Benedictine cathedrals would again be the norm, and indeed at Canterbury, the southern metropolitan see, and at Winchester, a seat of government, and elsewhere, monastic cathedrals were re-established. Yet this was to be far from universal. Even some Norman Benedictines preferred their cathedrals to be served by communities of secular canons. This was the case when Remigius moved his Mercian see from Dorchester-on-Thames to Lincoln in 1072 and when Osmund moved the West Saxon see from monastic Sherborne to Old Sarum six years later. This was how cathedrals were everywhere in western Europe apart from England.[2] And in practical terms it made sense to appoint to cathedrals clergy not under monastic vows, free to undertake additional responsibilities outside the close as administrators, lawyers, teachers and men of state. Significantly the earliest rules from an English secular cathedral, the early eleventh-century *regula* of St Paul's, London, the nation's busiest city, seem to provide for a chapter of canons who, while living communally and maintaining the *opus Dei*, were also likely to be occupied in a variety of business about the city.[3]

It has been suggested that the secular constitutions of Lincoln, Salisbury and York were consciously formalised during the period from 1089 to 1093 when, between the death of Lanfranc and the accession of Anselm, the see of Canterbury was kept vacant and 'milked' by William Rufus.[4] During this brief period able bishops, no longer answerable to a Benedictine metropolitan, took the opportunity to put in place secular constitutions that lasted to the Reformation; indeed, some elements have survived to the present day. So it was that by the twelfth century nine of England's seventeen cathedrals were secular:

Chichester, Exeter, Hereford, Lichfield,[5] Lincoln, London, Salisbury,[6] Wells[7] and the northern metropolitan minster of York.[8] In these cathedrals, though there were no child oblates, there were certainly boy choristers.

The earliest evidence comes from Exeter. When Leofric moved his cathedral from Crediton to Exeter in 1050 he introduced the enlarged rule of Chrodegang as the basis for the canonical life of his new cathedral.[9] Here the canons lived in one house, with refectory and dormitory, and the boy choristers lived in their own apartment, or possibly a separate house, under the care of a senior canon of proven probity, 'in order that their vulnerable years should be spent under ecclesiastical discipline and not in wantonness (*luxuria*)'.[10] The next evidence, though less secure, is from Salisbury. Two documents relate to the establishment of Osmund's cathedral and its chapter at Old Sarum, both attributed to the year 1091. The foundation charter gives every impression that its form, date and contents are genuine. But it refers only to the cathedral's canons and their endowment. No boys are mentioned. The other document is the so-called *Institutio* of Osmund. This goes into some detail about the life of the cathedral and its officers. A cantor, later to be called precentor, was to rule the choir and the chant, either in person or through his assistant succentor; and a chancellor was to rule the school. The *Institutio* deals in its antepenultimate clause with the treatment of disobedient or rebellious canons. Part of their penance was that in choir, having been temporarily expelled from their stalls in the highest row, they were to stand '*in choro ultimi puerorum*' – in the lowest place, after the most junior boys. Here, almost accidentally, is confirmation that the Salisbury community included boys. But the earliest surviving form of Osmund's *Institutio* cannot be certainly assigned to a date much earlier than 1220. By then its original form had clearly been tampered with, being updated to conform to how things were a century later than its attributed date. Some of these later interpolations can be confidently identified, but there is no reason to suppose that boys were a later addition. The most reasonable assumption is that boy choristers were there from the foundation.[11] In the course of the twelfth and thirteenth centuries evidence shows boy choristers to have been part of the establishment of all nine secular cathedrals.[12]

It might be wondered why the secular cathedrals had boys who were certainly not oblates in their communities at all. There was more than one reason. In the first place, they were there because boys had always been part of the scheme of things in western Christendom, and in England back at least to the time when Canterbury had been a secular cathedral under Augustine. Secondly, they were irreplaceable: the sound of young choristers was deemed to resemble the pure sound of the angels.[13] Hence the service books, when they begin to appear, reveal roles particular to the boys as singers, readers and, in their teens, acolytes. Their very juniority had, as we shall see, liturgical significance. Further, there was evidently a strong demand from parents to place their sons in the cathedrals' choirs and schools, particularly in the early medieval decades when, outside the monasteries, sound elementary schooling could only be had in the cathedrals. Boys beyond the statutory numbers were often to be found in school and quire alongside the choristers proper. Parents with aspirations that their sons should be literate, learned, cultured and capable of going on to higher studies, and ultimately employable as lawyers or civil servants, could look to the cathedral song school as a first stage. And of course a choristership (as it was not yet called) could also be the first step in a career in the church itself. After their voices broke, boys often remained in quire as singers with young broken voices 'in the second form', subsequently becoming anything from humble vicars choral to mitred bishops. We are not talking of large numbers. The most reliable figures from the late twelfth to the early fourteenth century are:[14]

Exeter and Salisbury	14
Lincoln	12
Chichester	10, later 12
Lichfield	probably 8, later 12
St Paul's	8, later 10
York	7, later 12
Wells	6 + 3 *tabellarii*
Hereford (always the poorest secular cathedral)	5

The circumstances of the boys' lives in the earliest post-Conquest centuries must be to some extent speculative. It is almost certain that the secular cathedrals from the first intended that their communities, though not monastic, should live a common life under rules such as those at Exeter. The bishop was the head of the community. The later cathedral dignitaries of dean, precentor, chancellor and treasurer seem to have been largely twelfth-century innovations, importations from Norman practice. With the possible exception of St Paul's, the earliest references to deans come from the 1090s and most offices appear only from the mid-twelfth century.[15] Meanwhile, with the almost certain exception of Hereford,[16] the canons lived together, sleeping in a common dormitory, eating at a common table in the refectory, fed from a common kitchen. Such a way of life was, according to Hugh the Chanter, imposed in the 1070s by Archbishop Thomas on his canons at York.[17] The boys, too, must have lived in this way. It was a secure, stable mode of life; but it was not to last.

Even in a community, canons were not expected to take vows of poverty and were able to own property.[18] Whereas the earliest benefactions to endow cathedrals seem mostly to have been made to the common fund, gradually gifts to individual canons appear in the records.[19] Soon the pressure for canons to build and live in their own houses became irresistible. Exactly when this change happened at the secular cathedrals is uncertain. Until the archaeologists have dug further into the grass at Old Sarum, the hill at Lincoln and the undercroft at York we shall remain in ignorance.[20] It is, however, certain that very soon after the foundation stones of Bishop Richard Poore's new Salisbury cathedral had been laid in the salubrious grassland of the Myrfield in 1220, the foundations of canonical houses began to appear on the ample building plots provided for them.[21] But this was the death-knell of the protected common life of the choristers. Now the boys were shared around the houses of the resident canons, houses that were in any case small *familiae*, accommodating relatives, minor clergy and servants. With a resident canon and a well-ordered household it may have been a satisfactory, even a pleasant, alternative to the former common life. But not all the houses were well-ordered and, most significantly, canons tended increasingly not to be resident.

Most canons were funded by prebends, the estates given to provide their income. One of the widespread practices of the medieval cathedral was the use of prebends to fund diocesan or episcopal or royal or even papal administrators. It led to non-residence on a massive scale. The richer the prebend, the more senior the cathedral officer, the more likely it was that the prebend would be used to fund administrators, clerks, lawyers and diplomats, or to add to the remuneration of higher clergy who accumulated benefices in plurality. To quote just two examples to do service for thousands: the bishop of Durham from 1099 to 1128 was the notorious Ranulf Flambard. For part or all of that time he was also dean of the royal chapel of Hastings, dean of Christchurch (Hampshire), and canon, possibly dean, of St Paul's, where he never resided.[22] Later, in the fourteenth century the greatest pluralist of all may well have been William of Wykeham, future bishop of Winchester. His principal occupation was in government as lord privy seal. In addition he was archdeacon and canon of Lincoln, provost of Wells and holder of prebendal stalls in the cathedrals of Lincoln, London, Salisbury and York. These benefices, in none of which was he resident, brought him in an enormous income, approaching £900 a year, from the proceeds of which he founded New College, Oxford, and Winchester College, whose headmaster was salaried at £10 a year.[23]

From the point of view of the choristers the least helpful absenteeism was that of the precentor. He was supposed to be directly responsible for their care and training; indeed at Exeter throughout the middle ages his title was *dux puerorum*.[24] Yet Lincoln was without a resident precentor from 1304 until at least 1340, and the precentor of Salisbury from 1244 to 1270 was a papally provided non-resident foreigner.[25] By this time, however, the bishops or chapters had become aware of the neglect arising from prolonged absence by precentors and other canons and were appointing surrogates. In place of the precentor a succentor was given responsibility for the care and conduct of the choristers, whilst vicars choral began to be appointed to undertake the attendance in quire of the non-resident canons.[26] We find a succentor at Salisbury by about 1150, at Wells in the 1160s and at Lincoln at the close of the twelfth century.[27] But whilst this undoubtedly kept the liturgy and music going, it failed to ensure the proper domestic care of the boys. The situation at Salisbury was vividly described by Bishop Roger Martival or Mortival in a letter of September 1322:

> When like little children they asked for bread but could not find anyone to break a piece for them from any quarter, they were compelled of necessity to go round flocking to crave a beggar's dole each day in the dwellings of resident canons so as to get enough victuals to keep the wolf from the door.[28]

It is also clear from other comments by Martival that the boys were expected to work as domestic servants in the houses in which they were lodged.

The earliest surviving evidence of endeavours to put things right comes in fact from Lincoln. There too in the first half of the thirteenth century the choristers, having no fixed lodging, were dependent for their maintenance on casual almsgiving from the chapter.[29] But in 1264 Bishop Richard Gravesend provided a house in the close for the corporate accommodation of the choristers under a warden. Twenty-five years later his successor, Oliver Sutton, appropriated the rectory of one parish and part of another for the maintenance of the twelve boys. The rectory was, in the spelling of 1115, that of 'Ascbi'. By 1291 it had come to be known as 'Askeby parvorum chori Lincolniensis' (Ashby of the boys of the choir of Lincoln) and subsequently, as it still is today, as Ashby Puerorum.[30] Twelve years after Lincoln a house was provided at Exeter to the south west of the cathedral's west front where the fourteen choristers were to live with the succentor, himself not a canon but a vicar choral. They were fed from the kitchen of a neighbouring canonry. Alongside the boys' dormitory was the room where they were taught song and reading.[31] In 1307 the maintenance of the York choristers was made a charge on Brodsworth church.

Salisbury is the next cathedral from which we have evidence of reform. At a time when, for almost a century, the deans were papally-provided absentee Italian cardinals, Salisbury was fortunate to have in succession two bishops of the first order, Simon of Ghent and Roger Martival. Both were outstanding scholar administrators, both had been chancellors of Oxford university, both had been archdeacons and canons at Lincoln, and indeed Martival had been an assiduously resident dean there. Both took a profound interest in their new cathedral. It was almost certainly during their time, in the first two decades of the fourteenth century, that Salisbury's prodigious tower and spire went up above the thirteenth-century crossing.[32] Yet both had the time and interest to care for their choristers. In May 1314 Simon of Ghent secured a royal patent providing the rent from 'a cellar under a hall in the town of Salisbury in a place called

Fysschamels' (Fish-shambles), as well as rent from neighbouring shops, 'for the sustenance of fourteen chorister boys of the church and of a master to instruct them in grammar'.[33] Within a year Simon of Ghent had died and it was Martival who then revealed a particularly humane concern for and interest in the welfare of the choristers. At Lincoln he had observed choristers properly cared for, and he set about ensuring that the same should be the case at Salisbury. In 1319 he drew up a set of statutes for the cathedral. Statute 45 required that the choristers should live in a designated house in the close, which was for the first twenty-five years on the site of the house known today as the Hungerford Chantry, and thereafter a house close to the gate to the Bishop's Palace. The choristers were to be in the charge of a warden, a resident canon who should be, Martival subsequently specified, 'an honest man, well-grounded in grammar and able to build [the boys] up in letters and behaviour' and 'a man commendable for moral character and manners', together with an assistant master and a resident servant. The warden's title came more often to be *magister choristarum* – and here at last we find singing boys called by the name that has been theirs ever since: choristers.[34] About 1322 the bishop improved the boys' endowment by appropriating to them the revenues from the church of Preshute, near Marlborough. In September 1322 Martival wrote to the master of the choristers, Alexander de Hemingsby, setting out his intentions for the boys:

> The boy choristers and their master shall pass their time in an honourable sort gathered together into one society, living in common and having all necessity for begging, and all excuse for wandering about, and those other inconveniences which we have mentioned before, done away. And there may the boys more freely attend diligently to the ministry committed to them, and also to the study and pursuit of manners and learning because they have befitting maintenance; ... and being adorned with the jewels of the virtues in the flower of their age, may by the grace of divine mercy receive the increase of honour and exaltation.

At Wells statutes dating from 1338 deal with choristers' behaviour, forbidding them to play or throw stones in the cathedral, the cemetery or the cloister. Shortly after this date a new choristers' house was built for them. In fact twelve boys lived there with their master: the six statutory choristers and a further six older boys, some certainly ex-choristers with broken voices, some at least of whom were kept on as altarists and acolytes, others perhaps as singers. The master had his own room. The boys slept in a single dormitory with just four (large) beds for the twelve (small) boys: a pair of younger boys with their heads at one end, an older *tabellarius* with his head at the other end, all six feet inter-mingling in the middle. Meanwhile in London, St Paul's, uniquely amongst the secular cathedrals, had chosen the almonry, a twelfth-century addition to the cathedral's buildings, conveniently adjacent to the bakehouse and brewery, for the housing of its choristers. In addition to distributing food to the poor and arranging for pauper burials, the almoner was to house, feed and clothe eight chorister boys, and, without charge, to teach them (or cause them to be taught) the liturgy, grammar and morals. Provision for them at the almonry must have been pretty basic, as the chapter gave instructions that when the boys accepted hospitality in canons' houses they must eat sitting on the floor in order not to become dissatisfied with their conditions in the almonry.[35] The housing of singing-boys in the almonry was later to become a widespread practice in Benedictine monasteries.[36] Lichfield seems to have made no proper provision for its choristers' accommodation until the sixteenth century; even then it took some three decades for funds to be sufficient for a house to be completed and occupied in the late 1520s.[37] Hereford, with only five choristers, perhaps had least motive for housing them centrally. They were lodged and fed individually throughout the middle ages. As late as 1526 a cathedral chapter act required that when a canon was absent from Hereford he should make arrangements to board his chorister with another canon. This must have had a deleterious effect on the coherence of the choristers as a team.[38]

From the growing number of documents concerning the life of choristers from the fourteenth century onwards,[39] it is clear that the need to give the boys a proper education became an increasingly important factor in the improvement in their domestic circumstances and in changes to their daily schedule. Up to the eleventh century what might be called primary education was provided from and for the liturgy by a liturgist, the precentor. In the centuries that follow, for a cluster of reasons this ceased to be good enough. First, within the quire itself, ever more varied and taxing demands were being made by an increasingly elaborate liturgy. No doubt more importantly, society was demanding a growing number of literate men. Parents of choristers expected their sons in due course to enter that cadre. So some at least of the young choristers needed an education that would prepare them for transfer, after voice-break, to the grammar school. These can already be traced in the eleventh century at Exeter, Lincoln, London and Salisbury.[40] By 1138 London had three established grammar schools and we find the acting bishop of London taking perhaps the earliest of what were to become widespread steps to check the spread of unlicensed schools.[41] In 1179 the third Lateran Council decreed that every cathedral must appoint and fund a master to teach without charge the cathedral clerks and other poor scholars, under the direction of the cathedral's chancellor. It was to these grammar schoolmasters that choristers were to proceed, either when they had ceased to be singers or when they had exhausted the educational resources of their song school. Some song schools managed to enhance their resources. Early evidence of specialist rather than generalist teachers – an issue that was to be unresolved until the twentieth century in some choir schools – comes from Lincoln where, some time between 1397 and 1407, the chorister school had a teacher of grammar, a teacher of song and a character (the 'steward') who acted very much like a housemaster-cum-bursar.[42] On the other hand, from about 1300 there is evidence that some choristers were, throughout, being educated not in a song school but by the grammar schoolmaster or indeed at the grammar school.[43] The heart of the matter was how much grammar should be taught, 'grammar' being the learning of Latin vocabulary and syntax and, usually at the secondary stage, the reading of its literature. Very little emphasis is found at this period on the teaching of writing. Usually the curriculum would be pragmatic, dependent on the quality of teaching and teachers available. One of the best must have been the early fourteenth-century almoner of St Paul's cathedral, William de Tolleshunte. In his will he left all his grammar books to the almonry boys and his more advanced books on history, medicine and law as a library from which former almonry boys could borrow.[44] But the provision could be deplorable. At Chichester in 1402 the bishop, in his visitation, reported the lack of any master 'diligent in teaching the choristers grammar', whilst later in the century Thomas Gyldesburgh, schoolmaster at Chichester for over thirty years, was 'over eighty, right corpulent, with a malady in his leg' and also in prison for debt.[45] Clearly at Lincoln around 1400 the song school was in excellent hands and doing what might be thought of as grammar school teaching; elsewhere grammar schools undertook some 'elementary' work, as they were to do for centuries. It is, in any case, dangerous to assume that the nature, or even existence, of a medieval school at one date can be taken as guarantee that its nature or existence are to be presumed at any other date.[46] A rigid distinction between the two might well be thought to be anachronistic; yet it was no later than 1315 that the master of the grammar school at Warwick complained to the chapter of St Mary's church that the master of their song school was teaching Donatus,[47] thereby encroaching on his curricular territory. The matter was firmly settled by chapter decree that the song school master must teach his boys only 'their first letters, the psalter, music and song'.[48]

There certainly did come to be an assumed level of elementary education that was regarded as necessary to permit entry to grammar schools with academic aspirations. William of Wykeham's statutes of 1400 for his college at Winchester require that a boy to be admitted as a scholar, not later than his thirteenth year, should have a sound grounding in reading, song and elementary (Latin) grammar. Wykeham's own college choristers would need this if they were to proceed, as it was intended they should, to the college in due course.[49] Such was also the case at Eton two generations later.[50] And even little boys seeking entry to the song school would be expected to have mastered the very basics: the abc, elementary reading skills and the commitment of the *Pater Noster* and other simple prayers to memory. In the eleventh and twelfth centuries the song school might well have no books beyond those used by the master. Alphabets and words might be found written on the whitewashed schoolroom wall, as in the (later) example that still survives in the vestry of St Michael's church, North Cadbury in Somerset. But from the thirteenth century text books do appear. Numerous copies survive of the little primers that contained prayers and simple devotions such as the Hours of the Virgin. At the same time availability of service books for the mass and the office was becoming widespread, although the choristers would still be expected to sing from memory. Unlike the canons and vicars choral of the two upper rows, the boys in quire had no bookstand.

It was here, in quire, that what Martival had called the choristers' ministry was chiefly fulfilled. Throughout the medieval centuries the round of worship in the secular cathedrals was closely similar to that observed in the monasteries. There were a morrow mass and the principal mass of the day, alongside subsidiary masses said or more rarely sung at the numerous side altars and the ever-increasing chantries. And the full round of the office, matins (or nocturnes), lauds, prime, terce, sext, none, vespers (or 'evensong' as it was called in some secular cathedrals) and compline, was sung by day and by night in quire. Furthermore, the cathedral quire was a private area, the private chapel as it were of the bishop, chapter and clerkly community. Insofar as the public did come into medieval cathedrals it was to the nave, with its Jesus altar, or the Lady chapel. In the later middle ages it was in these areas that additional services tended to be held, particularly in connection with the cult of the Virgin, for whom a daily mass became common from the twelfth century.[51] The public would also be drawn to witness the great processions that marked the holiest days and the acts of liturgical drama that were, from the fourteenth century, to find their way outside the church into the close or the market place.

No two cathedrals celebrated exactly the same liturgy. The honouring of local saints, William at York, Hugh at Lincoln, Chad at Lichfield, Richard at Chichester, to name but a few, brought discrete rites to individual foundations. Nor was there one uniform 'Use'. Around a core, common to all, Hereford and York in particular maintained idiosyncratic liturgies until the Reformation. Nevertheless, in the course of the medieval centuries the Use of Sarum achieved a grip on English, and on Welsh, Scottish and Irish,[52] non-monastic worship that made it a sort of standard.[53] Its very richness made it paradigmatic. 'Among the churches of the whole world, the Church of Sarum shines resplendent, like the sun in his full orb, in respect of its divine service and its ministers, and by spreading its rays everywhere makes up for the defects of others', wrote the thirteenth-century bishop Giles of Bridport, not without partiality.[54] Sarum Use was adopted in the royal and university chapels during the fourteenth century. St Paul's cathedral changed from its own to Sarum Use in 1415, Chichester changed shortly after this, and in the sixteenth century it was to the Sarum texts that Cranmer turned when creating the English Book of Common Prayer. Texts, not text: because there never was a single document. The body of liturgy was too vast to bind within one pair of covers and the Use was itself continuously under revision. New celebrations, such as that of *Corpus Christi* from 1264, were added, enrichments accreted, until Wycliffe came to rail against the whole elaborate structure as an abomination. Eventually the Council of Trent was to cut this overblown liturgy back to its essentials. But it is from the Use of Sarum, with some thirty extant thirteenth- to fifteenth-century sources in manuscript, as well as early printed antiphonals, graduals, hymnals, missals and processionals, and above all from its ordinals and customaries, that we can most readily learn what young boys were called upon to do, and how they were to do it, in the liturgy of the medieval cathedrals.[55]

It is likely that in the earliest centuries the boys were expected to sing the whole daily mass and office along with the canons. But there seems to be no evidence either to support or refute this supposition. By the time of the Sarum Customary and Consuetudinary,[56] dating probably from the early thirteenth century, after Richard Poore had moved his chapter and was building his cathedral in the valley, it is explicit that not all boys were required to attend all services. Even here, however, the documents are far from unambiguous. The annual programme of mass and office was immensely complex; the Customary and Consuetudinary are not always in accord with one another. Indeed, one is tempted to suspect (as has been said of other areas of medieval history) that if the matter appears to become clear one can be sure that one is on the wrong track.

Nevertheless, the Customary requires attendance by *all* boys as follows:[57]

> Let it be noted that the boys are required to observe all double feasts, Sundays, and feasts of nine lessons with a triple invitatory antiphon, by their presence at vespers, compline, matins, at the first of the day hours [prime] and mass; also at vigils of the dead whenever the corpse is present and at trentals [thirty-day commemorations following the death of dignitaries] and anniversaries.

The obligations begin with vespers, that is *first* vespers, which was sung with compline on the eve of every feast, the celebration ending with second vespers followed by compline on the feast day itself. There were approaching eighty feast days in the above categories, ranging from principal doubles like Christmas and Easter to such secondary feasts as St Peter *in vinculis* and St John *ante portam Latinam*, and fifty-two Sundays (though some would coincide with feasts). Trentals and commemorations of the recently deceased were, of course, unpredictable in number. Nevertheless, the implication is that all the boys were required for at least four offices and the main mass on somewhere between a third and half of all the days of any year, with first vespers and compline sung on a further hundred or more days (allowing for some overlaps). It will be noticed that there is no reference to the shorter offices of terce, sext and none; but on all Sundays and most double feasts, some eighty occasions a year, terce and sext could be sung as an introduction to the liturgy of the mass. On feast days the morning offices, procession and mass would rarely take less than two hours, often more. The evening offices were briefer.

The main mass of a Sunday or a major festival was indeed a splendid occasion, preceded, following the end of prime, by a procession, for which the boys on great feasts wore silk copes in the liturgical colour of the day. The procession was led by a chorister carrying the holy water and then, according to the rank of the feast, by increasingly many crucifers and thurifers, in addition to the usual acolytes, sub-deacon, deacon and celebrant. The bishop, when present, processed last of all. The officiant sprinkled each altar as it was reached, the choir singing antiphons, responsories and hymns. From the font, before the west doors, the procession returned up the central aisle, making a station at the rood between nave and quire before re-entering the quire from the west. The boys filed eastwards alongside their bench, junior canons (when there were any) in the lead,[58] the very youngest boys at the rear, followed, as we have seen, by any clergy under penance. The boys sang with the men the plainsong chants (one selected from many available sets) for the ordinary of the mass,[59] that is to say, the *Kyrie, Gloria*,[60] *Sanctus, Benedictus* and *Agnus Dei*. Similarly they sang with the men the greater part of the propers particular to the day, antiphons, responsories, graduals, alleluias and hymns. For these items the opening *incipits*, often with later repetition, were sung by soloists and small groups, sometimes men, sometimes boys. Whereas the adults stood for part and sat for part of the liturgy, the boys stood for virtually everything: 'Now the clerks sit and the boys, whether canons or not, stand in front of the others', states the Consuetudinary at one point;[61] and, with reference to vespers, the Customary specifies, 'The boys, indeed without exception, remain standing throughout, except in Easter week'.[62] The office rites, as in the monasteries, entailed primarily the chanting by full choir of psalms, along with canticles such as *Magnificat* at vespers and *Nunc dimittis* at compline, along with mostly shorter responsories and antiphons. Soloists and small groups ranging from two to seven voices brought brilliant variety to the singing of the office and the mass *incipits*. On the greatest feasts the solemnity of the day was marked at most points by the seniority of the soloists: the precentor himself or canons rather than vicars. Nevertheless, for example, at Easter vespers three boys sang the Alleluia, and on All Saints' Day five boys sang the responsory to the eighth lesson, *audivi vocem*. On some lesser feasts pairs of boys would leave their bench and stand either at the step just east of the choir or upon the rood screen or *pulpitum* which separated quire from nave and sing from there. Even when the main body of boys was not present, the Use still required two choristers on simple feasts and one chorister on ferias (non-festal days) to sing *incipits*. Often, but not invariably, these boys would be the hebdomadaries, boys listed on the precentor's or succentor's *tabula* or notice-board to sing listed solos for the week.

We have already seen how Maundy Thursday was marked in the monasteries by a night office that included twelve short lessons, each preceded by an antiphon and followed by a responsory. As each antiphon and responsory ended, so a candle was extinguished, ultimately leaving the building in total darkness. This office, in the Sarum Use, was one of those attended by all the boys and there was a really touching addition to that prescribed by the *Regularis concordia*. After the extinction of the last candle, as in the Benedictine rite, the responsory was sung (at Sarum by the boys only): '*Christus dominus factus est obediens usque ad mortem.*' (Christ the Lord was made obedient even unto death). Then, in the darkness, *unus puerulus* (one *little* boy) was to say or chant in a pure voice, *mortem autem crucis* [even the death of the cross]; and the whole community prostrated themselves and said the *Pater Noster*. Such a moment of dramatic solemnity cannot easily have been forgotten.

Yet the most memorable celebration for the boys happened four days previously, the procession of palms on Palm Sunday preceding high mass, a ceremonial of particularly rich pageantry.[63] It provided, especially at the various 'stations' *en route*, a liturgical replication of Christ's entry into Jerusalem. Indeed its origins go back to Jerusalem itself. Some time in the early fifth century a redoubtable Spanish nun, Egeria, made a great pilgrimage to the Holy Land and was present in Jerusalem on Palm Sunday. In her extraordinary diary she describes how a procession formed on the Mount of the Ascension and moved down towards the city, all the children bearing olive branches and palm fronds, the people chanting '*Benedictus qui venit*'. Here is the earliest account of what would become perhaps the church of Jerusalem's most significant contribution to the liturgy.[64] It took a firm hold on western Christendom. At most cathedrals and monasteries there was a procession out of the church and into the town to another church.[65] Here the palms and fronds were waiting and to this church, ahead of the main procession, a small group representing Christ and his apostles brought some of the cathedral's most hallowed relics along with a pyx carrying the consecrated host. Here they were joined by the larger procession, representing the Palm Sunday crowd. At Hereford, for example, the processions went out to an unspecified location outside the city walls.[66] The Use of Sarum prescribes processions which circumambulate the cathedral but do not venture outside the Close. Unfortunately for the scholar, the Sarum documents are the least clear: they are mutually inconsistent, probably reflecting a changing and developing rite; and at points they appear to conflict with the cathedral topography. Nevertheless, they are emphatic about the vital roles played by boy choristers.

Palms and fronds were blessed, sperged and censed before the high altar. Then the larger procession set off around the outside of the church. The first station at Sarum was, in the earlier centuries, at a location difficult to identify, but by the fifteenth century it was certainly at the churchyard cross, outside the north transept. There three prophecies were sung by a chorister stationed in a high place, then, 'Postea evanescit' – after that he vanishes![67] By the early sixteenth century he was appearing dressed in suitably prophetic clothing and bearded.[68] Here they were joined by the second procession, Christ meeting the crowd. The processions then moved around the east end of the cathedral to the canons' cemetery and there a second station was made, graves were sperged and seven boys sang the hymn, Gloria laus, once again 'in eminentiori loco'. This eminence may have been a parapet of the cloister roof.[69] The boys sang the opening verse; it was repeated by the crowd; then the boys sang each of the following verses, the crowd responding each time with Gloria laus as a chorus. By contrast, at most cathedrals and monasteries Gloria laus was sung at the next station, either as they re-entered the Close with boys atop the gate or as they re-entered the cathedral. At York a temporary high platform was built for the choristers at the West Front. At Wells it was sung from an interior balcony above the cathedral's west doors through purpose-built apertures still there, to the responding procession, waiting below to enter the cathedral. The mystery is that there is an almost identical balcony at Salisbury with apertures, now once more in use on Palm Sunday. Yet none of the Sarum documents places Gloria laus here.[70] When the procession did enter through the west door it passed, in another act of memorable drama, beneath the canopy held aloft with its relics and the host: the crowd entering Jerusalem where Christ, in the form of the consecrated bread, was waiting to welcome them. A fourth and final station was made at the rood screen before re-entering the quire.

The manuscripts and printed texts of the Sarum Use about this and every other service and ceremony imply that almost everything sung was monodic.[71] However, it is well known that, at least from the tenth century, experiments were being made with touches of harmony, first by way of improvisation, later from notated scores. Recent research appears to have established beyond doubt that until virtually the end of the fourteenth century part-singing was exclusively the province of small ensembles of adult males.[72] This being so, it may be thought that the role of no more than a hundred or so cathedral choristers at any one time, albeit sometimes as soloists, did not amount to very much. Yet it was critical. For some two centuries, from about 1150 until about 1350, only in the secular cathedrals and the larger collegiate churches were boys' voices heard singing in choir anywhere in Britain. These few choristers provided the vital thread of continuity for a tradition, traceable back to Augustine, that was to burst into splendour in the two centuries prior to the Reformation.

4

The Great Flowering

The last two medieval centuries were not easy times in England. Following from the wave of plague associated with the Black Death came severe population decline, monetary inflation and civil unrest; a century of war with the French brought no lasting advantage; the monarchy and the aristocracy tore themselves apart in a seemingly unending civil war; and the church was unsettled by a papacy in schism and the early rumblings of theological upheaval that were to culminate in the Reformation. Yet it was during these two centuries, approximately between 1350 and 1550, that the church's music, indeed one might simply say *music*, underwent a transformation greater and more fruitful than can be found in any comparable period before or since, more revolutionary than the creation of the symphony orchestra or the birth of jazz: the invention of what has ever since been the standard form of chorus, composed of treble, alto, tenor and bass voices. For this ensemble, choristers were an essential element.[1]

During these centuries there was a huge expansion in the number of churches and chapels in which choral music with choristers was to be heard. The monasteries, which had banned boys from their quires, brought them back, sometimes literally through the side door, into their Lady chapels and naves. It has been estimated that by the fifteenth century there were some forty or fifty monastic Lady chapel choirs, mostly Benedictine and Augustinian.[2] Even more important was the growth of choral foundations in colleges, schools and chantries, and in aristocratic and royal chapels. Coincidentally, the tentative ventures into music sung in two or three parts by solo voices as ornamentation to a tenor plainsong line broke out of their straitjacket: by the late fifteenth century there were whole choirs singing polyphonic music, ultimately freeing themselves from any strand of plainchant and opening into richnesses of five, six or seven parts from high treble to low bass.[3] As a consequence, instead of choir stalls being filled with clergy who happened to be able to sing, singers were musicians first and clerks, increasingly lay clerks, second. Skill in music became the chief criterion in the selection of boy choristers: to get hold of the best boys there was fierce competition, bribery, kidnap even. Many factors combined to bring about this revolution, but underlying all else were changes in devotional emphasis and practice.

It might be assumed that the mother of Jesus had always held a significant place in Christian teaching and reverence, yet this is not so. Outside the gospels there is no reference to St Mary at any point in the New Testament other than a single tangential mention in the first chapter of Acts. She seems to have been of no interest, even unknown, to Paul. Nor is the mother of Jesus referred to in any non-biblical writing during the first two Christian centuries, apart from the second-century *Protoevangelium* of James.[4] Only from the fifth century did church councils begin to concern themselves with Mary's place in the scheme of salvation. Her virginity was not made Catholic doctrine until the fifth General Council of 553.[5] Church dedications to Mary in Anglo-Saxon England, so far as can be judged from the patchy evidence, were less numerous than those to saints Peter, Paul, Andrew, Gregory and Michael. No pre-Conquest English cathedral church was dedicated to her.

Following the Conquest the picture rapidly changed. The new cathedrals of the 1080s at Lincoln and Salisbury were both dedicated to St Mary; from the eleventh century onwards, church dedications to her greatly outnumbered those to any other saint.[6] Most significant for the purposes of this history was the development of masses votive to the Virgin. In the eleventh and twelfth centuries these tended to be celebrated on one day in the week, frequently on Saturdays. But a daily Lady mass was introduced before 1140 at Bury St Edmunds and Tewkesbury;[7] in the course of the twelfth century there was a daily celebration in more and more collegiate churches. By 1235 Abbot William de Trumpington of St Albans could write that 'in all the noble churches of England a Mass of the Blessed Mary is solemnly sung by note daily'.[8] At first such masses were sung at a Mary altar; but chapels dedicated to her honour began to be added, and built with increasing architectural beauty and splendour. The earliest Lady chapel to be added eastwards of the quire was at Winchester between 1189 and 1204. Slightly later, the Augustinian abbey at Bristol had a Lady chapel built in the other favourite position, north of the quire, to be replaced by a yet more splendid one east of the quire in the following century.[9] Thirteenth-century Lady chapels were added to such great monasteries as Chester, Oxford, Peterborough, St Albans and Southwell, at the monastic cathedrals of Norwich and Worcester, and at the secular cathedral of Exeter; by about 1300 Chichester had rebuilt and doubled the length of its existing eastward chapel. Even more lavish were the great fourteenth-century Lady chapels of Ely, Lichfield, Wells and York. Several of these were to attract particularly destructive attention from the Puritans. At Ely, above all, can be seen both the depth of the devotion to Our Lady that produced a chapel of exceptional proportions and decorative richness, and the subsequent angry iconoclasm that ravaged an incomparable sculpted panorama of the life of the Virgin.

Honour to the mother of Christ came to be expressed in all the art forms. There was a florescence of images in glass and stone and painted wood, and of literature in her honour. Chaucer's Canterbury Tales again and again express his personal devotion to Mary.[10] But this spiritual devotion also found expression in the new music for her masses and other acts of worship, such as the office of Our Lady first found at Bury St Edmunds about 1120,[11] and the antiphons, effectively anthems, sung before her images at the close of the day. Two factors encouraged and facilitated this musical outpouring. First, the Lady chapel, not being the conventual or canonical quire, was open to the public: it was the *capella familiaris* where lay associates of the monastery or cathedral and, increasingly, the people of the town could come. Secondly, and for the same reason, boys, banned from the monastic quires, were welcomed to sing in the monastic Lady chapels.

As it happened, a supply of boys was available. When child oblation became unacceptable, the tradition of monastic song schools died. Some large houses continued to maintain grammar schools outside the precincts, but nowhere beyond the twelfth century is a monastic song school to be found.[12] Yet education had clearly been one of the charitable functions, alongside hospitality and care for the destitute, that Benedict had envisaged as proper for a monastic community. As it was, all flourishing monasteries had, by their main gate, an almonry where the poor and sick were received, tended, fed and blessed.[13] We have seen how the oblate boys had a role in the washing of the feet of the poor. Here, in their almonries, monasteries began the practice of accommodating a small number of poor boys, often the apostolic thirteen, in order to provide elementary grammar schooling not otherwise available.[14] It is difficult to say where or exactly when this practice started. All early references are to schooling that was already up and running. Claimant for first place used to be Ely (1314), 'the earliest in England'.[15] In fact evidence from two Kentish cathedrals, Canterbury and Rochester, proves the existence of almonry boys as early as the final decade of the thirteenth century.[16] Even they seem not to have been the first. A single sheet of parchment of Norwich provenance found, surprisingly, in the archives of Worcester cathedral priory in the early 1990s produced this new candidate for earliest almonry school. The Norwich document is a mid-fourteenth-century copy of an original that derives from the priorate of William de Kirkby, that is, no later than 1288/9.[17] There were to be thirteen poor boys, not physically handicapped, apt for being taught, under a master to teach them grammar and morals and a servant to provide for their domestic needs. For idleness or misconduct a boy could be dismissed following the conventional third warning. From the fourteenth century references to almonry boys appear increasingly frequently in monastic accounts: at Westminster from 1317, at St Albans before 1335 and at Durham during the 1350s.[18] By this time the practice was becoming general amongst the larger Benedictine and Augustinian houses and even established itself in smaller houses. In some cases, Worcester is an example, the monastery used its almonry merely as a boarding house and sent its boys for education to the local grammar school.[19] Information about the existence of such schools can be incidental: a report that in November and December of 1378 the monks of St Peter's Abbey, Gloucester were dislodged from their normal refectory while Richard II's parliament met there, the monks for two months being forced to eat in the schoolroom, has been cited as evidence of an almonry school there, though the evidence is not conclusive.[20]

It has sometimes been assumed that the almonry boys were there from the first to sing in the Lady chapel.[21] But recent research makes it virtually certain that in most if not all foundations, for some decades at least, the boys performed no choral function, but were there as beneficiaries of charitable schooling (often alongside fee-paying supernumeraries) and available to serve as acolytes at altars outside the monastic quire, including that of the Lady chapel. This latter role became pressing as votive masses increased and Benedictine rules insisted that priest-monks, when celebrating, must be served by trained acolytes.[22] Only later, at most foundations, is there evidence of the use of almonry boys as singers. At Westminster Abbey boy trebles are known to have been singing in the Lady chapel from 1384.[23] At Worcester, where boys had been taught in the almonry probably from the 1340s, two of these boys in the 1390s were attending upon John Ylleway, Custos of the chapel of the Blessed Mary, as *pueri de capella*.[24] More significant of the trend was an endowment in 1402 by Alice, widow of John Tolmache, to fund a cantor and four choristers for the enhancement of the daily Lady mass at the cathedral priory of Winchester.[25] Norwich seems again to have been ahead of other foundations. The chapter ordinance referred to above, datable from before 1290, specifies that on Sundays and feast days, after lessons in school coincident with conventual mass in quire, the almonry boys were to go to the church of St Mary in the Marsh, which lay within the cathedral precincts, where they were to chant the psalms and assist with the readings, divided into *decani* and *cantoris*, one set being singers, the other set readers '*secundum quod deus dederit eis facultatem*', that is, as God has given them aptitude.[26] It is striking that they went to sing in their parish church within the precincts but not in the cathedral's own Lady chapel. In the course of the following century, however, the boys' role was indeed changed to that of singing the daily Lady mass.[27] Almoners' accounts from the late fourteenth century refer to them as *clerici beate virginis*, *clerici beate Marie* or *clerici sancte Marie*. If Norwich was the earliest foundation at which almonry boys may have sung, at the opposite extreme amongst the major Benedictine foundations was, perhaps, Winchester. Although there had probably been almonry boys there since at least 1312,[28] no reference to them as singers can be found before 1340, when John Tyes, not himself a monk, was appointed 'to be of service to the convent by playing the organ and singing at the daily mass of Blessed Mary [at her altar] ... and by instructing the convent [almonry] boys in chant on the understanding that their number will never exceed four'.[29] This development was presumably funded by Alice Tolmache's endowment. Two years later the duty to sing a Marian antiphon and *de profundis* daily in William of Wykeham's chantry chapel was added. Before the end of the century the terms of the master's contract include the teaching of polyphony to the now *eight* boys – notwithstanding the earlier insistence that they should not exceed four. The development of the use of boys as Lady chapel singers is illustrated particularly clearly at Christ Church, Canterbury. Here a daily Lady mass had been celebrated from at latest 1200. By the late thirteenth century it was specifically being sung by the monastic precentor and seven monks, although an almonry school was in existence. At some point in the fourteenth or early fifteenth century the critical change was made; from 1438 there were eight boys forming the Lady chapel choir under a secular master and cantor, the composer Lionel Power. Three decades later the musical transformation was complete: the boys, together with adult male singers, were being trained to sing virtuosic, state of the art polyphony.[30]

It was not only in the Lady chapels that special choral honour was done to the Virgin. Everywhere in the later medieval decades there were choristers closing the day's worship at dusk with the singing of a Marian antiphon in the nave of the building before an image of the Virgin, in the presence of what may often have been large numbers of devout lay people.[31] Indeed, it was not principally from the monasteries themselves that the drive to make these dramatic changes came. The pace was being set in remarkable private foundations. Before turning to these, it will be proper to give attention briefly to the nunneries, albeit that the evidence is thin. No medieval nunnery produced a chronicle, comparatively few names have survived and virtually all references to children in nunneries come from sources external to the houses themselves, from such documents as bishops' visitations, family correspondence and contemporary literature.[32]

The English nunneries had enjoyed a golden age in the last two Anglo-Saxon centuries. Honoured by kings, they had been beneficiaries of rich endowments and had attracted able recruits from among whom were drawn a number of famous abbesses. For reasons not wholly clear, the Conquest seems to have brought this period of distinction to an end. Shaftesbury was a notable exception, to the extent that in 1326 the house was instructed to admit no more novices until their numbers had reduced to 120. But most nunneries in the thirteenth and fourteenth centuries were small, many very small indeed. Many were also very poor, living from hand to mouth and desperate for any available source of income. Education provided an obvious opportunity for earning money. Thus it is that, despite the canonical banning of child oblation, children, chiefly girls but also sometimes young boys, were to be found as part of the nunnery communities in these centuries. Most often they were maintained respectably as pupils boarding in the abbess's household, but episcopal visitations make it clear that sometimes they were maintained less respectably with the community of nuns.[33]

Nunnery children were found in two categories, though – as so often in the middle ages – the categories are often impossible to distinguish, the one blending into the other. Most girls and all boys at medieval nunneries were there primarily to be educated. In many cases the nunneries were the medieval dame schools, teaching the alphabet and going on, if only up to a point, to teach the familiar song school curriculum. The twelfth-century Hugh of Lincoln sent five-year-old Robert of Noyon to the nuns of Elstow 'to be taught his letters'.[34] A decade before the Dissolution Sir John Stanley provided in his will for his son, together with appropriate servants, to be looked after and educated by the abbess of Barking until the age of twelve, before proceeding to Westminster School. But, for all that canon law banned the practice, nunneries went on accepting small numbers of very young girls who had been implicitly, even if not explicitly, oblated to the house or were certainly intended by their families to be taking the first steps towards a lifelong vocation. Despite sixteen being the youngest canonical age for a novice, the seven-year-old Katherine de Beauchamp was in the nunnery of Shouldham in 1359, described as a 'nun'. William Greenfield, an early fourteenth-century archbishop of York, licensed the nunnery of Hampole to receive Elena Sperri at the age of eight. Bishop Alnwick, in 1441, found three 'nuns' all under fourteen at Ankerwyke.[35] These are examples of an unknown number of little girls who grew up in English nunneries in the later medieval centuries. Parental piety doubtless encouraged such placements. But there were less honourable motives. There is an account of a nine-year-old heiress being made oblate so that her family could secure the benefits of her inheritance for themselves.[36] Cardinal Archbishop Thomas Wolsey placed his illegitimate daughter with the nuns of Shaftesbury. As with the earlier boy oblates these child nuns spent many hours a day singing in quire. Children in nunneries specifically as pupils almost certainly joined the nuns in quire for some at least of their liturgy.

It would be wrong to assume that such girls faced a life of deprivation. A well-run nunnery could provide the setting for a deeply fulfilled life. The thirty or forty children at Polesworth were recorded at the Dissolution as having been 'right virtuously brought up'; and after the Dissolution the Protestant Thomas Becon regretted the universal closure of places where girls were 'godly brought up to be discreet, chaste, housewifely and good'. One must also add that after 1536 the opportunity to sing in quire was absolutely closed to girls until the twentieth century.[37] On the other hand, many of the nunneries struggled to survive, and bishops' visitations are full of attempts to prevent lapses of good order. Girls *and boys* were not to sleep in the nuns' dormitory at Flamstead (1530); the young nuns at Ankerwyke (1441) had nobody capable of teaching them reading or song; in the diocese of Lichfield individual nuns had taken to keeping children with them. Other sources paint even more telling pictures. Little Bridget Plantagenet was sent to St Mary's, Winchester, when her parents were posted to France. It can hardly be doubted that on occasions she attended mass and offices in quire, though the repeated requests in the abbess's letters to her mother, alongside requests for clothing, for 'two matins bookes' almost certainly have nothing to do with the quire liturgy. 'Matins book' was the popular name for the little books of the hours of the Virgin which were widely used in the later middle ages for private devotions.[38] Bridget was not happy, however, and indeed was so unhappy that after two or so years the family steward removed her because she was 'very spare and hath need of cherishing'. This reads like a very early case of schoolgirl anorexia. Perhaps most touching of all is the tale from Caesarius of Heisterbach, to be found at Appendix 1.

No evidence has survived to indicate that the music of the nunneries was anywhere remarkable. There was no English Hildegard of Bingen. To find the most advanced music in fifteenth-century England one must look to the royal and aristocratic domestic chapels and the chapels of the recently established educational foundations. Royal and aristocratic houses had always had chapels.[39] In the early medieval centuries, and in the less affluent houses, the chapel might be little more than an embrasure within the thick castle wall, staffed by a single priest-chaplain who could celebrate a daily mass. But by the fifteenth century most aristocratic families demonstrated their prestige by building substantial chapels, large enough to accommodate a numerous household, with a chapel staff imitative of that of the Chapel Royal or of a modest cathedral.[40] A small song school with a master would be maintained in order to provide a team of choristers, essential once polyphony was taken up in the chapel. One of the earliest recorded as including boys was that of John of Gaunt (1340–1399). Lady Margaret Beaufort, the mother of Henry VII, at Collyweston near Stamford, and Edward Stafford, duke of Buckingham, both employed choirs with from ten to twelve boy choristers in the late fifteenth century. Around 1500 Lady Margaret's choristers were recruited from as far away as the west country; they were provided with hose, surplices and grammar books; and, above all, careful provision was made for their future education at schools including Eton and Winchester. One of her boys, Thomas Bury, later became a Gentleman of the Chapel Royal.[41] From the same period the *Regulations and Establishments of the Household of ... the Fifth Earl of Northumberland* shows boys and men singing daily mass, matins and vespers, including polyphony in up to five parts at Leconfield.[42]

Most remarkable of all were the chapels of the new educational foundations. Like the Lady chapels, they too derived from a change in popular devotion and theology. The doctrines of purgatory and of the validity of votive prayer, and especially the offering of the mass with the intention of lessening the time spent by souls undergoing purgation, became hugely influential in the later middle ages.

Prayers for the Christian dead had, of course, a long history. Peter had written of Christ preaching to the spirits in prison and Paul provides a vivid description of purgatorial fires at work in his first letter to the Corinthians.[43] But doctrine about the state or states of the dead took centuries to develop: not until 1274 did purgatory find a place in conciliar teaching and only at the Council of Florence in 1439 did that teaching become Catholic dogma. For centuries mourners had been content that the names of their dead should simply be added to a foundation's obit list. Associating such prayers with the offering of the mass can, however, be found as far back as the fourth-century Cyril of Jerusalem, who wrote that the souls of the departed would 'obtain the greatest help if we make our prayers for them while the holy and most awesome sacrifice is being offered'.[44] In the high middle ages money was frequently donated to pay for a priest to say a votive mass: often large numbers of named masses would be said each day at subsidiary altars. As has been seen, the almonry boys at Norwich were 'tabled' on the duty list to serve at such masses. In 1235 a small chapel was endowed in Lincoln Cathedral specifically for the saying of perpetual masses for the soul of Bishop Hugh of Wells, the earliest recorded case of a practice that was to become widespread amongst the pious wealthy.[45] Exactly a century later, in the north choir aisle of the same cathedral, a chantry for Bishop Henry Burghersh was founded on a lavish scale, serviced by five priests, a benefaction that also provided education for six boys later to be metamorphosed into choristers. To this day some six of the Lincoln boys enjoy endowment from this benefaction and continue to be called 'Burghersh chanters'.[46] Although such chantries were sometimes founded by wealthy laymen, most notably and gorgeously by King Henry VII at the eastern end of Westminster Abbey,[47] the great majority of those located in cathedrals were for the benefit of the souls of deceased prelates. Winchester cathedral has the finest surviving group of these in the country.

The whole matter of chantries and votive masses can appear unseemly. Preachers, especially perhaps the friars, were all too ready to prey on the susceptible with vivid pictures of fire, brimstone and agony which, in return for alms, might be abbreviated by a commensurate number of days. Even as learned and sympathetic a man as Sir Thomas More could write of the fire that 'as far passeth in heat all the fires that ever burned upon earth, as the hottest of all those passeth a feigned fire painted upon a wall' in a place where the purgatorial minders were 'cruel, damned sprites, … despiteful tormentors, and their company more horrible and grievous to us than the pain itself'.[48] When one couples this with the remembrance that Henry VII endowed his chantry chapel sufficiently to pay for the saying of ten thousand votive masses, the modern reaction is likely to be one of revulsion. And indeed, even before the dissolution of all chantries by Edward VI's Protestant ministers, the practice of endowing chantries was in decline. Chantries were replaced by the endowment of schools and almshouses as the preferred form of *post mortem* fire insurance, good works being deemed more efficacious than a multiplicity of masses. Eventually the Elizabethan Thirty-Nine Articles of Religion were famously to describe Purgatory as 'a fond thing vainly invented, and grounded upon no warranty of Scripture, but rather repugnant to the Word of God'.[49] Nevertheless, for a few centuries, serious, pious, admirable people with capital available, gave generously towards the foundation of chantries where perpetual masses were said to relieve the purgatorial sufferings of the souls of their forebears, their loved ones, their colleagues and themselves, believing Purgatory to be an example of God's loving generosity, a second chance to purge those wilful sins that they might have failed sufficiently to confess and repent of in this life. Such chapels often had a direct impact on the singing boys, as was the case at Winchester, where eight almonry boys were required to sing a votive anthem daily in William of Wykeham's chantry chapel from the day of his death in 1404.

Some chantries were established outside existing buildings: they were freestanding collegiate foundations. In 1415, for example, Edward, duke of York, took over the parish church of Fotheringhay and rebuilt and endowed it as the mausoleum and chantry of the house of York. The college was to consist of a master, twelve chaplains, eight clerks and thirteen choristers who were to be trained by a skilled musician. Similar foundations were those of the earls of Lancaster and Derby at the Newarke, Leicester and the Cromwell family collegiate church at Tattersall in Lincolnshire, the former maintaining six choristers and the latter eventually ten. At the Newarke and at Tattersall the chantry also supported an almshouse, symptomatic of the growing tendency to provide for works of mercy alongside votive prayer.[50] There was another form of provision that might be established alongside a chantry, of far greater national impact than a local almshouse. When William of Wykeham set up his chantry chapel in Winchester Cathedral he had already established two chantries on a far more substantial scale: they were 'the College of Saint Mary of Winchester in Oxford', commonly called New College, founded in 1379 and, three years later, 'the College of the Blessed Virgin Mary of Winchester near Winchester', commonly called Winchester College. Both these foundations were collegiate chantries with educational facilities attached.[51] At Oxford, alongside the warden, fellows and scholars, there were to be ten chaplains, three singing clerks and sixteen choristers. At Winchester, where there were also a warden, fellows, scholars and two schoolmasters, there were to be three chaplains, three singing clerks and sixteen quiristers.[52] The teaching and study to be undertaken at each foundation were, however, subsidiary to the chapel, where the whole gamut of Catholic liturgy, mass and office, with nine sung services a day, was to be performed to the glory of God and for the good of the soul of the founder and his kin. Indeed, should William's foundations fall upon hard times, the school and college were to be disbanded before the chapel and its body of clergy were touched. What is especially striking is that at both foundations the number of choristers provided was sixteen, far in excess of the five at Hereford and ten at St Paul's; more even than the fourteen at Exeter and Salisbury, the most generously choristered of the secular cathedrals.

Half a century later, in 1440, the pious, nineteen year old, Henry VI determined on a similar foundation: a pair of chantry chapels, one with an associated school, one with an associated university college. He spent twenty-four hours at Winchester, hearing mass, dining with the warden, fellows and headmaster, above all looking into the detail of the establishment. Winchester and New College were very precise models for Eton and King's College, Cambridge. The statutes of these royal foundations were based on those of William of Wykeham; Henry even persuaded the headmaster of Winchester, William Wayneflete, to come to Eton to plan the foundation in detail and to become its first provost. Henry VI's original intention at Eton had been to convert the parish church into a collegiate chapel with associated school and almonry. The foundation charter of October 1440, reflecting the 1352 constitution of St George's chapel in Windsor Castle, just across the river,[53] provided for just four singing clerks and six choristers with a schoolmaster, twenty-five scholars and twenty-five poor and infirm men. But in 1443, under Wayneflete's influence, the establishment was increased to a provost, ten fellows, ten chaplains, ten clerks 'skilled in chant' and sixteen choristers, with a master and usher to teach seventy scholars. The almsmen were reduced in number and subsequently suppressed altogether. King's College at Cambridge was to be similarly staffed with a provost, seventy fellows and scholars, ten priests, ten chaplains, six singing clerks and sixteen choristers.[54] William Wayneflete was himself, in turn, to found and then more generously refound Magdalen College, with an associated school adjacent, at Oxford.[55] The chapel of Magdalen College was likewise to be served by sixteen choristers. In a later chapter we shall give detailed consideration to a particular Magdalen tradition, the singing from the top of the college tower on May morning, whose roots may go back to the sixteenth-century topping out ceremony when the tower was completed. These five foundations, Winchester and New College, Eton and King's College and Magdalen, all inspired by William of Wykeham, employed between them eighty singing boys, almost matching the ninety-seven required by the whole body of English secular cathedrals at their height. Inevitably one wonders what had motivated Wykeham to determine upon so large a complement of choristers.[56]

The monasteries, including the monastic cathedrals, reintroducing boys for the Lady mass and Marian evening devotions, chose to use relatively few boys. The Lady chapel choir of one of the country's most prestigious monastic establishments, Westminster Abbey, had just four boys in the late fourteenth century,[57] a not uncommon figure, subsequently increased to six. We have seen that Winchester's rose to eight. Numbers in the secular cathedrals, as listed in the previous chapter, ranged from five at Hereford to fourteen at Exeter and Salisbury. Amongst the grandest of the aristocratic chapels, that of Henry Percy, fifth earl of Northumberland, with a dean and subdean, some ten chaplains and ten lay clerks, employed only six choristers.[58] The thirteenth earl of Oxford had twelve boys employed in his chapel. Even Cardinal Wolsey, who set out a decade later at York Place, Westminster, to imitate the royal style, staffed his household chapel with thirty-two men but only twelve boys.[59] The twelve clerks and ten boys in the domestic chapel of Lady Margaret Beaufort, the mother of Henry VII, were described by Bishop John Fisher in 1508 as 'a grete nombre of clerkes and chyldren'.[60] Nor did the Chapel Royal itself exceed these numbers.

The English Chapel Royal is as old as the English Christian monarchy. An essential part of any Christian royal household was its chapel. And, like the medieval kings, the Chapel Royal was peripatetic: where the king was, there was his chapel. For nearly a century after the Conquest it was habitual for the king to hold court in Winchester at Easter, in Westminster at Whitsun and in Gloucester at Christmas. Hunting lodges like Odiham and Lyndhurst equally played host to the Chapel Royal, and when the king went abroad the chapel went with him. So the medieval Chapel Royal was a function or a department, not a place. The earliest mention of boy choristers is 1303 when the calendar of patent rolls records two recent Chapel Royal choristers, Richard of Nottingham and Thomas Duns, being sent to Oxford for further education. Thirteen years later twelve former Chapel Royal choristers were being educated at the King's Hall, Cambridge.[61] Partly, perhaps, because it was so unstatic, the complement of boys employed in the Chapel Royal seems to have been exceptionally variable. In the last two decades of the fourteenth century never fewer than two and never more than six boy trebles are recorded. Then suddenly at Christmas 1399 the number leapt to nine. Through the first half of the fifteenth century the number again seems to have varied widely, but it only once dropped below six, rising to more than double that number in the final year of Henry V's reign, 1421/22, and settling about 1442 to a standard number of ten, the number referred to in the Master of the Children's terms of appointment of 1449.[62] There was an increase to twelve in 1526. So it is clear that even the most prestigious chapel in the land had not been a model for William of Wykeham in 1379. The specification of sixteen boys first at New College and then at Winchester was ground-breaking. With it, Wykeham set a standard that was to become the template for the most ambitious choral foundations of the future, not exceeded until Stainer's doubling of boy numbers at St Paul's in the 1870s.[63]

In part, no doubt, the motive was conspicuous display. At the close of the four-teenth century fine music became 'a means of advertising the glory of the patron as well as that of God'.[64] More significant, however, was a dramatic change in the music itself. Throughout the earlier medieval centuries church music had been monodic plainsong, with occasional elements of discant or *organum* sung exclusively or almost only by the men. A century later, in the most ambitious collegiate chapels and aristocratic and royal households, but also in some monastic Lady chapels and secular cathedrals, polyphony for five parts and upwards could be heard. In the few foundations in which boys significantly outnumbered men, boys might be expected to sing as many as three of the five parts.[65] And whereas, in the early fourteenth century, there might have been some fifty prestigious choral foundations including boy choristers, by the close of the fifteenth century there were approaching two hundred professional liturgical choirs with boys in England.[66]

It is not easy to determine when individual choral foundations began to engage their boys in polyphony. Indisputable evidence only emerges with the appointment of a master of the choristers charged specifically with teaching his boys that art. By the mid-fifteenth century something like a standard form of words had developed. One example comes from Wells, where Richard Hygons was appointed master of the choristers on 7 December 1479, obliged 'diligently and zealously to instruct to the best of his powers the Choristers and Tabulars in good and virtuous behaviour, in plainsong, prick-song and descant, and also in organ-playing according to their disposition and ability'. Wells was not unique in making the teaching of good morals the prime duty of the master of the choristers. 'Descant' was, of course, the singing and often the improvising of a part above the melody, the melody being, until the close of the fifteenth century, invariably given to the tenor voice: the tenor *held* (*tenuit*) the melody. Prick-song was the novelty: the ability to read a line from a written score. The 'tabulars' or 'tabellars' at Wells were the senior boys whose role it was to read out the weekly *tabula* of duties to be performed by the boys.[67] Of course, the appointment of a master charged with the teaching of polyphony did not mark, or need not have marked, the start of polyphonic singing: but it confirmed that it was happening. It may well have been happening for some time. Nevertheless, the contracts of appointment cannot be gainsaid and the information they give is a critical pointer.

The earliest contract – and this might be cause for surprise – comes from the monastic cathedral of Durham. As early as 1415/16 the account rolls record a payment of 2s. 2d. to the cantor, the eponymously named William Chantour, for 'instructing the youths in polyphony'. Indeed, he is later described as 'the master of the polyphonists'. 'Youths', *iuvenes*, however, implies novices or young monks. But in December 1430, still earlier than at any other foundation, John Steel, a married layman, is contracted 'to instruct to the best of his ability eight secular boys [and some monks] in the whole art of music, including

Pryktnote, Faburdon, Deschaunte and Counter,[68] and playing the organ. Steel was to receive £3. 6s. 8d. a year, together with food, clothing and a house, for his responsibilities.[69] Thereafter appointments came thick and fast. In 1449 the *Liber Regie Capelle* records that the Chapel Royal has a master of song employed to teach the ten Chapel Royal boys 'and duly instruct them *in cantu plano et organico*', *organico* being not the organ but polyphony.[70] Two years later there was polyphonic singing by men and boys at Lincoln under a comprehensively skilled director.[71] In the 1470s, at much the same time as the appointment at Wells, Winchester Cathedral appointed Edward Pynbrygge to teach the eight boys chant and descant. There were similar appointments at Salisbury in 1467, Worcester in 1484 and from the early sixteenth century at St Peter's abbey, Gloucester, and at the secular cathedrals of Hereford and York.[72] Doubtless there were many more, for by now the singing of polyphony by choirs of boys and men was universal in suitably staffed foundations.

It might be thought that collections of polyphonic music would provide evidence of choristers' participation. But there are difficulties. Early polyphony, although written on five-line staves, gives no indication of pitch. Anything with up to a fifteen-note span could be performable by an adult trio or quartet. Inventories, if they go beyond simply listing books as 'music', normally record only that a volume contains 'polyphony'. Furthermore, the overwhelming majority of pre-Reformation written and printed music was destroyed in the sixteenth century, either by puritan intention or because the replacement of the Latin liturgy by the vernacular had made existing church music unusable, except for secret Catholic worship or private Protestant cultural enjoyment. Indeed, by the Act against Superstitious Books and Images of 1550 it was made illegal to possess 'all books ... heretofore used for service of the Church' on pain of fine or imprisonment.[73] Much of what remains is in small fragments, used as binding for books, or comes from chance survivals in bundles of miscellaneous material, or found in overseas collections where destruction was not habitual. Nevertheless, two major gatherings have been preserved.

The Old Hall Manuscript, probably incomplete and now in the British Library, may have been compiled during the second decade of the fifteenth century, possibly or partly for the Chapel Royal, possibly or partly for Thomas, duke of Clarence, younger brother of Henry V.[74] His domestic chapel at Woking Palace until 1419 (when it moved with the duke to France) had a choir of sixteen lay clerks and four choristers, under the direction at this time of the composer, Lionel Power. Its earlier items are all for three voices, most probably three men. The second layer has pieces for three upper and three lower voices and looks as if it has been composed with a large group – a full chorus – in mind, not just for a sextet of soloists. Even here there is no evidence to determine that boy choristers were singing.

The Eton Choirbook was probably compiled in the first decade of the sixteenth century for Eton College, in whose library it remains: 'a grete ledger of prick song ii folio *tum cuncta*'.[75] Originally containing ninety-three items, in the time of Edward VI it was disparaged for its 'untrue and superstitious anthems' and almost a hundred leaves of the book were lost. Nevertheless, sixty-four items have survived: fifty-four Marian motets, nine magnificats and a setting of the Passion of St Matthew by Richard Davy, which, with its choral crowd passages, is an early presage of the *oeuvre* that was to culminate in the masterpieces of Bach. The dominance of Marian antiphons is explained by a foundation statute which required the sixteen choristers with their master to process, each evening at dusk, into the nave to sing a Marian antiphon before the image of the Virgin. In later decades it seems that the choristers would have been joined by the Eton lay clerks.[76] In the Eton Choirbook there are works that would have been unperformable without boys singing the upper parts. There is a range of three octaves, the top line requiring the use of the characteristic English trebles. Here we find incontrovertible evidence of what late fifteenth-century choristers actually sang.

Late medieval and early Tudor choristers sang parts designated either for 'meanes' or for 'trebles'. The meanes sang that part or those parts sounding next above the highest of the adult altos or counter-tenors. A boy singing the upper meane part might be expected to sing between the B flat below middle C to F on the top line of the modern treble stave. The treble, and this seems to have been a peculiarly English requirement, was asked to sing within a range about a fourth above that of the highest meane, up to a high B flat above the stave. It was this sound that could so excite susceptible foreign visitors.[77] The finest of this music is by any criterion, and certainly in comparison with monodic plainsong, a truly thrilling sound.[78] It is music by sophisticated composers to be sung by skilled, professional men and boys. The *Magnificat on the 8th Tone*, from the Caius Choirbook, now thought to be by William Cornysh the elder, master of the Westminster Abbey Lady chapel boys, has a *Gloria* whose concluding *Sicut Erat* is a series of duets, starting with the bass and tenor and ascending through the voices in increasing complexity. On p. 51 see what was asked of the trebles and meanes at its climax: 'a breathtaking display of vocal agility'.[79] We are considering now a quite different breed of singing boy from the monastic oblates or the earlier medieval cathedral *pueri*. The best of these skilled choristers were boys to be fought over and bargained for.

From as early as the time of Henry V the Chapel Royal, in its determination to maintain the highest musical standards, had acquired the right to 'impress' boys into service in its choir stalls. In 1420 the Chapel Royal was with the king in Normandy. One of the chapel's singing clerks, John Pyamour, was commissioned 'to take boys for the said Chapel and bring them to the King's presence in his

Magnificat on the 8th Tone

duchy of Normandy', and it is known that he impressed two boys of high quality from the choir at Lincoln.[80] Twenty years later Henry VI licensed the dean of the Chapel Royal himself to impress as many boys as he thought necessary from anywhere in England.[81] When, however, Thomas Wolsey was dean of Lincoln, as a precaution he secured in 1514 letters granting to the Lincoln chapter immunity from having boys impressed for service to any foundation, except that even Wolsey could not win immunity for Lincoln from impressment for the Chapel Royal. Henry VIII's determination to have an unmatchable choir led him in 1518 to set up a competition between his chapel and Wolsey's household choir. It took the form of a test of sight reading ('*ex improviso*') and it was 'better and more surely handlydde' by Wolsey's choir. Henry was not one to be upstaged. Only three years earlier Sagudino, secretary to the Venetian ambassador, had written of the Chapel Royal, 'High Mass was sung by the king's choristers, whose voices are more divine than human, *non cantavano ma giubilavano*': not so much singing as jubilating.[82] As a consequence, Henry impressed Wolsey's best treble, 'Robin my boy', and, the royal secretary, Richard Pace, wrote to Wolsey, that but for the king's personal affection 'surely he wolde have owte off your chapel not children oonly, but also men'.[83] The king was not let down. Some time later it was reported that 'Cornysh, doth greatly laud and praise the child ... not only for his sure and clean singing, but also for his good and crafty descant'.[84] 'Crafty' descant implies skill in decorative improvisation. Robin was evidently a star chorister.

Meanwhile the endeavour to find and then hold onto the best boys continued. In 1528 Eton and King's College, Cambridge, secured letters of immunity, but here too with exclusions: in this case not only the Chapel Royal but also Wolsey's chapel could impress choristers from Eton and King's. St George's Chapel, another royal foundation, also had licence to impress. About 1460 Thomas Rolfe, master of the Windsor choristers, was paid 3s. 4d. for riding to London '*pro Willelmo Tylly chorist*'. In 1527 one John Wenham was paid 13s. 4d. for taking a boy and a vicar from London and a second boy from the Lady chapel choir of Winchester cathedral for the Windsor choir.[85] How wide the hunt for good singers could go, and how underhand the whole business might become, is shown by the record from 1492/3 of Richard Pomeroy, keeper of the fabric at Wells, bribing the king's servants 6s. 8d. 'not to take away three choristers', an even larger bribe being paid for a similar purpose a decade later.[86] This form of recruitment for the royal foundations was to continue for some centuries. But it was not only for royal choirs that boys might be poached. In 1491/2 St Augustine's abbey, Bristol, paid 20d. for escorting a boy from Windsor, presumably an above-board transaction to acquire for its Lady chapel choir a trained chorister. Twenty years later the abbey was not conducting itself so honourably. Richard Bramston, *alias* Smyth, was relieved of his duties as master of the choristers at Wells in 1509 and accepted a similar appointment at Bristol. The following year he was spotted at Wells 'in privye and disgised apparel to have hadde awey one of our best queresters, that is to say, Farre, and therewit takyn'. Notwithstanding this high-handed behaviour Bramston was welcomed back to Wells in 1512, was subsequently reinstated as master of the choristers and held the post until 1531.[87] St Augustine's, Bristol, clearly had difficulties in recruiting good boys.

It is evident that by the later decades of the fifteenth century there were other kinds of fruitful cross-pollination between major choral centres involving boys, lay clerks and composers and directors of music. Lionel Power was in the duke of Clarence's household until 1421 and is found at Canterbury cathedral by 1438. Walter Lambe was not alone in crossing the Thames between Eton and Windsor. James Denton and Thomas Fitzherbert, respectively dean and precentor at Lichfield in the 1520s, when polyphony was being most vigorously encouraged and the choristers were being properly looked after there for perhaps the first time, had both been students at Eton and at King's Hall, Cambridge. Christopher Tye had been a lay clerk in King's College chapel before becoming master of the choristers at Ely; John Sheppard went from being *Informator Choristarum* at Magdalen to the Chapel Royal. So one could go on. It is an extraordinary foretaste of the fruitful career mobility in the choir stalls and on the organ benches of the twentieth century. This brilliant musical scene of the decades either side of 1500 looks and sounds like a golden age. Yet it was to be the gold of autumn. By 1550 ferocious winter storms were to threaten and almost bring down the entire structure of liturgical choirs.

5

At Work and Play

So far the medieval chorister has been a shadowy, anonymous figure. This is not surprising: even from as prestigious an establishment as the Chapel Royal, methodical lists of choristers were not kept until 1893. In the earliest centuries only the famous, whose childhoods happen to have been recorded, have left us their names, as with Bede, the historian and Turgar, the boy hero of Croyland. Nevertheless, in the later medieval centuries choristers' names begin to appear. The Norwich almoners' accounts show fee receipts between 1378 and 1382 for the sons of John of Beverle and William Elys.[1] From Wells we have a complete list of late fourteenth-century boys resident and being educated at their newly built choristers' school.[2] The 'altarists, tabulars and choristers of the cathedral church of Wells' who contributed or on behalf of whom was contributed 4d. each to the poll tax of 1377, probably in order of seniority, were:

John Newman	Thomas Farlegh
John atte Well	Robert Hawe
Thomas Taket	John Cokscomb
Stephen Blannicomb(?)	Richard Leddred
Richard Ludeford	Joseph Taillour
Thomas Hullyngh	Walter Benet

Nine of these were singing boys, *choriste* and *tabularii*, three were altarists, ex-choristers remaining at the school for education and at the cathedral to serve at side-altars. Which boys fell into which category was not recorded. The Chapel Royal accounts contain the names of eleven boys for whom liveries were provided for the funeral of Henry VII:[3]

William Colman	Arthur Lovekyn
William Maxe	Henry Andrewe
William Alderson	Nicholas Ive (or Ivy)
Henry Meryll (or Merell)	Edward Cooke (or Coke)
John Williams	James Curteys
John Graunger	

From what sorts of family did these boys come? At Ely we know that the almonry boys were chosen by the monks in rotation for four-year periods. Many will

have been the sons of relatives or neighbours.[4] Continuing entries from the
Norwich almonry accounts early in the following century suggest that we are
encountering chiefly sons of Norwich burgesses and Norfolk landed gentry.
From the very end of the Middle Ages we know that Exeter chorister parents
were husbandmen, yeomen, a merchant, a brewer, a miller, a weaver and a widow
and that two choristers were sons of gentlemen, one illegitimate.[5] Some almonry
boys for whom fees were not payable may have been recruited from poor families.
Was the obligation to sweep the cloisters, that was placed on some at least of
the Norwich almonry boys, a mark of social inferiority? A.F. Leach, the great
authority on medieval education a century ago, concluded that the requirement
for the Winchester College quiristers to make the fellows' beds, wait at table in
hall, and dine off the fellows' and scholars' left-overs was indication that they
were 'gutter children'.[6] Leach drew a determined contrast between the scholars
of Winchester who, though supposedly *pauperes et indigentes*, had to declare only
that they had less than five marks a year of spending money (that being a third
of the headmaster's salary!), and the college quiristers who were likely to have
been from seriously poor homes; but it is doubtful whether the evidence supports
such a contrast. King's College choristers and, for that matter, Eton scholars,
were required to serve at the fellows' tables, though ironically Eton choristers
were specifically excused that indignity. Both the Eton and Winchester choristers
were to have priority in election to College once their voices had changed, and
the choristers of Henry VI's twin foundations, all of whom were supposed to
be 'poor and needy', albeit 'of respectable birth',[7] were frequently elected to
College at Eton when their voices had changed and equally frequently went on
to Cambridge or Oxford. Similarly, at Magdalen, Oxford, Edward Wootton was
at the choristers' school or class in 1503 and proceeded naturally from there
to Magdalen College School proper and from there to the College.[8] So it is no
surprise that Thomas Roke, one of the first choristers at King's in 1447, is found
as a scholar at Eton the following year. Many must have come from families with
expectation of a sophisticated education for their sons, who will have prepared
them seriously for their choristerships. The King's choristers, albeit 'poor and
needy boys' (the usual formula), could not expect a place unless they already
knew competently how to read and sing. The families were equally prepared
to have them educated far from home: amongst twenty Etonians, all ex-King's
choristers listed in the fifteenth- and sixteenth-century school registers, are boys
found with homes in Northamptonshire, Sussex, Shropshire and Warwickshire
as well as Cambridge itself.[9] The most favourable treatment for superannuated
choristers was to be had at the Chapel Royal where provision was made for
selected ex-choristers to proceed in due course to one of the royal colleges at
Oxford or Cambridge. Edward II had founded the King's Hall at Cambridge
specifically to house at any time twelve former choristers or young clerks from

the Chapel Royal. His purpose was to train future Chapel Royal clergy. Indeed, from the late fourteenth century it is possible to trace eighteen, of twenty-four known choristers, proceeding to King's Hall, and of the sixteen who survived their Cambridge education seven returned to the Chapel Royal as clerks.[10] But, to return to Wells, the choristers' surnames give us few clues as to their social class. There are several topographical names. Joseph Taillour may indeed have been the son of a garment maker. There is even the boy with the unflattering patronym Cokscomb.[11] But there seems to be no evidence that could credibly identify 'gutter children'.

Other early names that have survived in the records do so in less than happy circumstances. In 1519 a serious outbreak of the plague afflicted the Close at Salisbury and several choristers fell victim. The accounts tell the story in detail:

> Paid to a woman for keeping Lewis Chorister at the time of his [in]firmity for 10 weeks besides eatables and drinkables etc. 6s.8d. And to a man for the healing for the disease of pestilence of the said Chorister 2s. And in pence paid for hiring a horse for 2 days to send the said Chorister to his friends 12d. With pence paid for his expenses at home 12d. And in pence paid for the hiring of a horse to send another Chorister to his father and mother that is to say, Potecary querestre 5d. And in payment for medicines bought for 2 other Choristers for the plague of pestilence 4d. And for two women for keeping the said Choristers 4 days, 20d.

Worse follows:

> And in pence paid to the Priest of the Morrow Mass for burying a Chorister whose name was Mote. For his funerals etc. 23d.[12]

The daily occupations of the late medieval choristers come to light from a multitude of sources. Perhaps the most comprehensive single document, from Wells (but a century later than the list above), is the set of rules for the daily life of the choristers, drawn up by their Master, Robert Cator or Catur, before 1460, commonly known as Bishop Bekynton's Statutes and Ordinances.[13] It is clear that the school was expected, under its master and under-master, to provide a course that was both elementary and also adequate to prepare suitable superannuated choristers for entry to university. The master, in particular, is to be skilled in grammar as well as in music, the latter still the heart of the song school curriculum and purpose. Aptly, it is fragments of musical notation that have survived on the remains of a medieval wall blackboard in the erstwhile choristers' schoolhouse in Windsor Castle.[14]

Just as the first responsibility of the master was to teach his boys morals, so the most serious problem facing schoolboys was moral failure. In practice there is very little contemporary evidence of late medieval chorister misbehaviour. Episcopal visitation records are full of reports of slackness and immorality by a minority of lay clerks, vicars choral and sub-deacons. But one has to dig hard to find choristers being criticised. The six choristers of the collegiate church of the Newarke at Leicester in 1440 were found to be 'roaming about as it were without a leader, spent their time gadding abroad and in other unruly deeds, making no progress in virtues.' Early in the following century there were complaints that the dean of the Newalke was selecting boys as choristers without regard to their musical or intellectual abilities, boys who were 'wholly unteachable ... to the damage of divine worship.'[15] At Southwell Minster the boys seem to have been even worse. In 1503 the choristers' vestments were 'disgracefully torn', the boys themselves 'rave and swear', disturb the chantry priests and 'need a good whipping'. This may have been due to the fact that their master, Laurence Pypys, a vicar, himself frequently shirked choir, omitting to celebrate his chantry masses and 'teaching his boys ... at irregular times and to the disturbance of the other clergy'.[16] In some foundations there was little continuity in the office of chorister master: for instance, at St George's, Windsor, prior to 1416 the office of master of the choristers seems to have changed hands half-yearly.[17] Perhaps a lack of consistent pastoral care there accounted for the goldsmith's bill for 8d. for repairing the great censer 'broken by the choristers' (note the significant plural). But there is more scandalous evidence of magisterial failure at fifteenth-century Windsor. In most, perhaps all, medieval choral foundations choristers earned money. Sometimes it was what might be called 'casual earnings': pennies for special services or secular entertainments; habitually they would receive payments for funerals and obits; sometimes they earned something very like a wage. At Windsor, the choristers received whatever had not been spent on them from the five marks a year rendered to their master for their maintenance. It was to be put into their individual money-boxes against the day when they left the choir. The master kept charge of the money-boxes. From 1407 to 1408 one William Pounger was master of the Windsor choristers. In 1408 he died. But ten years later the boys had still not had the £20.5s.3d. that had accumulated in their six money-boxes. Pounger's executor was taken to court and ordered to pay off the debt in instalments. Even at the Chapel Royal it could be difficult to extract boys' expenses from the Exchequer, and the occasional practice of putting senior boys in charge of distributing the choristers' dues would raise modern eyebrows.[18]

Things were better ordered at Wells where strict rules governed the care of the choristers' savings. Their named purses were to be kept in a chest secured by two keys, one held by the master, the other by the precentor. Whenever moneys were paid into the chest the boy must be present as witness; and, when the boy came to leave, his savings were to be paid to him in the presence of both the precentor and the master. In another significant way things were better managed at Wells. Robert Cator was master of the choristers for several decades, so he knew his boys, their characters and likely failings. He condemns all 'rascally conduct, swearing, lying, brawling, quarrelling, fighting, contention, raucous laughter, jeering' and any other dishonourable, unnatural or unseemly behaviour.

He is well aware that some boys will be less able than others and that the slower ones will need special attention:

> Another hindrance or obstacle to teaching is a want of intelligence which is called denseness or stupidity. Since this defect is a product of nature rather than the boy's own fault, one must pity it rather than be angered at it, unless the boy should happen to be not only dense but lazy too. So if any boy is affected with denseness ... the Master must give to such a boy a short, concise lesson, capable of being carefully impressed ... more surely upon his memory. Then straightway [the boy] must have constant and careful recourse to one of his fellow-pupils having a more intelligent perception and who appeals to the dull one's imagination and interest.

This was not the only use made of responsible senior boys. Two were to be appointed each week to look out for and report on disciplinary failings in school, and two 'more skilled in singing' to perform a similar function in quire. The foundation statutes of King's College, Cambridge, detail the sort of failings for which such quire monitors would have been on the lookout: 'mutterings, chatterings, jeerings, laughter, discussions or indiscreet noise in any way whatsoever, lest ... the devotion and concentration of those singing ... might in any way be disturbed.'[19] Back in class, if denseness is to be treated with patience, a much more vigorous approach was called for when laziness is encountered. First, indeed, there can be a gentle admonition; then, at a second offence, a sharp reprimand will be necessary; and should there be a third offence then the stick should be applied, as recommended by king Solomon. Evidently a particular problem of the late fifteenth century, 'our present wanton age', was a boyish urge to wear outlandish clothes, even in quire: 'pointed slippers, long hose, strait doublets and short cassocks barely covering the buttocks'. If discovered, the offending items were to be confiscated and converted by the master into acceptable pieces of clothing. In fact, choristers' accounts from elsewhere show that even legitimate clothes were becoming more varied and sophisticated. From Salisbury we can read that, where at one time the boys had made do with a hooded robe and a set of footwear, by the late fifteenth century they were being equipped with coats and caps, shirts and stockings, boots and shoes, with a laundress paid ten shillings a year for washing and darning.[20]

Special attention was given by Cator at Wells to conduct in dormitory and refectory. Rising after sleep, most likely at the sound of a bell,[21] whether in the morning or for the midnight service, required 'good, salutary and holy discipline'. Those getting up in the morning:

shall rise from their beds and say Mattins two and two together, and while they say it
they shall dress themselves, make their beds, tidy their lockers, wash their hands and
straightway go to school peacefully and quietly, and sit down there without making a
noise, and await the arrival and presence of the Master or Under-master.

The teacher worked on their plainsong and pricksong, appropriate to the pitch of
their voices. Breakfast was taken just before prime, which was attended by some
but not all of the boys. Some sang in quire and some continued their lessons
until 11 a.m. when dinner was taken. Lessons continued through the afternoon
until time for evensong. Once again, some went to sing, others remained in
school. This use of small numbers of tabulated boys to sing the lesser offices was
widespread, perhaps universal, in the secular cathedrals and meant that school
lessons were almost always missed by some boys, different boys on different days
or weeks. Add to this the wide age-range and the fact that some were undertaking
just the elementary syllabus while others were expecting to be prepared for
university and it is clear that education in the secular cathedrals' song schools
must have necessitated constant 'differentiation'. The boys must have been
working almost individual syllabuses. But then at Wells there were just twelve
boys being taught by a master and an undermaster, with habitual assistance from
senior boys.

After evensong it was time for supper and after supper the boys went out to
play. Here, for the first time since the ninth-century Hildemar,[22] is documentary
evidence that play and recreation did form part of a chorister's programme.
Normally play-time was restricted to thirty minutes; but 'on feast days it is right
for them to have more time for games and recreation': some after morning dinner
and more after supper, subject always to the 'wise administration' of the master
or undermaster. The boys must not invite outsiders to play with them, least of
all 'any persons of a dissolute nature'. Nor must there be 'any swearing, fighting,
quarrelling, or any vestige of raillery'.

Meanwhile, table manners received particular attention from Cator. The boys
processed into the refectory, youngest or smallest first, oldest or tallest last. They
remained standing to say grace together then in silence took their seats. There
was to be no leaning on the table, they 'must not deliberately or wantonly soil or
spoil the cloth'. Then come some very precise instructions:

> They must cut their bread or break it decently, not gnaw it with their teeth or tear it with
> their nails. Also they must drink with their mouths empty, not full and eat their food
> decently, in moderation and not quickly. On no account are they to raise their knives to
> their mouths with their food, nor pick their teeth with their knives. If ... there is anything
> lacking ... they must ask for it softly, not loudly, not in English but in Latin; and they
> must consider themselves satisfied with what is provided without any murmuring or
> disapproval.

So the day came to its end. Having said their Hail Mary, *De profundis* and evening collect in the schoolroom, the boys processed in pairs to the dormitory, said their private prayers on their knees at their beds' foot, then quietly undressed and slipped into bed: three to each bed, as noted earlier. Thus they were 'to lie and rest in silence, not making a noise' until waking time. Furthermore, in the dormitory 'all the decencies are to be observed'. But not every chorister had a good night's sleep every night. At Durham, and doubtless at other Benedictine foundations, there was a custom which is unlikely to appeal to modern sensitivities. One chapter of Fowler's *Rites of Durham*[23] is concerned with 'The Ryte … in Buryinge of Mounckes'. It describes how, on the night before a monk's burial, the corpse is removed to St Andrew's chapel until eight in the morning. Two monks 'either in kindred or in kindness ye nerest unto him' kneel throughout the night at the feet of the corpse. But they are not alone.

> Then were ye children of thaumerey [the almonry] sitting on there knees in stalls of eyther sid ye corpes appointed to read Dav[id's] spalter all nyght … incessantly till ye said [hour of eight in the morning].

Such a regulation is unlikely to have applied to the choristers of Wells or of the other secular cathedrals.

It will have been noticed that Cator has virtually nothing to say on curriculum beyond the requirement for his boys to be taught Latin grammar and song. In fact no curriculum as we would understand the word existed prior to the early sixteenth century. Then in the 1530s Convocation issued guidelines for the teaching of grammar and ten years later Henry VIII imposed something akin to a national curriculum by ordering the use of the Grammar largely written by William Lily, High Master of St Paul's School. The biggest single change to what was taught to choristers in the last two medieval centuries was, however, the infiltration of the English language into the classroom. In earlier times everything curricular, whether sung, said or read, would have been in Latin. But by the late fourteenth century wills and merchants' letters began to be written in English, increasing numbers of private letters in English survive from around 1400, and by the closing decades of that century parliamentary statutes were written in English. So it is that from the fifteenth century Latin grammars are found with explanations in the vernacular, and from about 1530 there has survived the earliest English/Latin dictionary. Indeed, from about 1340, in many elementary schools, instruction would have been given at least in part in English.[24] It is significant that Cator has to remind his boys that the formal language of the refectory is Latin. Perhaps the earliest surviving English/Latin text book dates from before 1420 and was written in Bristol (though not for St Augustine's).[25] It contains *vulgaria*, that is, sets of English sentences with Latin translations used to illustrate points of Latin grammar, such as:

'Me comyth to scole yn the mortyde'
'Children stond yn a row, sum wel a-rayd, sum evel a-rayd'
'My fellow were e-bete with a byrch gerd, y ham to be bete with a whyppe'

This is primitive material compared with the developed *vulgaria* that were written towards the close of the century. In this work of text book production the great powerhouse was Wayneflete's Oxford foundation, Magdalen College, under a series of great masters, notably John Anwykyll and John Stanbridge.[26] Stanbridge, in particular, wrote eight grammatical works that quickly found their way into print and were in use at Eton, Winchester and St Paul's, amongst other places. There can be no doubt that for many of the older and brighter choristers about Britain at the dawn of the sixteenth century Stanbridge's works would have been standard text books. Thus it was from one of the choral foundations that the most significant steps forward from medieval to Renaissance education were made.

Several of the features dominant in the life of the late medieval chorister, the life of the classroom, the cult of the Virgin and the development of the Mary-antiphon, come together in remarkable conjuncture in the tale put by Chaucer into the mouth of his Prioress. The Prioress's Tale is not original. It is a conflation of several accounts, historical or legendary, of the supposed murder of Christian children by Jews, the best-known English examples being the deaths of the twelve-year-old St William of Norwich in 1144 and of the nine-year-old Little St Hugh of Lincoln (not the famous bishop) in 1255. What are specially remarkable in the Prioress's Tale are the richness of the expression of the Prioress's devotion to Mary, the telling detail of classroom practice and the picture of a little boy captivated by the beauty of one particular plainsong chant, Chaucer's boy 'a litel clergeon, seven yeer of age'. Notwithstanding that the Oxford English Dictionary gives, and at least one recent editor uses, 'chorister' as a synonym for 'clergeon', in two important respects he seems not to have been a chorister. He is never encountered singing in quire; and he lives at home with his widowed mother.[27] But the details of the schooling he undergoes and the music taught must be closely similar to those found in song schools known to Chaucer, and the 'little clergeon' gives us moving insights into the educational experiences and frame of mind of a chorister of the time.

He attends class in a single schoolroom where children of different ages are taught, 'children an heep' in small groups alongside each other. At the age of seven, his work is elementary,

> This is to seyn, to syngen and to rede
> As smale children doon is [t]here childhede.

He had been taught by his mother to show special reverence to the Virgin, 'oure blissful lady, Cristes mooder deere', singing *Ave Mary* whenever he saw her image. As he sits at work, learning his primer, the little clergeon is distracted by the song being taught to a group of older boys.

> This litel child his litel book lernynge
> As he sat in the scole at his prymer,
> He *Alma redemptoris* herde synge
> As children lerned [t]hire antiphoner.

So the clergeon, distracted from his own work by the special beauty of what will have been the Sarum form of the Marian antiphon, *Alma redemptoris mater*, listened 'til he the firste vers koude al by rote'. Later, he is frustrated because he knows the Latin words and the music but does not know what they mean, so he begs, on his bare knees, one of the older boys to translate the words for him. The older boy's response is famous, quoted in every history of education:

> This song, I have herd seye,
> Was maked [for] our blisful Lady free,
> Hire to salue, and eek hire for to preye.
> To been oure help and socour whan we deye,
> I kan namoore expounde in this mateere.
> I lerne song, I kan but smal grammeere.
>
> And is this song maked in reverence
> Of Cristes mooder?" seyde this innocent.
> 'Now, certes, I wol do my diligence
> To konne it al, er Cristemasse be went.
> Though that I for my prymer shal be shent,
> And I shal be thries beten in an houre,
> I wol it konne, Our Lady to honoure!

So the little clergeon learns the whole antiphon, and sings it 'ful murily' to and from school,

> The swetnesse [hath] his herte p[i]erced so
> Of Cristes mooder, that to hire to preye
> He kan nat stynte of syngyng by the weye.

But his route to and from school takes him through the Jewish district, and his singing brings the story to its crisis. He is murdered and thrown into a ditch. That, however, is not the end. His distraught mother comes searching for him and a miracle happens:

> O grete God, that parfournest thy laude
> By mouth of innocentz, lo, heere thy might!

Ant. 5.

A L- ma * Redemptóris Má- ter, quae pér-

vi- a caéli pórta má- nes, Et stél- la má- ris, succúrre

cadén- ti súrgere qui cú- rat pópu-lo : Tu quae genu- í-

sti, natú- ra mi-rán- te, tú-um sánctum Ge-ni- tórem :

Vír- go pri- us ac posté- ri- us, Gabri- é- lis ab ó-re

súmens íllud Ave, * peccatórum mi-seré- re.

Alma Redemptoris Mater

> This gemme of chastite, this emeraude,
> And eek of martirdom the ruby bright,
> Ther he with throte y-korven lay upright   [y-korven=cut]
> He *Alma redemptoris* gan to synge
> So loude, that al the place bigan to rynge.

So he was found and taken on a bier to the nearby abbey, still singing all the way. After mass, on the way to burial, the little clergeon explains to the abbot that Mary herself, 'this welle of mercy, Cristes mooder sweete', had bidden him sing the antiphon as he lay dying, placing a grain upon his tongue that 'may I synge *O alma* loude and cleere'. So the abbot gently opens the boy's mouth, finds and removes the grain 'and he gaf up the gost ful softely'. Then 'his litel body sweete' was taken and 'laid in a marble tomb'.

One important development that had its early roots in the choral foundations – in their schools and, even earlier, in their liturgies – was the drama. As has been seen, on Palm Sundays, choristers acted out the roles of Old Testament prophets and of the palm-bearing crowds in Jerusalem. By the close of the sixteenth century choristers, at least in the metropolis, would be forming the casts of famous theatre companies.[28] The earliest recorded incidents of dramatic representation in Britain are to be found in tenth-century ecclesiastical Winchester. Contemporary documents describe or reproduce the *Visitatio sepulchri* trope, the acorn from which subsequent liturgical drama grew. It was to be found throughout western Christendom and an astonishing five hundred manuscripts survive containing this sequence, some eighty of them from the twelfth century or earlier. In exact detail they show widespread variations, yet an unmistakably distinctive fingerprint is found in them all.[29]

As Easter matins came to its close, dawn light breaking, the normal static formality of the office was interrupted by a leap into drama. The visit to the sepulchre by the three Maries, as described in the gospels, was presented in dramatic form as an extension to, yet part of, the liturgy. Here are the instructions as given in chapter 51 of the *Regularis Concordia* of Ethelwold:[30]

While the third lesson is being read, four of the brethren shall vest, one of whom, wearing an alb as though for some different purpose, shall enter and go in stealthily (*atque letenter*) to the place of the sepulchre[31] and sit there quietly holding a palm in his hand. Then, while the third respond is being sung, the other three brethren, vested in copes and holding thuribles in their hands, shall enter in their turn and go to the place of the sepulchre, step by step, as though searching for something. Now these things are done in imitation of the angel seated on the tomb and of the women coming with perfumes to anoint the body of Jesus. When, therefore, he that is seated shall see these three draw nigh, wandering about as it were and seeking something, he shall begin to sing, softly and sweetly (*mediocri voce dulcisone cantore*), 'Quem queritis?'

Angelica de Christi Resurrectione :

Quem que – ri – tis in se – pul – chro, (O) Chri – sti – co – lae?

Sanctarum Mulierum responsio :

Ihe – sum Na – za – re – num cru – ci – fi – xum, O ce – li – co – la.

Angelice vocis consolatio :

Non est hic, sur – re – xit si – cut pre – di – xe – rat; i – te, nun – ti – a – te

qui – a sur – re – xit, di – cen – tes:

Sanctarum Mulierum ad omnem clerum modulatio :

Al – le – lu – ia, re – sur – re – xit Do – mi – nus ho – di – e; le – o for – – tis, Chri – stus

fi – li – us De – i! De – o gra – ti – as; di – ci – te, E – – ia!

Dicat Angelus :

Ve – ni – te et vi – de – te lo – cum u – bi po – si – tus e – rat Do – mi – nus. Al – le – lu –

– ia, al – le – lu – ia.

Visitatio Sepulchri

And so begins the most touching dialogue.[32] The angel asks the women whom they seek: '*Quem queritis in sepulchro, O Christicolae?*' They respond: '*Ihesum Nazarenum crucifixum, O caelicola.*' Then, with an astonishing musical shout, a rising fifth which then rises even higher, the angel cries, '*Non est hic!*' – 'He is not here, he is risen'; and the women turn to the choir and sing, '*Allelulia! Resurrexit Dominus!*' The empty sepulchre is revealed to the community, the choir sings *Te Deum*, and all the bells of the church sound in joyous medieval cacophony.[33]

It is clear from *Regularis Concordia* that at Saxon Winchester the roles of the angel and the Maries were sung by monks, dressed as it were in women's clothes. But in later centuries it seems that, in an age when women had no liturgical part to play, a better similitude of the Maries could be achieved by boys with unbroken voices. A recent writer, describing the drama in great household chapels of the later middle ages, with particular reference to the *Visitatio*, is confident that boys had been performing these plays for centuries.[34] This must be a strong probability, yet evidence of choristers taking part in the *Visitatio sepulchri* seems to have survived only in continental sources, as at sixteenth-century Bamberg where choristers sang the Maries at the sepulchre (operatically, 'with querulous voices').[35] A sibling of the Easter play developed, however, in the *Visitatio praesepe*, the Office of the Shepherds, visiting the stable at Bethlehem. This too occurs at the close of matins, as a sort of prelude to mass. Records, again continental, are full of choristers singing and acting appropriate roles. At Clermont Ferrand two chorister angels question the shepherds, '*Quem queritis in praesepe, pastores, dicite?*' Other boys play two (non-biblical) midwives, attending at the manger. At Rouen seven choristers, holding staves '*in similitudinem pastorum*', act as shepherds, while three others in albs sing the angels' words. It is in this Christmas liturgy that we have proof that practice in England reflected that in Normandy. At Salisbury five choristers (not three, as at Rouen), went up into the vaults of the cathedral, singing *Gloria in excelsis* from the angelic heavens.[36] The Exeter Ordinal provides a more detailed example of Christmas liturgical drama performed by the choristers:

'There the first eight words of the respond were sung by a boy with a good and clear voice', who came from behind the altar holding a lighted torch in his left hand. At the words *caelorum rex* he pointed with his right hand to heaven, at *de virgine* he turned to the altar and held out his hand towards the image of the Virgin, and at *dignatus est* he genuflected. While the choir sang the rest of the respond, three boys came from the south door of the quire and three from the north door and stood at the choir-step. The solo boy joined them and all sang the verse, turning towards the choir, and then walked slowly through the quire and out by the main quire-door.[37]

The twelfth-century statutes of Lichfield Cathedral make it clear that the *Visitatio Praesepe* drama took place there also, though there is a frustrating lack of information as to who played what role.[38] Thirteenth-century Beverley had choristers acting in the play of Zaccheus.[39] There is a striking circumstance in 1378 of a petition by the cathedral of St Paul, London, against 'certain inexperienced persons' infringing their boys' monopoly of presenting the History of the Old Testament at Christmastide. Fifteenth-century Ely almonry accounts record tips for their choristers acting in the Play of St Nicholas during December.[40] In 1487 the almonry boys of St Swithun's, Winchester, presented a miracle play of Christ's descent into hell while Henry VII ate his Sunday dinner.[41] Once into the sixteenth century examples multiply, presumably because surviving records multiply, but also because acting by choristers and other schoolboys became more widespread. Perhaps the most comic example comes from Lincoln where, in the Drama of the Prophets, a boy was tied beneath a real donkey, from which unbecoming position he was required to speak (or perhaps sing) the words uttered by Balaam's ass.[42]

The Chapel Royal was one of the foundations whose choristers were to become something akin to professional actors. The roots of this development can be traced in some detail.[43] The earliest evidence of Chapel Royal boys taking part in dramatic performances comes from 1501, when they performed in the pageants that formed part of the celebrations that accompanied the marriage of Katherine of Aragon to the ill-fated fifteen-year-old prince Arthur, eldest son of Henry VII. First, four boys sang from the turrets of a mock castle. Later there appeared 'a glorious town or tabernacle', drawn along on wheels, on each side of which walked a mermaid and beside each mermaid 'a Childe of the Chapell singing right sweetly and with quaint harmony.' Later in that decade there is evidence of the performance of plays rather than mere pageants, at first with adult actors. The children went on appearing in pageants, but at Christmas 1515 or 1516, early in Henry VIII's reign, we find the Chapel Royal choristers taking more demandingly theatrical parts, including the roles of Troilus, Pandor and Ulysses, in the play of *Troilus and Pandor*.[44] The key to this development is the fact that the designer of the pageants and author of the plays had also been, from 1509, master of the children who boarded with him in his residence: William Cornysh. He was a man of immense ingenuity, musician, writer, designer of elaborate stage sets; and from 1517 he had in his house a body of bright, intelligent, eager boys, selected by impressment from the best in the land, who will have delighted in being drawn into dramatic service to perform before Henry VIII and his court. Throughout this time there are records of the boys performing in pageants and plays at court, notably in September 1519 when, after a sumptuous banquet, one of Cornysh's entertainments was put on, with seven choristers in star parts: Sun, Moon, Wind, Rain, Summer, Winter and Lust! But the choristers' most exciting experience was yet to come.

In the summer of 1520, as the climax of peace negotiations between the kings of England and France, there took place a meeting between the two historic enemies, with celebrations planned by Wolsey on an unprecedented scale. To the east of the then English enclave, the pale of Calais, lay a valley, the *Vallis Aurea* or, as it was to become known, the Field of the Cloth of Gold.[45] Here, at the boundary between English and French territory, were erected a fairy-tale palace, a jousting-field with stands for the spectators, splendid marquees, tents and pavilions with accommodation and provisioning for the five thousand persons in each of the two royal suites. All the highest and grandest of the lands were to be there. Chapels were erected for the daily singing of mass and the office, for which purpose the French royal chapel and the English Chapel Royal were in attendance, the latter complete with all ten choristers, for whose provisioning 2d. per day for sixty-two days was provided.

After the formal peace-making on 7 June there began a fortnight-long party, with jousting and tilting, wrestling and sword-fights. Henry VIII and François I themselves took part, until Henry sprained a wrist and François suffered a broken nose and black eye. There was of course competitive feasting: banquet after banquet, each nation determined to outdo the other – 'so much food that many choked themselves' – not to mention a fountain that spouted wine for five hours free for all comers.[46] The banquets were accompanied by revels, the English pageants devised by William Cornysh. Most likely, the boys will have been members of the casts of these entertainments.

But the boys' moment of glory came on the final Saturday. Overnight, the jousting field had been stripped of all its military and sporting paraphernalia and prepared for high mass. For the altar and reliquaries, 'costly and all glittering with gold', Wolsey had ordered 'the best hangings, travers, jewels, images, altar cloths etc that the King has' and instructed that the finest available set of vestments, gifted by Henry VII to Westminster Abbey, should be used. Thrones were built for the two kings. Between the thrones and the altar, facing each other, were the two royal choirs, each with their positive organ and organist. The liturgy began at noon, when the English choir sang the office of terce. The solemn high mass itself, *de Trinitate*, was celebrated by Cardinal Wolsey, with English bishops assisting him as gospeller and epistoler. There were two French cardinals and twenty other bishops, eight British and twelve French, robed and mitred. The music of the ordinary is said to have been by the otherwise unknown Perino, sung with organs, trombones and cornets, 'very magnificent'. The French and English choirs did not sing together, but divided the mass between them. Each sang an introit, then the French choir undertook the *Kyrie*, *Patrem* and *Agnus Dei* and the Chapel Royal the *Gloria*, *Sanctus* and *Benedictus*, each choir carefully brought in by their own respective organist.[47] Instrumental accompaniment to the *Patrem* was provided by the French king's *cors de sabuttes et fifes*. At the close several motets were sung.

All this must have been thrilling enough for the boys. But at the climax of the mass something extraordinary happened. We have two accounts, which do not agree in detail. 'After the elevation,' wrote the Mantuan, Soardino, 'the Eucharist was seen in the air floating over the tilt-yard, no one perceiving whence it issued nor who propelled it, to the height of a tall tower.' The other account comes almost certainly from a French source: 'While the Preface [to the prayer of consecration] was being said a great artificial salamander or dragon, full of fire, appeared in the air from Ardre[s]. Many were frightened, thinking it a comet, or some monster, as they could see nothing to which it was attached. It passed straight over the chapel to Guisnes, as fast as a footman can go, and as high as a bolt from a crossbow.' What can have been going on? Soardino clearly thought that it was a miracle, maybe a sign of divine approval. But the French account is open to less innocent interpretation. The salamander, a lizard that cannot be consumed by fire, was the personal heraldic badge of François I. Passage from Ardres to Guisnes was from French territory to the English pale. Was it perhaps a symbolic representation of the French claim to the territory?[48]

All in all, it must be wondered whether any group of English choristers has ever experienced, indeed played a central part in, a more extraordinary sixty days. Soardino certainly thought not: 'Thus ended these games and pageants, which were very grand and magnificent, ... nor is it to be supposed that in our time a similar display was ever witnessed, or that the like will be seen for many a day to come ... for it could not be expressed by any memory, however vivid, though aided by the readiest of pens.'

There was one other form of drama, far more homely, in which English choristers played the chief roles, probably the best known feature of the medieval chorister's life: the office of the Boy Bishop. Strictly speaking one should be referring to the Boys' Bishop, *episcopus puerorum*. That is how he appears in most English sources. But he is also found as the Nicholas Bishop, the School Bishop, the Almonry Bishop, the Little Bishop, the *episcopellus*.[49] However, in recent times he is almost universally spoken and written of as the Boy Bishop. The Boy Bishop celebrations formed part of what was widely known as the Feast of Fools, the most curious and surprising feature of the whole medieval liturgy. On several days after Christmas the liturgical roles of bishops, cathedral canons and other senior clergy were taken over in a kind of parody by the deacons, sub-deacons, vicars choral and choristers of the choral foundations. The deacons had their day on 26 December, the feast of St Stephen (who had himself been a deacon); 27 December (St John the Evangelist) was allotted to the vicars choral; 28 December (The Holy Innocents) to the choristers; and 1 January (the Circumcision of Jesus) to the sub-deacons. The evidence for these celebrations goes back at least to the early tenth century.[50] The term 'Feast of Fools' is sometimes, as in Brewer's *Dictionary of Phrase and*

Fable, following wide-spread medieval custom, used broadly to refer to the whole period from Boxing Day to New Year's Day; but the term particularly referred to 1 January, in part perhaps because of its association with ancient, pre-Christian revels on that day, in part because the most outrageous misuse of the liberties given to them was habitually taken by the sub-deacons. Of those in major orders it was the sub-deacons who were likely to be the youngest, the least educated, the least restrained and most high-spirited. It was, of course, possible for the festal offices to be conducted with decency and solemnity by these surrogate priests and bishops during this post-Christmas week. But all too often the services revealed what Chambers has called 'an ebullition of the natural lout beneath the cassock'.[51] The services were frequently occasions for impious larks; sometimes the liturgy on 1 January became a scandal.

From at least the twelfth century the church authorities set about forbidding the entire tradition. In 1207 Innocent III directed a decretal to a Polish diocese where the problem had caused particular outrage; a quarter-century later Gregory IX incorporated Innocent's decretal into universal canon law. But, as so often, canon law proved ineffective in competition with popular custom. As late as 1445 the Faculty of Theology at the University of Paris reported:

> Priests and clerks may be seen wearing masks and monstrous visages at the hours of office. They dance in the choir dressed as women, pandars and minstrels. They sing wanton songs. They eat black puddings at the horn [corner] of the altar while the celebrant is saying mass. They play at dice there. They cense with stinking smoke from the soles of old shoes. They run and leap through the church, without a blush at their own shame. Finally they drive about the town and its theatres in shabby traps and carts; and rouse the laughter of their fellows and the bystanders in infamous performances, with indecent gestures and verses scurrilous and unchaste.[52]

Local English bans are found, as in the1230s at Lincoln and Beverley. They seem to have been more effective than some continental ones. After the thirteenth century the Feast of Fools drops out of the records of the English church; but with one vital exception. The festivities on Holy Innocents' Day, the choristers' day, the day when the Boy Bishop ruled, escaped the bans and continued in an ever-increasing number of foundations well into the sixteenth century.

There is evidence to suggest why the festivities of the Boy Bishops escaped the otherwise universal ban. It was generally less unseemly, indeed frequently an occasion for rather special devotion; it had a potent charm about it, and it could be shown to have a sort of evangelical authority. Jesus himself had brought a little child to him and said, 'Truly, I say to you, unless you turn and become like children, you will never enter the kingdom of heaven'. Had Jesus not rebuked the disciples when they tried to keep children away from him?[53] It is quite clear that it was enormously popular. Foundations had to try to take steps to control the press of people who thronged the churches on these occasions. The 'insolence of the disorderly multitude' was specially noted in 1263 at St Paul's, for instance.[54] Four elements of this festival need to be considered. First, there is the election of the 'bishop' by the choristers, normally on 6 December, the feast of St Nicholas, patron saint of children. Then events moved to 27 December, the eve of the feast of the Holy Innocents, when, again usually but not quite universally, the 'bishop' was enthroned at first vespers, and he and his 'canons' usurped the places of the higher clergy and presided at the offices for twenty-four hours. Thirdly, coincident with these liturgies the 'bishop' and his 'canons' were feasted. Finally, but by no means invariably, an episcopal 'visitation' might take place in the course of January, to the delight of the populace and the considerable financial benefit of the Boy Bishop.[55]

It was the privilege and responsibility of the choristers to elect their own bishop. By holding the election in December not only was the feast of the children's patron saint given an added significance, but the boy selected was also given time to prepare himself for the responsibilities that lay ahead. The preferred method of election was 'scrutiny': votes, either oral or written, were collected by appointed scrutators, a majority of votes determining who should be bishop. Far from this child-suffrage being a problem, the statutes emphasised and protected it. There was an occasion at Salisbury in 1449 when the precentor, Canon Nicholas Upton, decided to intervene in the election of the Boy Bishop. He had good reason for being worried. The previous year, when the boys, accompanied by an unruly crowd of vicars choral, were returning to their house from feasting at one of the canonries, the merriment had got out of hand, with wild misuse of sticks. As they reached the choristers' house, a canon's servant, who was supposed to be overseeing the walk back, was injured and subsequently died. The precentor, judging that the Boy Bishop had not been properly in charge, wanted to be sure that a boy with dependable leadership qualities should be selected in 1449. He offered them three names, Thatcham, Knyton and Bokebynder. But there was uproar. The matter was referred to chapter and chapter voted for the boys' rights against the wishes of their own precentor.[56] Only at York do the boys seem to have been disenfranchised. There in 1367 the chapter register requires that the Boy Bishop must be the boy who has served longest and been most useful to the cathedral. There is also a curious proviso: the boy chosen must be *corpore formosus* – of handsome appearance. The phrase reflects a verse from first vespers of the Holy Innocents that the Boy Bishop is required to sing: *'Speciosus forma pre filiis hominum.'*[57]

At the two foundations of Henry VI, albeit not themselves episcopal establishments, boys were elected bishop: at King's it was to be a chorister, at Eton, by contrast, one of the scholars. Their election was to be for one day only, the feast of St Nicholas.[58] Elsewhere the real festival ran from first to second vespers of the

Holy Innocents, with the major liturgical interest on the eve of the feast. Earlier in the day the Boy Bishop, assisted by his 'canons', had the responsibility of drawing up the *tabula* or list of duties for the feast. This might cause problems. There was a temptation for the choristers to award the most junior functions as acolytes or book-boys to the most senior clergy, and sometimes deans, precentors and other principal persons failed to appreciate the joke. It may, indeed, have provoked unseemly mirth to have the dean and chancellor processing into quire as mere candle-bearers. In 1263 the chapter of St Paul's passed a statute forbidding the boys to list the dignitaries as acolytes.[59]

The services presided over by the Boy Bishop were not meant to be comedies: they were to be serious acts of worship. First vespers began with a procession. At Salisbury the choristers, dressed in silk copes and with lighted candles, led the procession to the altar of the Holy Trinity, eastward of the quire (where in churches not dedicated to the Virgin the Lady chapel would usually be found). There the Boy Bishop, clothed in full pontificals, mitred and with episcopal ring on his finger, began the first responsory in praise of the children murdered by Herod. It was taken up by the choir of boys, three of whom then sang the verse, '*Hii empti sunt*', followed by all the boys singing ten verses of a prose. Each ended on the long-held syllable '*ee*', and while the boys held that syllable the 'chorus' – presumably the men of the choir – repeated the responsory as a kind of descant to it. Then the Boy Bishop proceeded to cense the altar and, behind it, the image of the Holy Trinity. This part of the office concluded with the 'bishop' singing the collect and a prayer in honour of the Virgin. The procession then moved round the aisles to the outside of the quire, where the lay people would be likely to throng, and entered the quire by its west door. In quire, the boys claimed the upper row of canonical stalls, the rest of the clergy taking their places in inverse order of seniority. And, states the rubric, 'from this hour until the end of the procession on the following day, no cleric is to occupy the upper stalls'.

At this point we have a problem. Throughout western Christendom the climax of the office occurred during the singing of the vespers canticle, *Magnificat*. At the critically significant verse '*Deposuit*: He hath put down the mighty from their seat and hath exalted the humble and meek', the Boy Bishop ascended the bishop's throne, was handed the pastoral staff and gave his episcopal blessing to the people. But the Sarum Processional and supporting Breviaries make no reference whatsoever to '*Magnificat*'.[60] Yet it must have been sung: it was the very heart of the office. So when was the Salisbury Boy Bishop enthroned? Wordsworth's edition says that he entered his stall '*tunc*' – the supremely unhelpful adverb 'then'! From the crucifer he received the pastoral staff and, later, in the course of the antiphon *Princeps ecclesie*, he undertook a series of benedictions: of the clergy, of the people and of the altar. But we can only presume that at Salisbury, and at the innumerable places that followed Salisbury's Use, the climactic moment of enthronement came at the verse *Deposuit* during the vespers canticle. Later that evening, at compline, and on the feast of the Innocents itself, at matins, lauds and second vespers, the Boy Bishop in silken cope and mitre sang versicles and, at lauds, 'in a modest voice, as if reading' sang the 'chapter' from the book of Revelation. At mass, the Boy Bishop censed the altar and the people, preached a sermon and gave the blessing. One sermon, on the text 'Except ye be like little children' written at Gloucester for John Stubs, 'Querester', and 'pronownsyd' by him in 1558, the very last year of the catholic rite, has survived – and it includes a passage very revealing of what his fellow choristers at Gloucester had been up to:[61]

> I kan not let this passe ontouched how boyyisshly thei behave themselves in the church, how rashly thei cum into the quere without any reverence; never knele nor cowntenaunce to say any prayer or Pater Noster, but rudely squat down on ther tayles and justle with ther fellows for a place; anon thei startes me owt of the quere agayne, and in agayne and out agayne … but only to gad and gas abrode, and so cum in agayne and crosse the quere fro one side to another and never rest.

There is no evidence that a Boy Bishop was ever called upon to celebrate mass, whatever the legislation abolishing the ceremony, and abusive puritan pamphlets, might subsequently assert. Celebrating mass would have been an unimaginable act of sacrilege. He did, however, receive the offerings, although various attempts were made by chapters and precentors to divert the money to more virtuous uses. The Salisbury chapter in 1390/91 took half of it 'for the fabric of the church'; in 1405 the Boy Bishop had to beg for it. In the fifteenth century the Salisbury chapter put it aside to pay for the Boy Bishop's subsequent education, a kind of bursary fund. The sums, incidentally, ranged from £2.6s. in a bad year to £5.6.8d. from the most generous congregation,[62] substantial sums of money at a time when a fifteenth-century master of the choristers at Wells earned an annual stipend of £4.13.4d. So far as the liturgy is concerned, the ceremonies ended with second vespers.

The fun happened outside the cathedral. The 'bishop' and his 'canons' were to be feasted by one of the senior clergy. We actually have the menu of the feast given to the Boy Bishop and his 'canons' at York on 27 December 1396. It included veal and mutton, sausages, two ducks, twelve chickens, eight woodcocks and a plover, forty-six field fares and assorted small birds, pears, honey, spices, mustard and flour for bread. The cook's fee was sixpence; the sum spent on wine, two shillings and three pence. No wonder things got rowdy. In fact the Boy Bishop celebrations at York became thoroughly out of hand. The fourteenth-century 'bishop' and his 'canons' were allowed to go on episcopal visitation for the best part of a month following Holy Innocents' Day. The compotus accounts for 1396 show total expenses of £6.14s.10d. However, the Boy Bishop had received gifts totalling £7.16. 4d., so he ended the month eleven shillings and sixpence in pocket. Meanwhile he had extracted money from the chancellor, precentor and treasurer of York, along with several of the diocesan archdeacons; accompanied on horseback by some of his 'canons' he had visited and begged alms from all the major monasteries and nunneries of Yorkshire; he had won substantial sums from the leading aristocracy and in addition charmed a gold ring from the countess of Northumbria and another in a silk purse from the Lady Marmeon. This was the least acceptable feature of the tradition and in due course, in most foundations, the Boy Bishop's visitation was banned. As early as 1319 Roger de Martival had stopped it at Salisbury. But the festival itself seems to have increased in appeal right to the close of the middle ages. In the first half of the sixteenth century it spread from the cathedrals, monasteries, great houses and colleges even to parish churches and schools. This spread of popularity may in the end have been its undoing. It was too widespread and obvious an affront to the Protestant mind, which could not tolerate the cohabitation of religion and fun. The only thing to do, when 'children be strangelie decked and apparayled to counterfeit priestes, bishoppes and women, and so be ledde with songes and daunces from house to house, blessing the people and gatheryng money, and boyes do sing masse and preache in the pulpitt, with svch other unfittinge and inconuenient vsages, rather to the derysyon than to any true glory of God', was to have the whole business 'clerely extinguished'; and so it was, by royal proclamation on 22 July 1541.[63]

One choristic jape did, however, survive the Reformation: the ancient privilege accorded to choristers, or some would say to the most junior chorister, of challenging for spur money any gentleman rash enough to enter the sacred precincts wearing spurs. There was an escape route. The offending gentleman could then require the challenging chorister to recite his Gamut, his *ut, re, mi*. If the boy failed, no fine was payable; if he succeeded, then five shillings in medieval and Tudor times, five guineas in Victorian times (when the Duke of Wellington seems to have been a frequent victim, especially at the Chapel Royal), would be demanded by the triumphant boy. That the practice is still alive today – but in strikingly different circumstances – is evidenced in chapter 16.

6

Turmoil

By the early decades of the sixteenth century, some degree of reformation of western Christendom was all but inevitable.[1] Laxity, corruption, superstition, misappropriated wealth, conspicuous ecclesiastical grandeur: all these and other faults were coming to seem intolerable to a wide range of society without any particular theological axes to grind. Alongside the numerous laymen who objected to the church's shortcomings was a growing body of biblical scholars and their educated followers, many directly inspired by the writings of Luther, to whom the practices of the contemporary church and the theology which lay behind its practices seemed deeply at odds with the life and worship of the earliest Christians as portrayed in the New Testament; at odds with the recorded words of Christ; and, above all, at odds with Paul's explications of Christ's teaching. In England events developed a special urgency due to the failure of Catherine of Aragon to produce an heir to Henry VIII and the papal refusal to countenance annulment. So the groundswell of calls for reform meant that by the 1530s the question was not so much whether there would be reform as what shape it would take. In the event it was to take manifold forms. By the time the Catholic Church set about its own reform programme at the Council of Trent irreparable multiple fracture had already occurred.[2]

The part that choristers should play in a reformed church was problematical. Indeed, for those reformed groups that followed the teaching of Calvin, choristers could hardly have a place at all: all music in church, apart from unison melody for congregational singing of biblical texts, was suspect and likely to be banned, as it was at Geneva.[3] Yet the first, and in some ways most dramatic, act of church reformation in England had no effect on the life and work of choristers. This was the abolition of papal authority over the English church in the summer of 1534, making Henry VIII and his heirs, 'the only Supreme Head in earth of the Church of England'.[4] This move left the church's liturgy and worship almost wholly unchanged. Some forty-five martyrs, notably John Fisher and Thomas More, paid for their loyalty to Rome with their lives; but the generality of the church in England survived the breach with Rome intact. All choral foundations continued to sing the traditional offices and the mass. Most choristers, apart perhaps from the almonry boys of Rochester, who lost their saintly bishop, may scarcely have been aware that anything significant had happened.

Later in the 1530s, however, 'a huge and urgent problem [for which] radical action ... was both necessary and inevitable'[5] was addressed with the suppression of the nunneries and monasteries. Although, like the abolition of papal authority, it left the liturgy and the Catholic theology on which it was based largely unchanged, the suppression had a major effect upon a large number of choral foundations. By the two Acts of Dissolution, that of the lesser houses in 1536 and that of the greater monasteries in 1539,[6] every group of children who sang in nunnery or monastery underwent either abolition or reconstitution. The girls suffered total disbandment. How many girls were affected it is impossible to say: precise records do not exist and probably never existed. Only the larger houses had girls in such numbers that they could have been regarded as any sort of a choral force, and even to describe them as such is anachronistic. Nevertheless, to quote just two cases, the community at St Mary's, Winchester, at the Dissolution, included twenty-six boarding children, mostly, perhaps all, girls; Polesworth nunnery was bringing up over thirty.[7] The children must have engaged to some extent in liturgical singing. Other large houses of nuns likewise accommodated girls. By 1536 most and by 1539 all had been dispersed. Daily liturgical singing by girls was abolished until the late twentieth century. The actual sixteenth-century loss can have been, numerically, only very minor. But the loss *in principle*, over a period of four centuries, needs at least to be on record as matter for regret. The Act that closed almost all the nunneries also dissolved a large number of 'lesser' monasteries, those whose income fell below a yearly value of £200. Here, as with the nunneries, it is impossible to say how many had maintained almonries with boys singing in their Lady chapels. It has been estimated that in total there may have been 1500 boys educated in almonry schools just before the Dissolution.[8] Not all these boys, however, would have been choristers. Often four, sometimes six, rarely as many as eight, are recorded as singing in monastic Lady chapel choirs. So we may be considering a few hundred singing boys. The 1536 Act was, however, only a stage in a process. Three years later the second Act of Dissolution, that for 'the Dissolution of the Greater Monasteries', closed all surviving monastic houses. In fact, by that time, February 1539, all but twelve had already been persuaded to surrender to the crown. With the surrender of Waltham Abbey on 23 March 1540 the abolition of monasticism in England was complete.

Those monastic houses that were seats of bishops – Canterbury, Carlisle, Durham, Ely, Norwich, Rochester, Winchester and Worcester – survived as refounded secular cathedrals. Prior to the Dissolution a grand scheme was considered to provide a cathedral for every county.[9] Had this been implemented, the boys of the Lady chapel choirs at Bury St Edmunds, St Albans, Waltham and some ten others would have been maintained. In the event, only five became the seats of new bishoprics: St Augustine's, Bristol; St Werburgh's, Chester; and three abbeys dedicated to St Peter at Gloucester, Peterborough and, for a decade,

Westminster.[10] A further new diocese of Oxford was established with its seat at the Augustinian abbey of Oseney, just west of the city, to be moved after three years to the chapel of Christ Church, the Oxford college refounded by Henry VIII after the fall of Wolsey, whose foundation as Cardinal College it had been.[11] Every other monastery was forced to surrender, including, along with the three mentioned above, such distinguished houses as Glastonbury, Ramsey, Reading, Abingdon and Tewkesbury.[12] Here indeed were to be, 'bare, ruin'd choirs where late the sweet birds sang'.[13] It must, nevertheless, be reiterated that boys in monastic churches, even those churches that were the seats of bishops, had since the twelfth century sung only at the daily Lady mass in the Lady chapel and evening Marian devotions in the nave, almost never in quire.[14] For the larger Benedictine and Augustinian houses the Dissolution wrought two contrasting effects. On the one hand, in abbeys such as Waltham, where Thomas Tallis was in charge of the music, the choral foundations were closed down completely. Their choral forces, including boy choristers painstakingly trained in the singing of sophisticated and beautiful polyphony, were disbanded and scattered. Most of the boys must simply have been sent home, but there is a record of three shillings being paid to each of the two boys at Nocton Priory in Lincolnshire and others may similarly have been compensated.[15]

In those abbeys that had been or became the seats of bishops, boy choristers did not merely survive but had their roles extended and in some cases their numbers increased. The boys were to find themselves singing in quire with the men. All former monastic cathedral re-foundations were established with between six and ten boys, that is, with former Lady chapel choir numbers in some cases maintained, in some cases increased; nowhere were they decreased. Indeed, perhaps the most surprising feature of the dissolution of the 'cathedral' monasteries is the continuity of personnel from the Benedictine or Augustinian community to a college of secular clergy. With the single exception of Canterbury, at every one of the former monastic cathedrals the monastic prior became the secular dean. Substantial numbers of his monks also became either prebendary canons (usually the university graduates, as at Durham,[16] where all had Oxford or Cambridge degrees) or minor canons or singing men. The reformed choral force of secular clergy simply carried on where they had left off as monks.

That in some foundations the continuity of personnel extended to the choristers is virtually certain, with the singing of at least some of the liturgy almost or even absolutely unbroken. Other foundations suffered a hiatus while the new establishments were proposed, agreed and legitimised. Unfortunately there is a shortage of clear and unambiguous evidence. As to choristers, the evidence is particularly thin. Clerks rarely troubled to record or administrators to retain lists of choristers. Durham is a glowing exception. From there, as noted by an antiquarian of the 1690s, we have a list of ten Durham boys said to have been on the strength at the time of the re-establishment in May 1541, listed, as was usual, in order of seniority. They were:

Christopher Mayer	Richard Stott
Thomas Whitehead	William Chapman
William Sim	John Watson
John Hunter	Robert Biddick
Edward Raw	Oswin Chapman

Of these boys it is known that William Sim was aged about twelve in 1541. It is probable that at least he and those (presumably older) boys listed above him had been amongst the six or eight almonry choristers. Hutchinson's History of 1823, using a seventeenth-century source, recorded that the daily mass of Our Lady, sung, of course, by the choristers, continued without a break.[17] Recent research at Durham confirms that worship and the management of income were maintained throughout the period of transition by over twenty of the monks under Hugh Whitehead, the last prior.[18] Such continuity may not have occurred everywhere. At Norwich, the first cathedral monastery to surrender (May 1538), where fifteen of the monks not required or unwilling to serve in the secular cathedral had been pensioned off, difficulty was certainly encountered in building up its post-Dissolution choral forces.[19] Indeed, it would have been difficult for any choral foundation to muster from scratch at short notice an entire team of ten boys with the educational and musical skills necessary for commencing a choristership. But the likelihood is that the new choirs of most if not all of the episcopally refounded monastic houses included at least some boys who had been almonry choristers, knew the liturgy of the mass and had received training in polyphonic singing.[20] Even at Norwich payments of forty shillings in 1538 to Thomas Daryes, master of the boys of the chapel of the Blessed Virgin Mary, and ten shillings for the upkeep of two of those boys, may suggest continuing maintenance of at least some of the almonry singers. Certainly by 1542 Thomas Crewe had been appointed as 'Maister, instructor and teacher of the eight syngyng chyldern within the said Cathedral Church'.[21] At Ely, the schoolmaster, Ralphe Holland, continued in post as head of the refounded King's School.[22] A Winchester lay clerk, Richard Wynslade, was being paid 'pro the dyette, rayment and other necessarys' for the choristers, of whom he had been made master, as early as 1541;[23] and the unique survival from Worcester of a royal nomination of a master of choristers antedates the issuing of the cathedral statutes.[24] It is, indeed, hard to believe that great churches like Canterbury, and even more so those many places like Durham and Norwich whose priors and monks had submitted to Henry VIII as Head of the English church and were clearly willing to continue as secular deans and predendaries, simply lay unoccupied and silent, no masses said, no offices sung, while the details of reappointments were worked out.

Even at some of the new cathedrals there seems to be evidence of continuity. At Westminster the choir of twenty-six men and ten boys under their master, William Grene, seem to have included a nucleus of those recorded as singing there in January 1540.[25] From Chester, where the abbot continued living in his lodgings up to the point when he was about to become bishop,[26] we have a list of eight choristers from November 1541:

John Traver	Rafe Becket
Thomas Parker	Edward Morecroft
Matthew Wright	Richard Hough
Thomas of Prestbury	Thomas Wilcock

At Gloucester a collegiate establishment bridged the period between monastery and cathedral, making continuity of personnel likely. Here the five boys of the Lady chapel were to be increased to eight cathedral choristers, though there is evidence that the post-Dissolution complement was generally only six.[27] On the other hand, one cannot assume continuity of personnel at all churches that were to become cathedrals for the first time.[28] At Augustinian Bristol, for instance, the monastery was dissolved on 9 December 1539, its abbot and eleven canons being pensioned off, the abbot to a comfortable retirement on one of his former estates at Abbots Leigh. A receiver was appointed to administer the monastic estates on the king's behalf. A decision was taken to pull down the whole of the part-rebuilt nave of the church. It was not until June 1542 that Bishop Bush was consecrated and a further twenty-five months before statutes were drawn up for the new cathedral.[29] Here, at an institution whose future was uncertain, it is unlikely that a team of singers, men and boys, would have been maintained during three and a half years of hiatus. Indeed, when steps were taken to have the newly designated cathedral church staffed, it was found that the school building was 'ruinous'. Cathedral funds intended for charity had to be diverted for three years to pay for the repair or rebuilding of the schoolroom.[30]

Detailed statutes were drawn up for each of these 'New Foundation' cathedrals, both those that had formerly been monastic sees and those that became cathedrals. The earliest, as might be expected, were for Norwich in April 1539; the latest for Bristol in June 1542. All the rest were issued between December 1540 (Westminster) and January 1542 (Worcester), with five sets issued within days of each other in August and September of 1541. Norwich had been in a rush to surrender and seems to have paid a price in the narrowness of its provision, perhaps before the government's schemes for the former monastic cathedrals had been fully worked out. A set of eight choristers was proposed, to live with and be maintained by their master; but a proviso added that the cathedral might have to manage with just 'four of them that are most fit to serve in choir, until the table in the Common Hall be provided for them'. Further, no money payments are stipulated for the choristers, only an annual livery gown. More seriously, there was to be no grammar school, a neglect not rectified until 1547.[31]

Apart from the provisions at Norwich, all other sets of statutes share a common template, albeit individualized at certain points. That template reveals that the drafters were, like Henry VI's clerks before them, familiar with the statutes of William of Wykeham's foundations. The numbers of choristers to be maintained reflected the prestige and economic and financial standing of each cathedral. The specification seems to have been to match the number of singing men, that is vicars choral and lay clerks, by approximately half that number of boys, a strikingly different balance from that deemed desirable in cathedral choirs of today. A notional norm seems to have been eight boys, as at Norwich, a number also stipulated for Chester, Ely, Oxford, Peterborough, Rochester and probably also Gloucester. Two foundations were deemed to be unable to sustain this number and were to maintain just six choristers each: Bristol and Carlisle; this seems to have been the number actually maintained at Gloucester. Five grand foundations were thought to need and be able to provide for ten boys each: Canterbury, Durham, Westminster, Winchester and Worcester. Nowhere did Henry VIII come near to matching the sixteen boys to be found serving the college chapels of Eton and Winchester and at the three great medieval Oxbridge choral foundations.

In preparing his subjects to accept his huge acquisition of ecclesiastical property and wealth, Henry VIII and his ministers uttered expansive and expensive intentions for the foundation of grammar schools across the land. In the event the king reneged on these undertakings and far fewer schools were established, nearly all those established being refoundations of existing monastic grammar schools. Eight English cathedrals had their monastic schools refounded as royal grammar schools, along with Coventry (a sometime cathedral) and Brecon in Wales.[32] In practice, these grammar schools had only tangential impact on the choristers, with the probable exceptions of Chester, Peterborough and Westminster Abbey. At Chester and Peterborough, although the boys lodged with their master, there is some evidence that from the start they attended academic lessons at the king's grammar school. Similarly, Elizabeth's foundation charter of May 1560 for Westminster School clearly implies that the choristers were part of that foundation and required that 'when they can write moderately well and have learned the eight parts of speech, they are to proceed to the Grammar School for two hours a day at least'. The grammar schools had one other importance for chorister boys in almost all the New Foundation cathedrals: ex-choristers were to have priority over non-chorister candidates for free places, that is to say, to be King's Scholars. Such priority is explicit in the statutes of several foundations and was probably intended at the others.[33] Indeed, one of the first promulgations of Edward VI's reign was a set of royal injunctions for cathedrals (exercising his royal power as Head of the Church in England), of which Injunction 20 required every cathedral that did not have a free grammar school to establish one, and Injunction 22 required them to educate 'choristers as have served in the church five years or more, and have their voices changed, at some grammar school and give them yearly £3 6s. 8d. out of the revenues of the common lands for the space of five years'.[34] Nevertheless, Durham's slightly later Marian statutes of 1555 hedged the priority a little: if the choristers 'are duly qualified, and have made good proficiency in music, and have faithfully served in the Choir, we ordain that they shall be chosen in preference to others'. This expectation, explicit or implicit, that choristers should proceed to the grammar school was supported by the further provision, in almost all the statutes, that, whereas for the generality of candidates the upper age-limit for entry was the boy's fifteenth year, in the case of choristers this restriction should be waived until the point 'when their breast changeth'; that is, a chorister was expected to continue singing in the choir until his voice broke, whatever his age. Only after he had stopped singing would he have time to undertake the grammar school curriculum.

For the singing-boys, with the possible exceptions noted above, quite separate and supposedly appropriate educational provision was made. They were to be taught everything they needed to learn by the master of the choristers. Here, as an example, is the core of the relevant chapter from the Henrician statutes for Canterbury:

Of the Choristers and their Master
    We do appoint and ordain that in our Church [of Canterbury] there shall be by the election and appointment of the Dean and Chapter or, in the Dean's absence, of the Vice-dean and Chapter, ten Choristers, boys of tender age, both with musical voices and apt for singing, who shall serve, minister and sing in the Choir.
    For the instructing and imbuing these boys as well with modesty of manners as with skill in singing, and playing artistically (*artifioso pulsandi*)[35] on musical instruments ... one [Minor Canon or Clerk] shall be chosen by the Dean and Chapter, or, in the Dean's absence, by the Sub-dean and Chapter, who shall be of good character, of upright life, and skilled in singing and playing on the Organ, who shall diligently employ himself in playing at proper times upon the organ, and in chanting the divine services, and shall also apply himself to the teaching and instructing of the Choristers ... And if he be found careless or slothful in teaching, after the third warning, let him be deposed from his office, by the votes of those by whom he was elected. And he shall be bound by an oath faithfully to perform his office.[36]

Flesh is put on these bones in some of the documents. Throughout, musical potential in the boys and musical skill in their master far override concerns about academic abilities. At every foundation candidates for a choristership were to be, 'boys of tender age, both with musical voices and apt for singing', as

at Canterbury. At Westminster an additional talent required of candidates was
'*ad musica instrumenta pulsanda apti*'; and there is an expectation expressed that
the Master of the Choristers will be either a Doctor or a Bachelor of Music. At
Canterbury, however, representations must have been made during drafting of
the statutes that the organist was not a suitable man to have care of the boys, so
a long, awkward clause (omitted above) emphasises that it does not necessarily
have to be the organist who is elected master. The Durham statutes tackle the
problem of priorities for a man who has to sing, play the organ and look after the
boys. 'That he may the more diligently apply himself to the charge of instructing
and supervising the boys we permit him to be absent from the choir on ordinary
days (feria), provided he attend upon Sundays and Festivals.'

These statutes, insofar as they apply to the choristers and their masters, are
not impressive. They look backwards rather than forwards and are strewn with
landmines that were to explode intermittently for more than three centuries.
The imprecision concerning the choristers' academic schooling, in an age
when education was in the course of being broadened and transformed, could
be helpful in that it gave chapters flexibility, but it could be and sometimes
was disastrous, inviting culpable neglect. A consequence was that well into
the nineteenth century the choristers of some choral foundations were hardly
educated at all. The imposition upon one man, most often the organist, of the
obligation to provide musical and academic education and pastoral care was
already becoming anachronistic by 1540: the boys of St George's, Windsor,
had a schoolmaster distinct from the organist as early as 1527. Yet no statute
authorised funding for a choristers' schoolmaster, a 'master of grammar', as
such. More generally, the expression of salaries as fixed money sums rather than
as the products of specific endowments was to wreak havoc during the inflation
of the Elizabethan years and was to lead directly to reductions in chorister
numbers. The expectation that choristers would eat at the common table with
other members of the foundation derived from an age when clergy were celibate
and single. Once it became usual for clergy and singing men to be married there
would cease to be a common table at which the boys could eat. Gigantic rows were
to arise over whether choristers did or did not have rights to grammar schooling.
Finally, the statutes were very imprecise regarding the requirement on the boys
'to attend, minister and sing in the choir'. What exactly were the boys obliged to
sing in these no longer monastic churches?

The question needs to be set in context. The Benedictine monastic churches
had sung their mass and their office according to the Use of St Benedict, which,
by the thirteenth century, wholly excluded a liturgical role for boys. So the
New Foundation cathedrals had no experience of boys singing other than the
Lady mass and Marian devotions and, probably in some of the most affluent
establishments, polyphony in quire on high feast days. At the Dissolution

the Use of Benedict became obsolete in England. Early in the 1540s we find episcopal injunctions being issued requiring the New Foundation cathedrals to adopt the Use of Sarum. The New Foundation cathedrals had somehow to adopt this liturgy, to equip themselves with multiple books (still, so far as music is concerned, mostly in manuscript, despite the invention of printing) and to acquire or commission music. It was a daunting task. Bishop Heath of Rochester, for example, enjoined in 1543 that all the ministers of the church (including the choristers) 'shall endevour theryself as myche as they can to do everything within the Churche wich is appointed by the ordinal of Sarum to be done'. This entailed boys singing extensively, including many passages for solo boys or small groups of boys, at high mass and at least four offices, on between a third and half of the days of the year; but not on ferias.[37] This explains the Durham provision that excused the master from singing the Office in quire on ferias when the choristers would be in school. Nevertheless, Bishop Heath's injunctions make substantial demands on the boys, even though Rochester was not a 'grand' cathedral. They were to sing a Lady mass with polyphony with their master every day of the year, joined by the priests and clerks on lesser holy days. On principal and greater double feasts, with their vigils, they were to sing the whole gamut of high mass and office and were to add, after compline, a 'prycksong anthem'.[38] Rochester Cathedral in the years immediately following its secular reconstitution was evidently to be full of the sound of boys singing plainsong and polyphony. It was in these final years of Henry VIII's reign that composers such as Tallis, Sheppard and Tye produced much of their finest music.[39]

This high noon of the late medieval choral liturgy was short-lived. Already, the radical winds of Lutheran and Calvinistic theology were blowing in from the Continent, affecting not only the former monastic establishments but every choral foundation in England and Wales. Revulsion against the veneration of saints' relics had already led to the destruction of such shrines as those of Becket at Canterbury, Swithun at Winchester and Oswald at Durham. In 1538 the almonry boys of Winchester saw their cathedral's reredos attacked, its incomparable array of carved saints hacked out by iconoclasts. Injunctions began the removal of minor feasts from the calendar. From 1543, lessons at matins and vespers, formerly read or sung in Latin, for which tasks choristers took their turns, were to be read in English. The following year, the archbishop of Canterbury, Thomas Cranmer, replaced the various Latin processional litanies by a single one in English to a text and quasi-plainsong melody of his own devising, 'not full of notes, but, as near as may be, for every syllable a note', as he famously wrote to the king.[40] A further series of suppressions, this time of chantries and collegiate churches, began during the early 1540s. Nevertheless, the king was determined to hold the dykes against the flood-tide of Protestantism flowing in from the Continent. Choristers at St George's Chapel at Windsor in 1543 may well have witnessed the burning of three professed Calvinists, Peerson, Filmer and the foolish Robert Testwood, 'who with more ingenuity than taste had altered the wording of an anthem so as to protest against the worship of the Virgin Mary'.[41] And the choristers must surely have known that their own organist, later to be their schoolmaster, John Merbecke, only narrowly escaped the same fate.[42] The collegiate clergy were aware that only the king's conservative theology prevented an increasingly radical Cranmer from imposing sweeping liturgical change, change which many of them, persuaded already by Protestant theology, would have welcomed and worked for. Thomas Becon, sometime chaplain to Cranmer, was soon to write:

> There have been (would God there were not now!) which have not spared to spend much riches in nourishing many idle singing men to bleat in their chapels, thinking so to do God on high sacrifice … A Christian man's melody, after St Paul's mind, consisteth in heart, while we recite psalms, hymns and spiritual songs, and sing to the Lord in our hearts … All other outward melody is vain and transitory, and passeth away and cometh to nought.[43]

It was Becon's opinion that 'music is a more vain and trifling science than it becometh a man born and appointed to matters of gravity to spend much time about'.[44] He was not alone in thinking this. Hanging over the choral foundations was the threat – some thought it the likelihood – that radical change, when it came, would sweep away all choirs.

Henry VIII died on 28 January 1547. His nine-year-old heir, Edward VI, was placed under the regency of a Protector, his late mother's brother, Edward Seymour, earl of Hertford, soon to become duke of Somerset. Seymour was of Protestant inclination and Cranmer was given a freedom he had never enjoyed under Henry VIII to refute much of Catholic doctrine and dismantle the liturgy that expressed it. Church worship was to be by the people, not primarily by clergy on behalf of the people, and the language of all worship was not to be the Latin of the learned but the vernacular of the congregation. It followed that a multiplicity of daily offices would have no useful place; more significantly, the essence of the mass must be the personal communion of the faithful, not the votive offering of a supposed sacrifice. Altars were to be replaced by a modest table, of which not even the grandest church would have need of more than one. Liturgies expressing devotion to the saints, above all to the Blessed Virgin Mary – in which, of course, boy choristers had played a central part – were to be discontinued. Anything that smacked of non-scriptural superstition was to be removed, opening the floodgates to the destroyers of relics, saints' tombs, images, statues, painted glass, books of music; indeed, to the slighting of a whole millennium of Christian history and heritage.

The first stage of this transformation took place from early 1547 until October 1552. The central pillar was the Act of Uniformity that contained orders of service to be used everywhere from 9 June (Whitsunday) 1549.[45] But both before and after this Act, other legislation, royal injunctions and episcopal injunctions imposed significant changes. Bizarrely, the first impact on choristers of the new Edwardine reforms concerned their haircuts. Since the earliest Christian days, when boys became choristers they had been admitted to the lower orders of the clergy as exorcists, lectors or acolytes. This admission required them to be tonsured, the hair on the crown of their heads to be shorn. In the course of 1547, Visitors under royal authority were sent to the cathedrals, their requirements being recorded in sets of injunctions. Thus, Injunction 25 for Canterbury Cathedral reads: 'Item, the choristers to have from henceforth the crown shaven no more; their heads nevertheless to be kept short'. Injunction 5 for Winchester cathedral reads similarly: 'Item, that all manner of choristers of this said Church shall from henceforth suffer their crowns to grow and be no more shaven, but only their hair to be rounded and clipped short.'[46] The characteristic tonsured medieval singing boy was to be a thing of the past. In future it was to be 'short back and sides': choristers were to be ordinary schoolboys who happened to sing. There must have been a brief period of a few weeks when they all looked very comical. But within a month or two the chorister in the street was tonsorially indistinguishable from any other little Tudor boy.

In more important respects 1547 was to be a year of change, uncertainty and diversity, to the extent that individual deans and canons did or did not embrace reform theology and local iconoclasts varied in the vehemence with which they felt free to strip churches of Catholic apparatus. Thus it was that, almost coincidentally in Lent 1547, at St Paul's Cathedral Cranmer and the cathedral choir sang a requiem mass for the soul of François I of France whilst the dean, William May, ordered the pulling down of the high altar.[47] Discrete suppressions during the early 1540s culminated in legislation for the wholesale abolition of chantries in 1547,[48] with the consequent disbandment of collegiate and choral foundations such as Beverley and Ripon, the Newarke at Leicester and St Mary's at Warwick, St Stephen's at Westminster, Fotheringhay, Tattersall (where John Taverner had been master of the choristers), Bishop Grandison's foundation of Ottery St Mary in Devon and the secular collegiate church with a complement of some ten to twelve singing boys and men at Wallingford in Berkshire.[49] This latter has a singular significance due to one boy, a chorister at Wallingford shortly before the dissolution of its choral foundation in 1548. His name was Thomas Tusser. In 1575 his Five Hundred Pointes of Good Husbandrie was published, prefaced by some stanzas of metrical autobiography.[50] These explain how Thomas, an Essex boy, came to be a chorister at Wallingford, and how from there he went on to a second and more interesting and profitable choristership.

It came to pass, that borne I was
Of linage good, of gentle blood,
In Essex laier, in village faier,
      that Riuenhall hight ...

I yet but yong, no speech of tong,
Nor teares withal, that often fall
From mothers eies, when childe out cries,
      to part hir fro:
Could pitie make, good father take,
But out I must, to song be thrust,
Say what I would, do what I could
      his minde was so.

O painfull time, for euerie crime,
What toesed eares, like baited beares!
What bobbed lips, what ierks, what nips!
      what hellish toies!
What robes, how bare! What colledge fare!
What bread, how stale! What pennie Ale!
Then Wallingford, how whart thou abhord
      Of sillie boies!

Thomas Tusser was to be saved from the horrors of this small and clearly inadequate choral foundation by the rights of impressment that had been granted to the Chapel Royal where he was taken to become one of the choristers, often peripatetic with the Court ('now there now here'). Finally he transferred to the choir of St Paul's, where the gifted John Redford was Master of the Choristers.

Thence for my voice, I must (no choice)
Away of force, like posting horse,
For sundrie men, had plagards then,
      such childe to take:
The better brest, the lesser rest,
To s[e]rve the Queere, now there now here,
For time so spent, I may repent,
      and sorrow make.

But marke the chance, my self to vance,
By friendships lot, to Paules I got,
So found I grace, a certaine space,
      still to remaine:
With Redford there, the like no where,
For cunning such, and vertue much,
By whom some part of Musicke art,
      So did I gaine.

St Paul's saw to it that after his 'brest' change Thomas went on to Eton. From there he proceeded to Cambridge which, after Eton, was, in his words 'heauen from hell'. These brief verses cast an interesting light on the poor quality of at least one small, no doubt underfunded, collegiate foundation. They also show that impressment of an apt chorister could be a great blessing.

Just three of the collegiate churches with choral foundations survived the dissolutions of 1547/8: Southwell Minster, whose collegiate foundation was thought to be useful in a county that had no cathedral; and the parish churches of Ludlow and Newark-on-Trent,[51] whose choral foundations were deemed not to be chantry-based. Each of the three had a formal establishment that included six choristers, though Ludlow parish church found it hard to maintain that number of boys through the sixteenth century.[52] Although the Chantries Act specifically excluded from its provisions chantries associated with Oxbridge colleges, Eton College and Winchester College, St George's Chapel, Windsor, and the Chapel of the Sea (a royal foundation in the Isle of Ely), some at least of the Oxbridge colleges had to fight to maintain their choral establishments. At Oxford, Doctor Cox, dean of Christ Church, tried to get Magdalen College's school with its choristers suppressed, but the fellows, supported by citizens of Oxford, successfully defended it 'as a Norisshe to trayne up their youth in vertue and lerninge'.[53] Cranmer moved with care, hoping to hold together Catholic- and Protestant-minded men. He had for some time been working on drafts of an English service book to replace the Latin missals, graduals, breviaries and the like.[54] The Chapel Royal, with its committedly Protestant dean, Richard Sampson, was used as a testing ground for some of his ideas. Within two months of Edward's coronation an English form of compline was sung there. The following year, as uncertainty spread through the English church as to what forms of service should be used, Somerset wrote to the vice-chancellor of Cambridge University ordering that, until a new prayer book was published and made obligatory, the chapels and churches of Cambridge should follow the order of mass, matins and evensong 'such as is presently used in the king's majesty's chapel, and none other'.[55]

It was not until January 1549 that Parliament approved for use by Whitsun 'The Booke of the Common Prayer and Administracion of the Sacramentes, and Other Rites and Ceremonies of the Churche after the use of the Churche of England'.[56] This first of Cranmer's two Prayer Books was in many ways a conservative document. The liturgy of the Church of England was to consist, as before, of office and eucharist. The multiplicity of eight short offices was ingeniously and beautifully transformed into an extended matins, drawn from the texts of the Sarum matins, prime and lauds; and an extended evensong, drawn similarly from the texts of vespers and compline. Cranmer's urge towards comprehension is vividly demonstrated by the multiple title given to his liturgy for 'The Supper of the Lorde and the Holy Communion, commonly called the Masse'. The ordinary of the Catholic mass he left largely intact, though with additional scriptural material and a substantial section of prayers preparatory to the reception of the communion in both kinds inserted after the consecration. Most strikingly, provision was still made that 'the clerkes shall syng' the traditional choral sections, *Introit, Kyrie, Gloria, Credo, Sanctus* with *Benedictus, Agnus Dei* and post-communion. Here appeared to be authorisation for undiminished choral worship. But there was, of course, a gigantic problem: the whole text was now in English; the entire corpus of existing music for office and sacrament had been made obsolete at a stroke. The clerks and choristers were to sing, but to sing with no music, there being none. Emphasising this, legislation also required that all copies of former service books – 'antiphoners, missals, grails, processionals, manuals ... whatsoever heretofore used for service of the church' – were to be 'utterly abolished, extinguished and forbidden for ever to be used *or kept*'.[57] Enforcement was joyously assisted by iconoclasts, with the consequence that the overwhelming majority of pre-Reformation music, including the entire corpus of some composers (the existence of whose music is known only from library inventories), has been irrecoverably lost.

What, then, did the choristers and the men behind them sing in this unmapped landscape? Four kinds of musical setting can be distinguished. Some pre-Reformation music survived reworked to English texts: for instance, the *Gloria, Credo, Sanctus* and *Agnus Dei* from two of Taverner's five-part Latin masses appeared, set to the English words of the 1549 Prayer Book, and his *Mater Christi* was transformed into an English anthem to the words *God be merciful to us*.[58] Secondly, some foundations attempted to put together a plainsong fudge, endeavouring to adapt the new English words to the old 'Gregorian' modes. This seems to have been the preferred option, a model having already been set in Cranmer's own Litany of 1544. The royal injunctions for Lincoln Minster of April 1548, for instance, require that 'they shall from henceforth sing [anthems] only of our Lord, and them not in Latin; but ... shall turn the same into English, setting thereunto a plain and distinct note for every syllable one'.[59] Indeed psalms were to be sung to varieties of this quasi-plainsong for decades. Within a year of the Prayer Book's publication there was an official solution in this genre to hand. At Windsor, John Merbecke had been at work, presumably under commission from the prayer book committee of Convocation, setting the entire choral sections of the Prayer Book of 1549 to music. He did so with exceptional skill and diligence, using melodic phrases recognisably drawn from the plainsong modes, yet set to reflect the distinctive emphases of Cranmer's English prose. It should have been a best seller, as it was indeed to become in the twentieth century after four hundred years of neglect. But until modern times it appeared in only one edition, *The Book of Common Praier Noted* of 1550, because it was cut down in its infancy when the 1549 Prayer Book was withdrawn in 1552. This was indeed a warning to other composers setting out, by a fourth route, to pen original music for English liturgical texts, free from plainsong models. We cannot know how much was written during these years, so much has been lost. Of the twelve or so composers known to have written for the new Prayer Book texts, Tallis, Tye, Shepherd and Mundy were the most distinguished. The fullest surviving contemporary sources, the so-called Wanley part-books,[60] contain some ninety works, all but seventeen by unidentified composers. Most are for men's voices only, suggesting that the collection may have been gathered for a London or provincial church, served normally by men, that could call on a neighbouring body of choristers to add splendour to the music of high days. In addition to the Taverner adaptations, there are original works, including complete settings of the 1549 texts for the choral sections of the communion and the matins and evensong canticles, along with anthems identifiable as by Tye, Shepherd and Tallis. The need for learning so much new music may account for the extreme simplicity of such settings as Tallis's Short Service of about 1550, a work that has survived in the repertory to the present day.

If the period from 1547 to October 1552 was one of upheaval, the twelve months that followed were to be cataclysmic. Following the fall of the Protector Somerset, his successor, Robert Dudley, sometime duke of Northumberland, enabled Edward's ecclesiastical advisers to give the Calvinists a free hand. In November 1552 Cranmer's first Prayer Book was withdrawn and replaced by a second book, radically more Protestant and quite evidently anti-choral. Evensong became 'Evening Prayer'; in it all references to singing by 'clerks' at the communion were removed, apart from what seems to have been an oversight at the *Gloria*, introduced by the phrase 'Then shalbe sayd or song'.[61] Bishops, like John Hooper of Gloucester and Worcester who had been in Zurich in the 1540s, issued local injunctions which sometimes went further than the apparent intentions of the Prayer Book, prohibiting polyphony and ordering the removal of organs. Pressure to do away with choral foundations became intense. Many have thought that events in the summer of 1553 signalled the death throes of the English choral tradition.[62] Indeed, since the 1530s a Protestant tide had been flowing, stemmed briefly by Henry VIII but then unchecked after his death, moving with seemingly inexorable force towards a Calvinism that had no use for the professional choir of men and boys. Yet eight months after the introduction of the new book, Edward VI was dead, to be succeeded by his half-sister, the Catholic Mary. By December 1553 all the Edwardine legislation had been repealed and forms of worship returned by statute to those that had been in use in the last year of Henry VIII's reign.[63] All music written to English texts was in its turn made obsolete, with Latin once again the universal language of liturgy. If choristers who had sung only in Latin had found it difficult to adjust to singing church music in English, how much more difficult must it have been for those who had sung only in English to master the texts of the Latin mass and the Latin matins, prime, terse, vespers and compline.

There is a frustrating lack of precise, local, archival or anecdotal evidence about specific groups of choristers or individual boys and of what happened to them during these upheavals and reversals of the 1550s. It has been noticed that much of what Tallis wrote to 1549 texts, presumably for the Chapel Royal, is for altos, tenors and basses only. Yet there were twelve choristers on the Chapel Royal strength at this time. Perhaps, for a period, the boys could not cope with the overwhelming new demands. Perhaps they concentrated on quasi-plainsong psalms and the like. Similar questions are raised for the early years of the Marian reaction. It is from this period that the Gyffard part-books come, containing music almost certainly written for the Chapel Royal.[64] Once again, much of it is for men only, suggesting that the Chapel Royal boys, who were literally the pick of the land by impressment, could not cope with Latin polyphony.[65] From another royal foundation, St George's, Windsor Castle, there is gloomier evidence. Item 27 of the royal injunctions of February 1550 states,[66] 'Also, because the great number of ceremonies in the church are now put away by the King's Majesty's authority and Act of Parliament, so that fewer choristers be requisite, and the College is otherwise more charged than it hath been;[67] we enjoin that from henceforth there shall be found in their College only ten choristers', a reduction, that is, of three. During the same period there was a reduction in chorister numbers at Salisbury where, by 1550, the statutory fourteen had been very nearly halved to eight.[68] Worse still was happening at Cambridge, the nursery of English Protestantism. At King's College the entire choral establishment was in course of being disbanded. The choristers were reduced in January 1549 from sixteen to fifteen, in August to twelve, in 1550 to ten and by 1552 there were no choristers at all: just one priest and one clerk to maintain non-choral services.[69] Then, with the Marian reimposition of Latin liturgies and the encouragement once more of polyphony, there followed a frantic search for choristers. John Wickham, 'conduct' or priest, in March 1554 was paid twenty-six shillings for riding to Peterborough, Boston and Newark-on-Trent to find and presumably impress actual or potential choristers. Clearly he was successful: the two choristers of January 1554 had by mid March become nine; by June, twelve and September, thirteen. A year later the full statutory sixteen had been enrolled.[70] It looks very likely that Wickham had been appointed *informator chorustarum*: early in 1555 he was receiving a further extra payment for caring for 'Roose egrotante', a sick chorister. Amongst many of the adult singers there must have been great delight at the return of multi-part polyphony, giving them the chance to exercise again their true skills. Canterbury lay clerks certainly knew where to lay their hands on secreted copies of the old music: the chapter subsequently reimbursed them for no less than seventy-nine items.[71] Surviving accounts from Exeter Cathedral tell of repairs to retrieved Catholic books of music and purchases being made in London.[72] During Mary's brief four-year reign some of the most splendid music in the old style was composed. The antiphon *Vox patris coelestis* for four trebles (two high and two 'meane') and two basses by William Mundy (who had been head chorister at Westminster Abbey in 1543) has been described as 'perhaps the finest composition of the whole Marian genre ... the apogee of the grandiose Marian antiphon'.[73] And the music for high mass celebrated at St Paul's Cathedral on Christmas Day 1554, sung by the combined choirs of the English Chapel Royal and the Spanish *Capilla Real*, in the presence of the supposedly pregnant Queen Mary and her consort, Philip of Spain, is widely assumed to have been the climax to a half-century of English festal masses,[74] Tallis's dazzling seven-part *Missa Puer Natus Nobis*. At Cambridge an entirely new choral force was established at Trinity College and throughout the country choirs were being rebuilt, with choristers once more learning the Latin liturgy and rising to the complex challenges of brilliant polyphony.

Meanwhile, some three hundred Protestants were going to their martyrdom at the stake. Canterbury choristers may well have watched, on 19 June 1557, as three men and four women were consumed for their faith in a single conflagration there. Within six years John Foxe's popularly-called *Book of Martyrs*, a copy of which was available for public reading in the Canterbury quire, had ensured that Mary, following her early death in November 1558, was to be the most reviled sovereign in English history.[75] At Canterbury, as at every other choral foundation in the country, the chances of England's laws of royal succession and the bloody memory of Mary's reign soon condemned the dizzied choristers to yet another liturgical upheaval.

7

From Elizabeth I to Cromwell

Students of English Reformation church music will be familiar with the provocative hypothesis that it was the accession of a Catholic monarch in 1553 that secured the future of the choral tradition of the Anglican church.[1] A few more years of Edwards VI's reign, the argument holds, would have seen the choirs closed down. But the undisputable saviour of the English choral tradition and its choristers was not the ephemeral Mary.

The heir to Mary's throne was her half-sister Elizabeth. That the English choristers survived the upheavals of the sixteenth century is due directly to her. Elizabeth I's coronation on 15 January 1559 was a Catholic Latin ceremony. In the weeks that followed, however, it became clear that this daughter of Henry VIII and Anne Boleyn, a Catholic by baptism but a Protestant by nurture, was going to reject the Marian settlement and the authority of the papacy and restore a reformed vernacular liturgy. There is some reason to believe that Elizabeth would have been most happy reintroducing the 1549 Prayer Book with its many Catholic elements, including frequent occasions for choral music.[2] But her strongly Protestant Parliament and Convocation made it clear that no Act of Uniformity based on the 1549 book would be acceptable to either the secular or the ecclesiastical powers. So a Book of Common Prayer was issued in 1559 which, at almost all points,[3] replicated that of 1552. That book, it will be recalled, had provided virtually no role for choirs. Left to Parliament and Convocation the English choral heritage might well have withered to extinction. But Elizabeth was musical and had experienced 'the beauty of holiness' through music in church. So the issuing of the 1559 Prayer Book was accompanied by a set of fifty-five explicatory royal injunctions, of which Injunction 49 reads:

> Item, because in divers Collegiate[4] and also some parish Churches, heretofore there have been livings appointed for the maintenance of men and children to use singing in the church, by means whereof the laudable science of music has been had in estimation, and preserved in knowledge: the Queen's Majesty, neither meaning in any wise the decay of anything that might conveniently tend to the use and continuance of the said science, neither to have the same so abused in the church, that thereby the common prayer should be the worse understood of the hearers, willeth and commandeth, first that no alterations be made of such assignments of living, as heretofore hath been appointed to the use of singing or music in the Church, but that the same so remain. And that there be a modest

distinct song, so used in all parts of the common prayers in the Church, that the same may be as plainly understood, as if it were read without singing, and yet nevertheless, for the comforting of such that delight in music, it may be permitted that in the beginning, or in the end of common prayers, either at morning or evening, there may be sung an Hymn, or such like song, to the praise of Almighty God, in the best sort of melody and music that may be conveniently devised, having respect that the sentence of the Hymn may be understood and perceived …[5]

The future of the English chorister was secured, therefore, by an extraordinary injunction which seems to be plain contradictory to the intentions of the Prayer Book that it sets out to explicate. Throughout her reign Elizabeth was to intervene personally, as 'Supreme Governor', to ensure that the Church of England would survive as a *via media* between the extremes of Catholicism and puritanism. Against Catholicism she was to wage international war; against puritanism there was to be an unceasing domestic struggle. Thereby, in the course of a reign of over forty years, the Church of England found itself secure, reasonably consistent, and developing a unique personality, unlike that of any other church in Christendom, which by the time of the queen's death in 1603 many people had come deeply to relish and love. Cranmer's beautiful offices of matins and evensong were to be the staple of its liturgy; and as sung by choirs of boys and men they were to be amongst its glories.

The importance of Elizabeth's 49th injunction can be measured from the table that follows. Here is a list of the thirty-four cathedrals and collegiate churches or chapels in which choral forces with choristers maintained the offices of matins and evensong daily (or nearly daily) in 1560. It is an extraordinary circumstance that today the choral office continues to be maintained by choirs with boys (and in some cases also with girls), on from four to six weekdays in addition to Sundays, throughout the year apart from vacations, in all but four of these foundations. The figures indicate the number of choristers maintained at each foundation about 1560.[6] The four that no longer sing daily offices appear in italics.

TABLE 1

Cathedrals of the Old Foundation:	
Lincoln	8 + 7 Burghersh Chanters = 15
Exeter	14
York	12
London, St Paul's	10
Chichester	8 (but 'no more than 4 on duty in any one week')[7]
Lichfield	8

Cathedrals of the Old Foundation (cont):

Salisbury	8 (but + or − 2) (a significant reduction from the medieval 14)
Hereford	7 (5 on the foundation + 2 funded by the College of Vicars)
Wells	6

Formerly monastic Cathedrals of the New Foundation:

Canterbury	10
Durham	10
Winchester	10
Worcester	10
Ely	8
Norwich	8
Rochester	8
Carlisle	6

New Henrician Cathedrals:

Chester	8
Oxford	8
Peterborough	8
Bristol	6
Gloucester	6

Royal Peculiars:

The Chapel Royal, Whitehall	12
Westminster Abbey	10
Windsor Castle, St George's Chapel	10, but reduced to 8 in 1638

Collegiate Chapels of Schools and Universities:

Eton College	16
Winchester College	16
Cambridge, King's College	16
Oxford, Magdalen College	16[8]
Oxford, New College	16
Cambridge, Trinity College	10 by intention but often less[9]

Collegiate Churches:

Newark-on-Trent	6
Southwell	6
Manchester, Christ Church	4 (from 1555)

It must not be assumed that the continuance of these choral foundations between 1560 and their total abolition by Parliament in the 1640s was easily achieved. The earliest evidence that the choral foundations might be in decline is found in a Jacobean treatise now in the British Library.[10] Its anonymous author surmises that 'the first occasion for the decay of music in cathedral churches and other places where music and singing was used … began about the ninth year of Queen Elizabeth', that is from November 1566. This, he asserts, but with gross exaggeration, 'was the cause that all endeavour for teaching of music or the forming of voices by good teachers was altogether neglected, as well in men as in children …' That *all* endeavour was not in practice neglected was due, literally, to a 'battle royal' to preserve it. Throughout the years from 1559 until the 1640s, cathedral worship was under attack from 'puritanism', a dangerously loose term but one too handy not to use.[11] Most puritans detested liturgy. It enchained the spirit. So the Book of Common Prayer, even the 1559 version, was 'unperfect … picked out of that popish dunghill the mass book, full of all abominations'.[12] Puritans wanted preaching and spontaneous prayer, not versicles and responses, canticles and collects. Most puritans were also deeply worried by beauty; by anything that stimulated the aesthetic sense. The architectural splendour of cathedrals was a distraction; music carried the taint of sin. When attempts in the 1560s to persuade Convocation to do away with cathedral worship failed, the puritans turned to Parliament. In 1572, under the leadership of Thomas Cartwright, sometime Professor of Divinity at Cambridge, they submitted their first open manifesto, *An Admonition to Parliament*, in a direct attack upon 'Cathedrall churches':

> the dennes of all loitering lubbers, wher master Deane … Canons … the cheefe chaunter, singing men … squeaking queresters, organ players … live in great idleness, and have their abiding. If you would knowe whence all these came, we can easely answere you, that they came from the Pope, as oute of Troian horses bellye, to the destruction of Gods kingdome. The churche of God never knewe them …[13]

And here is an irony, for Cartwright was in a tradition that went back at least as far as Amos, the earliest of the Hebrew prophets, who wrote 'Take thou away from me the noise of thy songs: for I will not hear the melody of thy viols'.[14] Thus in condemning respectively high cathedral and high temple culture, both Cartwright and Amos were unable to avoid using language which is itself high culture invective. By the narrowest of margins Convocation and Parliament rejected these attacks. A proposal put to Convocation in 1562 'that the use of organs be removed', organs being particularly disliked, was defeated by a single vote. But the attacks continued, and where a bishop or a dean or a chapter were strongly Calvinistic, local injunctions could and did damage the choral liturgy. Puritan canons at Norwich broke down the organ about 1570, the year in which

William Byrd was instructed to limit his organ playing at Lincoln to simply sounding the pitch for the canticles and nothing more. Robert Horne, bishop of Winchester, in 1571 banned polyphony from his cathedral and abolished the office of organist at Winchester College. More seriously, the recently established choral force at St John's College, Oxford, was wholly abolished in 1577.[15]

Curiously, the lassitude at some foundations in Elizabeth's later years and the subsequent encouragement of the choral liturgy during William Laud's archbishopric in the early seventeenth century seem to have had little obvious impact on the well-being and proficiency of the choristers. Throughout this eighty-year period from the 1560s to the 1640s chorister numbers remained remarkably stable. The factors chiefly affecting the choristers appear to have been: foremost, the calibre and stability of the man or men who held direct responsibility over the boys; secondly, the level of interest and supervision maintained by dean and canons, indeed, whether these principal persons were at all often present in an age of growing pluralism;[16] thirdly, the level of maintenance, that is board and lodging, provided for the choristers; and finally, the calibre and nature of the schooling given to the boys and the extent to which, between services, they were occupied or idle. They had been effectively reduced to singing just two services a day. English canticles for matins and evensong, with an English anthem alongside musically bland psalmody and litany, were the sole harmonic choral diet during a period when holy communion, whether sung or said, was usually 'dry' (terminated after the creed) and was celebrated less and less frequently. Canterbury Cathedral was entirely typical when celebrations of communion were reduced to one a month from 1563. Precisely this frequency, or, it might seem, infrequency, was required by Hereford's new statutes of 1583.[17] These factors affected the choristers in varying ways from foundation to foundation and from time to time. For example, King's College, Cambridge, between 1606 and 1622 when John Tomkins was organist and intermittently master of the choristers, was exemplary, and the cynosure of 'town and gown'. Yet within little more than a decade, under Tomkins's successors, things fell apart and in 1639 Laud's Visitors reported that 'Quiremen cannot sing and are very negligent. Choristers are half mute and come without surplices'; neither choir nor congregation showed any reverence.[18]

Choristers were seriously affected by the constraints that stemmed from the roaring inflation that saw prices double twice in the course of the sixteenth century. Their medieval predecessors had been most often looked after by resident canons until, in the fifteenth century, well-qualified lay instructors became more common. By the reign of Elizabeth, however, clergy with a vocation to choral minor canonries were becoming hard to find. St George's, Windsor, had noted about 1550 that 'the choir cannot now be so well furnished with priests that are cunning singing men, for the rareness of them'.[19] Their replacements, lay clerks, were particularly severely hit by price inflation, having nothing tangible to sell. As a consequence, all too often they came to be appointed from 'a class of man totally unfitted, either by character or education, for the responsibility of teaching [choristers] music or caring for their bodily wants'.[20] One response to poverty was for lay clerks to seek supplementary employment and be only part-time employees of their chapters. An anonymous early seventeenth-century document complains of choirmen who are 'tailors and shoemakers and tradesmen, which can sing only so much as hath been taught them since they were men', implying that they had not themselves been brought up as boy choristers.[21] Increasingly they were married men, not keen on dining in the common hall along with the choristers, but preferring to eat at home with wife and children. To give one example from many: the Bedern at York, where the vicars choral had long lived and dined, was closed in 1574.[22] Even at the Chapel Royal courtiers and their servants began eating in their own quarters during the sixteenth century and the common hall was closed shortly after the restoration of the monarchy.[23] Chorister residence inevitably suffered. Lichfield gave up its short-lived provision of boarding, the chorister house being leased out and the boys lodged locally; by the end of the sixteenth century there were not even funds available to pay the choristers their customary pensions.[24] Carlisle was forced to abandon residence for its choristers. The boarding house at Lincoln went bankrupt in 1560 and was closed, albeit temporarily. Although Salisbury retained a house for its boys, by the early seventeenth century only one boy lived there.[25] Provision of residence with its precinctual care was abandoned at Canterbury during the 1580s: sums for maintenance were paid directly to the boys themselves from 1587/8. The Exeter choristers were 'placed abroad' from 1608. No payments for maintenance appear in any college accounts at King's, Cambridge. Perhaps most surprising of all is the Chapter Act of St George's Chapel, Windsor, in 1633 wherein 'it was decreed that the ten choristers should be fed and looked after by their friends, if any friends are judged by the Chapter to be suitable for this, and they are to receive 9s. 7d. a month for each boy'.[26]

Not all foundations gave up boarding their choristers, but the calibre of some of the masters in charge was such that their boys would surely have been in better hands at home. At Dr Ackworth's visitation of New College in 1566 it was reported that the boys, apart from three, 'could not and had never been instructed to sing'. The schoolmaster, John Serrel, was found to have fled so was declared contumacious and suspended but, characteristically, he was not dismissed, remaining in office for a further five years.[27] There were serious problems with the masters of the choristers at both Lincoln and York in the second decade of the seventeenth century. But the most consistently unsatisfactory foundation with resident boys under unsuitable masters was almost certainly Chichester.[28] It was the general practice there to appoint one of the lay singing men to combine with his singing duties the office of organist and that of *informator choristarum*. In the 1570s William Payne held these offices in combination and was accused of neglect of his duties. His response was to assault the verger and threaten that if anyone else spoke against him he would 'fill his skynne full of hayleshotte'. A generation later one of Payne's successors, John Cowper, was admonished for failing to teach the choristers adequately; nine months later the same complaint was coupled with the frequency of his haunting alehouses. Within a further six months Cowper only narrowly escaped dismissal. The boys, in any case, rarely had their voices tested before admission as choristers, and it had to be suggested to Cowper that the choir would sound better if they *stood* to sing the music.[29]

Worse was to come. In 1602 the chapter appointed to the same combined post the organist from Winchester College.[30] This was Thomas Weelkes, one of the most distinguished and innovative composers of the age. At first all seems to have been well. But in 1608 he was suspiciously absent throughout Bishop Andrewes's visitation and in 1611 there is an episcopal decree enjoining Weelkes to teach his boys for at least three hours a day on pain of deprivation. Thereafter the complaints piled up, chiefly for neglect of duty and drunkenness. By 1616 the drunkenness seems to have become habitual. Weelkes was charged by chapter 'that he hath been, and is noted and famed for a common drunkard and a notorious swearer and blasphemer'. He denied the charges and was given the chance to find witnesses to swear to his sobriety. Nobody came forward. Weelkes was dismissed.[31] The marvel is that in circumstances such as this any parents submitted their sons to choristerships. The problem, however, was general. Virtually all the lay clerks at Chichester were admonished regularly for absenteeism, idleness, bringing their dogs with them to evensong or arriving in quire tipsy. At Wells, in the last decade of the sixteenth century and the first of the seventeenth, there was a long catalogue of failings by the men of the quire stalls: debt, affray, fornication, adultery, absence from duty, keeping an alehouse in the cathedral close, all-night gambling.[32] In the midst of all this, choristers were supposed to be brought up in virtue and godliness; and, although one must not apply current preconceptions of decorum to the far more rumbustious Elizabethan age, these goings-on did not facilitate high standards in quire.

Salisbury, too, had similar problems. In 1568 Salisbury's Bishop Jewel found it necessary to call on the chapter to take action against their master of choristers, Thomas Smythe. Smythe was frequently 'quarrelsome in choir in the time of divine service and author of dissention and brawling between the vicars of our church, and was a swearer and a drunkard and up all night and player of dice openly and publicly in the market-place with many looking on'. Quarrelsome, also, one might add, with vicars' wives. In 1566 he had been called before chapter to explain how he came to engage in a stone fight with Agnes Chamberlayne, wife of the organist, outside the choristers' house. Jewel recalled that two married women had had occasion to 'make grave charges' against him. Following a bout of fisticuffs with another of the singing men in the precinct cemetery, the two men had gone to evensong and, while the choristers were singing, had shouted abuse at each other across the quire. More seriously, he was entirely unfit to teach the choristers who 'under him utterly mock at work to the disgrace of our Church'. Smythe was imprisoned for two days, relieved of responsibility for the choristers – yet retained as a lay clerk.

In October 1571 chapter appointed John Farrant (one of several musicians of that name) as a probationary lay clerk. Subsequently he was to become also organist and master of the choristers. He too had difficulty in living at peace with his colleagues, having a churchyard fight with another lay vicar in 1575. Above all, he had difficulty living at peace with his wife, Margaret, who happened to be a niece of the dean, Dr John Bridges. Margaret was in the habit of going to her uncle to seek counsel. Eventually, early in 1592, Dr Bridges summoned up courage to call Farrant to discuss these problems with him. Farrant's response was aggressive. He ended his interview with the dean by saying that 'he would deal with him elsewhere if he could find him alone'. Farrant's anger continued to boil within him. On Saturday, 5 February, at evensong (not attended by the dean), immediately before the second lesson, Farrant suddenly called to him a senior chorister, William Deane, handed him a service book and ordered him to follow him out of quire. In their surplices they left the cathedral and made, westwards, for the then deanery, the organist leading, the boy, book in hand, behind. What happened next was recorded by the chapter clerk, immortalising the seventeen-year-old chorister's vivid words and breathless syntax.

And soe going presently in surplice to Mr Dean's house [Farrant] went up into the dining chamber, I following him, and then sent me up to Mr Dean, being in his studie, to tell Mr Dean that my Mr Farrant would speak with him, which message being delivered, Mr Dean being then writing in his Studie, willed me to desire my Master to hold him excused because he was then busy about his sermons, and to come to him the next day (being Sundaie) in the afternoon and then he would speak with him. I went down and told my Master what answer Mr Dean made him: then the said Farrant commanded me to tell Mr Dean that he *would* speak with him. Whereupon I, going up the staires again to Mr Dean, my Master, the said Farrant, came after me and said: 'By God I will speak with thee' and going into the studie in furious and angry sorte threw off his surplice and his gown and immediately drew his knife out of the sheath and, stepping to Mr Dean, took him by the collar of his gown and said: 'Thou goest to take away my living but, God's Wounds Ile cutt thy throat.' Then Mr Dean said 'What, Vilane wilt thou kill me', and strived with the said Farrant to thrust him from him; and then Mr Dean willed me to call up some of his men … but I could not because my Master kept me back. At length Mr Dean, having with striving gotten without his studie dore on the steares and slipped off one of his sleaves of his gown, I helping him to do so, Farrant pulled back Mr

Dean upon the steares and tore away his gown of his back, Mr Dean presently leaving his gowne behind him rann down into his dining chamber, and, thinking to go down into the hall found the dore made fast that he could not. Whereupon ymedietaly Mr Dean went into his bed-chamber and made fast the dore after him; Mr Farrant, in the meantime being left in the studie, took up his gowne and surplice and willed me to go before and turne to the Anthem, and presently he came back to the Cathedral again and sange part of the anthem.

Farrant was, of course, summoned to appear before chapter. Repeatedly called, he was each time unavailable. Finally the chorister house was searched but he was, in the words of his wife, 'above half a hundred miles out of the Town'. So he was dismissed, not for attempting to murder the dean but for having broken his contract. Nevertheless, within two months he had been appointed to Hereford Cathedral – as master of the choristers – where he was soon once more at odds with his colleagues and resigned. It might be added that his son, John Farrant 'the Younger', who had been a Salisbury chorister under his father in 1585, became organist there in 1598 and performed his role in exemplary manner until his early death in 1618. As for young William Deane, who had played some part in saving the life of Dean Bridges and had witnessed perhaps the most extraordinary half hour in the experience of any English chorister before or since, nothing more is known.[33]

It has been written of this period that the quality of the boys determined the quality of the whole choir.[34] What is clear from the experience of Chichester and Salisbury is that the quality of the boys was wholly dependent on the quality of their master. Indeed, in the course of 1630 at Salisbury, in consequence of a long-drawn-out dispute as to who should have occupancy of the Chorister House and its schoolroom, there were for some months no choristers at all.[35] Happily, Chichester and Salisbury occupied only one end of a spectrum. Durham exemplifies how satisfactory things could be when fine masters trained fine boys who in their turn became fine masters.[36] John Brimley was organist and master of the choristers at Durham from 1541 to 1576. (As such he managed to change his theological coat under Henry VIII, Edward VI, Mary and Elizabeth without loss of office.) With one exception, all Brimley's successors in post for over a century were former Durham singing boys. When his immediate successor, William Brown, was appointed, the young man was still a chorister, aged between eighteen and twenty, to be described in due course as 'an excellent Master of Musicke'. Of his choristers three became organists of Durham, one organist of York, one a Gentleman of the Chapel Royal and one was very likely the Richard Nicholson who went on to be *Informator Choristarum* of Magdalen College and composer of the exquisite *When Jesus Sat at Meat* in honour of the college's patroness. No less than four more of his pupils wrote music that found its way into the cathedral repertoire, whilst another former chorister was William Smith of Durham (the nephew, not the 'Elder' uncle) whose office responses are to this day the very staple of cathedral evensong settings. Only one of these appointees seriously disgraced the record, concluding a brawl with a lay clerk by clouting him on the head with a candlestick, thereby wounding him 'verie dangerously'. The high quality of musical instruction and, doubtless, performance at Durham did not prevent the boys from having fun. One former chorister, George Dobson, published in 1607 a book of reminiscences, *Dobsons Drie Bobbes*.[37] This catalogues his escapades, in several of which a fellow-chorister, Rakebaines, features. Dobson stole his pudding, locked him up in the candle cupboard (and when Dobson was punished by his uncle for this, he got his uncle and aunt tied up overnight in their orchard) and, after Rakebaines had been disciplined by Brimley's assistant for mischievously firing an arrow, Dobson caused the assistant to be caught by the dean and chapter in compromising circumstances. Bright choristers have rarely been short of initiative and ingenuity.

That many choristers in this period went on to become distinguished musicians should be no cause for surprise. A choristership provided, as it has continued to do, a unique form of education preparatory to mature training for a musical career. It is clear from the obligations placed on masters of choristers that the boys were expected not merely to be able to read music but also to improvise descants and decorative versions of melodic lines, in the way we expect 'authentic' performers to sing Baroque operatic *da capos* today. There is one famous report of just such a performance in 1592. Frederick, Count Mömpelgard, duke of Württemberg, visited St George's Chapel, Windsor, on Sunday 20 August in that year. After describing the organ and other instruments used during the service, he adds, 'And there was a little boy who sang so sweetly, and *lent such charm* to the music with his little tongue, that it was really wonderful to listen to him …' The phrase in italics is a translation of the German '*colorirt*', 'embellished', and describes precisely the skill of improvised decoration.[38] Here, then, was a form of early training in musical invention. A boy who could do this could not fail to want to compose.

It is frustrating that almost nothing is known of the childhood of many Tudor composers. There are unconfirmable claims that Byrd was a chorister at St Paul's (where two of his brothers certainly were), or that he sat at Tallis's feet as a Chapel Royal chorister, or (perhaps the most probable) that he started at the former and went on to the latter.[39] Tomkins may have been a boy at the Chapel Royal (he claimed Byrd as his teacher) and Weelkes at Winchester (where a Thomas Wikes was a chorister in the early 1580s). It is certain, to name only some of the more distinguished, that Thomas Morley and Thomas Ravenscroft were choristers at St Paul's, William Mundy at Westminster Abbey, Orlando Gibbons at King's and Robert White at Trinity, Cambridge. Orlando's son, Christopher, was at the Chapel Royal, Adrian Batten at Winchester (where Gardiner's chantry still bears the *graffito*, 'ADRIAN:BATTIN:1608'), John Bull at Hereford and William Lawes at Salisbury; and Robert Parsons surely must have sung as a boy in the collegiate choir of his home town, Newark.[40]

Of all the choral foundations that can be deemed to have been in good shape in this period the Chapel Royal was in a brilliant class of its own. It was an expression of the splendour of the royal court of which it was a part.[41] There it gathered to itself the finest musicians in the land, drawn to be Gentlemen of the Chapel and, once appointed, allowed, even encouraged, to retain or accept other coincident posts. Many, for instance, held appointments as secular court musicians. Of those mentioned above, all but Batten, Ravenscroft and Weelkes became Gentlemen, along with such luminaries as Tallis, Tye and Sheppard, Edmund Hooper and Richard Farrant. They were well paid, with stipends increased to take account of inflation. It should, therefore, be no surprise to observe that Chapel Royal records are almost wholly free from charges of misbehaviour on the part of Gentlemen. As a consequence, the choristers were admirably cared for. The Chapel Royal was not immune to the problems of inflation, to the extent that in 1583 William Hunnis found the courage to write to the queen's officers bemoaning that, so small was his stipend, he had to spend his own money on the care of his boys.

May it please your honors, William Hunnis, master of the children of her highness Chapel, most humble beseecheth to consider of these few lines. First, her majesty alloweth for the diet of twelve children of her said Chapel daily six pence a piece by the day, and forty pounds by the year for their apparel and all other furniture. Again there is no fee allowed neither for the master of the said children nor for his usher, and yet nevertheless he is constrained, over and besides the usher still to keep both a man servant to attend upon them and likewise a woman servant to wash and keep them clean. Also there is no allowance for the lodging of the said children, such time as they attend upon the court, but the master to his great charge is driven to hire chambers both for himself, his usher, children, and servants. Also there is no allowance for riding journeys when occasion serveth the master to travel or send into such sundry parts within this realm, to take up and bring such children as be thought meet to be trained for the service of her majesty. Also there is no allowance nor other consideration for those children whose voices be changed, who only do depend upon the charge of the said master until such time as he may prefer the same with clothing and other furniture unto his no small charge ... [and] ... although it may be objected that her majesty's allowance is no whit less than her majesty's father of famous memory therefore allowed: yet considering the prices of things present to the time past and what annuities the master then had out of sundry abbeys within this realm, besides sundry gifts from the king, and divers particular fees besides, for the better maintenance of the said children and office: and besides also there hath been withdrawn from the said children since her majesty's coming to crown ... other allowances incident to the office ... The burden hereof hath from time to time so hindered the masters of the children ... that notwithstanding some good helps otherwise some of them died in so poor case, and so deeply indebted that they have not left scarcely wherewith to bury them. In tender consideration whereof, might it please your honors that the said allowance of six pence a day a piece for the children's diet might be reserved in her majesty's coffers during the time of their attendance. And in lieu thereof they be allowed meat and drink within this honourable household for that I am not able upon so small allowance any longer to bear so heavy a burden. Or otherwise to be considered as shall seem best unto your honorable wisdoms.[42]

Hunnis's plea was graciously received and an endowment of lands was made, the income from which must be presumed to have solved his financial problems.

Hunnis's petition made reference to the costs incurred in touring the country to impress the finest choristers from other choirs. It is natural today to regard this as an outrageous form of child kidnap, but that is wholly to misjudge things. A boy brought to the Chapel Royal found himself in a brilliant environment, in a company of elite children, nurtured by leading musicians, singing music from the cutting-edge of sixteenth- and seventeenth-century composition, and admirably cared for. When his 'breast changed' his future was secured, either by placement in another choir as a secondary or, probably more frequently, sent with royal funding to Oxford or Cambridge. There was a famous case in the 1580s when a Wells chorister, John Pitcher, was impressed into the Chapel Royal. Near the close of the decade a letter was written to the dean and chapter of Wells stating that [John Pitcher's] 'voice beginneth to change' and 'he is become not so fit for our service' and 'recommending' him back into the Wells choir for a vacant vicar choral's place with an appropriate salary, accommodation and provision. The dean referred the request in writing to his chapter. They took umbrage and pushed the dean into declining to accept the young man. This was outrageous. A letter came from court, signed in person by the queen, not asking but *ordering* them to appoint John Pitcher a vicar choral. The dean wrote to his chapter, 'If I had written to any other church in the realm in like case, her majesty should not have been made to have written herself in so small a matter.' Pitcher became a vicar choral.[43]

The Chapel Royal was the seed-bed of a major compositional development at this time that gave new opportunities for virtuosity on the part of the choristers: the development of the 'verse anthem' and 'verse service', settings with verses in which, supported always by free-standing instrumental accompaniment, 'a sweete Melodious Treble or Countertenor singeth single and the full Qire answereth (much more when two such single voices and two full Qires enterchangeably replie one to an other, and at the last cloze all together)'.[44] Byrd was certainly among the first composers of the verse anthem and it was precisely this innovative use of accompanied singing that led the puritanical Lincoln chapter to forbid such use of the organ.[45] This was to be a form richly fruitful in the future, leading, by way of Mundy, Richard Farrant, Morley, Weelkes, Gibbons and Tomkins to the accompanied splendours of Purcell. Orlando Gibbons in London had trebles

Gibbons, *See, see the Word is Incarnate*

who could tackle such challenges as the brilliant extended dialogue between solo treble and alto in *See, See, the Word Is Incarnate* and the sparkling duet for two solo trebles towards the end of *O All True Faithful Hearts*.[46] It was not only in verse anthems and services that the Chapel Royal excelled: few other foundations could have tackled at all adequately the massive demands of such settings as Byrd's ten-part Great Service, 'the finest service ever written for Anglican use',[47] or Gibbons's eight-part Ascensiontide anthem *O Clap Your Hands*.[48]

Nevertheless, although the Chapel Royal was musically far superior at this period to any other choral foundation in the land, it is going too far to suggest that singing standards throughout the choral foundations at this time were 'deplorably low'.[49] We have already noted how consistently good Durham was. For at least much of the time fine music was also well sung at Canterbury and at St Paul's. Although the nave was a public thoroughfare and gathering place, frequently filthy and disorderly, nevertheless a sentence from *The French Schoolemaister* of 1573 read, 'See whether we may get to the quier, and wee shall heare the fearest voices of all the cathedral churches of England'.[50] George Herbert, the poet-priest, himself musically skilled, could not have walked across the water meadows to Salisbury Cathedral twice every week and found evensong there 'his Heaven upon earth' if the quality of singing had not been such as to lift his spirits. But for the provincial cathedrals there is a serious shortage of evidence as to how well the boys and men actually sang, and such evidence as there is must be read with caution. In the year after George Herbert's death the Salisbury canons responded to Laud's archiepiscopal visitation. Several of the canons declared that 'the Choristers have not been well ordered and instructed in singing ... and they have not been catechised and instructed as they ought'; but Canon Seward insisted that 'the choristers are well ordered ... I never knew them better ... all save two sing their parts perfectly.[51] Which report is one to believe? At Worcester in 1619 cornetts were brought in to supplement the 'meanes'. Perhaps about the same time the organist, Thomas Tomkins, wrote six four-part anthems for men's voices only. Can one deduce from this that at Worcester there was either a shortage of boy choristers or that they were seriously weak?[52] There was just one cathedral enthusiast from the 1630s who, with a pair of friends, undertook two tours of the kingdom, was drawn to cathedrals as by magnets, and kept a full diary: an otherwise unknown Lieutenant Hammond.[53] At each cathedral his method was first to describe the architecture, then the organ, then to comment on the choir. Of course he was a soldier, not a musician; of course his judgements were subjective; and of course even the best cathedrals have their off-days. His description of Ely, where 'most of her Inhabitants have butt a turfy s[c]ent and Fenny posture about them, which smell I did not relish at all' (so he did not stay for evensong), suggests that he was not wholly immune from prejudice. Nevertheless, it is reasonable to assume that his judgements, if subjective, were consistent with each other. Furthermore, where he was seriously disappointed there are reasons for our not being surprised.

Hammond's harshest criticism was directed at Carlisle where 'the organs and voices did well agree, the one being like a shrill bagpipe, the others like the Scottish tone'. Carlisle was probably the poorest cathedral in the land, its lay clerks paid less than £3 a year as against Durham's £16 13s. 4d., itself less than half the Chapel Royal rate.[54] Chichester and Peterborough failed to impress him, with 'voyces but indifferent'. We know what the problems were at Chichester. Bristol, another modestly endowed cathedral, had merely 'indifferent good quiristers'.[55] Rochester was satisfactory: 'Her Quiristers, though but few, yet orderly and decent'. The singing in each of the eight remaining foundations in which he worshipped and on which he makes significant comment clearly moved him. Canterbury had 'a deep and ravishing consort of Quiristers'.[56] York, the northern metropolitical cathedral, also had 'a deep and sweet snowy row of quiristers'. At Durham, as one would expect, he relished the 'orderly, devout and melodious harmony of quiristers'. At Winchester Hammond attended service at both the cathedral and the college, describing both the cathedral and college boys as 'Quiristers'.[57] At the cathedral, 'where they sing sweet and heavenly Anthems', the 'Quiristers were skilful and the voices good'. At the college Hammond found the full complement of sixteen singing boys, 'all in their Collegiate surplice Habit … reading and singing as solemnly as at the cathedral'. At Lichfield he clearly heard a verse anthem or verse service, because the 'deep and sweet' voices included two trebles, two counter-tenors and two basses who 'most melodiously acted and performed their parts'. The 'orderly snowy crew of quiristers' at Hereford sang in 'a deep and sweet diapason', but then Hammond and his friends had just been entertained by the vicars choral, one being his landlord, and had 'freelie tasted of their choral cordiall liquor' which may have coloured his judgement. Finally, at Exeter something special must have been going on because in addition to the 'tunable Voyces' and the 'rare Organist' there were 'Vialls and other sweet Instruments'. (There is no indication that the viols were used to accompany the voices.) The effect was profoundly moving, 'a melodious and heavenly Harmony, able to ravish the Hearers Eares'.

Hitherto this history has focused primarily on the choristers' choral duties, and to some extent on their education and leisure, but not on instrumental music. From the second half of the fifteenth century, however, contracts for masters of choristers increasingly often required them to teach not only singing. As early as 1430 at Durham John Steel is to teach 'the whole art of music' which included instruction in playing the organ; but, as some of his pupils were young monks, we cannot be sure that choristers were given organ lessons. When Robert Hygons was appointed master of the choristers at Wells in 1479, however, he was unambiguously required to teach the boys 'in plainsong, prick-song and descant, *and also in organ playing according to their disposition and ability*'.[58] By the early sixteenth century instruction in playing the organ to choristers deemed apt for the skill was standard form. Significantly at Lincoln in 1539 the song master's obligation was extended to teaching 'organ and clavy-cords' and at Hereford in 1583 new statutes required the choristers to have 'instruments for instruction … in the practice of the harp or virginals'.[59] In the 1540s there was a further development: first from the Chapel Royal, then from St Paul's comes clear evidence that choristers are being taught to play viols. In 1550 on 17 May the dean and chapter of Exeter bought a set of 'vyalles' for the choristers and a week later appointed Lewis Mugg to be instructor on the viols.[60] In the course of the second half of the century the teaching of viols to choristers is recorded at Ely, Lincoln, Newark and Westminster Abbey,[61] though sparsity of evidence on the subject may or may not indicate that whilst most choristers learned keyboard skills not all foundations offered string tuition.

Why did this development take place? More precisely, why did chapters *require* chorister masters to teach instrumental music? Probably the reasons changed. From the earliest days of the monastic oblates certainly until the Reformation boys in quire were viewed as apprentice clergy. In the later middle ages organs were developing in sophistication and coming to be deemed essential accoutrements of worship, not to accompany singing – that never happened – but for short instrumental interludes between sung verses or items and to provide what might now be called voluntaries at appropriate points; in particular, to 'jubilate' on high occasions. Secondary organs were provided in Lady chapels where the boys sang most, sometimes all, of the music. Instruction to particularly apt boys was perhaps primarily to keep up the supply of organ players in future years. It was part of their apprenticeship for future church service. Later the teaching of instrumental music was also seen to be vocationally useful for those who might not become clergy. The Hereford statutes of 1583, quoted above, go on to explain that ability to play musical instruments could help a chorister whose voice had changed in 'liberal employment not unworthy of a respectable man, and suited to earn his livelihood hereafter'. That might be equally true of learning the viols. But viols were different. In the first place, even in the seventeenth century, when organs increasingly accompanied singing, viols never fulfilled that role in church. They made the wrong sort of sound and were too quiet; what is more, as Charles Butler observed at the time, they were 'often out of tune … in our Chyrch solemnities onely Winde instruments (whose Notes ar constant) bee in use'.[62] Indeed the *only* reference to viols being played in church in this period (and that not about them as accompanying instruments) is Lieutenant Hammond's experience of 'vialls and other sweet instruments' during service at Exeter in the autumn of 1635. Apart from the organ, the instruments most frequently used in the Tudor and Stuart church were cornets and sackbuts, called upon for those special occasions when 'grett and solompne' music was required.[63] An Italian visitor to Canterbury in 1589 encountered such an occasion and was amazed at the 'solemne Musicke with the voices and organs, Cornets and Sagbutts'. Never in his life had he 'heard a more heavenly sound'.[64] Early in the following century archbishop Laud was to put the Canterbury cornetters and sackbutteers onto the foundation.[65]

The earliest and the most frequent notices of choristers playing viols come from the metropolis, chiefly from the Chapel Royal and St Paul's Cathedral. These boys were increasingly in demand for the provision of secular musical entertainment. The development of chorister viol consorts was coincident with the development of chorister acting troupes. What was common to choristers as actors and choristers as viol players was that the boys displayed themselves as prodigies. Indeed their three skills, singing, viol-playing and acting, were frequently proffered in combination. Almost all the plays written for the chorister troupes included opportunities for singing and instrumental playing. But free-standing consort performances by choristers were, for perhaps two decades from around 1550, immensely popular. In 1549 the St Paul's choristers attended the annual dinner of the Merchant Taylors' Company and entertained them with viol music. Clearly the word got round the City, because it was not long before they were providing similar entertainment for the Goldsmiths and the Grocers. 'And all ye dynner tyme ye syngyng children of Paules played upon their vialles & songe verye pleasaunt songes to ye delectacion and reioysynge of ye whole companie.'[66] And the finest composers in the land, mostly themselves ex-choristers, including Bull and Byrd in lavish profusion, provided consort music of the highest order, a foretaste of Telemann's *Tafelmusik* and Mozart's serenades, wordless polyphony to be used as aural wallpaper, heard against the clattering of cutlery and a crescendo of wine-lubricated conversation. And of course, afterwards, in such places, the boys were themselves wined and dined.

Encouragement of viol-playing seems to have come chiefly from the masters of the choristers rather than from the chapters. At St Paul's, for instance, the set of viols and their chest were the personal property of the master, Sebastian Westcott. In his will, and he was by no means a poor man, he left them to the boys.[67] The Hereford chapter saw instrumental tuition as vocational. The metropolitan choral foundations were able to recruit boys from families with higher aspirations or to impress outstandingly musical children. For them, music had become by the mid-sixteenth century part of a liberal education. All round London, and in the great houses in the counties, music was becoming a sophisticated recreation. This explains how from some composers, notably Byrd, Bull, Gibbons and John Dowland, much of their music, in some cases almost all of their music, was written for domestic performance rather than for the liturgy. Here, from these mostly former choristers, came the first great flowering of

English instrumental music. Many of these composers will have first encountered secular viol, clavichord and consort music in their days as choristers. Most of the music published under the royal monopoly enjoyed by Byrd and Tallis was intended for the court and the many homes where sophisticated music-making was a prime leisure delight. In the 1630s the poet-parson George Herbert, before returning to his rectory at Bemerton after Salisbury Cathedral evensong, would stay in the town for a private 'Musick-meeting', where he would sing and play the lute or the viol.[68] Such gatherings were widespread and continued unabated through the Commonwealth and beyond. For a chorister to leave his choir school without such skills would by 1630 have indicated a neglectful education.

There was another benefit that instrumental tuition provided. Medieval choristers had sung up to eight services on many days in the year. Post-Reformation choristers were required to sing just two. Even with more sophisticated schooling they would still have had time on their hands. Instrumental music helped to fill that time. Further, masters of choristers must also have found it more congenial to teach instrumental music to their boys than to struggle to teach Latin grammar, in which they themselves may have been less than competent. Here again, foundation varied very much from foundation. From this time until well into the twentieth century chapters puzzled as to what form of education to provide for their choristers. They could provide a school of their own which taught the full classical syllabus in preparation for university; or they could send their choristers to the local grammar school, not of their foundation; or they could require their chorister master to be both musician and educator, offering the basics in preparation for a trade or craft apprenticeship. At Cambridge, King's and Trinity provided high quality grammar schooling. Orlando Gibbons became a chorister at King's in 1596 and left, apparently without a break, a graduate of the university in 1603. Several of the Henrician cathedral foundations found it easiest to educate their choristers in the grammar school set up by the royal statutes: Peterborough and Chester seem consistently to have done this. On the other hand, the King's School at Canterbury, despite its statutes, declined from the start and continued to decline any responsibility for the education of either the cathedral choristers or ex-choristers. In the city of Lincoln, in the second half of the sixteenth century, there were intermittently a grammar school and a free school, and equally intermittently the chapter sent their choristers to one or the other. There, as at Hereford, the boys were constantly on foot between services and music lessons at the cathedral and secular education some distance away at the school. At Salisbury there was a move, not consistently followed, away from education provided by the chorister master towards sending the boys to the mostly good local grammar school. St George's, Windsor, on the other hand, by its injunctions of 1550, provided a master from amongst its own chapel staff, appointed or reappointed annually 'to be grandsire of the Choristers: to teach

Catechism, principles of Grammar and to write, and also to see to their manners' from 6 a.m. to 8 a.m. and from noon to 2 p.m. daily; the rest of the day, outside the singing of the offices, was to be devoted to learning vocal and instrumental music. At the Reformation the teaching of Latin lapsed, but in 1636, to facilitate entry to university, the Windsor Chapter appointed their librarian to teach the choristers Latin grammar for the first two hours of each morning.[69] At Salisbury about 1570 we find the first hint of the inevitable clash between cathedral duties and educational demands, that was to become a growing problem. Anthony Nicholas, headmaster of the grammar school in the Close, complained that those of his pupils who were choristers spent too much time singing and not enough at their grammar. The chapter considered the problem and sent back the baffling obfuscation that 'those who were found fit [singers] should be sent back to the Grammar School on condition that they should serve the cathedral in turn'.[70]

That there were places where it all worked well, however, is implied by a charming piece of historical fiction published in 1938 and summarised here at Appendix 2. Derived from detailed research, the author has reconstructed a day in 1573 at Christ Church, Oxford, where an actual Christ Church chorister, John Milton, father of the poet, benefits from a richly fulfilled boyhood. He enjoys a challenging classical education, learns several musical instruments and relishes the singing in quire, the varied music for the morning and evening canticles and the exquisite English of Coverdale's psalter. We certainly know that sixteenth-century Christ Church, under the *informator* William Blitheman, sang a wide repertoire of liturgical music. In just this way, across the country, the steady rhythm of Cranmer's offices was becoming familiar and loved.

The greatest celebration of Anglican cathedral worship and its music was to come from the pen of Richard Hooker in his magisterial defence of the Elizabethan church settlement, *On the Laws of Ecclesiastical Polity* (1594).[71] Music, he wrote in Book Five, touches 'that very part of man which is most divine':

> A thing which delighteth all ages and beseemeth all states; a thing as seasonable in grief as in joy ... that carrieth as it were into ecstasies, filling the mind with an heavenly joy and for the time in a manner severing it from the body. So that although we lay altogether aside the consideration of ditty or matter, the very harmony of sounds being framed in due sort and carried from the ear to the spiritual faculties of our souls, is by a native puissance and efficacy greatly available to bring to a perfect temper whatsoever is there troubled, apt as well to quicken the spirits as to allay that which is too eager, sovereign against melancholy and despair, forcible to draw forth tears of devotion if the mind be such as can yield them, able both to move and to moderate all affections.

'Church music', wrote Hooker, 'is in truth most admirable.' 'They must have hearts very dry and tough' who do not draw spiritual delight from it.

Those with dry, tough hearts were already at work on its destruction.[72] In

August 1642 Parliamentary soldiers entered Canterbury Cathedral and wrought their 'godly orgy of retributive plunder', their response to the High Anglicanism of Archbishop Laud, disseminated through high-church appointments to deaneries and chapters, and tied inextricably to the uncompromisingly 'Thorough' policies of Strafford and Charles I. At Canterbury music books were rent and scattered about the cathedral floor, the organ was damaged and soldiers on horse-back acted a parody of the Anglican service before riding off. Following the battle of Edgehill in October 1642, Windsor Castle was occupied and the chapel personnel, including the choristers, expelled. Two months later Winchester Cathedral was entered, all the prayer books and music books were burnt and the organs wrecked. Similar havoc occurred further east at Chichester just after Christmas, the music scattered in shreds all over the cathedral floor. 1643 witnessed widespread destruction: in the spring, for example, Peterborough Cathedral was rifled and defaced, the organs broken 'with strange, furious and fanatick zeal' and the choir books torn up. This was the year when the choristers and clergy were ejected from Norwich and the choral establishments at Cambridge were 'purified' by the notorious iconoclast, William Dowsing, witness the record in the Trinity College accounts for 1643 of the payment to their loyal servant, Chambers, of fifteen shillings 'for *not* blowing the organs a whole year'.[73] Among the later targets were Hereford, York and Exeter, whose choristers were driven out with the jeering cry, 'Boyes, we have spoiled your trade, you must go and sing Hot Pudding Pies'. Of Westminster Abbey,[74] the Puritan divine, John Vicars, could write:

> Whereas there was wont to be heard nothing almost but Roaring-Boyes, tooting and squeaking Organ-Pipes and the Cathedral-Catches of Morley, and I know not what trash; now the popish Altar is quite taken away, the bellowing Organs are demolish'd and pulled down, the treble or rather, trouble and bass singers, Chanters or Inchanters driven out; and instead thereof, there is now set up a most blessed Orthodox Preaching Ministry.

For the first and only time since the coming of Augustine in 597 the sound of boys' voices singing in quire was utterly silenced throughout England.[75]

8

Chorister Actors

In the course of the sixteenth century two groups of London choristers, the boys of the Chapel Royal and 'the Children of Paules', developed parallel roles as theatre companies. There is some uncertainty about how this came to be. In both cases their commercial public performances were offshoots of their 'royal command' entertainments at court. Choristers had long undertaken acting roles, either within the drama of the liturgy or in the presentation of court revels;[1] but what emerged in the metropolis in the mid sixteenth century was stage performance on a wholly new scale. This phase in the development of Elizabethan drama was to culminate in the works of Shakespeare and the flourishing of theatres such as the Globe. Drama was one of the great glories of the Elizabethan age: choristers were at its heart. The story falls into two separate periods: the first from the 1550s until 1590; the second from 1600, a shadow of the earlier phase.[2]

The group that had most frequently performed at court was, of course, the Chapel Royal. The gentlemen and boys were part of the court, often peripatetic with the monarch. Early in the sixteenth century, William Cornysh had been both master of the choristers and master of the king's revels. As early as 1515, before he had become master of the revels, the 'chylldern of ye chappell' played the stories of 'troylous and pandor' and 'kaukas and cryssed' before the king at Christmas-tide, trained by 'Wyll kornyche'. Cornysh was the author of at least eight lost but identifiable plays.[3] His successor, William Crane, master from 1523 to 1546, was similarly active in the writing and production of court plays using boy actors. His texts too are lost, but the Venetian ambassador described in May 1527 how eight Chapel Royal boys, four personifying *Amor* and four *Richezza (Riches)*, recited verses prior to a mock battle by knights.[4] That Crane's successor, Richard Bower (master 1545–61), was able to continue to present the choristers in court plays over the Christmas holidays during the reign of Edward VI is evidence that puritan anti-theatrical sensibilities had not reached the court. Indeed, the plays of Christmas 1547 and 1549 may well have been weapons of anti-papal propaganda.[5] Edward Seymour, duke of Somerset, Protector for the first three years of Edward's minority, had himself commissioned the boys of St Paul's to provide an entertainment – a 'disguising' – at a family celebration of his own.[6] Performances continued in Mary's reign, though theatre was not one of her enthusiasms. Throughout the early Elizabethan years there are records of court plays by the Chapel Royal boys on Twelfth Night and at Shrovetide. Although the London seat of government was the palace of Whitehall, dramatic performances most frequently took place in the great halls at one or other of the 'suburban' palaces to which the court withdrew in holiday times: Greenwich, Hampton Court or Windsor Castle.[7]

Performances also seem sometimes to have been given at Whitehall in the Chapel Royal itself. This is implied in the oft-quoted puritan broadside of 1569:

> Plays will never be suppressed, while her Majesty's unfledged minions flaunt it in silks and satins. They had as well be at their popish service, in the Devil's garments. Even in her Majesty's Chapel do these pretty, upstart youths profane the Lord's Day by the lascivious writhing of their tender limbs, and gorgeous decking of their apparel, in feigning bawdy fables gathered from the idolatrous heathen poets …[8]

Dramatic performance in church, of plays not exclusively biblical or even religious, common enough in the middle ages, continued to take place in Tudor times. There is a detailed account of Queen Elizabeth, while visiting Cambridge in 1564, attending three plays given on a stage, specially constructed to the west of the organ screen, in King's College Chapel.[9] Whether this was an entirely adult production, or whether the choristers of King's performed, is not recorded. In 1542 Bishop Bonner of London had issued an injunction against the performing of plays in ecclesiastical buildings in his diocese, but it was clearly ineffective. As late as 1580 another puritan pamphlet, Anthony Munday's *Second and Third Blast of Retrait from Plaies and Theaters*, had remonstrated against actors 'permitted to publish their mametree in everie Temple of God … unto the horrible contempt of praier. So that now the Sanctuarie is become a plaiers stage and a den of thieves and adulterers.'[10]

Evidence has survived of the logistic arrangements for the transport and provisioning of the boys from their London base literally up and down river for their performances.[11] Some of these records of commercial expenses tell a human story. Thus, from 1573/4:

> To Bruton of Powles Wharf for a Bardge and vi ores with ii tylt Whirreys that caryed the Masking geare and Children with theier tutors and an Italian woman … to dresse their heads as also the Taylers, ppty makers and haberdashers. xxiiii s.

> Expenses at Kingston [for] lodging, ffyer, and vittells for the Children and Women who waited tattyer them with others who were appointed to stay till the Mask were showen and for their dynners the nexte daye being Shrove-tewsdaye there xiiii s viii d.

> To Bruton for his Bardge and ii whirreyes to cary the children and stuff to London and for his wayting daie and nighte to cary the children betwene the Coorte and King[s]ton xxv s vi d.

To Thomas Totnall for ffyer and vittells for the children when they landed some of them
being sick and colde and hungry vi s vi d.

Which group of acting children is referred to here is not specified. It may well
have been the children of the Chapel Royal.[12] William Hunnis, as we have seen,
bemoaned that as master of the children he had personally to fund such journeys.
But performances at Elizabeth's court were by no means exclusively given by the
Chapel Royal. School troupes from Merchant Taylors', Elizabeth's refounded
Westminster School and the grammar school of St Paul's all gave entertainments
from time to time.[13] There were also annual dramatic entertainments at Windsor
Castle between 1566 and 1576 by the boys of St George's Chapel under Richard
Farrant.[14] Above all, the choristers of St Paul's Cathedral – 'Pawles boys' – were
clearly court favourites. Their natural point of river embarkation would have
been 'Powles Wharf'.[15]

Early in the sixteenth century it is unclear whether by 'St Paul's boys' was
meant the choristers or the grammar school boys or a mixture of the two. When
Thomas Wolsey hosted the Venetian ambassador at Epiphanytide 1528, after a
sumptuous dinner 'the scholars of St Paul's, all children, recited the *Phormio*
of Terence with so much spirit and good acting that [ambassador Spinelli] was
astounded'. At the close of the entertainment 'a little boy, who had already recited
with great applause the prologue of the comedy, delivered a Latin oration ... The
grace with which this little fellow delivered [it] could not be imagined'. It is not
unreasonable to assume that the performers were grammar school boys together
with at least one precocious chorister.[16] Well into the latter half of the century
choristers of St Paul's were taught grammar at the senior school if their needs
exceeded the teaching powers of the choir school. Thomas Gyles, on his appointment as master of the 'quiristers' in 1584, was to teach the boys their catechism
in English, their writing and music, and then to 'suffer them to resort to Paul's
school that they may learn the principals (sic) of grammar' before returning to
learn the catechism in Latin 'and other good books' under Gyles himself.[17]

When John Redford, composer, organist, poet and dramatist, was master of the
St Paul's choristers in the closing decade of Henry VIII's reign, he wanted 'to make
his boys pre-eminent in the entertainment of the sovereign'.[18] By the early 1550s
it becomes clear that the description 'Paule's Boys' implied a cast fundamentally
of choristers.[19] Under Sebastian Westcott, Redford's successor and an enthusiastic
play-producer, their acting was further developed. Indeed there is indication that
he undertook charge of their dramatic work whilst Redford was still master of the
choristers. In February 1551/2 he was paid £4 19s. toward the cost of transport
of the children and their costumes for a performance before Princess Elizabeth
under house arrest at Hatfield Palace.[20] It seems to have been a crucial success.
From the time of her accession in late 1558 until 1581, and again from 1584 until

1590,[21] the St Paul's boys became Elizabeth's favourite company, performing at court more often than any other troupe, never less than once and sometimes as often as three times each year. In the paragraphs that follow, much attention is given to performances before audiences other than the court. But it must be emphasised that court performances remained the chief acting responsibilities of these boys and must have been their greatest thrill. Elizabeth's court, like that of her father, was a place of special splendour. The cream of society was gathered there in an atmosphere of high culture, ostentatious wealth and sophistication, with, at its centre, that extraordinary, compelling queen, 'the fountain of power and influence, magnet of all eyes'.[22] Here, before the greatest in the land, these little boys appeared, playing to an audience that was more often noisily participatory than quietly attentive.[23] Yet those audiences and their monarch thought the boys wonderful, and had them back again and again.

Nevertheless, it was not only at court that they played. The cathedral almonry, where the master and his choristers lived, lay in the churchyard to the south of St Paul's Cathedral.[24] Here was an astonishing cluster of buildings. Attached to the southern wall of the cathedral proper were, from west to east, St Gregory's, the precinctual church sometimes used by the boys as their school room; the almonry, where the master and his choristers lived; and the cathedral cloisters which embraced the chapter house. Higgledy-piggledy with these were shops, lodgings, workshops, booths and market stalls.[25] The churchyard, along with the cathedral itself, was one of the great gathering places of Londoners. In November 1556 Sebastian Westcott secured a ninety-nine-year lease on a large part of the west churchyard. Three years later he was granted the almoner's house for life. Sophisticated facilities for rehearsal of the plays to be presented before the queen by the St Paul's boys were made available somewhere in this area south of the cathedral.[26] By some point in the 1570s there existed, broadly in the region of the cloisters and almonry, a raised stage large enough for some fifteen actors together with entrances on two levels; a tiring-house (green room) or at any rate rear access to such a facility; and seating for audiences of perhaps a hundred people. In theory this was where the boys rehearsed their royal command performances. In practice it was where Londoners in large numbers gathered, almost certainly on weekdays after evensong,[27] paying from twopence to sixpence a seat, to watch plays that became the talk of the town performed by the choristers.

Westcott was deeply committed to his boys. In his will he left substantial furnishings and his violins and viols to the almonry. Also, alongside bequests to adult colleagues, including his 'deere friende' Henry Evans, he left £1 each to his existing choristers, and similar donations to seven named ex-choristers: 'Bromehame, Richard Huse, Robert Knight, Nicolas Carleton, Bayle, Nasion and Gregory Bowringe', and the large sum of £6 14s.4d. to Peter Phillipe, a former chorister still in some capacity on the cathedral foundation. The casts have been described as made up fundamentally of choristers. There can be no doubt that we are dealing with choir school plays and players. The cathedral theatre was within or adjacent to the choristers' boarding house; and the productions were promoted by, in Westcott's days possibly written by, and always subject to, the oversight of the chorister master. Most of the actors will have been his choristers, but not all. Evidence for this comes from the plays themselves. Up to 1581, out of some eighteen named plays, predominantly moralities and histories, all but three or four have been lost. From 1583 to 1589, under Thomas Gyles, Westcott's successor as master, six comedies mostly derived from classical sources were commissioned from the gifted writer John Lyly.[28] All six have survived. They have casts of some twenty characters, but, with doubling, none requires more than fifteen actors. Except when the St Paul's and Chapel Royal boys briefly undertook combined productions, however, there can never have been as many as fifteen choristers available to act: ten was the statutory number throughout the period under consideration. So even if all ten choristers acted, five more actors were required. There were two likely sources. We have seen how at late medieval Wells superannuated choristers remained in the choir school, supporting the cathedral liturgy in ways other than on the front bench of singers. At St Paul's it is not unlikely that boys remained at the song school after their voices had broken. There may be an implication in Westcott's legacies that superannuated choristers were still under his charge and actively in his casts. Alternatively, or in addition, the school may have taken in non-chorister pupils. Notoriously, about 1600, boys were recruited to the Chapel Royal school specifically to act rather than to sing.[29]

There is evidence from Lyly's *Endymion* (1588) that one character was strikingly taller than some of the others. A comic knight, Sir Tophas, 'a braggart, ridiculously armed and accoutred', encounters Dares and Samias, a couple of young pages. As with everyone and everything he meets, he threatens to kill and eat them. At first he pretends to mistake them for a pair of larks. His servant corrects him:

'Larks? Are you blind? They are two little boys.'

To which Sir Tophas responds:

'Birds or boys, they are both but a pittance for my breakfast. Therefore have at them …'

The pages insist that they are old friends of his, but Tophas refutes the suggestion on the grounds that they are so tiny compared with him:

'Now, my pretty companions, you shall see how unequal you be to me. But I will not cut you quite off; you shall be my half friends, for, reaching to my middle, so far as from the ground to the waist I will be your friend.'[30]

Even tinier may have been the huntsman's impertinent servant in *Midas*. This little boy appears in only one scene. Lyly names him 'Minutius', and the huntsman at one point likens him to 'a small pebble'. Clearly Lyly knew the choristers well and wrote parts for individual boys.

Lyly plucks frequent entertainment from the fact that seeming-girls in his plays are in fact little boys. The comedy becomes yet more convoluted in *Galatea* (1585), when two seeming-girls are obliged, unknown to each other, to pretend to be boys (which of course they are). Each, dressed as a boy, then falls in love with the other, believing 'him' *actually* to be a boy, which the audience knows him both to be and not to be. 'It is a pretty boy and a fair,' says Phillida of Galatea. 'He might well have been a woman, but because he is not, I am glad I am.'[31]

In writing for a children's cast Lyly set out to entertain adults, first and foremost the queen, who is unfailingly flattered by him, explicitly in prologue and epilogue and implicitly through characters in the play designed to represent her. But in writing for child actors a price was paid. No attempt was made at the representation of deep emotion, for that would have been beyond the children's capacity. Although Shakespeare was to borrow several of Lyly's devices, including the cross-dressing of boy-girls, Lyly's plays are emotionally a world away from *Romeo and Juliet* a decade later. Also absent from Lyly is the slightest hint of bawdy. His plays are proper and moral. Sexual love is a farcical passion, an emotion to be laughed at. The real qualities to be admired are true friendship and loyalty, well understood by boys, and of deep significance to a queen who had constantly to be on the watch for perfidy. On the other hand, a benefit of writing for these particular children is that Lyly's plays are full of music: solo songs; part-songs, such as trios for a treble and two meanes; and instrumental pieces. In his very first play for St Paul's, *Campaspe*, Lyly includes a song by one boy 'who signes like a Nightingall' and by another, 'Trico', who has a 'high stretch minikin voice'. All of these instances would have been vehicles for showing off the boys at their most gifted.

In his final year of writing for the St Paul's boys, Lyly turned from these comedies, occupying a wholly imaginary world of fickle gods and fragile mortals, to something more serious and contemporary. In his play *Midas* (1590),[32] drawn still from the classical authors, the central figure, Midas himself, is clearly intended to represent Philip II of Spain, recently routed at sea by the English. The sophisticated court audience was to understand the play as an allegory. This was all very patriotic and loyal; but elsewhere in London plays acted by adult companies over the past decade had begun to be more dangerous. Sides were taken in the bitter religious contentions that racked society. The Marprelate Controversy,[33] a violent Calvinist attack on episcopacy, raged through 1588 and 1589 and the playwrights joined in. Foolishly, Lyly was one of these, publicly advertising that he would write a play featuring the bishops and a disguised but recognisable Martin Marprelate. Although there is no certainty that such a play was actually written, let alone performed, both the court and the City became increasingly alarmed. In the course of 1590 the authorities shut down the playhouses, including that at St Paul's.[34] For some ten years, despite pleas for remission, the Children of Paul's ceased to be an acting company.

Meanwhile a third group of choristers had, on a smaller scale, been moving into dramatic performance: the boys of St George's Chapel in Windsor Castle. In the early 1560s at Windsor there had been three masters of the choristers in as many years. A measure of stability was restored in 1564 with the appointment as their master of one of the Chapel Royal gentlemen, Richard Farrant.[35] Farrant is best remembered as a musician: singer, organist and composer. But he was also an entrepreneur willing to take risks. He had a keen interest in the theatre and wrote plays for his boys to perform. Within three years of his appointment he had the boys sufficiently well drilled in dramatics that they were ready to act before the queen. For a decade they performed under Farrant's direction annually each winter. None of Farrant's plays has survived, but the titles of which we have record suggest that he favoured histories from classical sources, such as *Ajax and Ulysses*, *Quintus Fabius* and *King Xerxes*. As with Lyly's plays for the St Paul's boys, Farrant's included opportunities for showing off the boys' singing and instrumental skills, notably in the form of songs by Farrant himself for solo boys with polyphonic viol accompaniment. Then in 1569 his fortunes took a new turn. While remaining master of the Windsor choristers, he was called back to the Chapel Royal. It is uncertain exactly what his role there was,[36] but he seems to have had coincident responsibilities over two of the leading sets of choristers in the land from 1569 until his death in 1580. He continued to produce the annual Windsor performances until 1577, in which year, uniquely, he put on a play at court performed jointly by boys from the two royal choral foundations, *The History of Mutius Scevola*, a characteristic Farrant choice. Meanwhile, at the close of 1576, he had taken a venturesome step.

On 20 December Farrant took a lease on what had formerly been the refectory of the Dominican house of Blackfriars in the City from its freeholder, Sir William More. His declared purpose was to use it as a schoolroom for the Chapel Royal children. But in fact he pulled down its partition wall and furnished the space as a theatre with a stage and seating.[37] Within months he was presenting plays there to public audiences. One cannot be sure what had led Farrant to such a course. It may be that the puritan complaints of the 1560s had been effective in closing down the boys' theatrical presentations in their chapel. Certainly we hear no more of them from 1570. But the Chapel Royal boys continued to perform at court and indeed elsewhere. In 1565 they performed *Damon and Pithias* before the lawyers at Lincoln's Inn, under their then master, Richard Edwards, himself a member of the Inn. *Damon and Pithias*, of which Edwards was the author, is an 'Upstairs/ Downstairs' play, in which the serious action is mirrored by rustics in a comic sub-plot.[38] It may be that Farrant found himself back in London with nowhere to give performances other than at court, perhaps even with no adequate rehearsal space. Yet it seems more likely that Blackfriars was a speculative commercial venture from which Farrant hoped to draw significant financial benefit, using a cast of boy actors who charged no fees. The Blackfriars Theatre was indeed a popular success and ran until 1584, surviving both an attempt by the lord mayor to close it in 1578 and the death of Farrant in 1580.[39] But Farrant's death left his widow, Anne, with ten children to maintain, her husband's debts to pay off, and the uncertain asset of a lease on a London theatre. So she sublet the theatre to the boys' surviving master, William Hunnis. His takings from performances, however, failed to match the rent due to the widow, so Hunnis in turn sublet the theatre to Farrant's former friend, the scrivener Henry Evans.

The Windsor boys had entirely ceased acting. Farrant had virtually abandoned them in favour of the Chapel Royal. After his death in 1580 there is no known Windsor chorister master for five years. Even then we find no record of dramatic performances by the Windsor boys, though there was a Christmas play at the castle in 1582, 'a comedy devised on a game of cards', performed under William Hunnis's direction by the Chapel Royal boys.[40] Then for a year from January 1583 performances at court seem to have stopped entirely.[41] Even the favoured St Paul's boys took no play to court for over a year. But in January, March and December of 1584 early plays by Lyly were performed by casts drawn jointly from the Chapel Royal and St Paul's at the Blackfriars theatre, under the patronage of the earl of Oxford and calling themselves 'The Earl of Oxford's Boys'. It was an unwise association. Edward de Vere, seventeenth earl of Oxford, was 'light-headed, a fop, … talented, with a taste for literature and the society of players, dissolute and with no head for money whatever … [and] the mentality of a failed gambler'.[42] Throughout this period the theatre's lease passed in rapid succession from Hunnis to Evans, to the earl of Oxford and, finally, during the summer, back to Sir William More, the freeholder. At this point Thomas Gyles extracted his St Paul's boys from the partnership and resumed their performances of Lyly's plays at St Paul's and at court.[43] But for the Chapel Royal boys it was the end. They were to do no more acting for some sixteen years. So, for the final decade of the sixteenth century it must have looked as if the days of the chorister acting companies were over: their closing lines spoken by the St George's boys in 1577, by the Chapel Royal boys in 1584 and by 'Paule's Boys' in 1590. It was during the last decade of the century that the adult theatre companies came into their own. James Burbage acquired, rebuilt and reopened the Blackfriars theatre in 1596 for an adult company; the first Globe Theatre was opened two years later. By 1600 Shakespeare had staged twenty-two of his plays.

Astonishingly, by 1601 both the Chapel Royal and the St Paul's companies were up and running again. The Paule's Boys revived first, in the autumn of 1599 under the new and enthusiastic master of choristers, Edward Pearce, with financial backing from William Stanley, sixth earl of Derby.[44] Pierce turned to a young and untried poet, John Marston (?1574–1634), as playwright, and in the prologue to their opening play, *Antonio and Mellida*, a sort of *Romeo and Juliet* with a happy ending, his cast beg for tolerance of their inexperience:

> For wit's sake doe not dream of miracles.
> Alas, we shall but falter, if you lay
> The least sad weight of an unused hope
> Upon our weakness.[45]

In two respects Marston's work resembles that of Lyly: every opportunity is taken for the cast to show off their skill in singing; and he wrote with specific St Paul's choristers in mind. The title role of Antonio was given to a senior boy whose voice had already broken. Early in the play Antonio disguises himself as an Amazon. He worries that his broken voice will give him away but is assured that a virago-like voice will pass well for that of an Amazon. As in Lyly's plays, very little boys are teased about their smallness: 'Balurdo calls for your diminutive attendance' says one page to another.[46] But in other respects *Antonio and Mellida* is very unlike the work of Lyly. Marston was a poet and, apart from some comic scenes, he wrote in pentameters. There are vulgarities that Lyly would never have indulged in. Rosaline's speeches are full of *double entendres*; the two pages mentioned above are named Dildo and Catzo, both Elizabethan slang for the penis. The *double entendre* was appropriated for facile jokes in the text, scarcely suitable for the use of young boys. Marston also used the boys' plays for scoring points against his rival, Ben Jonson, and for mocking the adult acting companies.[47] After 1601 Marston, who had already had books of satires ordered to be burnt, by Bancroft, bishop of London, was replaced by more substantial writers such as Thomas Middleton, Thomas Dekker, John Webster and the great partnership of Beaumont and Fletcher. These plays no longer show clear evidence of having been written for child actors, and there must be a growing supposition that the casts were partly composed of former St Paul's choristers with hopes of acting careers. They continued to play at court, now of course before James I, until July 1606 and in London a little after that. London, however, was becoming a cauldron of religious ferment. A recent play by Middleton, *The Puritaine*, had blatantly mocked the contention surrounding the nearby church and congregation of St Antholyn's, which had been conducting services after the Geneva fashion for some years. It might have been a trivial matter but Middleton's play, acted by the St Paul's troupe, brought things to the boil. To the north of St Paul's cathedral was a wide area with a public pulpit, known as Paul's Cross. Here crowds came, particularly to hear puritan sermons. One such, preached in February 1608 by William Crawshawe,[48] contained a violent attack on the theatres: 'What are they but a bastard of Babylon ... a hellish device (the divel's owne recreation to mock at holy things)?'[49] Furthermore, 'he that teacheth children to play is ... a spoiler and destroyer of children'. Soon after this all City theatres were closed. In 1609 Edward Pearce accepted a 'softener' of £20 in exchange for an undertaking never again to dabble in drama. The St Paul's boys' acting days were finally over.

A very similar development had been happening at the Chapel Royal. They resumed public and court play production in 1601. By now the master of the choristers was Nathaniel Gyles. As his father, Thomas, had done at St Paul's before him, he called in Henry Evans to help him prepare for the production of his boys' plays at the newly reopened Blackfriars Theatre. But they were to be in trouble from the beginning. Gyles had rights of impressment for Chapel Royal choristers; Evans wanted the best possible boys for his acting company. On 13 December 1600 a little boy, Thomas Clifton, was walking through the City from home to school. On his way he was kidnapped and carried off to the Blackfriars theatre.[50] The choice of this boy for impressment cannot have been accidental, but it could hardly have been less judicious. Thomas's father, Henry Clifton, a gentleman of Toftrees, Norfolk, but clearly with a second home in London, got wind of what had happened and rushed to Blackfriars to recover his son. There he was met by Evans, Gyles and an associate, James Robinson. They refused to hand the boy over, Gyles quoting his royal commission to impress whomsoever he wished. Indeed Evans, in front of the father, threatened to whip the boy if Thomas was not left with them and handed Thomas a scroll of paper with lines to learn by heart. But they had misjudged Henry Clifton. He was a man who knew his rights and had the determination and connections to set about securing them, which he did with singular skill. He submitted a petition of complaint to the queen which was heard before the Star Chamber the following December. Designed to win royal support, it was not simply a plea to recover his son: it was expressed as 'for the better furnisheing of your Chappell Royall with well singing children'. He conceded that Nathaniel Gyles had the right to impress children for his choir. But Thomas had not been so impressed. Indeed, they could hear for themselves that young Thomas had absolutely no singing voice. He was 'noe way hable or fitt for singing, nor by anie the sayd confederates endevoured to be taught to singe'. If a boy such as Thomas had been impressed for the choir, then it could only have been to the Chapel Royal's detriment. But, claimed Clifton, Thomas had been impressed solely 'to exercise the base trade of a mercynary enterlude player, to his utter losse of tyme, ruyne, and disparagment'. Clifton's petition went on to list six other boys who had been impressed in similar circumstances: John Chappell from a school near Cripplegate; John Motteram from Elizabeth's own Westminster School; Alvery Trussel (who may have been taken from St Paul's cathedral); Phillip Pyman and Thomas Grymes who were apprentices; and – of particular interest – two remarkable boys, Nathan Field, a pupil at St Paul's Grammar School, and Salman or Saloman Pavey. Clifton, one assumes,[51] duly recovered his son. Henry Evans, soon after, resigned or was removed from his partnership, selling his share in the theatre's lease to his son-in-law, though he was later to return to the scene.

Some, possibly all, the other boys remained at Blackfriars. For Field and Pavey it was, indeed, the right place because both had exceptional acting talents. Nathan ('Nid') Field went on to be a distinguished principal actor at the Globe and a playwright of some note.[52] Saloman (or Salathiel) Pavey might have had an even more brilliant career, but at the age of thirteen he contracted either consumption or the plague and died, to be eulogised by Ben Jonson in a famous and touching epitaph:[53]

Weepe with me all you that read
This little storie:
And know, for whom a tear you shed,
Death's self is sorry.
'Twas a child that did so thrive
In grace and feature,
As heaven and nature seem'd to strive
Which owned the creature.
Yeares he numbered scarce thirteene
When fates turn'd cruell,
Yet three fill'd Zodiakes had he beene
The stage's jewell;
And did act (what now we mone)
Old men so duely,
As, sooth, the Parcae thought him one,
He play'd so truly.
So, by error, to his fate
They all consented,
But viewing him since, (alas too late)
They have repented.
And have sought (to give new birth)
In bathes to steepe him,
But, being so much too good for earth,
Heaven vows to keepe him.

It is clear from this that by no means all the Blackfriars acting team were Chapel Royal choristers. One at least was categorically not a singer; two were old enough to have been apprentices and Field had been recruited at the age of thirteen and went on acting at Blackfriars for several years. When, however, the Chapel

Royal boys played before the queen, which they did three times in 1603, it was to Nathaniel Gyles, their master, that payment was made. It looks as if there were already two separate groups of boys: one of actors and one of singers who still sometimes acted. Indeed, in 1604 the Blackfriars company called themselves 'Children of the Revels of the Queen' (being under the patronage of James I's queen, Anne of Denmark) and later, simply 'The Children of the Revels', seeming to distinguish themselves from the chapel choristers. In 1606 Nathaniel Gyles's writ of impressment was withdrawn. A new writ continued to give him authority to impress Chapel Royal choristers. But it expressly commanded that 'none of the said Choristers or Children of the Chappell so to be taken by force of this Commission shalbe used or imployed as Comedians or Stage players or to exercise or act any stage plaies Interludes Comedies or tragedies for that it is not fitt or decent that such as should sing the praises of God almightie should be trained up or imployed in such lascivious and prophane exercises'.[54] The Puritans had won. Meanwhile, by 1606 the Blackfriars theatre had yet again been closed down, its most recent plays having been deemed so insulting to the English and French monarchy that they could no longer be tolerated. The company's intermittent revivals thereafter clearly involved no choristers at all.

Looking back over this extraordinary saga, one cannot help concluding that the people who come consistently well out of it are the boys. Not all the men were reprehensible: Sebastian Westcott in particular managed to be an effective entrepreneur and at the same time to undertake his role as master over the boys efficiently and caringly. But others were little more than rogues. Richard Farrant, although a writer of fine church music, seems increasingly to have used his salaried posts at both Windsor and Whitehall chiefly to facilitate his ill-founded ventures as a dramatic manager and promoter. His lack of concern for the music and the boys of St George's Chapel sank to the point of complete neglect. Nathaniel Gyles allowed himself to be drawn into serious abuse of his rights of impressment. His choice of business partners could scarcely have been worse. The seventeenth earl of Oxford was a spendthrift dandy; Henry Evans seems to have brought the kiss of death to every venture in which he was involved.[55] Even the playwrights used the boys, in the end, as vehicles for pushing their own contentious political or religious predilections. Meanwhile the choristers, not for the first or the last time in this history, survived the influence of their corrupt seniors. It is clear that at their peak the child actors, especially the choristers of St Paul's up to 1590, additional to their singing role in the cathedral, had developed into an acting troupe of outstanding ability and lasting cultural significance. No wonder that when the children of St Paul's and the Chapel Royal returned to the stage at the turn of the century they irked Shakespeare into writing about them. In *Hamlet*, in the prince's dialogue with Rosencrantz about 'an aery of children, little eyases, that cry out on the top of the question, and are most tyrannically clapp'd for't',

Hamlet wants to know whether they will act 'no longer than they can sing'.[56] In the event they were to sing far, far longer than they acted. But there had been a short period, between 1560 and the mid-1580s, when the development of the English theatre rested almost wholly upon the skills of two small troupes of unbroken-voiced boy choristers.

9

Restoration

Charles II entered London in triumph on his thirtieth birthday, 29 May 1660. The restoration of the Stuart monarchy consequentially restored the Church of England, returned its buildings and required the resumption of its liturgy, not least the musical liturgy of its choral foundations. This could not be achieved immediately. Certainly there survived from the 1640s significant numbers of organists, singing men and former choristers now with adult voices. These necessarily ranged from the middle aged to the elderly, though presumably few were older than William Burt, who rejoined the Winchester cathedral choir in his eighties. But critically, there was not a single boy in the land who had been trained in or had experience of liturgical choral singing. In their treble departments the choirs had to be rebuilt from scratch. The immediate need to fulfil the statutory requirements was for some 330 choristers nationwide, of whom almost a hundred were needed in the Thames Valley between Oxford and London. There were, of course, boys who had been taught to sing. Secular, domestic music making had expanded during the Commonwealth.[1] Oliver Cromwell himself had maintained a musical establishment in his household with boy singers whose repertoire surprisingly included the Catholic Latin motets of his favourite composer, Richard Dering.[2] Many schools that had hitherto educated some or all of the boys of a choral foundation had also remained in operation throughout the Commonwealth. This was particularly the case with Henry VIII's and Edward VI's refounded grammar schools, such as the cathedral school at Bristol and the King's schools at Gloucester and Peterborough; but also, for example, the school in the Close at Salisbury, with its direct link back to the medieval choristers' school, continued to function.[3]

In the event, the choral foundations gathered teams of boys with commendable speed. Most recruited locally and benefited from the long tradition of family commitment to the choir stalls. Men who had sung in cathedral choirs in the 1640s and clergy who were admitted or readmitted to canonries in 1660 now had sons who were offered for the consideration of their chapters. Surviving cathedral schools must have been recruiting grounds. Lincoln may be taken as an example of how things went. Three of their musicians had survived the Commonwealth and became respectively organist, master of the choristers and steward of the choristers. A new dean, Michael Honywood, was installed on 12 October 1660.

A fortnight later six further junior vicars were appointed. Before the end of October a bellows-blower was engaged, suggesting that musical services of a sort were on the point of resumption. By the second week of December 1660 seven choristers and seven Burghersh Chanters had been recruited and were admitted, amongst whom at least two were sons of lay vicars.[4] At Gloucester the list of eight singing boys appointed in 1660 includes the son of the master of the choristers.[5] Eleven choristers were elected in 1661 at Durham, eight at Chichester and Ely and choristers once more shared the single dormitory with the King's Scholars at Eton. At Henry VI's other foundation, King's College, Cambridge, ten boys were recruited as early as 1660, though it was not until 1666 that chorister numbers reached the statutory sixteen.[6] Elsewhere, bishops' visitations in the early 1660s report chorister places filled, as at Canterbury and Chester by 1663. At Westminster Abbey there were no choristers available for the December 1660 funeral of Charles II's sister, Mary; but by the time of the coronation in April 1661 Westminster Abbey boys joined those of the Chapel Royal to sing fittingly splendid music.

This rush to appoint a whole team of boys immediately could generate its own problems if the boys were of a similar age: there was a danger that their voices might all change about the same time, generating in due course another large set of vacancies. No Gloucester chorister left the choir for five years, then, within three years, six of the eight boys had to be replaced, five lost by voice change and one by death. When the two who went in 1665 had not been replaced for twelve months, perhaps because there had been a change of organist and master of the choristers, the bishop stepped in. At his 1666 visitation Bishop Nicholson ordered the chapter to seek suitable boys against the time that the entire 1660 intake would need replacing. One of those appointed in 1667, Jesse Painter, is of special interest. His father had been a Gloucester chorister in 1638 and became, at the Restoration, a lay clerk. The father was also a glazier, one of the pair who undertook the huge task of replacing the cathedral glass wrecked during the Commonwealth. This may explain why in the 1660s he was admonished for frequent absence from services. Nevertheless he remained a lay clerk until his death in 1696 when he must have been in his seventies.[7] The son, Jesse, the younger of two chorister brothers, having been appointed to sing treble in 1667, apparently continued to do so until 1679. He may have been one of those, not unknown in the seventeenth century, whose treble voices held until they were eighteen or nineteen. Or he may have been occupying a nominal chorister's place whilst singing alto – or even playing the cornet. Cornets appear frequently in the records during the early years of Charles II's reign, used to strengthen inadequate treble tone. At York, where chorister recruitment was a serious problem, Roger North observed that wind instruments were used 'to supply the want of [boys'] voices'.[8] And at Durham, where after strong initial recruitment a similar shortage of boys developed, Alexander Shaw and Matthew Ridley, two of the boys recruited in a rush in 1661, were appointed sackbutteer and cornetter respectively as soon as their voices broke in 1664.[9] Awards of grants to leaving choristers sometimes reveal the quality of the boy. At St George's, Windsor, in 1678 James Garroway, after serving as a chorister for eight years, received a clothing grant of £5, 'the youth having all along behaved himself very civilly'. Not so John White who, three years later, had a grant of just five shillings to help him find an apprenticeship, being a chorister who had 'become altogether useless'. (Nevertheless, he reappeared at St George's Chapel in 1684, appointed sexton.) At the other extreme was his contemporary, John Golding, chorister from 1675 to 1684. By July 1685 he was recalled to St George's 'to assist the [very aged] organist upon all necessary occasions and diligently instruct the choristers in the art of singing'.[10]

By far the most remarkable gathering of choristers was the initial provision of the statutory twelve boys at the Chapel Royal. In June 1660, within a month of the return of Charles II, 'Captain' Henry Cooke, a former chapel musician of Charles I and sometime officer in the royalist army, was appointed to a variety of duties in the Private Musick of the court.[11] By September he was Master of the Children of the Chapel and set about gathering a group of the most extraordinarily gifted boys.[12] Indeed, Cooke's successful gathering of this brilliant team is one of the most remarkable feats in the entire history of the English chorister. Amongst the initial twelve were Pelham Humfrey and Michael Wise aged thirteen, John Blow aged eleven, William Turner aged nine and Thomas Tudway of a similar age.[13] They were to become the leading musicians in the land. Between them, as adults, they were to run the music at the Chapel Royal, Salisbury, St Paul's, Lincoln and King's College, Cambridge, and all became significant composers. One could say that in the latter part of the seventeenth century the Chapel Royal was the nearest Britain had to a Royal Academy of Music and that its choristers were the student body. That particular group of boys must have been a hive of mutually stimulating musical endeavour. Whilst choristers, Blow, Humfrey and Turner joined together to write the so-called 'Club Anthem' for the chapel; and, while still trebles, Pelham Humfrey had five and John Blow three anthems published in Clifford's *Divine Services and Anthems* of 1664. As composers these two at least were to outshine their master.[14]

Not all the twelve were to become professional musicians. We do not know from where Tom Edwards was recruited. The earliest mention of his name is 12 August 1664, when he is noted as having suffered a voice change. He was, perhaps with special haste, given a suit of leaver's clothes already delivered for Michael Wise whose voice had also broken.[15] The clothes were urgent because Cooke had a placement in sight for him. Cooke had first met Samuel Pepys, the naval administrator and diarist, at a midday dinner party four years before. Acquaintance developed, and in May 1664 Cooke seems to have suggested to Pepys that he might in the future consider taking one of his chorister leavers as a household 'boy'. Pepys comments in his diary: 'I think, if I do find it fit to keep a boy at all, I had as good be supplied from him with one as anybody'. Early in August Cooke wrote to Pepys, commending Tom Edwards to him. Pepys went to Whitehall, spoke with Cooke and, after evensong, was introduced to Tom, who struck him as 'a good willing boy'. Later Pepys met the boy again at Cooke's house and on 17 August Pepys came home from work to find Tom Edwards there, ready to begin his new life. Hence, from Pepys's pen, we have a vivid portrait of a Chapel Royal chorister immediately following his voice-break: 'a very schooleboy that talks innocently and impertinently; but at present it is a sport to us, and in a little time he will leave it'. Later, 'pretty it is to see how our boy carries himself, so innocently clownish as would make one laugh'; by November Tom is described as 'a very droll boy and good company'. But Pepys's greatest joy was that Tom was musical: 'then the boy and I to singing of psalms, and then came in Mr Hill and he sung with us a while; and he being gone, the boy and I again to the singing of Mr Porter's motets, and it is a great joy to me that I am come to this condition, to maintain a person in the house able to give me such pleasure as this boy doth by his thorough understand[ing] of music, as he sing[s] anything at first sight'. Tom not only sang. Unable to sleep one night, he woke about 4 a.m. and 'in bed lay playing on his lute till daylight'. Pepys had Tom trained as one of his Navy Office clerks. He married one of Pepys's maids, Jane Birch, and went on in 1678 to be appointed Navy Agent at Deal.[16]

The facilitator of this happy outcome had been Captain Henry Cooke. As master of choristers he stands supreme in his century and beyond. It is unfortunate that detailed terms of his appointment have not survived. The nearest we can get is a tangential reference to a warrant of 14 October 1662 that provides for the annual payment of £30 'for the Diet, Lodging, washing and teaching of each of ye Children of ye Chapell Royall' to Henry Cooke and his successors.[17] This seems to put certain responsibilities beyond doubt; though, as we shall see, it is not clear to what extent he was permitted or chose to delegate some of these responsibilities. First of all, he was to identify and acquire musical boys. Cooke had, of course, the advantage of rights of impressment and he used these assiduously throughout his years in office. Whereas most cathedrals recruited locally, Cooke used the grapevine of the Chapel Royal's incomparable network of musicians, many of whom held provincial positions in plurality, to help him fish the cathedral ponds for boys. Thus Michael Wise was recruited from Salisbury, John Blow had been a Newark boy, Pelham Humfrey was from Windsor and William Turner from Christ Church, Oxford. Over the years Cooke put in travelling claims for recruiting boys from Newark and Lincoln (1661, presumably relating to his acquisition of John Blow); Windsor and Canterbury (1664); 'going into the countrie looking after boyes for the chappell for a half year' (1665); 'fetching and bringing up boyes from several places' (1669); Rochester, Lincoln, Peterborough and Worcester (1670) and 'Westchester', Lichfield, Canterbury and Rochester (1671). Some foundations will have been proud to see one of their boys go off to join the most prestigious choir in the land. Some were furious at losing their most promising boys. We have noticed that in 1664 Cooke lodged a claim for the cost of travelling to Windsor. He had heard from Dr William Child, organist, and Matthew Peniall and Nathaniel Watkins, singing men, all of whom had feet in both camps, that the choir of St George's Chapel included two particularly promising boys. He went there and took them by impressment. The chapter of St George's believed themselves to be immune to such theft and brought all four men before the Lord Chancellor 'for stealing away two of the choristers without any special warranty contrary to the privilege of this place'. Child, Peniall and Watkins, doubtless with an eye to their Windsor appointments, apologised. But there is no record of Cooke apologising and it looks as if he kept the boys.[18]

Once he had recruited his choristers, the master's two prime responsibilities were 'keeping' his boys (housing, feeding and laundering them) and teaching them singing and musical theory. Because no precise 'job specification' for any master of the Chapel Royal choristers has survived from this period, some uncertainty exists as to whether Cooke accommodated the boys himself. It has been suggested[19] that the choristers lived, scattered, in various homes in London. But, quite apart from the inconvenience and unsuitability of such an arrangement, costs of such hospitality are wholly missing from the accounts. Cooke did put in reimbursement claims for maintaining boys. Regular items in the Lord Chamberlain's accounts refer to the four trebles kept at Whitehall for the king's 'private musick' over whom Cooke was also master. These were the successors of Cromwell's boys, trained to entertain the king (in distinction from the choristers proper, the 'Children of the Chapel'; though there are indications in the accounts that from the 1670s some private music trebles may have doubled as chapel choristers).[20] From the first year there are recurrent claims by Cooke at £20 per boy per year for keeping and teaching two boys and claims by other musicians, for instance Thomas Lanier, for keeping and teaching the other two.[21] There are also claims by Cooke for *continuing* to maintain Chapel choristers following their change of voice. He was, as we have seen, maintaining Tom Edwards, and it was to Cooke's house in August 1664 that Pepys went to discuss with Tom the possibility of the latter becoming his household 'boy'. Cooke periodically incurred and claimed reimbursement for the substantial costs of taking his boys to Windsor, for the St George's Feast or when the court moved there for the summer months, primarily in the seventeenth century to escape the high risk of plague in London. Typical costs of taking and maintaining himself and his boys there are those of 1671:

> To Captain Henry Cooke for himself and twelve boys at Windsor 14 days and himself and 6 boys there 7 weeks and 3 days, 25 May to 15 July at 10s. per day for himself and 4s. per day for each boy.

But Cooke never claimed for maintenance of the twelve or thirteen singing Chapel boys at Whitehall; indeed, the cost of their Whitehall maintenance never appears in the accounts at all. The likely explanation must be that 'keeping' the Chapel Royal boys, along with training them in singing, was the essence of Henry Cooke's appointment and that for these duties he received accommodation, maintenance and a salary that covered the costs of living for him, his family and the choristers, the £30 a head stipulated in 1662. Above all, there is evidence that Cooke occupied accommodation at Whitehall large enough to be a modest choristers' boarding house. In 1669/70 Ralph Greatorex drew up a ground plan of the Palace of Whitehall. In some surviving copies a very substantial property within Whitehall is identified as 'Captain Cooke's House', large enough, one would have thought, to have accommodated him, his family, their servants and some dozen or more singing boys.[22] Further, in October 1673, by which time Pelham Humfrey had succeeded his former teacher as master of the children, there is a revealing instruction to Christopher Wren: '[It is] his Majesty's pleasure that you cause to be made & opened a Doore out of ye present Dwelling house of Mr Pelham Humfryes into the Bowleing green for the perticular use of Him and ye Children of his Majestys Chappell.'[23]

Notwithstanding that Cooke had lodgings at Hampton Court, which were given as his domicile in his will and where he died on 13 July 1672,[24] it seems overwhelmingly likely that residence in 'tied' accommodation at Whitehall was both a perquisite and an obligation of his mastership, as would be expected and necessary; and that the accommodation passed on to his successors, and that the choristers were equally obliged to live there with their master. At a time when many, perhaps most, of the Chapel Royal staff were pluralists, singing or playing the organ part-time elsewhere in London or in provincial cathedrals,[25] Cooke devoted his time exclusively to the music of the chapel and court and in particular to the boys of the Chapel Royal and Private Musick.[26] Indeed, his single-minded sense of responsibility towards his choristers is strikingly revealed in an entry in the Chapel's Old Cheque Book of 1662 which records that Captain Cooke accepted office to be steward of the annual Gentlemen's Feast in 1663 'on condition that this choise should be no p'cedent to binde his successors for the future whilst they are Masters of the sayde Childern … it being never the custome … nor … meet or convenient for the Master of the Children to beare that office'.[27]

Cooke's periodical claims for reimbursement of expenses are interesting as much for what they omit as for responsibilities they identify. A typical half-yearly bill is that from April 1665:

> £115 10s. 6d to H. Cooke for – Latin, writing, violin, organ, lute stringing and penning their harpsichords fire and strings in the musique room at the Chappell disbursement for cloathes for Michael Wise[28] for going into the country looking after boyes … and for nursing of three boys that were sick of the small pox.[29]

One can understand how payments for heating the chapel music room, repairing instruments, travelling to recruit choristers and providing care of the sick appear as disbursements, additional to Cooke's regular responsibilities. But why was he claiming academic and instrumental teaching of the boys as expenses? One answer can be found in March 1662, when Cooke lodged a claim for £45 'by him expended to masters for teaching the said children to write and to learn and speak Latin from Michaelmas 1660 to Lady Day next'. So at the Chapel Royal (unlike many other foundations) the master of the children was not also their grammar master; but it *was* his responsibility to employ and pay a grammar master, subsequently recovering the cost. The claim for expenses for teaching the boys violin, organ and lute is more surprising. These duties were standard in most if not all seventeenth-century choirmasters' responsibilities. Nowhere in the Lord Chamberlain's accounts do we find mention of anyone delegated to undertake instrumental teaching to the choristers. The probable solution is that Cooke did teach his boys their instruments but that only the teaching of singing and theory were covered by his salary as chorister master.

Another of Cooke's responsibilities was the clothing of the boys. Each year sets of summer and winter liveries were ordered. Here is the list from February 1671:

> 12 tunicks, vests and breaches of scarlet cloth lined with sky shalloone, laced in silk (silver)
> 36 shirts
> 36 half shirts
> 48 plain bands and cuffs
> 24 laced bands and cuffs
> 36 handkerchiefs
> 12 silver hose [prs]
> 24 worsted hose [prs]
> 36 gloves [prs]
> 24 hats
> 36 shoes [prs]
> 12 sashes

Cooke himself paid the supplier for these liveries and submitted an account for reimbursement. But Charles II was allowing, indeed encouraging, his household to spend far beyond the royal income and bills were simply not paid. By the summer of 1668 Cooke was owed £385 for liveries, and he seems to have given up ordering further sets of clothes: on Sunday 19 January he had refused to allow the boys to sing in Chapel because their clothes were 'in tatters', as they were again two years later. At his death Cooke was owed by the crown more than £1600 in unreimbursed expenses.[30] He was lucky enough to be a man of property who could keep himself afloat, unlike some court musicians who, unpaid, borrowed themselves into penury.[31] Matters got worse in the 1680s. By 1686 the huge sum of £2848 16s. 4d. was owed for liveries, some of it going back to Cooke's time. A solution was found in September of that year when an order was made for the liveries arrears to be paid directly from new taxes on tobacco and sugar.[32]

Clothing was part of the generosity shown to Chapel Royal choristers after their voices changed: 'two suits and cloaks and with double portion of all lynnen and other necessaries'.[33] The Chapel took seriously its responsibility to see the boys settled in life after their choristerships, though there seems to be no evidence of continuance of the earlier practice of sending them on to university with scholarships. Cooke maintained several such boys at a cost of £30 a year, presumably in his lodgings, 'during the King's pleasure'.[34] Some found continuing employment at court. One of Cooke's minor appointments at court was Master of the Pages of His Majesty's Chapel Royal.[35] In December 1666 three boys whose voices had changed, two of them lodging with Cooke, became 'pages' of the Chapel, whatever that may have entailed. More significantly, some of the finest boy musicians went straight on from their choristerships to senior court appointments, most notably Henry Purcell, whose voice changed about Michaelmas 1673 when he was 'gon from the Chappell' and who had already, the previous June, been appointed 'keeper, maker, repayrer and tuner of the regalls, organs, virginals, flutes and recorders and all other kinds of wind instruments whatsoever, in ordinary, without fee, to His Majesty and assistant to John Hingston; upon the death or other avoydance of the latter, to come in ordinary with fee'.[36]

That Cooke, Humfrey and their successors taught singing and musical theory to the choristers cannot be in doubt. Cooke's skill in this field was the source of his lasting fame. Charles II brought back with him from his exile in France a passionate love of the French and Italian styles of church music, rich in florid solos and accompanied as much by strings as by the organ. Church music in the 'English Baroque' style had already made an initial appearance before the Civil War. Charles II gave powerful momentum to its development, making clear his preferences when he attended chapel, and requiring all or a select number of his 'four-and-twenty violins' (in imitation of Louis XIV's *Vingt-Quatre Violons du Roi*) to attend and play in chapel on Sundays and high days, often himself somewhat obtrusively beating time to the music. Henry Cooke wrote an anthem for Charles's coronation that required violins in four parts to play a substantial introductory 'symphony' and several *ritornelli*. As early as 1663 we find Cooke teaching the boys to play the (Italian) violin, no longer the (English) viol. The new style of music made wholly new demands on boy choristers. We have encountered Pepys and Tom Edwards singing motets by Walter Porter. Porter (d. 1659) had studied in Italy under Monteverdi. His *O prayse the Lord*, although itself probably intended for domestic rather than liturgical use, shows how virtuosic a Chapel Royal chorister could be expected to be, introducing (see below) the *trillo* or tremulo, a figured bass accompaniment (a skill talented choristers would be expected to master), as well as the helpful novelty of regular bar lines.[37]

Walter Porter, *O prayse the Lord*

Cooke was himself a master of the Italian style of singing and he undoubtedly taught this style to his boys. He was a prolific composer, and his work, though it has not stood the test of time, appealed to contemporary taste: 'To Whitehall chapel … After sermon a brave Anthem of Capt. Cookes, which he himself sung, and the King was well pleased with it'.[38] One of his anthems, *O Give Thanks*, gives evidence of the Chapel Royal choristers' ability in depth, the trebles being divided into three parts for most of the anthem, in both the choruses and the verses.[39]

Between 1670 and 1676 William Tucker, a gentleman of the Chapel Royal and precentor of Westminster Abbey, undertook the task of 'pricking' in fifteen books the music and words of nineteen services and sixty-five anthems that were in the chapel's repertoire, presumably additional to those already to hand.[40] Eleven of the anthems were by Tucker himself, a pardonable indulgence. Apart from one each by Batten, Byrd, Hooper and White, all the other anthems and all but one of the services were by post-Restoration composers. In other words, in part to gratify the taste of the king, almost all the music sung liturgically by the Chapel Royal boys was contemporary. They were learning or sight-reading 'modern' music. While Tucker was pricking out the anthems John Playford was publishing his *Order of Performing the Divine Service*. Here were included 'common tunes' for singing the psalms and, on days when 'settings' were not appropriate, the canticles. These common tunes were a sort of half-way stage between Merbecke's simplified plainsong and the modern single chant. The Chapel Royal was their seedbed, and from there they rapidly spread around the choral foundations. One of the most committed composers of such tunes was former Chapel Royal chorister William Turner, who has been called the father, if not the inventor, of the Anglican chant.[41] Fitting beautiful but unwieldy words to rigid ten-note melodies was another skill the boys had to learn. It was to be a long time before any choir sang chanted psalms tidily. As Roger North wrote: even when the psalms were sung with care,

> the pronunciation is at best a huddle unintelligible, as if all strove to have done first. And for this reason, where the organ is not used which keeps the choir upright, the chanting is scandalous, such a confused din as no one living not pre-instructed could guess what they were doing.[42]

The psalms, of course, were never the main attraction. Notwithstanding that very little of the repertoire is ever heard today, Chapel Royal services became a great draw. Society flocked to hear the music, watch the king and compare notes with friends. Not everyone approved. John Evelyn's appalled comment of December 1662 is well known:

> After which, instead of the ancient, grave, and solemn wind-music accompanying the organ, was introduced a concert of twenty-four violins between every pause, after the French fantastical light way, better suiting a tavern, or a play-house, than a church.[43]

But the English Baroque had come to stay. It was to be the style of all Cooke's ex-chorister composers and was to triumph under the genius of Henry Purcell. Pelham Humfrey survived Cooke by just two years and a day; but another of

Cooke's original team of boys, John Blow, proved an admirable successor: able, assiduous and a far finer composer than his master. Among the brilliant boys he recruited were Jeremiah Clarke and William Croft. Surely the outstanding musical occasion in this period was the coronation of James II at which Purcell at the Abbey and Blow from the Chapel Royal combined to produce a service of unparalleled splendour. Nine musical items were sung, all but one composed by former Chapel Royal choristers and including two eight-part masterpieces, Blow's *God Spake Sometimes in Visions* and Purcell's equally massive *My Heart is Inditing*. It was to be the climax and the end of a great period of English church music from a unique centre of excellence.[44] Significantly it was not for the Chapel Royal but for the St Cecilia's Day Festival of 1694 in St Bride's church in Fleet Street, that Purcell wrote his great *Te Deum and Jubilate in D*. In what was to be the final year of his life, here is the former chorister recalling the thrill that can be achieved, surely nowhere more splendidly, from the sound of high trebles, cherubim and seraphim, singing in thirds: see p. 138.

John Blow was less single-mindedly devoted to the Chapel Royal than his predecessors had been. Without resigning from the Chapel he accepted in 1687 an appointment as almoner and master of the Children of St Paul's and six years later he succeeded Purcell as organist of Westminster Abbey. Thus by 1695 he was virtually running the whole of London's front-line church music. One reason why he felt able to do this was that by 1695 high demands at the Chapel Royal were over. So long as Charles II reigned the Chapel Royal choir and its choristers flourished. With the death of Charles royal interest in the court chapel disappeared. James II was a Catholic and preferred to attend his Catholic queen's chapel, where there was a separate but far less distinguished musical establishment. William of Orange, a Calvinist, and Mary II simply were not interested. A consequence and evidence of this comes from Henry Purcell, the most distinguished composer from amongst the former Chapel Royal choristers: from 1688 he produced almost no music for liturgical use, turning his attention almost exclusively to opera, incidental theatrical pieces and songs and chamber music for the drawing room. At the same time, royal determination to modify court expenses had its impact on the Chapel. The staff of men was substantially reduced and the number of choristers was cut to ten. String players began to absent themselves so that Princess Anne, who did worship at the Chapel, had to demand their attendance. Similar absenteeism on the part of singing men reached the level of 'notorious neglect of duty' as references to fines from the 1690s confirm.[45] When in 1691 an order was made that 'the King's Chappell shall be all the year through kept both morning and evening with solemn musick like a collegiate church',[46] it was a sad admission that the Chapel Royal ought to maintain the standards of worship of the English cathedrals. Those standards were, by and large, deplorable.

Henry Purcell, *Te Deum in D Major*

The bishops and their new cathedral chapters had greeted their rebirth in 1660 with high hopes. The Book of Common Prayer of 1662 was seen as both a necessity after the wholesale puritan rejection of liturgy and as a bulwark against Roman Catholic accretions. Although puritans, led by Richard Baxter, and High Church Anglicans, spoken for by bishops Cosin of Durham and Wren of Ely, tried to have the Prayer Book modified in their preferred directions, in the event Convocation and Parliament authorised a book closely modelled on that of 1559. In particular, attempts to recast the communion service in directions anticipatory of the American Episcopal Prayer Book of 1935 or, indeed, of Order One in the current Common Worship, failed.[47] To the 1559 book were added a number of occasional services and some modest rubrical changes designed to add dignity and reverence to the liturgy. The bishops and chapters now directing the Church of England wanted a liturgy that would match and enrich 'the moderate, sober and dignified devotions of the moderate, sober and dignified English people'.[48] Yet these fine intentions rapidly faded. As early as 1676 Thomas Mace, a lay clerk of Trinity College, Cambridge, wrote of the 'Deficient, Low, Thin and Poor' state of the choral worship of most cathedral choirs; and by 1720 Thomas Tudway, sometime chorister of the Chapel Royal and from 1671 to 1728 organist of King's College, Cambridge, could bemoan 'that contempt, which [the] Cathedral Service is fallen into'.[49]

Both men had views on how this decline had come about. Tudway had a dislike for the Baroque with its 'Levity and wantonness of style', which he saw as 'the corruption of that solemn and grave style which was established as only proper to be used in divine service'. That was a matter of personal taste. More fundamentally, both Mace and Tudway saw the root of the trouble as stemming from the low calibre of men and boys recruited into cathedral choirs, this in turn being due to the fall in the purchasing power of fixed remuneration. And both saw that the most serious consequence of ill-paid men was absenteeism and neglect. According to Tudway:

> Deans & Chapters, since ye Reformation, tyeing their Clerks down to ye same allowance, now, when money is not a 5th part in value, to what it was then, have brought a generall neglect of ye service, & a very mean, & lame way of performing it, for want of encouragement; I can't forbear to say, it was an oversight at ye Reformation, to constitute a dayly service, for Chanting and Singing of Hymns, &c, & not provide a sufficient maintenance, for those, upon whom ye performance of that duty lay; whereas before ye Reformation, their Clerks were provided for, in their way in ye Colleges and Cloysters, and in wch they were Establish'd, & had their meat, drink, lodgings, &c provided ... This insufficient provision, I take to be, the source of ye decay of Cathedrall Service.[50]

Boy choristers could hardly absent themselves; but the frequent absence and carelessness of the men had an inevitable impact on the demeanour, standards and reverence of the boys. The music suffered. As Mace observed, here were magnificent buildings and rich foundations yet the music was deficient. There was a general thinness: often just one man to a part due to the absenteeism of men who were in any case 'inferior-low-capacitated', singing for just £10 or £12 a year and forced to supplement these wages by cobbling, tailoring, barbering and such like. All cathedrals were required by statute to have a number of ordained vicars choral on the foundation; but such clergy were hard to appoint and almost invariably combined their cathedral stall with a parish responsibility to which they gave priority on Sundays, when the cathedral music was supposed to be at its best. They were among the worst absentees. At Chester in 1687 the precentor and minor canon, Otway, supposedly responsible for the music and the liturgy, was threatened by Bishop Cartwright with dismissal for 'his neglecting services and anthems, and his teaching of the quire; and he refusing to amend, and be the packhorse, as he called it, to the choir and choristers'; despite which Otway was still in office in 1694.[51] Durham in the previous century had been in famously good shape. John Cosin, first as dean and then, after the Restoration, as bishop, was determined to keep it so. Yet within ten years of his death the rot had set in. Dean Granville noted in 1681:

> Boyes running up and down the Quire rudely and unseasonably, without any manifest necessity or reason, and sometimes quite contrary to command. The Quiristers carrying Anthem Bookes and sometimes Common Prayer-Bookes very impertinently and troublesomely to those that do not desire nor need them.
>
> The Quiristers, and sometimes the Singing-men staring, gazing, and laughing, indecently lolling, and sometimes scandalously sleeping not only during the sermon but also the service.
>
> A great part, if not the greatest part, of Singing-men and boyes many times not joining in at all in the responses, and sometimes not at all in the very Creed and Lord's Prayer, or at other times gabling them over, and out-running the Precentor and others in the Quire.[52]

Some foundations, as an economy, had reduced their number of choristers: St Paul's to eight, Chichester to six; Salisbury, where the medieval foundation had maintained fourteen choristers, by 1681 also had only six. Most dire of all was Llandaff, where funds became so short that in desperation the dean and chapter in 1691 disbanded the entire choral foundation, including their statutory four choristers.[53] Elsewhere, where numbers were maintained, we find complaints of poor quality. Lincoln after the Restoration gathered fourteen, but by 1666 only two or three were said (by Dean Honeywood) to be worth keeping; and ten years later, coincident with public rudeness and rows extending to fisticuffs among the men, the boys were (not surprisingly) irreverent in their demeanour about the quire. Indeed, John Cutts, master of the choristers, was dismissed, having, in quire, struck another junior vicar, John Jameson, so violently on the head that he 'not onely broke the Complainants head but also shiver'd and broke his stick or Cane'; this because Jameson had reprimanded Cutts for having his dog in quire with him.[54] Repeated misbehaviour by the Chichester boys in the 1670s found its way into the records. Recruitment was sometimes a scandal. At Southwell Minster, choristers had priority in election to closed scholarships to St John's College, Cambridge. Around 1700 the chapter were allowing themselves to be cajoled into electing as choristers wholly unmusical and over-age boys whose parents were determined that they should secure the scholarships. Elsewhere chorister education was being scandalously neglected. At Canterbury, where the King's School had no interest in admitting choristers, their 'education', exclusively in the hands of the master of the choristers, consisted of almost nothing but music. No grammar master was to be appointed to teach them until 1845.[55] No wonder that Mace made what was, for the age, the astonishing proposal that the chorister problem would be best solved by replacing boys with females.

It is impossible to know how general the decay of cathedral music had become by 1700. First, it should be recorded that during the time when so much was supposed to be in decline, new demands for choristers were being made. Bangor cathedral's music had been in bad shape: of a service in 1684 it was reported that 'the choir sang scarce half the service'. But the following year an endowment was made for the maintenance of the choir; and the new dean, John Jones, in 1691 had the office of organist endowed, ensured that by 1698 there were four singing men, and in the same year enhanced the value of the scholarships for the four leading choristers to £5 a year. By 1703 they were able to sing an anthem on every Sunday, holy day and vigil.[56] Of great significance for the future, at St John's College, Cambridge, in 1671, Peter Gunning, the High Church bishop of Ely, whom Charles II had nominated to the college as master, assigned certain room rents to the provision of two counter-tenors, four trebles and a music master; and in 1680, by his will, Gunning provided, for the benefit of 'the choir begun to be founded in St John's, £100 for the better provision of male voices ... whereby God's services may be more solemnly performed and decently sung', a gift enhanced the following year when a donor added tithes to Gunning's endowment.[57] How good the music actually was at Bangor and St John's it is impossible to know. Contemporary accounts of choral services are few and contradictory. Tudway praised the standards at St Paul's (where the lay clerks were decently remunerated), yet when Pepys was there in February 1664 he was 'most impatiently troubled at the Quire, the worst that ever I heard'. Under Tudway himself, it cannot be doubted that King's College, Cambridge, maintained standards, and in 1693, possibly uniquely for that period, the college built a new house and school for its choristers.[58] The choral worship at Christ Church, Oxford, under the deanship (1689–1710) of the deeply musical Henry Aldrich, was maintained in exemplary form. One of his guiding principles was 'never admit a chorister who had not undergone some preparation, and never without a trial'. Weekly choir practices, unknown in some cathedrals, were held at the Deanery, where 'the Spirit of the Music' was complemented by generous refreshments, except for any who arrived late, whose drink was limited to small beer.[59] Eton College had re-established their choral services in December 1660 and by 1699 a public appeal for funds had beautified the quire and ensured seating there for the whole college community. But the Eton choristers continued to be put to additional service as high table waiters, as they were at Winchester and New College, and their low status at Magdalen, Oxford, is indicated by the move to have them lodged in the homes of college servants.

There is a revealing picture of conditions at Salisbury in 1686 from Bishop Trelawney of Bristol, writing to Archbishop Sancroft:

> I wish to tell your grace what I observed at Salisbury. By reason of the deane's supporting the choir against the Bishop there is a scandalous neglect in the performance of the service. The day I rested in the town the singing-men refused to sing an anthem which was then desired by the bishop's nephew and Canon Hill, and in the afternoon the organist (which, they say, happens often) was absent, and the prayers performed without the organ.

The quarrel between the dean and Bishop Seth Ward was vitriolic and long lasting. It was said to have hastened the bishop's death. The reference to the anthem being requested by the bishop's nephew is symptomatic of the nepotism for which Seth Ward was notorious. But it also reveals a practice that by the 1680s had become almost universal: the anthem was chosen at the last minute, sometimes even in the course of the service, so that the men and boys were expected either to know it or sing it at sight. As for the absent organist and master of the choristers, this was, and had been from 1668, Michael Wise, who as a boy had been one of Henry Cooke's brightest pupils. Salisbury under him should have been in fine shape. But in 1676 he had accepted appointment in plurality as a counter-tenor at the Chapel Royal. Thereafter he became increasingly irascible and disorderly, drunken and profane, often at odds with his men and negligent of his boys. On the occasion of Bishop Trelawney's visit he may have been at the Chapel Royal or he may have been 'incapacitated'. In either case he had failed to appoint a deputy. A year later he became embroiled in a row with a nightwatchman of the Close who, in self-defence, struck Wise with his bill, causing a fracture of the skull from which Wise died. The refusal of the men to sing, possibly encouraged so to do by the dean in order to slight the bishop's nephew, reveals conditions of indiscipline and disorder which must have made it extraordinarily difficult for the choristers to fulfil their roles with any sort of reverence.

From Salisbury comes a particularly vivid example of much of what has been described. In the course of a service in the mid-1680s, Michael Wise (as so often) was away, but a deputy was sitting at the organ. A chorister, John Freeman, was waiting by the organist during the reading of the first lesson to find out which setting of the canticles the choir was to sing. Not until the end of the lesson, according to the boy's evidence, did the organist decide,[60] so Freeman rushed to the stalls to convey the decision to the men and boys. But a particularly petulant vicar choral, William Powell,

> reacht over the Seate and caught him by the haire and pulled his head back against the Seate, and struck his face agst the Seate with such force as caused his mouth to bleed, and called him 'Bastard' which caused him presently to cry.

And, one might add, caused his affronted father to make a great fuss (these being the days when bastardy was matter for considerable shame). Powell's defensive account was not identical. John Freeman, he said, had been playing at the quire door

> when he should have brought me notice which service was appointed, and did not, by which means I could not tell whether I should begin before y^e Organ or not but in truth did begin before y^e Organ (wch as it happened I should not have done) and being thereby $somw^t$ provoked I confess I did pull y^e said Freeman by the haire, and called him Rascall ...

Whether the organist was late in making his decision or whether Freeman had lingered at the quire door, the picture is clear: inefficiency and impatience on the part of deputising organist and vicar choral, and misery for the chorister.[61]

It is not surprising that the judgements of Mace and Tudway have been broadly confirmed by subsequent historians and musicologists: in most choral foundations the last three decades of the seventeenth century were years of distressing decline.

10

Georgian Nadir

The century and more following the accession of George I in 1714 has been seen, even from Georgian times, as the nadir of the fortunes of the cathedral choral tradition and, perhaps even more so, of the choristers who served that tradition. There are some incontrovertible facts supporting this view. No choral foundation formally increased its chorister numbers during this period; some allowed numbers to shrink and one disposed of its choristers altogether. No new choral foundation with choristers was established between 1700 and 1850. Fewer choristers sang daily services in colleges and cathedrals between 1750 and 1850 than at any time since the early thirteenth century, the years of the Commonwealth only excepted. As to the choristers themselves, it is widely believed that they were ruthlessly exploited, were forced to undertake menial tasks such as pantry work and boot cleaning, were hired out for their masters' pecuniary benefit to sing in unseemly secular locations, in short that almost everywhere their treatment lay between 'scandalous neglect and brutal ill-treatment'.[1]

Determining to what extent this broad disparagement of the circumstances of the eighteenth-century chorister is sound meets an immediate problem. In the records of many foundations from the Georgian decades the choristers seem to disappear. The historians of Bristol Cathedral School and of the Prebendal School, Chichester, have been unable to find a single piece of evidence about their eighteenth-century choristers.[2] In the archives of St George's, Windsor, from 1732 there commences 'a lengthy silence on the singing-boys' affairs'.[3] No eighteenth-century York Minster chorister's name seems to have been recorded: two survive by chance mention during their adult lives. Indeed, contemporary references to choristers from all foundations are at best patchy: they give only the occasional snapshot, leaving long gaps without evidence. As a consequence modern histories of eighteenth-century cathedral music tend to make little or no mention of the choristers. The eighteenth-century volume in Blackwell's 1990 *History of Music in Britain*[4] has a bibliography listing over a thousand books and articles relevant to British eighteenth-century music. Not one item is directly about boy choristers; few refer to them at all.

Nevertheless, despite huge lacunae in the evidence, helpful sources do exist. From this period come the earliest autobiographical recollections of choris-terships, notably those of Richard Stevens of St Paul's and John Harding of

Salisbury.[5] Between 1781 and 1794 the Hon. John Byng, later to become Fifth Viscount Torrington, kept a series of pithy travel journals, and, like Lieutenant Hammond a century and a half before him, Byng delighted in visiting cathedrals and recording his impressions of the services and their music.[6] Finally, between 1817 and 1827, at the very close of the period, Maria Hackett published comparative analyses, albeit often brief, of the work and education of choristers from almost all the choral foundations.[7] From these, and from fragmentary local sources, it is possible to form some picture – incomplete, sketchy, not always reliable – of the conditions within which Georgian choristers lived and sang.

A richly fulfilled choristership, such as has been observed in fourteenth-century Salisbury and fifteenth-century Wells, at Christ Church, Oxford, in 1573 or the Chapel Royal a century later, needed to be lived out in a place of worship where the liturgy was cherished and meaningful and the music stimulating and uplifting, with a musical education that embraced singing, theory and instrumental skills, alongside an academic education that was thorough and appropriate, all within what would today be called an environment of pastoral care, preferably in a single residential establishment. Before judging the extent to which the lives of the Georgian choristers met these criteria, it is essential to bear in mind the broad circumstances that coloured the ecclesiastical, musical, educational and social life of the period.

One cannot expect to find in eighteenth-century quires the passion and colour of liturgical worship that characterised the fifteenth century or is to be found in today's cathedrals, enriched as they have long been by the Oxford Movement. The predominant religious mindset of the period was rational and latitudinarian, not spiritual or liturgical.[8] Even the great new religious movements of the time, Wesleyanism and the associated evangelical revival, left the cathedrals largely untouched. Outside the London Catholic embassy chapels, rarely were beauty or splendour of worship deemed necessary or particularly desirable in the ordinary daily liturgy. There were exceptions: what might be called Laudian survivals. At Canterbury there was a continuity of High Church liturgy and devotion from Stuart times until the Oxford Movement.[9] At Durham, perhaps uniquely, a weekly choral celebration of Holy Communion was maintained throughout the eighteenth century: a charming sketch of about 1780 shows such a celebration in progress with the surpliced choristers devoutly kneeling around the well-dressed altar. There was a determination to maintain good music and look after the choristers well.[10] But these were the exceptions. Elsewhere few clergy, including the deans and canons and prebendaries, put attendance at the office or the rarely celebrated communion services high in their list of priorities, even in what were technically their times of 'residence'.[11] All too often absence by singing men also went overlooked. Many deans and chapters expected their choirmen to live on a pittance and frequently turned a blind eye or did not notice when they failed to report for duty, an increasingly widespread trend. It is well known that for evensong on Easter Sunday 1834 the new organist at Hereford, S.S. Wesley, guessing that the dean's butler would be the only choirman to turn up to sing, wrote – or perhaps rearranged – a masterpiece for boys and a single bass.[12] The prime use of cathedrals was as centres of political stability, places for large-scale civic occasions and for the funerals and monuments of the wealthy.[13] Choral services were almost everywhere attended by few clergy and fewer if any laity. 'How few people attend!' wrote John Byng when visiting Lincoln in 1791.[14] 'Any attendance will soon cease: and I shall live to see when none will be present at a cathedral service, but a reader, a verger, and two singing boys, who will gallop it over in a few minutes.' The choral services were maintained because they were by statute obligatory. Inertia kept them going. Few principal cathedral clergy were musical, and even the musical could be unmoved. At York Minster for more than a third of the eighteenth century, from 1762 to 1797, the precentor, the man responsible for music and liturgy, was William Mason, a church music enthusiast, author of four essays on the subject and editor of a substantial collection of anthems, eight of them of his own composition. Yet of his multiple benefices, including a chaplaincy to the king, his York precentorship was the post he least relished. He was obliged to reside for three months of the year, which he wrote of as his 'ecclesiastical imprisonment', attending upon a congregation composed of a few 'decayed tradesmen and card playing old gentle-women', together with (when all were present, which was rarely) six singing men and five or six boys. Whenever possible he would arrange his York residence to coincide with his period of royal chaplaincy, so that he could give priority to the latter.[15] Towards the end of Mason's time at York, John Byng attended matins, subsequently writing of the 'tiresome' anthem.[16]

In eighteenth-century England opera flourished, musical societies abounded, choral societies provided opportunities for large numbers of men and women to sing oratorios, and music was an almost ubiquitous form of entertainment in taverns, such that it has recently been argued that England was the *most* musically active country in the world in the second half of the eighteenth century.[17] Yet this florescence of musical activity had negligible impact on the daily music of the choral foundations. In the sixteenth and seventeenth centuries every leading composer had begun his musical training as a chorister and had devoted at least a major part of his career to liturgical music. But of the leading men writing music in the eighteenth century not one had trained as a chorister and their main focus was upon music for other than the Church of England liturgy. Charles Avison and J.C. Bach concentrated almost exclusively on the composition of secular music; and ironically, two composers of promise, Thomas Arne and Samuel Wesley, when not writing secular music were composing for the London Catholic embassy chapels.[18] Above all, the dominating giant of eighteenth-century English music, Handel, wrote almost nothing that could be used, as he wrote it, in the ordinary course of cathedral worship. His church music was either the grand anthem for the special occasion, such as his inspired coronation anthems, or was written for the only choral foundation in England that regularly employed orchestral accompaniment, Cannons, the Edgware seat of the 1st Duke of Chandos.[19] It is, of course, the case that choirmasters took to arranging oratorio music for cathedral use. Durham Cathedral had movements from *Messiah* copied into their part-books, and there is a reference to the young Thomas Ebdon, later to become organist, singing 'I know that my Red[eeme]r [liveth]' as a chorister in 1752.[20]

By contrast, the characteristic composers writing service settings and anthems for the eighteenth-century cathedrals do not bear comparison with such predecessors as Tallis and Byrd, Gibbons and Purcell, even though the best works of Blow and Croft, Boyce, Crotch and Attwood still find a place in today's cathedral repertoire, and recent writers have been urging a revaluation of the work of Maurice Greene.[21] Most of the music sung in provincial Georgian cathedrals was the work of local organists with minimal training, small talent for composition and little sensitivity for word-setting. Few today are familiar with any of the music of Thomas Kelway or James Kent, Philip Hayes or Thomas Kempton, Benjamin Cooke or James Hawkins the elder (still less, the younger). If the name of Charles King is better known, it is because his chorister pupil at St Paul's, Maurice Greene, gave this prolific composer of services a specious immortality by dubbing him 'a Serviceable man'.[22] His canticle settings were to be the staple diet of eighteenth-century cathedrals, yet as early as 1776 John Hawkins was describing King's compositions as 'restrained within the bounds of mediocrity',[23] while today's comments range from the generous 'merely commonplace'[24] to the damning 'vapid ... musical dysentery'.[25] Further, for reasons that will be made clear, eighteenth-century masters of the music tended to encourage a repertoire of the shortest and easiest music available. One of William Savage's anthems for St Paul's ran to just seventeen bars.[26] At St John's College, Cambridge, Handel's fifty-bar chorus, *But Thanks be to God*, was abbreviated to twenty-two bars.[27] In the endeavour to get matins and evensong over as quickly as possible, James Hawkins the elder, organist of Ely from 1683 to 1729, devised the antiphonal 'Chanting Service', applying something of the style of the early Anglican chant to the canticles, quickly taken up also at Norwich, Peterborough and Lincoln. His C minor *Magnificat* might be termed eighteenth-century minimalism.[28] The number of such undemanding settings actually in use was in some foundations very limited. The most notorious case was that of Rochester. When Ralph Banks moved from Durham to be organist of Rochester cathedral in 1790 he found that for the past twelve years a mere seven anthems had been in the Sunday repertoire, while the morning and evening canticles on Sundays throughout that

Hawkins, *Magnificat in C Minor*

period had been Aldrich in G and Rogers in D, sung on alternate weeks.[29]

As to schooling,[30] it needs to be remembered that there was for children of chorister age throughout the eighteenth century no public education at all and relatively little private education. Henry Brougham, in introducing his abortive Education Bill to Parliament in 1820, estimated that only one child in fifteen in England underwent any form of schooling.[31] The charity school movement initiated by the SPCK about 1700 was in decline before 1800: the Church of England's National Schools did not begin to be operative until 1811. Hence a choristership that offered even vestigial education and an annual wage was, for a tradesman parent, a straw to be clutched at. As for the ancient grammar schools, for which many choristers were by statute supposed to have favoured candidate claims, many had closed and the surviving ones almost all suffered in the Georgian decades. There was no specific training for teachers and a good master might be followed by a disastrous appointment and vice-versa. Between 1789 and 1793 all the parents at a once distinguished Essex grammar school removed their sons. Thereafter, for seven years, the headmaster drew the endowed income and taught no boy, saying that he was there and available but that nobody applied to him to be taught.[32] When, a generation later, the notorious Robert Whiston was appointed to be headmaster of Rochester Cathedral Grammar School, where the cathedral choristers were supposed to be educated, he found there were no pupils enrolled. Whiston rapidly filled the school with boys, but doggedly avoided admitting any choristers.[33]

Finally, in assessing the quality of pastoral care the boys received in the eighteenth century it must be remembered that choristers were not the only children to suffer neglect and maltreatment at the time. Plenty of historical notice has been paid to boys of chorister age who worked in factories and mines or were sent to sweep chimneys: surprisingly little notice has been taken of boys who were sent to sing daily matins and evensong while their education, their morals, their manners and their general well-being might be neglected. This was how things were in a rough age, indeed a far rougher age than the middle ages, if one considers the care of child oblates advocated by St Benedict in the sixth century or the caring rules for the Wells choristers promulgated by Bishop Bekynton in about 1450. Not until late in the eighteenth century did a new sensitivity towards the young so much as begin to influence public attitudes, generate pressure groups and start to colour the views and intentions of those with charge of children, whether factory managers or masters of cathedral music. Coincident with Maria Hackett's concern for the state of cathedral choristers, legislation was being introduced in Parliament to raise the minimum age for chimney-sweepers' apprenticeships from eight to fourteen. Children continued to work long hours in dreadful conditions in the factories well into the nineteenth century. This has to be borne in mind when Richard Stevens tells us of his teacher at St Paul's 'chastising the boys almost to cruelty' and he himself being beaten 'most intolerably'. There were few eighteenth-century schoolmasters of whom this sort of disciplinary action was not typical; those who set out to be gentle were often, as we shall see, scorned by their pupils who could themselves be more savage with each other than were their masters at their most irate. It is against this background, liturgical, musical, educational and social, that the details of the life, work and treatment of choristers in individual foundations from which records have survived need to be set.

It is as well to dispose of the worst cases first. Llandaff, it will be remembered, had parted with its four statutory choristers in 1691. No steps were taken throughout the Georgian period to resume choral services, the choral endowment being spent on erecting between the aisles what Byng in fury called 'a modern building like a ballroom with venetian windows'. To keep anything at all going two vicars were supposed to 'reside', but there were no habitable residences for them. As a consequence, Byng found there to be hardly any services at all – 'all is in neglect and dishonourable to religion'.[34]

Something less barefaced and more devious was happening on the Thames. Eton College's foundation statutes provided for a choral force that included sixteen singing boys. In the fifteenth and early sixteenth centuries, when Eton's choristers were required to sing nine services a day, the need for them was self-evident. But by 1700 chapel services had become a minor function at Eton. In the 1430s, when Henry VI was planning the foundation of Eton, he had visited Winchester College and attended sung high mass. In 1762 when George III visited Eton and went to the chapel, no religious service was held, but a piece of music was performed there accompanied by a military band. So Eton had questioned why they maintained choristers. By the time of George III's visit there were in effect none.[35] With sleight of hand Eton convinced themselves that, by making payments of meat, bread and beer to the choristers of St George's Chapel, Windsor, in return for their singing evensong in Eton College Chapel on

Saturdays, Sundays, festivals and their eves in addition to their Windsor duties, Henry VI's intentions were being honoured. 'The choral services', wrote Provost Joseph Goodall to an exasperated Maria Hackett in 1821, 'are so diminished, it was thought expedient to allow the choristers, if they could obtain both appointments, to become members of the Windsor choir, as well as ours, by which their emoluments were increased.'[36] So the Eton choristers, it might be claimed, had not been abolished: they had been metamorphosed and had, as by smoke and mirrors, become Windsor choristers. Provost Goodall was, in 1821, describing how things had turned out to be, but there seems to have survived no evidence as to *when* the use of St George's choristers began, that is to say, as to when Eton stopped appointing choristers of their own. From 1713 until well into the nineteenth century, however, the master of the Windsor choristers was also organist of Eton, and the Windsor men sang at Eton. It could be that the 1713 appointment of an organist jointly to serve both foundations was the trigger for the amalgamation of the choristers. Be that as it may, the fact is that at some point during the eighteenth century Eton College disbanded their statutory choral foundation and eased their conscience by feeding the Windsor choristers: a daily pound of bread, a pound of mutton and a quart of ale, delivered to (and the latter usually drunk by) the parents.[37] In justice one should add a mitigating circumstance. In 1803 the Windsor chapter determined to establish proper educational arrangements for their ten boys who, for some years, had been in part-time attendance at local elementary schools.[38] In April of that year they 'ordered that a school be instituted for the instruction of the choristers in reading, writing and arithmetic and their duty to God and Man', with Francis Binfield, a former Windsor chorister, appointed to be schoolmaster. This is probably the earliest post-Reformation case of the establishment *de novo* of a school specifically for a small body of choristers, a step that was to be followed widely throughout the country in the course of the nineteenth century.

Sixty miles to the south west, Winchester College came close to replicating Eton's abandonment of their choristers. Here too the statutes called for sixteen. During the eighteenth century recruitment was allowed to slip and by 1770 there were only five. In any case, the college 'quiristers' were sometimes so inadequate that from 1720 cathedral choristers, who themselves now never exceeded six and sometimes dwindled to as few as four, were often brought in to supplement them, earning extra pocket money for doing so. From 1737 for 112 years the cathedral organist, as at Eton and Windsor, ran the music of both cathedral and college. Lay clerks also were often shared. The decline in the standing of the college quiristers was dramatically marked when, from the 1760s, they were removed from the main educational structure of the college and placed in a special form of their own – 'Second Book'. They were no longer boarded. Their gowns were removed and they were put into a page-boy livery of chocolate-coloured swallow-tail coat, giving them the status of a kind of servant. By the end of the century Second Book itself was closed down and the quiristers were sent to the local free school in the town, to be given, like the cathedral choristers, a grant when their voices broke to enable them to be apprenticed to some local tradesman. The founder's intention and subsequent expectation had been that able quiristers would proceed to become scholars of the college. One boy did so in 1784: thereafter no quirister was to become a Winchester scholar until 1948. The musical diet was stodgy, suited to the warden's preference: 'Novelty in services and anthems has no charm for me', he wrote in 1816, 'I hear the same anthems with satisfaction.' Meanwhile, the interest of the organist, Peter Fussell, in the cathedral's music had sunk to such a low point by 1782 that the chapter ordered the senior chorister to keep a record of the occasions when their master had and had not turned up to teach them, and to bring the record once a fortnight to the Chapter House for the chapter to see. No wonder that John Byng, joining a 'shabby congregation' at Winchester cathedral in August 1782, found the service 'more irregularly performed than I ever remember to have heard it'.[39] Yet things were to get worse, for under Fussell's successor, the infamous George Chard, between 1 December 1817 and 1 December 1818 Chard attended chorister practice just fourteen times.[40] Meanwhile the music of the college continued to decline.[41] It is not known whether there had been significant conversation between the powers at Eton and at Winchester to encourage the development of so parallel a situation. At least at Winchester some choristers were maintained; the choral foundation was, after a fashion, preserved.

By contrast, the Oxford and Cambridge medieval choral foundations continued to maintain their statutory number of sixteen choristers. At King's College, Cambridge, as we have seen, a new schoolroom had been provided in 1693; but by 1776 it was described as 'totally neglected'. The school itself fell into decline during the century, the curriculum from the 1740s being of the most elementary kind. The boys were typically recruited from the families of college servants or from other poor homes. They were accepted after a brief 'trial' at which they were expected to be able to write their name and home address, to sing a scale and to give proof of their voice projection by shouting in a crowd. No evidence survives of the standard of singing that such carelessly selected choristers achieved under the two unremarkable organists, Robert Fuller and John Randall, who successively directed the music from Tudway's death in 1726 until the last year of the century.[42] As for St John's, Maria Hackett was despairing. So eighteenth-century choral establishments were no great credit to Cambridge.

Oxford was a different story. Whilst the Cambridge choristers seem to have been elected locally from lower-class families and most if not all lived at home, at New College and Magdalen College in Oxford this was by no means the case. Gentlemen, both local and distant (for example, from Buckingham, Cheltenham and Wantage), would write to the Warden of New College seeking a chorister's place for their son or other relative or acquaintance. Clergy or men with Oxford connections especially feature. There is evidence of boys being admitted as young as six and as old as twelve. Certainly in the second half of the century formal voice trials took place and by no means every boy was accepted. In the early years of the century New College School, conducted in the University Church, was in fine shape, educating not only the choristers but also over a hundred other boys. But from mid-century the school fell into decline and in 1771 the decision was taken to have the choristers educated at Magdalen College School. Magdalen also seems to have been attracting able boys into its choir. Such was Andrew Etty: chorister from the age of nine, a scholar ('demy') of both the school and the college, then for eight years fellow of Magdalen, before settling from 1758 in the desirable living of Selborne. Indeed, it has been said that 'any [Magdalen] chorister of ordinary ability in the eighteenth century could look forward to a placid and unalarming career, supported through his university life by the college to which the interest of some fellow had given him entrée at the age of eight or nine, and thereafter standing a good chance of a comfortable living in which to end his days, as useful or as useless to his parishioners as he chose'.[43] Here were choristers who were not expected to go off to apprenticeships but to continue their education through to university. Whether at New College or at Magdalen, a chorister in the latter decades of the century would have been under the musical charge of the same man. Dr Philip Hayes had been appointed to New College in 1776 (daily services at 8 a.m. and 5 p.m.); later he added Magdalen (daily services at 10 a.m. and 3 p.m.) and finally St John's (evensong at 6.30 p.m.). Briefly Hayes even accepted the post of organist at Christ Church, and throughout this time managed also to be Professor of Music and a Gentleman of the Chapel Royal. Of course he delegated; but the care of the New College and Magdalen choristers must have suffered from this manic accumulation of offices. And even Magdalen was by the early nineteenth century no longer boarding its choristers communally but lodging them with college servants in houses in Holywell and Longwalk, with a sitting room shared with the family. Their unsupervised walks between lodgings and college were frequently the occasion for fights with gangs of town boys. Drinking and smoking were prevalent and some of the boys had pistols.[44]

From New College comes perhaps the earliest surviving autobiographical snapshot of a chorister in quire. At some point in the nineteenth century there was found a faded sheet of paper stuck behind the figure of a plaster angel in the chapel. It read:

When you find this, recall me to your mind, James Philip Hewlett, Sub-warden's chorister, April 26th 1796. Yeates just gone out of Chapel, making as if he were ill, to go to 'Botleigh' with Miss Watson ... Mr Lardner is now reading the Second Lesson ... Slatter shams a bad eye because he did not 'know' the English of the Theme and could not do it ... A whole Holiday yesterday being St Mark. Only the Subwarden of the Seniors at prayers.[45]

So here we have the names of three Oxford choristers, including one who malingered for nefarious purposes and another who slipped out of singing a 'verse' solo by feigning an ophthalmic infection; evidence also that in Georgian times fellows were no better than prebendaries at attending services. But one would dearly like to know who Miss Watson was and what she and Yeates were up to at Botleigh.

If Magdalen seems to have been, musically, educationally and pastorally, amongst the best of the eighteenth-century choral foundations, what evidence is there to identify the least good? As for the services, Byng had unhappy experiences at Christ Church, Oxford, in 1792 ('evening prayers miserably performed') and at Worcester in 1781 with matins 'very ill performed' and the psalms at evensong 'slurr'd over most irreverently'. At Hereford in 1787 he attended 'almost alone at a hasty, slovenly service'. Of the ten boys singing at Lincoln in July 1791 he reckoned that only one had a decent voice.[46] Carlisle, Chichester and Ely appeared to Maria Hackett to have virtually abandoned all attempt at chorister education. The boys at Carlisle had been for some time 'greatly neglected'; the six Chichester choristers received just one hour of musical instruction three times a week, none attended the cathedral's Prebendal Grammar School and no alternative educational arrangements seemed to be made; and at Ely, 'shabby and ill-kept', according to Byng, apart from the occasional boy who managed to gain admission to the King's School, no educational provision other than in singing was made by the chapter for their six choristers.[47] The York boys no longer boarded with their master. The Minster's educational responsibilities for them seem to have withered, as indeed they had at Canterbury, to instruction merely in music. For singing twice a day, at 9 a.m. and 5 p.m., the boys received £1 a quarter. No wonder that early in the nineteenth century the *York Gazette* reported that the choir were 'scarcely able to perform the ordinary choruses in the anthems, which were therefore omitted'.[48] Miss Hackett was careful not to utter criticisms that might land her in court for slander. Thus of St John's College, Cambridge, whose authorities had made no response to her enquiries, she says only that 'the accounts which have been transmitted to me respecting the present state of the School, under the superintendence of this Society, are such as I forbear to publish'. Byng, who had no intention of publishing – 'I shall never hazard a bookseller's window' – showed less restraint. The litany at Lincoln on 29 June 1791 was chanted 'by two lay-vicars with voices like bulls'. Brecon Cathedral in 1787 was 'a filthy display of Welsh dirt – every part like a hog's stye'. At Oxford in July 1781, where Byng and his companions had hoped to hear 'the famous singing boy of New College' (who he was is unclear), all they heard was 'the anthem very ill sung and the service most idly performed'.

The *Torrington Diaries* and Hackett's *Brief Account* are, however, sources that must be taken with caution. Both suffer from inevitable limitations. John Byng visited choral foundations at particular times on particular days. Thus at Canterbury, supposedly maintaining a strong High Church tradition,[49] on 23 September 1790 he found the morning service 'well performed' with 'a well-chosen Anthem ... well sung by two good Singing Boys'; yet evensong later that same day was 'as sadly slurr'd over as any Dissenter could wish'. So it is impossible to make a balanced judgement about Canterbury. As for Maria Hackett, at least in the early stages, before her personal visits began, she published only what she had been told. Sometimes her informants were the deans themselves, presumably truthful men but not likely to be over critical of their own establishments; sometimes, as at Cambridge, she was reliant upon what she herself called 'more questionable sources'. To Byng it was the service that mattered; to Maria Hackett, the condition of the choristers. This difference of concern gave rise to sharp conflicts of evidence. Byng thought that the choristers at New College were 'such persons as I should suppose had never learnt to sing or read'. Yet Maria Hackett avers that in the early years of the nineteenth century 'valuable and efficient members' of the cathedral communities of Canterbury, York, London, Durham, Chichester, Hereford, Norwich, Salisbury and Worcester had been trained in the choir of New College. It had been (presumably about the time of Byng's visit) the most remarkable training ground in the country. The Warden of the collegiate church of Manchester assured Miss Hackett that their choristers were selected exclusively for their musical talents which were then developed by the organist, and that they had access to the 'excellent Free School' where they studied English and Latin. Yet when Byng went to service at Manchester in June 1790 the singing was so bad that he gave up and left. All we learn from this is that no human organization is ever wholly good or wholly bad and that no observer gets the whole picture. It is perhaps from the boys themselves that we can most clearly see how like the curate's egg were the lives of eighteenth-century choristers.

Richard John Samuel Stevens, as an adult always known as R.J.S. Stevens, was to become one of the leading secular musicians of his time.[50] He had been born into a once prosperous family that had come down in the world. His father was musical and, forming a desire for Richard to have a musical education, sent him to St Paul's cathedral for a voice trial. By proving himself able to sing the Bellisle March in any key requested by William Savage, almoner and master of the choristers, Richard was admitted in 1763, aged six, first as a probationer and then as a surpliced chorister. The St Paul's boys were boarded in the house of the almoner at Paul's Bakehouse Court. Stevens has left an exact account of a typical day.

> We rose at six o'clock, in the Spring and Summer half year; at seven o'clock from Michaelmas to Lady Day. Our summons to our singing duty was the tolling of the Cathedral Bell to Morning Prayers at a quarter before [our rising time] … We sung our Solfeggi (or Solfaing lessons) and singing exercises for the improvement of the voice, for an hour; the head boy accompanying us on the Spinnet. Then came the Writing Master,[51] who in the summer half year staid two hours with us; and one hour in the winter half year. At nine o'clock we breakfasted upon a Porringer of Water Gruel; excepting on Sunday and Thursday, when we had bread and butter, and Small Beer. At half past nine we went to the Cathedral, and before eleven, we had returned to Paul's Bakehouse Court. We then practised singing until one o'clock, the head boy still accompanying us on the Spinnet: sometimes we sang together, sometimes singly, as our preceptor chose. At one o'clock we generally dined; and at three o'clock, again, went to the Cathedral. We returned home by four o'clock; and from that time till six o'clock, we practised singing, accompanied on the Spinnet by the Head Boys [sic]. From six to seven o'clock we were permitted to exercise ourselves in a large yard; except on Wednesdays and Saturdays, when we had sometimes an hour, sometimes two hours allowed us to fetch our clean linen from our parents' houses. At seven o'clock we supped upon Bread and Cheese and Small Beer; again exercised ourselves after supper until eight o'clock; when we invariably went to bed, unless engaged for the Evening at Concerts or other Musical performances. The two Head Boys only were permitted to sit up later, to practise from Eight to ten o'clock upon the Spinnet, various lessons, thoro' base, Services or Anthems; or to improve themselves in the theory of music. Twice or three [times] in a week (generally in the morning) Mr Savage used to hear the progress that each boy had made in his Singing.

Richard Stevens then goes on to describe in detail some facets of his life as a chorister. He was, as we have seen, unable to forget the cruel beatings that Savage administered to him and indeed to any boy who angered him. Nevertheless, he greatly admired his master's skills as a voice trainer.

> He was particularly attentive to forming the voice by singing exercises: the *intonation* he was rigid about to an extravagant degree; every vowel was to be pronounced with the greatest possible exactness: then the time was to be beaten by all the boys … the Shake, turn, inverted turn, Appogiatura … Bravura and Cantabile styles of singing were all practised every morning in our singing exercises: we used the French Solmisation, ut, re, mi, fa, sol, la, si, ut.

In 1768 Richard Stevens temporarily parted company from the cathedral due to his father taking him to Windsor for a weekend outing in flagrant breach of William Savage's orders. When they returned, Richard had been dismissed. Savage was, however, willing to have him back as a fee-paying music apprentice, at the generously low fee of ten pounds a year for ten years.[52] The apprenticeship included instruction in singing as well as in keyboard playing and it is clear that Stevens continued singing treble with other choristers until the age of sixteen. Mr Stevens, in a letter to his son, quotes Richard himself as saying that on 3 April 1776 he would be 'leaving the Surplice', his voice having broken. It is interesting that both father and eleven-year-old son were legal parties to the indenture, but that the dean and Chapter of St Paul's were in no way involved, although Richard continued to sing in their choir for five years. The indenture required William Savage to provide for Richard 'good and sufficient Meat, Drink and Lodging', which he indeed did, having him sleep with the other choristers in the dormitory. It was there, during his apprenticeship, that he narrowly avoided being murdered. Stevens had composed, and had sung second treble in, a vocal trio. So impressed by it was William Savage that he gave Stevens half a crown. A fellow chorister, Charles Hullatt, consumed with jealousy, took a case knife up to the dormitory and hid it under his bolster. That night the choristers had a pillow fight, in the course of which the knife fell to the ground, making public Hullatt's murderous intent, to which the petrified boy confessed. He was instantly despatched home to his parents, his choristership over.

Stevens writes lively accounts of concerts to which he and fellow choristers were taken to sing. The very first, at Haberdashers' Hall, seems to have been memorable chiefly for the soprano soloist's brilliant ear rings. In 1764, at the age of seven, Stevens was part of the chorus for the first performance of Battishill's opera, *Almena*. Other operas and oratorios in which he was a chorus treble took place at Covent Garden, Drury Lane and the King's Theatre. Less resplendent was the Feathers Tavern in Cheapside where the London Madrigal Society often held its meetings. William Savage was a member and here too he took selected boys along with him to sing, their reward being a Banbury cake or twopenny cheesecakes. Indeed, it was at one of these meetings that Stevens, then aged fourteen, first had two compositions of his own publicly performed. Thereafter, Savage would bring Stevens along to private dinner parties in order that his prize apprentice's compositions could be shown off. On one such occasion Battishill offered him half a guinea to write a piece especially for him; but when, some time later, Stevens fulfilled the challenge, Battishill, seriously drunk by the end of the dinner, completely forgot his part of the bargain. What is extraordinary about Stevens's recollections is that he has *absolutely nothing* to say about the services in St Paul's Cathedral that he sang twice a day for thousands of days, other than that they happened: a damning silent commentary on the boring nature of the liturgy, on his master's secular priorities, and on the clergy's failure to teach the meaning of worship to their choristers. At a time when, Stevens says, the boys were 'looked up to, as being possessed of a good share of musical knowledge', the whole experience of his choristership was of twice-daily drudgery.

Yet before his time things had been not so good and after his time they were to become seriously worse. Charles 'Serviceable' King had been master of the choristers in the first half of the century. He had virtually no control over his boys and allowed them to run riot:

> Indulgence ne'er was sought in vain,
> He never smote with stinging cane
> He never stop'd the penny fees,
> His boys were let do what they pleased.[53]

After William Savage's retirement in 1779, care of the boys collapsed.[54] His successor left after a year, the chapter having refused to reimburse him for expenses he had incurred in boarding the eight boys. To replace him they appointed Richard Bellamy, another vicar choral. Bellamy was frequently inebriated and his tenure came to a disastrous end by way of Bow Street magistrate's court when he was found to have indulged in 'great indecency' with some of his choristers. (Only by being huddled out of the court by the back door did he escape the murderous attention of a furious female lynch mob.) Finally, at the turn of the century, another vicar choral who was made almoner and master of the choristers, John Sale, refused to do anything other than teach the boys singing, which he was said to have done 'diabolically bad', and closed down the boarding facility, so that 'they were but 3 or 4 hours in the Course of the day at his house in Arundel Street in the Strand. They were suffered to run about the streets, and appeared in the Choir, dirty and disgracefully ignorant'.[55] It was these circumstances, 'the total neglect of their education, and the habits of idleness which they contract', that were to come to the attention of Maria Hackett and, through her, be brought to public notice.[56]

The ten Chapel Royal choristers also now lived and worked in circumstances much reduced from the security and stimulus of the days of Captain Cooke. They no longer lived in palace buildings but in the houses of their masters, where they were to be taught 'to sing, play on Harpsichord and organ' along with 'Writing, Arithmetick and compos[ition]'. Two such houses were 27 Craven Street, Charing Cross, in the days of John Stafford Smith (1805–17) and, jointly with the top four St Paul's boys, 7 Adelphi Terrace, the Strand, from 1817. Like the St Paul's boys they suffered (notwithstanding new regulations of 1804) much unsupervised wandering about the streets of London and had time on their hands. We shall see in the following chapter how a culture of bullying brutality had developed amongst the Chapel Royal children. Also, as with the St Paul's boys, a major occupation came to be singing at evening concerts. This was cause for some scandal. James Nares, the composer and their master from 1757 to 1780, was believed to earn £100 a year from the evening singing of his boys, from which he allowed them sixpence a concert with which to buy barley sugars. Under his successor,

Edmund Ayrton, the boys were so poorly fed – 'starving' was the word used – that the parents petitioned the dean of the Chapel, Bishop Porteous of London, for improvement. Although the bishop, on inspecting Ayrton's accounts, was forced to agree with the parents, no disciplinary action was taken. The Chapel Royal boys received no wages or pocket money. From the charitable Christmas boxes they had come to expect, often amounting to £30 each in the earlier eighteenth century, was deducted money for the man who cleaned their shoes and the man who cut and powdered their hair before Sunday services, leaving them, it was said, less than £3. Later in the century the Christmas boxes began shrinking 'because there is now so little Choir service'. Although in theory they still sang the daily offices, in practice this was only when the king was resident in London and not when he was at the increasingly favoured Kensington Palace or Windsor Castle.[57]

Even before their partial joint residence, the choristers of the Chapel Royal (and of Westminster Abbey) would have had occasional contact with the St Paul's boys, for they joined with them to sing the grand services that marked special occasions. It was Queen Anne who had established the practice of holding great services of thanksgiving in St Paul's Cathedral for great victories, not infrequent occasions during Marlborough's campaigns. Even more frequent were the annual gatherings of the Corporation of the Sons of the Clergy, which had begun with a sermon preached in St Paul's in 1655. In the years after the Great Fire these were held in various London churches, but since 1697 a festival service has been held in St Paul's annually without a break. Thus what had been a mere charity sermon in the seventeenth century evolved into a great musical function and one of the events of the London season during the eighteenth.[58] Once again it is believed to have been on the initiative of Queen Anne in 1709 that the then dean of St Paul's was persuaded to allow the occasion to become a choral festival. From 1772 not only did the service itself attract great crowds but so too did a full rehearsal on the previous day for which an entry fee was charged. Three years later there was an added attraction for the choristers: the stewards entertained the three choirs at the Queen's Arms hostelry 'with much Glee'.[59] From early years the music was on a grand scale and with orchestral accompaniment. The Purcell *Te Deum* and *Jubilate* in D (written originally for a St Cecilia festival) were sung regularly between 1697 and 1713. Thereafter Handel began to edge Purcell out. For half a century from 1775 Handel's *Esther* overture, his *Dettingen Te Deum* and *Jubilate*, the *Hallelujah Chorus* and a coronation anthem became fixed musical components. All attempts to vary the programme of the festival in the early years of the nineteenth century were vetoed by the Prince of Wales, who, as with others we have encountered, liked what he knew.[60] It is not difficult to imagine the thrill it would be for boys, reared on the predictabilities of the likes of King and Rogers, to find themselves singing Handel as a top line of thirty trebles, possibly outnumbering the men (because many London singers were members of two or even all three of the liturgical choirs), and pitting themselves against an orchestra of strings, wind and brass. Another unfamiliar experience provided by these festivals for the boys was that of being conducted; for ordinary quire services were never conducted, nor were they to be for many decades.

In only one area outside London did choristers enjoy the experience of joining with those of other choirs to sing in large groups and that was in the Severn Valley. Assiduous research has failed to establish exactly when the annual Three Choirs Festivals began.[61] The *Worcester Postman* of 14–21 August 1719 records that

> The members of the yearly Musical Assembly of these Parts are desired to take Notice, That, by their Subscription in September last at Gloucester, they are obliged ... to meet at Worcester, on Monday the last Day of this instant August; in order to [give a] publick Performance, on the Tuesday and Wednesday following.

and a manuscript of 1746, preserved in the British Library, refers to the

> three choirs [which] have for abt these 30 years last past annually met in September reciprocally with their Choirs to perform ye finest Piece of Music England can boast off ...

The initial impetus may have been a service of thanksgiving for the Treaty of Utrecht held at Worcester Cathedral in July 1713 at which Purcell's *Te Deum* was sung with violins and oboes.[62]

It is clear that from before 1720 an annual gathering of the cathedral choirs of Gloucester, Hereford and Worcester was taking place over two days in the summer at which, in the early years, matins was sung, with orchestral accompaniment to Purcell's *Te Deum* and *Jubilate*, and with the singing of anthems of a more extended nature than was normally felt appropriate, or even possible, for everyday use. There were also secular concerts in the town in the evenings. Significant early developments were the addition of a third day of choral singing and the enhancement of the cathedral choirs by a few local amateurs. These, presumably, were men: in consequence, as the *Gloucester Journal* of 14 September 1772 reported, the voices of the choristers of Gloucester, Hereford and Worcester, even in combination, were swamped by the sound of the massed altos, tenors and basses below them. Indeed, we know that in 1788 at Worcester the three cathedral choirs mustered just sixteen trebles as against thirty altos, tenors and basses, ten to each part. This implies that their ten youngest trebles were left out, only the experienced boys being brought to sing. What, then, must those boys have thought in 1772 (and thereafter) when they discovered that six female members of northern choral societies had been invited to come to Gloucester and help them out? And what would have been the reaction of those boys who read in the *Gloucester Journal* that 'the exact and spirited accompanyment [of the ladies] added greatly to the grandeur of the several choruses'? It was prophetic of the course the festival would take. By the 1830s the Three Choirs Festival, as it had become known, would feature concerts given by great choral societies with famous soloists. It is, of course, unlikely that the northern ladies ever sang matins. That would have been deemed an intolerable impropriety. By 1772 the choirs were singing the great oratorios – *Messiah* had made its first appearance in 1757 – and it would have been in these that lack of top line would have been especially noticeable. The performances made the groundbreaking move from the concert hall to the cathedral at Hereford two years later, acknowledging (against robust opposition for over a century) that non-liturgical music was not inappropriate in a cathedral setting.[63] Singing such music must have been a transforming experience for the choristers, even when they needed the help of some ladies. And the choristers continued to feature, free of female help, with the men of the three cathedral choirs singing matins, daily until 1783 and thereafter on the first morning. The loss of the second morning's matins is indicative of the low priority given to the liturgy by Georgian cathedral clergy. As at the festivals of the Sons of the Clergy at St Paul's, so at Gloucester, Hereford and Worcester, the choristers enjoyed the unfamiliar experience of singing together under a conductor, initially William Boyce, and later, first at Hereford in 1795, to the beating hand of their own cathedral organist.[64] By the close of the Georgian era, Gloucester, Hereford and Worcester were, in the judgement of Maria Hackett, caring comparatively well for their choristers. Gloucester and Hereford seemed to her to be among the country's four best. Of the education provided for the choristers at Worcester she wrote creditably and noted that 'there are few Cathedrals in the United Kingdom which can boast a greater number of distinguished names among those who received the rudiments of their musical education under the superintending care of the Dean and Chapter'.

One other provincial cathedral provides evidence of the way in which things could be both good and bad in differing ways. John Harding was a Salisbury chorister in the early nineteenth century. There too one Georgian chorister had tried to murder another. In June 1826 a singing boy with a particularly brutal temperament, John Langridge, had a violent argument with the head chorister, John Arnold, in the churchyard. It culminated in Langridge taking out his pocket-knife and stabbing Arnold. Chapter held an enquiry and the choristers *en masse* reported that they were terrified of Langridge. He too was expelled. In his place John Harding was awarded a choristership. The joint master of the choristers and organist at Salisbury at the time, and indeed until 1863, was Arthur Thomas Corfe. John Harding filled his later memoirs with praise for Corfe, who took his responsibilities seriously and was respected by his boys. He was consistently dutiful, 'never slackening his vigilance with regard to our behaviour and attention at Church or Singing School, being prompt to punish, yet ready to encourage and reward desert. Our training in singing and music was his constant care, whilst he also kept a watchful eye upon our conduct in the Choir.' It is clear that for John Harding the daily services in Salisbury Cathedral were a positive and meaningful part of his childhood. Maria Hackett had reported on Salisbury shortly before Harding began his choristership: after commenting on the high regard in which the cathedral's choral service had long been held, she praised the deportment and musical proficiency of the boys.[65] But at Salisbury it was the boys' education that was awry.

Corfe had no responsibility for the boys' academic training. This was in the hands of a tutor, one of the vicars choral, a Mr Greenly. From him the boys in effect learnt nothing. Latin was the sole subject of instruction. The boys would be issued with a book, for example Aesop's *Fables*, would struggle through a chapter or two, make no progress and so be issued with another book, then struggle ineffectually through those opening pages until that book was similarly abandoned. Mr Greenly, in consequence, taught in a constant state of anger. 'Gentlemen', he would say,

> you have chosen to learn nothing and I have foolishly refrained from punishing you as you have deserved; but now my patience is exhausted and I give you warning that on *Monday next* I begin in earnest, and every boy who does not say his lesson will be severely flogged.

But when Monday dawned Mr Greenly's housekeeper would appear to announce that 'You young gentlemen be to bide quiet – you be to bide quiet and do your excumcises. Master's abed.' (Gout or a bad cold had struck again.) Then the choristers would make mayhem in their schoolroom, which would be left with smashed windows and chaos everywhere. On the rare occasions when it looked as if Greenly's draconian threat might actually be fulfilled, the choristers had an escape route. By ancient custom the canon in residence could, during his three months' period of duty, award two full holidays to the boys. So, before reporting to school, they would rush to the residentiary's house, claim their due, and set out for a jolly day about town, or attempt to achieve a complete circuit atop the Close wall. The next day, back in school, Mr Greenly's threat would have been forgotten. Eventually Arthur Corfe intervened and, by way of punishment, stopped the choristers' pay. A little later the chapter brought in an elderly master three mornings a week to supplement Greenly's classical efforts with lessons in writing and arithmetic. He, too, was hopeless. So the chapter added their choristers to the half dozen pupils of yet another lay clerk, a Mr Biddlecombe, who, with his daughter, ran an elementary school in his cottage in the Close.[66]

Attempts at reform rarely stuck for long. At Lincoln in 1761 the chapter, in a sudden outburst of reforming zeal, laid down new regulations for the provision and education of their choristers, who were not to be 'look'd upon & treated as Menial Servants', but things soon fell apart again. One trivial but symptomatic detail is worth mention. In the late thirteenth century, when the chapter were concerned to see that their choristers were decently cared for, the tithes of Ashby, one of their rural parishes, were earmarked as an endowment for the singing boys. The village became known as Ashby Puerorum, as it still is today. Yet in 1801 those tithes were diverted by the chapter to provide for the maintenance of a priest vicar.[67] In 1816, visitors to a weekday evensong found the music 'so extremely bad that they were shocked and disgusted', even more so when, as they walked away down the nave, they found themselves chased by the choristers begging for a tip.[68] Nor did things improve at Lincoln: as late as 1836 it was deemed 'inferior to any other choir'.[69] Naves seem to have attracted misbehaviour. At Wells the choristers regarded it as their playground and used to kick balls and throw stones around the place. The ancient glass in particular suffered. John Turle, later to become organist of Westminster Abbey and the composer of favourite psalm chants, as a Wells chorister scored a direct hit on a glazed St Andrew, leaving a round hole where once his nose had been. Nobody bothered to repair the damage. Long after, the verger, showing visitors around, would delight in pointing to the hole in the glass and say 'That was done by the organist of Westminster Abbey!'[70]

In summary, evidence of the conditions in which the Georgian choristers lived, such as it is, suggests that brutal treatment and sweated labour, in so far as they existed at all, were not widespread. The Chapel Royal boys rather than being made boot-boys actually had their boots cleaned for them. Although Richard Stevens suffered severe beatings from his choirmaster, yet his overwhelming attitude towards his teacher was admiration and affection. The secular education of Stevens and Harding certainly seems to have been neglectful, yet they grew up to be writers of vivid and entertaining English. Harding's grasp of Wiltshire brogue anticipates the manner of Thomas Hardy. These two writers looked back on their chorister days at St Paul's and Salisbury with zestful affection. Stevens, who became a man of some wealth, made kindly benefactions to a later generation of St Paul's choristers. Of course Stevens and Harding were at St Paul's and Salisbury respectively under good choirmasters. At St Paul's, notoriously, things got very bad, and the cathedral had the misfortune – or good fortune, depending on the viewpoint – to have these circumstances made public. The St Paul's boys may actually have been the most neglected in England at that time. Certainly, in 1820, when the Prime Minister, Lord Liverpool, invited William van Mildert, the occupant of the poorest bishopric in the Church of England, Llandaff, to enhance his income by becoming additionally dean of St Paul's, he wrote, 'I understand that the Service is performed there in a much less creditable manner than in any other Cathedral in the Kingdom' and stated that both the archbishop of Canterbury and the bishop of London were looking for a new dean of St Paul's who would institute 'a thorough Reform ... in all these Particulars'.[71]

Nadir nevertheless remains the right word. Not only were chorister numbers at an absolute minimum, almost nowhere were the boys residentially maintained in the precincts. At Oxford for some of the time Magdalen and New College boys were boarded within the colleges. Elsewhere, at the Chapel Royal, at St Paul's for some of the period, at Lincoln some but not all of the boys boarded with their master. From some foundations there is no clear evidence. But at most places, where in earlier centuries careful residential maintenance had been of the essence of a choristership, the boys now lived at home or with friends or with hosts found for them by the foundation. Such was the case, for instance, at Christ Church, Oxford, and King's, Cambridge; at the metropolitan cathedrals of Canterbury and York; at Chester, Ely, Gloucester, Hereford, Norwich and nearly everywhere else. This was not cruel brutality: but it was at best casual, at worst neglectful. Some boys suffered by it, especially in London. We know that at St Paul's and elsewhere finance was a prime cause. In most foundations, deans and canons, often wealthy themselves, were adamantly unwilling to increase funds in line with inflation for the care of their boys and choirmasters.

More serious was the decline in the provision of education. This too was not universal. Some of the Henrician and Edwardian cathedral grammar schools continued to educate their choristers, in elementary classes when young and in classical studies when ready for them. Regulations of 1683 at Peterborough that 'the choristers shall go to the grammar school and be taught there at such times as not obliged to be at Church or singing school' seem to have been honoured throughout the Georgian period.[72] Maria Hackett was assured that grammar schooling was provided at Chester, Manchester, Christ Church, Oxford, Worcester and York, and it was an option for those apt for it at Gloucester, Lincoln and two or three other foundations. But the cathedral grammar schools at Canterbury, Rochester and Westminster ignored their statutes and kept their doors firmly closed to choristers or ex-choristers, as did Eton and Winchester. Where recruitment was overwhelmingly of boys unlikely to be suitable for grammar schooling some foundations provided sound, regular elementary education. Such for instance were King's, Cambridge, Durham, Exeter, Lincoln, Norwich, Rochester, Salisbury and Wells. But there were other places where the chapter seem to have washed their hands of all responsibility for education in anything other than singing. Bristol for much of the eighteenth century, Canterbury, Carlisle, Chichester, Lichfield until the very close of the period and Westminster Abbey fall into this discreditable category.

Perhaps the least discreditable feature of the life of the Georgian chorister was his musical education. This everywhere took priority over his academic schooling and in some places was evidently outstandingly good. Both the autobiographies vouch for this, as does the succession of cathedral organists and leading secular musicians who learnt their music first as choristers. Winchester Cathedral, diminished as its choral resources were, yet managed in the eighteenth century to set two boys on the their way to distinguished musical careers. James Kent, chorister from about 1707, was to become organist successively of Trinity College, Cambridge, and Winchester Cathedral. He was to be a leading church composer, and although Fellowes described his compositions as 'deservedly forgotten',[73] they were hugely popular in his day and included favourite anthems of George II and George IV. Half a century later Charles Dibdin was a chorister under Kent at Winchester. He had a famously successful career as a prolific song-writer and composer of operas and plays with music. Other Georgian choristers who became leaders of reform when it eventually occurred included John Goss and S.S. Wesley.

It is sad, then, that so many generations of choristers, well educated musically, spent their time in quire singing bland anthems and meretricious settings of the canticles in the course of services that were drab, routine, ill-attended and sometimes scandalously negligent. Charles Dibdin described his amazement when he first heard secular concert music.

> I have no power of expression that can give the faintest idea of what I felt when I heard the first crash of an overture. What an immense distinction between this electrical power and the clerical strumming I had been accustomed to in the country![74]

Well-paid pluralism on the part of chapter members was a prime cause of the evident lack of committed leadership, competent management, above all of a superintending care for the welfare of their choristers. William Paley, author of the celebrated *Evidences of Christianity*,[75] was an exceptionally able man. He had, said his headmaster at Giggleswick (who also happened to be his father), 'by far the clearest head I ever met with in my life'. After ordination he accumulated livings with exceptional zeal, including the rectorship of Bishopswearmouth, one of the richest in England, the archdeaconry of Carlisle, a prebend at St Paul's Cathedral and, in 1795, the subdeanship of Lincoln. Of this he wrote: 'Formerly the Dean of Lincoln had so much to do that he was obliged to have a subdean to help him; but now I cannot find out for the life of me that there is anything for either of us to do'.[76] So much for 'superintending care'. This, it may be recalled, was where Byng, four years earlier, had been led by the air of general neglect to anticipate that all attendance at cathedral service would soon cease.

11

The Seeds of Reform

The first real steps to transform for the better the life, duties and education of the English cathedral choristers were taken in the early decades of the nineteenth century. As with most reform movements there were both an underlying ground swell and some dynamic, visionary torch-bearers. Greater care for the choristers was a small part of far broader movements: the transformation of the English church (and not least the life and work of its cathedrals) and the growing humanitarianism that was to touch every facet of Victorian life. As for torch-bearers, there is something like unanimity of opinion that the initiating champion of the cause of the choristers was Maria Hackett.[1] She is widely known as 'the Choristers' Friend', the title on her memorial tablet in the crypt of St Paul's Cathedral. It has even been written of her that she reformed the choir schools 'just as Elizabeth Fry reformed the prisons'.[2] She was certainly a remarkable lady, with persistence her dominant characteristic. Miss Hackett's lone voice was first raised in protest at the neglected condition of the St Paul's choristers in January 1811, by way of a letter to the bishop of London. In the course of that decade she was to broaden her area of concern to embrace all the choral foundations, and she went on pressing her crusade well into the 1870s, by which time her voice was part of a chorus and the condition of most sets of choristers had already been greatly improved. To what extent she herself can be said to have been responsible for those changes in most of the individual institutions is, however, difficult to assess.

Maria Hackett was born in Birmingham on 14 November 1783. Her father, Joseph Hackett, died when she was four months old and the following autumn her mother married Samuel Capper, of a family of cloth merchants. When Maria was not yet four he too died. By 1800 mother, daughter and two sons of the second marriage had moved to the home of her uncle, George Capper, a successful London merchant, settling in due course at his house in Crosby Square, just off Bishopsgate, from where Maria became a regular worshipper at St Paul's Cathedral.[3] Of her education nothing is known, but it is clear that she was intelligent, fluently literate and a more than competent Latinist, or, as R.J.S. Stevens, who was touched by her persuasions, succinctly put it, 'a learned Clever Woman'.[4] Whilst not rich (at death she left just £300), in her earlier life she had financial resources beyond her immediate needs, sufficient to enable her to be generously charitable and, up to a point, to fight causes that stirred her.

In 1810, aged twenty-seven, she was moved to help a widowed relative of hers, by taking on the role of guardian to the widow's seven-year-old son, Henry Saxelby Wintle, and, in particular, arranging for his schooling. She managed to place him as a chorister at St Paul's Cathedral, believing that there he would be put in the way of a good classical education. In the course of his first months as a chorister she became horrified at how far the reality was from her expectations. He was in the hands of the grossly neglectful and incapable almoner John Sale, under whom residence had been discontinued, education was limited to a few hours of music lessons a day, and the boys were obliged to walk the streets of London unsupervised between Sale's house off the Strand, the cathedral in the City, and wherever their home might be, sometimes late at night after singing to 'nocturnal assemblies' where they might be 'exposed, unprotected, to the contagion of any society'.[5] Characteristically but, as might have been anticipated, unhelpfully, she took the problem to the top. On 12 January 1811 she wrote to the bishop of London drawing his attention to the condition of the choristers for whom he was, so she assumed, ultimately responsible. It was a courteous letter and was courteously acknowledged, before being passed by him to the dean of St Paul's, as the person 'whose immediate concern it is'. But Miss Hackett heard nothing from the dean. This is hardly surprising, because the dean of St Paul's, the Rt. Revd Sir George Pretyman Tomline, Bt, FRS, etc., lived on an exalted plane. Fellow of Pembroke College, Cambridge, theologian, canon of Westminster, bishop of Lincoln, he had until recently also been effectively, if not by title, private secretary to the Prime Minister. Further, he had extensive family estates to look after. He was a busy man, so busy that he visited St Paul's as seldom as possible, certainly knew nothing of its choristers and was not one to allow himself to be troubled by a naive and bothersome spinster.[6]

Nine ladies out of ten would have accepted the silent snub and admitted defeat. Not Maria Hackett. After waiting fruitlessly for four months she climbed down the scale of authority and wrote to one of the canons, the Hon. G.V. Wellesley, DD, leaving him in no doubt that she was angry: 'valuable weeks and months are wearing away and in that time the Children are wasting the inestimable gift which no future exertions can recall'. She pointed out, with more force than tact, that the cost of employing a schoolmaster to occupy the boys' wasted hours 'would be attended with an expense scarcely perceptible to the Chapter'. There was no reply. Then, within a week, when she found that the dean was, exceptionally, in residence, she wrote again:

> but, my Lord, if you knew the great disadvantage under which the children at present labour, the total neglect of their education, and the habits of idleness which they contract, I cannot think you would leave town without giving an order that they should be placed, as soon as possible, under the care of a Schoolmaster, who would instruct them during the interval between morning and evening service.

She was mistaken. The dean left town with no action taken and no acknowledgement of her letter made. Over the next several months she wrote to the cathedral chancellor, to the precentor, to a succession of canons, catching them as they took up their periods of residence. She tried shaming them by pointing out (not, as it happened, very accurately) that at Westminster Abbey, thanks to the 'unremitting exertions' of the Music Master, the choristers were now receiving instruction at Westminster School. Eventually, in August 1812, her patience was exhausted. She wrote again to the bishop of London, who had at least acknowledged her original letter. It was, she wrote, evident that the present deplorable condition of the choristers was how the chapter wanted it to be. She had retained copies of the unanswered correspondence and, unless something was done, she would give it wider circulation.

At about this time she had begun investigating in the British Museum the statutes and other documents concerning St Paul's and these convinced her that the dean and chapter had a statutory duty to maintain, feed, clothe, educate and care for their choristers. So her barrage of letters continued and, in the course of 1813, there began to be evidence that her campaign was not being wholly ignored. The canon chancellor offered to visit her when he was recovered from illness (though the visit never happened). There was another response, this time from Canon Hughes, stating that any complaint concerning a particular chorister would be dealt with by the residentiary of the day. This elicited (10 March 1813) perhaps Miss Hackett's most vitriolic riposte:

> There is no Residentiary of the Day. In your absence there is seldom anyone to whom an appeal can be made. The Dean's attendance for the past ten months has not amounted to so many days. I believe Dr Weston has not been in the Cathedral since July. Dr Wellesley rarely [attends quire] above thirty days in the year.[7]

There had, however, been a more encouraging development. In January she had drawn her concerns to the attention of the newly appointed almoner, William Hawes. He too acknowledged her letter (but spoilt the effect by sending it 'by hand of a juvenile messenger'). On his appointment the almoner's salary was raised beyond that of his predecessor, John Sale, specifically so that he could afford to board at his home the four senior choristers and employ a master to teach all eight boys reading, writing and arithmetic. Although William Hawes was to prove in some respects as neglectful of his choristers as John Sale had been, the changes made on his appointment provided the first indication that notice was being taken of Miss Hackett's complaints and that reform might be in the air.

Nevertheless, Maria Hackett's researches made her pursuit of justice for the choristers relentless. In April she wrote again to the dean, who was once more in residence, and for the first time her letter contained a threat: 'it is my intention, after the expiration of your Lordship's present month in residence, to plead the cause of these children before a more disinterested court'. And indeed, with the encouragement and help of her uncle and two half-brothers she determined to place before the court of Chancery the fruits of her researches. These had convinced her that endowments clearly intended for the benefit of the choristers were being misappropriated by the chapter for their own remuneration. In August of 1813 she wrote to the dean at his episcopal palace in Huntingdonshire, seeking permission – 'at the suggestion of [her] legal advisors' – to examine the cathedral's archives. When the dean – within a week – asked her by what right she sought such access, she replied that she was seeking a favour, not asking to exercise a right. Meanwhile members of chapter tendered an olive branch. On 3 August the chancellor and precentor jointly offered to make available a proportion of the revenues of their stalls for the provision of a classical education to the choristers.

It was not Maria Hackett's way to make threats that she did not intend to carry out. In September 1813 a first appeal was made to Chancery by her and her male relatives on behalf of the St Paul's choristers, followed in August 1814 by affidavits filed to the Master of the Rolls for the restoration of property left in trust for the choristers' maintenance. However, although the court indicated that the appellants probably had right on their side, the case was deemed to be outside Chancery jurisdiction. To take the matter further was beyond the financial resources of Maria and the Cappers and, despite moral victory, they had to accept practical defeat. For Maria, however, it was defeat on one front, but by no means the end of the war. She would, she wrote to Canon Hughes, continue to be 'an ardent and disinterested advocate' for the most powerless members of the choir so long as life and leisure were afforded her. And indeed in 1817 she published the *Registrum Eleemosynariae D. Pauli Londiniensis*, reproducing with commentary a Harleian manuscript from the British Library, identifying the charitable endowments of the cathedral and their supposed purposes. Then in 1832 she published her entire correspondence with the St Paul's clergy.[8] Long after Henry Wintle had left she continued to show kindness to individual choristers and ex-choristers, most fruitfully of all by paying for organ lessons to the young John Stainer. Her interest in St Paul's was far more wide-ranging than either support of the choristers or shaming of the chapter. Her researches led her to write and in 1816 to have published a *Popular Account of St Paul's Cathedral*, which proved so popular that by 1833 it had run to twenty-one editions.[9]

It was in 1816, having made as much progress on the St Paul's boys' behalf as under the present management she thought likely, that Maria Hackett turned her attention to the other choral foundations. In December of that month she wrote a letter to the *Gentleman's Magazine* pointing out the contrast between the widespread public interest in the *fabric* of England's cathedrals and the almost total ignorance of what went on within them – 'the celebration of Divine Service is passed over in silence, as a matter of perfect indifference.'[10] This ignorance M. H. (as she signed herself) was going to rectify: she would begin by describing to the readers of the journal 'the situation of the children belonging to the several Choirs'. She had, she wrote 'made application to individuals officially connected with the several Cathedrals in order to authenticate the information derived from more questionable sources'. Not every such individual had replied; so failing official communication, she would, as she put it, 'be compelled to avail myself of the most authentic information within my reach'. The detailed articles on individual foundations began to appear in March 1817 and concluded with a note about Ely in July 1819. Subsequently she was to gather and amplify the information into her *Brief Account of Cathedral and Collegiate Schools*, printed privately and circulated to all those with whom she was in communication about the choristers. It is clear from the form her articles took that Miss Hackett had sent to her correspondents similar or identical sets of questions concerning their foundations. Though none of these letters has, seemingly, come to light, it is not unlikely that somewhere in cathedral archives one or more of them may still be extant. Meanwhile, it is possible to reconstruct their main outline. Her questions ran more or less as follows:

How ancient is your choral foundation?
How many choristers do you have?
What are their ages?
How do you select them?
What services do they sing each week?
Who is directly responsible for them?
What provision is made for their academic and musical education?
What emoluments do they receive?
When do they leave?
What financial and/or educational provision is made for their future?
What careers have former choristers followed?

It is fortunate for the historian that Miss Hackett received far more courteous and helpful responses from most foundations than she had received (or, rather, not received) from St Paul's. They indicate, for instance, that several of the cathedrals felt proud of the way in which they cared for and nurtured their choristers in and about 1816. Many of the most fulsome responses came from what she called 'the highest authority', that is surely the deans themselves. Here, for example, is part of the response from Gloucester:

The Choristers, while they are with us, are always looked after by the Dean and Prebendaries, with all due care and kindness, making allowance for their youth; and aware of the unavoidable effect of that incessant attendance [at Divine Service in the

Cathedral every day, at eleven and four] in such cases, to relax their devotional regard by continual practice, which we know will affect persons older than themselves; so that on the whole we may do them all the good we can, and by proper advice and admonition may prepare their minds to make good citizens when they leave us. After their departure from the Choir, having had the benefit, if their parents please, of an education or much assistance towards it, in Latin, Greek, Writing, Arithmetic and Music, nothing hinders their going to the University ... whence they frequently come back again in the capacity of Minor Canons, of which many very respectable instances may be adduced. The sons of Clergymen are thus very often put in training for the Church, and become in time useful members and ornaments of it.[11]

Nobody replied from Lincoln promptly enough to be included in a *Gentleman's Magazine* article; but by the time Maria Hackett gathered the reports together for her *Brief Account* she was able to quote the following less pastorally sensitive but more factually detailed account of things there:

There are four Choristers, who are chosen by the Dean and Chapter; they are lodged and boarded with the Music Master, and receive salary with fees, amounting to £3 *per annum*. Their dress is a black cloth gown, faced with white, given them every second year. There are also six junior boys, denominated from the founder Burgherst [*sic*] Chanters; they are chosen by the Dean and Chapter, and receive a salary, amounting, with fees, to £2 10*s*. They wear white surplices, given them on their admission.

All the boys, as well Choristers as Bergherst Chanters, attend daily choral services at ten and three on weekdays, and at ten and four on Sundays. The Dean and Chapter provide for their instruction in writing, arithmetic and grammar; and those boys whose parents wish it, are allowed to attend the Free Grammar School, of which the Dean and Chapter appoint the Head Master. They attend these Schools from 11 o'clock to 12, from two to three, and from four to five. They attend the Music Master from seven o'clock in the morning in summer, and eight in winter, until prayer time. The Master derives no emolument from the musical talents of the Choristers, who are confined wholly to the Church Service. On leaving the Choir they receive a sum not exceeding £15 from the Dean and Chapter, as an apprentice fee. A medical attendant is allowed the Choristers in case of sickness.[12]

One circumstance which was common to Gloucester and Lincoln was the optional nature of part of the choristers' education. The chapter provided elementary schooling sufficient to set the boys on the way to apprenticeships; but if the parents wanted a classical education for their sons, designed to lead to university, that was up to them and, it must be added, up to the grammar schools to be prepared to accept and teach such unhelpfully part-time pupils. This sort of arrangement, not confined to Gloucester and Lincoln, was to become a problem as secondary schooling came to be taken more seriously in the course of the nineteenth century. Nevertheless, it is clear that at Gloucester and Lincoln the dean and chapter had a serious pastoral concern for the welfare of their singing boys. They were two of several foundations – Exeter, Hereford and Salisbury should also particularly be mentioned – for which Maria Hackett had nothing but praise; where she deemed there to be no reforming mission for her to undertake.

It was not so everywhere. She was critical of having received no communication from St John's and Trinity Colleges in Cambridge. The condition of the cathedral choristers at Bristol, Canterbury, Carlisle, Chichester, Rochester and Winchester and the singing boys at Winchester College gave Miss Hackett special cause for concern. As for Eton, she was appalled by the college's abandonment of its clear statutory duty to maintain and educate sixteen choristers. Eton became a particular focus of her endeavours, endeavours that had to wait half a century for fulfilment. From some of these foundations she had received no official information, and it was this, perhaps, that determined her to set out to see the establishments for herself, with evidence of her visiting St George's Chapel, Windsor, as early as 1818.[13] It was a move that was to transform her mission. She began to meet the choristers and to love them. By 1844 she had visited every choral foundation in England and Wales.[14] Thereafter she undertook a six-week expedition each autumn, managing thereby to take in all the foundations approximately once every three years, while at the same time fitting in some local culture: in 1818 Frogmore was combined with St George's, a visit to the Welsh cathedrals in 1837 saw her climbing Snowdon, and Salisbury in 1869 gave her opportunity to take in the Blackmoor Museum. But the choristers were always the chief purpose, and she would arrive 'always carrying with her presents for the choir-boys, whose names she well knew and kept in her diary – each got a book, a purse and a new shilling'. Sometimes she would get to hear of an able chorister whose family was too poor to afford instrumental lessons and she would quietly arrange to pay for them herself.[15] It was not only the boys she began to meet on these visits but also the clergy. In course of time the reaction of many of them towards her changed from suspicious, even belligerent, antipathy to respectful affection. 'I am ... happy to say that the bitter feelings which occasionally broke out were but transient; I was ultimately on friendly terms with most of my opponents, and though in my capacity as Solicitor-General for the choristers I now and then break the truce with their masters, we are always ready to renew our amiable relations', she wrote in 1841.[16]

Maria Hackett is not to be seriously compared with her celebrated contemporaries, Elizabeth Fry and Florence Nightingale. They worked for the benefit of many thousands and their achievements were of national and international significance. Maria Hackett was concerned (according to her own calculations of 1837) with just 236 boys or thereabouts at any one time. Elizabeth Fry and Florence

Nightingale directly brought about major reforms in respectively prisons and nursing. In contrast it is difficult to prove that Maria Hackett directly brought about reform in the lives of the choristers. By her generosity she undoubtedly set John Stainer on a brilliant career and no doubt others less famous. But of her more general influence it is difficult if not impossible to make an exact assessment. Of herself she could effect nothing: all she could hope to do was change the minds of those in positions of authority so that they would bring about reform. No chapter minute or college resolution was likely to attribute anything as a response to Miss Hackett's urgings. On some foundations she had no effect. Brecon and Llandaff had been brought irrecoverably low by poverty. Eton proved immovable for half a century. Canterbury and Rochester adamantly refused to contemplate admission of choristers or ex-choristers to their King's Schools. Ripon, when the dean eventually replied six years after Miss Hackett's original letter,[17] admitted that they provided nothing towards their choristers' schooling other than in music.

Occasionally, and significantly, the *Brief Account* itself reveals that reform had been afoot before she herself began her enquiries. In 1812 the authorities at Canterbury, where the chapter had no school of their own providing elementary education, undertook to pay any necessary fees for the education of their choristers in reading, writing and arithmetic at private schools in the city. More striking is this statement from Lichfield:

> 'till within a recent period, there has been no establishment in this Cathedral for any branches of education [other than in music]. There is an old foundation of a Free Grammar School in the adjoining City, and also a modern National School; but in neither of these could the Choristers be conveniently received on account of their attendance in the Choir and in the Music School. A School for their separate use was wanted; and in order to obtain the means of its establishment, the Dean and Chapter [have recently acquired the reversion of a lease that] has enabled them … to pay a Master for teaching them in reading, writing and arithmetic. But this School had its establishment a few years before the lease expired, *by the liberality of some of the members of the Chapter.* [My italics]

Here then is evidence of the groundswell at work before Maria Hackett began to give it greater impetus. It would be of exceptional interest to have notes of discussions within a chapter, finding itself unable to provide schooling for its boys, yet with canons so concerned for their choristers, and recognising the scandal of their condition, that some were moved to pay for schooling from their own pockets.

The one foundation where it is virtually certain that Maria Hackett had direct impact was, not surprisingly, St Paul's. It can hardly be doubted that the appointment of a schoolmaster to the choristers was a response to her urgings.

Right: 1. New College, Oxford, *c.* 1463, including (bottom left and right) the sixteen tonsured choristers.

Below: 2. A New College chorister carries victuals from buttery to hall, 14th century.

3. Almonry boys keep night watch over the body of a dead monk. 15th century.

4. Wynkyn de Worde's engraving of John Ankwyll, first master of Magdalen, Oxford School, with some of his pupils, *c.* 1480.

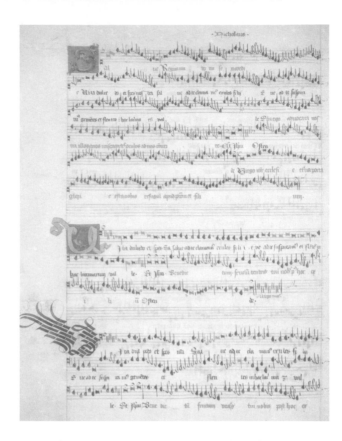

. The Eton Choir Book, *c.* 1500,
he earliest surviving polyphonic text
n which boys' voices are an essential
lement.

. Orlando Gibbons (1583–1625),
Chapel Royal musician and former
King's College, Cambridge chorister.

7. Henry Purcell (1659–95), Chapel Royal musician and former chorister, and organist of Westminster Abbey.

8. (Assumed to be) William Croft (1678–1727) musician, as a Chapel Royal chorister *c.* 1690.

9. Laudian survival: reverent Durham choristers at choral communion, *c.* 1780.

10. St Michael's College, Tenbury: the model choir school of the 1850s.

11a. Maria Hackett (1783–1874), 'The Choristers' Friend'.

11b. Sir Frederick Ouseley (1825–89), founder of St Michael's, Tenbury.

11c. Sir John Stainer (1840–91), St Paul's organist and former chorister, and Oxford musician.

11d. Reginald Couchman (1874–1948), master of the St Paul's choristers and founder secretary of the Choir Schools' Association.

12. Choristers of St George's Chapel, Windsor, c. 1852.

13. Chichester Cathedral, Owen B. Carter, 1853.

14. Conductor Sir Charles Groves as a St Paul's chorister with his mother *c.* 1920.

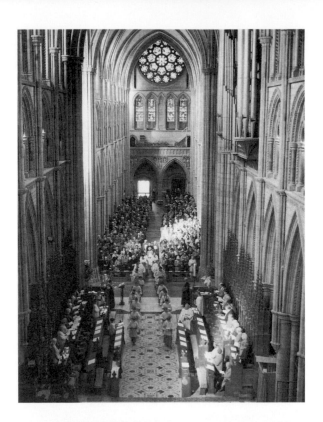

15. Truro Cathedral: Introit procession. Twentieth century choral worship.

16. Boy and girl choristers of Salisbury, 2002, including the successful spur money challenger.

Similarly, the restoration of income from some of the properties intended for the choristers' benefit followed directly upon her approach to Chancery.[18] But she got no further at St Paul's: in 1828 she complained that their arrangements for the choristers remained 'among the least creditable' and as late as May 1870 she is found writing to the leading churchman H.P. Liddon, newly appointed a canon there, bemoaning that non-resident choristers coming in from the suburbs daily were still provided by the cathedral with neither breakfast nor midday dinner. 'St Paul's contrasts unfavourably', she wrote, 'with the improved and improving condition of other capitular schools and in the watchful regard of the authorities for the welfare of their chorister boys.'[19] The changes that were to transform the lives of the St Paul's choristers later that decade, although they were the fulfilment of Maria Hackett's dreams, were the direct consequence of a new and determinedly reforming chapter.

It is possible that there is a direct connection between Miss Hackett's failure to elicit responses from St John's and Trinity colleges in Cambridge in 1817, reported in the *Gentleman's Magazine* of 1818 (where she praises the care shown by King's College for their choristers) and the actions taken by St John's and Trinity in 1819, as recorded in the St John's College Conclusions Book:

> Agreed that we do concur with the Master and fellows of Trinity College in the following arrangement respecting the choir: first that Dr Whitfield [John Clarke-Whitfeld] be employed to instruct in Music a sufficient number of Singing Boys for the service of the Chapels belonging to the two Colleges, and that he be paid ... £60 a year, *viz*: £40 by Trinity and £20 by St John's. Secondly that John Johnson be appointed Schoolmaster to instruct them in reading, writing and arithmetic, and in the Religious principles of the Church of England, with a salary of £24 a year, *viz*: £16 to be paid by Trinity and £8 by St John's College. Also that six boys to be so instructed be immediately put on our Establishment and paid the usual Salary.

The following year's accounts show St John's College spending money on schoolbooks for their choristers.[20] The joint arrangement between St John's and Trinity, which involved the sharing not only of choristers and organist but also of lay clerks, lasted until 1856 when the two colleges decided to go their own ways in chapel. Trinity's by then ten choristers and St John's' eight continued, however, to share one schoolmaster and schoolroom with a good library, as reported by Miss Hackett in the 1860s.[21]

At Chichester the prebendal rents that were supposed to fund their school brought in only £13 a year and its eighteen boys in 1866 were all aged under fourteen, nor is there evidence that any of them were choristers.[22] In the *Gentleman's Magazine* in 1818 Maria Hackett wrote that, with the exception of singing lessons, the patrons and guardians of the choristers did not 'interfere' in any way with their education. Could this damning comment have been the motivation that led the chapter to formulate new rules for their choristers in the following year? Later, in her *Brief Account*, she recorded despairingly that 'the Choral School of Chichester Cathedral has greatly sunk in public estimation', yet it was to be a further thirty years before the Chichester chapter set up a discrete school for their choristers. There simply is no evidence to show what part, if any, her visits to Chichester played in such a decision.[23]

All the same, it cannot reasonably be doubted that, in the fullness of time, her unremitting concern and her readiness to publish played a powerfully significant part in forming the growing public conviction that choristers needed good schooling and positive pastoral care. Over the decades during which she never ceased to make her visits and never ceased her correspondence with the clergy, masters and musicians responsible for the choristers, one by one the foundations, Chichester among them, took action to improve the conditions under which their boys lived, sang and were educated. Influential contemporaries in a position to know were certain that she had been a powerful force. In 1872 Frederick Ouseley contributed an essay on the education of choristers to J.S. Howson's *Essays on Cathedrals*. His final paragraph reads:

> In conclusion, the thanks of the writer of this Essay, as of all who sympathise with the cause herein advocated, are due to one who may be said to have been among the very first to draw attention to the status of our Cathedral Choristers, and to whom is due no small part of the improvements which have of late years been made in their treatment. With the name of no one could these remarks be more appropriately concluded than with that of the Choir-boys' greatest friend, Miss Hackett.[24]

A generation later, in his widely read and influential *History of English Cathedral Music*, John Bumpus outlined the improvements made between 1813 and 1830 in the condition of the St Paul's choristers. He added, 'These improvements were largely due to the exertions of that worthy, clever lady, Miss Maria Hackett, "the choristers' friend", who ... spent the greater part of her time in ameliorating the condition and education of the choristers, not only of St Paul's, but of those of every cathedral in England and Wales'.[25] Ouseley and Bumpus knew Miss Hackett well and their judgements cannot easily be gainsaid.

Meanwhile there were other forces for reform at work. The most potent of these was what came to be known as the Oxford Movement. In the 1830s, there was gathered at that university a remarkable group of young academic clergy, of whom the leading members were John Henry Newman, John Keble, Edward Pusey, Isaac Williams and, briefly, Hurrell Froude. They shared a horror of the slack, latitudinarian ways and theology of the Georgian Church of England and a deepening knowledge of their church's past. So they found themselves becoming a party, a movement that, on the basis of a shared patristic theology and a rediscovery of the Prayer Book's roots in pre-Tridentine medieval Catholicism, set out to return the worship of the 'Anglican' church to what they believed to be its lost seventeenth-century dignity.[26] They were, in the founding decades, in no sense ritualists, but they were serious liturgists and put prayerful and dignified congregational worship at the heart of their practice. They publicised their views in a series of *Tracts for the Times*. They were hugely influential, especially on several generations of young ordinands who were, first as curates, later as parish priests, ultimately as canons, deans and bishops, to spread their convictions and practice first to the parishes and later to the cathedrals. Unlike Maria Hackett, they had power to bring about direct change.[27] Well before they were to bring about reform to the worship and lives of cathedral choristers, young clergy fired by Tractarian convictions had created new choral foundations with teams of choristers in the parishes.[28]

The first indications of change occurred at the Margaret Chapel in Marylebone (later to become All Saints, Margaret Street) under the Rev. Frederick Oakeley, previously chaplain of Balliol College. There, from 1839, he established daily choral services sung by boys and men under the training of Richard Redhead, a former chorister at Magdalen College, Oxford. The boys wore surplices, virtually unheard of in parishes at that time, sang the psalms antiphonally and the canticles to choral settings.[29] Despite the boys being (in Oakeley's words) 'a mob of children from the lowest courts and alleys in the parish', they were painstakingly trained, all was meticulously rehearsed and the services were a model of orderly reverence. Growing daily congregations included the future dean of St Paul's, R.W. Church, and the future Prime Minister, W.E. Gladstone. Two years later, in 1841, the Rev. Dr. W.H. Hook introduced a robed choir of men and boys to his newly rebuilt parish church at Leeds.[30] Under the musical direction of S.S. Wesley the daily choral singing at Leeds Parish Church became nationally famous. A third and more influential place where daily choral services were sung by boys and men from the mid-1840s was the newly restored Temple Church in London, under the direction of former Chapel Royal chorister, E.J. Hopkins.

More significant still was the choral worship of the chapel of the Church of England's ground-breaking new teacher training college established at Chelsea in 1841, later to be known as known as St Mark's College. Here, the Oxford-educated Thomas Helmore was appointed vice-principal with the specific task of training the student-teachers of the college and boys from the college's 'model school' to sing the daily office in chapel, with a choir, to sing choral canticles and anthems, formed from the most musical students and the twelve best pupils at the school. Here, quite explicitly, was a missionary establishment for the dissemination throughout the land of the choral service – well before the cathedrals had awoken from their Georgian sleep of choral lassitude. As early as 1844 the choir were singing in a single week services by Tallis, Farrant, Gibbons,

Aldrich and Rogers as well as five separate anthems by Byrd.[31] Within three years they had a repertoire of seventy anthems drawn from Tudor to contemporary composers, German and Italian as well as English. It is not surprising that in 1846 Thomas Helmore was invited by the bishop of London to take on additionally the mastership of the choristers of the Chapel Royal, following the death of William Hawes, their master since 1817.

The Chapel Royal, once the crown of the English cathedral tradition, had, in the course of the eighteenth century, fallen into sad straits. Largely neglected by the monarchs, its choristers no longer maintained at St James's Palace, their condition in the early nineteenth century was pitiable. We have seen how William Hawes in 1813 had replaced the utterly neglectful John Sale as almoner of the St Paul's boys, and that, in his premises at Adelphi Terrace, the Strand, the chapter paid for him to board their four senior choristers. Four years later he had been permitted additionally to accept responsibility for boarding and training the Chapel Royal boys. Here, once again, there is an enigma. Hawes was a distinguished musician, full of initiative and at the heart of the music making of the capital; yet pastorally he was almost as neglectful as his disastrous predecessor.[32] Under him, a schoolmaster was brought in to teach reading, writing and the rudiments of arithmetic – predominantly the latter, according to John Goss, a chorister at the time – but on only two days a week for only an hour and a half on each of those days. Hawes's chief interests in life were directing the opera at the Lyceum, conducting the Madrigal Society, playing the organ at the Lutheran Chapel in the Savoy and, amongst other interests, running a music publishing business. Samuel Sebastian Wesley became one of his choristers in 1817, released from a home made miserable by poverty, by his severely depressed father, Samuel Wesley, and by his mother, Samuel's housemaid, the mistress who had displaced his wife. The Chapel Royal was the making of Sebastian. He was the apple of William Hawes's eye – 'the best boy I ever had' – and as a chorister he so impressed George IV that the king presented him with a gold watch. He loved the 'extra-curricular' music of the London theatres and concert halls to which Hawes took him. As a boy he sang in the first English performance of Bach's *Magnificat* and in an early, if not the first, English performance of the *St Matthew Passion* and he may have been amongst those who, under Hawes's direction, sang in the first modern performance of Tallis's forty-part motet. By his teens he was breaking new ground, playing Bach fugues. Yet for others Adelphi Terrace, under Hawes's neglect, was Hades. Frederick Walker was recruited to the Chapel Royal choir as a chorister in 1844. After eighteen months his father threatened to remove him on account of the unchecked bullying that went on.

> Two seniors would seize a junior and hold him down on his back, whilst a third would take hold of his nose and slit upwards with a penknife! … A junior boy was 'buried'. That

is, a sort of coffin was made with bolsters, pillows, blankets etc., and tied fast with sheets, so that the air was entirely excluded: this being done, he was hoisted upon the shoulders of his school-fellows, and tumbled into a large copper, and then, after dancing on the 'coffin' for about ten minutes, they dragged him out, generally in a fainting condition; but a copious supply of cold water brought him round.

Such is Walker's own account of his sufferings. At other times boys dressed only in their nightshirts were put out of the dormitory window onto the sill on bitter, frosty nights. And there was a fagging system that gave opportunity for other abominable cruelties.

All this barbarity stopped with the appointment as master of Thomas Helmore in 1846. The boys were moved from Adelphi Terrace to Helmore's home in Chelsea. Singing services at the Chapel Royal only on Sundays and high days, as they now did, they were found by Helmore to be seriously underemployed. He provided a rich daily academic programme embracing English, Latin, History, Geography, Euclid, Arithmetic and Scripture. They had daily choral practice and music theory and, most significantly, they became the stiffening in Helmore's treble line at St Mark's. Every day the citizens of Chelsea could see the twelve Chapel Royal boys, dressed smartly in their red-striped trousers and crown buttons, marching behind the equally smart Thomas Helmore to and from St Mark's College. It was this sight that drew the young Arthur Sullivan to pester his father until in 1854 he was himself allowed to become a Chapel Royal chorister.[33] Helmore's influence was to be felt primarily in the great wave of improved singing in parish churches. Some of these indeed became small choral foundations with choir schools. By far the most important of these, for the purposes of this history, was St Barnabas's, Pimlico, thanks to the vision, drive and wealth of one of its curates.

Sir Frederick Arthur Gore Ouseley, Bart, had not been a chorister.[34] Quite simply, sons of baronets did not become choristers. For one thing, the education would not do. So he was educated privately before going up to Oxford in 1843. Nevertheless, he was hugely musical, an infant prodigy. Perfect pitch was evident at seventeen months; aged about four he overheard a band playing a quarter-tone sharp and announced that the note they were playing was 'a kind of F but neither F natural nor F sharp'. Before he was three his sisters were able to write down little dance tunes he composed at the keyboard. Over two hundred compositions written before he was seven have survived.[35] As an undergraduate his intention was to seek ordination, and this intention was strengthened at Oxford by strong High Church influences. Also there, his musical talents were greatly extended and in his final year for several months he was acting organist of Christ Church cathedral. When staying in his family's London home, Ouseley began singing regularly in the choir of the Tractarian St Paul's, Knightsbridge, and there, as a deacon, he undertook his first curacy. When its vicar, W.J.E. Bennett, decided to build and run a daughter-church in the slum-filled southern part of his parish, Ouseley was asked to be one of its team of curates. The project was completed by 1849, and as well as the church (St Barnabas, Pimlico) it had also a clergy house, a large parish school and a residential choir school for twelve choristers who were to sing the daily offices.[36] Soon after the church was opened, however, it became the target of severe and famous anti-popery riots. These so distressed Ouseley that he resigned his curacy. Shortly afterwards St Barnabas was forced to close down its residential establishment of men and boys. But Ouseley was determined that the incipient group of choristers should not be disbanded. He managed to purchase property at Langley in Buckinghamshire and settle them there (as a sort of churchless choir school) under the charge of a fellow curate, with music instruction provided by an exceptionally gifted senior boy, John Hampton.

Ouseley himself went off for a year's tour of Europe to recover from the shock and to rethink his vocational future. In Germany he visited many churches, notably two with great choral traditions, the Kreutzkirche at Dresden and the Thomaskirche at Leipzig where Bach had been cantor. He found himself astonished by the quality of the choristers' singing. 'I have never heard anything equal or approaching to the excellence of their voices. The intonation is so true, and the style so tasteful and refined, and the quality so rich and round', he wrote. 'I am quite out of conceit with English chorister boys ... they are too often mere rabble.' When he pondered the reasons for the quality of these German boys, he concluded that they were drawn from a higher class of society than were typical English choristers. The root of the problem lay in the English choristers' homes where the boys were subject to 'very vulgarising, if not demoralizing, influences'.[37] He had for some time been pondering the establishment of a residential choral foundation and now the germ of the idea of what was to be St Michael's College at Tenbury began to form in his mind. He was determined that its choristers would be boys from Christian and cultured homes, sons of clergy and the professions, not from uneducated, low-class families as at so many British choral foundations. They would be taught Latin and Greek and they would go on from their choir school to good, academic public schools prior to university. Only in this way, he felt sure, could *musical* quality be assured.

When he returned to England his mind was formed and the six choristers and three probationers at Langley were his seed, ready in waiting for replanting in a suitable location. In 1852 he found what he deemed the right site, close to Tenbury Wells; in June he purchased the land. Later that year he was granted permission to build a church, which, whilst having a parish, could also operate as if it were the collegiate chapel of his intended foundation.[38] So, while at Langley the embryonic choir school was musically and liturgically active and growing in numbers, in north Worcestershire St Michael's College and its church began to rise. The church was consecrated on Michaelmas day 1856; in February 1857 the collegiate buildings were ready for occupation, his trebles came over from Langley and the round of daily services began.

Here was the ideal, hitherto so elusive in the established cathedrals and collegiate choral foundations. 'The object of the College', Ouseley would write, when in 1864 he conveyed ownership of the college to a board of trustees, was

> to form a model for the Choral Service of the Church in these realms ... [and] for the furtherance of this object to receive, educate, and train boys in such religious, musical, and secular knowledge as shall be most conducive thereto.

The essence was the church and its choral worship which was to be exemplary: a daily round of worshipful, dignified and seriously musical services – over five hundred a year – with an exceptionally wide repertoire of canticles and anthems. Only on Sunday mornings was the worship of St Michael's congregational rather than choral. The first requisite to achieve and maintain this exemplary worship was a choir school. To this end there were eight choristers (for whom no fees were paid) and eight probationers (who were charged a third of a fee) and all were required to be resident. Non-choristers, boarding and day, improved the educational challenges and brought in full fee income (apart from sons of clergy who enjoyed a 50 per cent rebate). Ouseley's vision of the centrality of the worship undoubtedly made its impact on the boys. Montagu Alderson, later to be a canon of Salisbury, was a chorister at St Michael's towards the end of Ouseley's time, of which he has written:

> Ouseley's chief aim and object in life was to make the worship of the collegiate church ... the focal point around which all other interests revolved. He made us, little boys as we were, to feel that we must put our whole being into this discharge of this Duty to God, and he inspired us with the beauty of this offering which we were called upon to make. Of course the music – the best of its kind at that time – made us love the august Prayer Book services. ... We sang to the praise of God and in the invisible presence of His Holy Angels. That privilege on our part could not be too highly prized.[39]

The college, largely unendowed and with full-fee paying pupils less easy to recruit than those on scholarships, was always financially insecure, indeed dependent upon Ouseley's readiness and ability to fund some half of the running costs.[40] So economies were made in the appointment of staff. A prime criterion in selecting teachers was their ability to sing, or even whether they were a tenor or bass. Ouseley himself sang alto. That the teaching was effective is to some extent confirmed by the range of careers to which his pupils proceeded: the church, the armed and colonial services, teaching, the law, engineering, banking, as well as farming and business. At least thirteen from Ouseley's time became professional musicians.[41]

Ouseley himself did not teach, not even music. He was warden and, of course, vicar of the parish, for which he cared assiduously. He had also, in 1855, accepted appointment as non-resident precentor of Hereford and election to the professorship of music at Oxford (a post that had been virtually a sinecure until he himself took things in hand). Although these roles and other concerns took him away from St Michael's from time to time, his pastoral and spiritual responsibility for the boys of his foundation was always paramount. They loved him, and as the years went by a significant part of his large correspondence consisted of affectionate letters from former pupils, always meticulously answered.

The impression given so far must be that early nineteenth-century reform of the lives and work of choristers lay entirely outside the cathedrals. Margaret Chapel, Leeds Parish Church, the Temple, St Mark's, Chelsea and St Michael's, Tenbury, were all new choral growths. But it would be quite wrong to conclude that there were no moves to improve the choral services and the circumstances of the choristers within the existing choral foundations themselves during the first half of the nineteenth century. There were musicians and there were clergy sowing seeds of reform.

When Samuel Sebastian Wesley went to Leeds in 1842 he had already given ten years' service to the cathedrals of Hereford and Exeter. As an organist he had no rival and as a composer he set out to transform the musical language of the cathedral quires, writing for his boys and men music more thrilling to sing than had been written by any English liturgical composer since Purcell. In 1832, after a year as organist of Hampton parish church, Middlesex, his vicar, John Merewether, was appointed dean of Hereford and Wesley found himself, aged twenty-two, head-hunted for the post of organist at the cathedral. Both there, and in his subsequent post at Exeter, however, Wesley was deeply frustrated by the circumstances in which he operated, battling with unsympathetic chapters who regarded musicians as the lowest form of cathedral life, with lay clerks and vicars choral who, when present, were often unbiddable, and with choristers who, to the brilliant Wesley, seemed unmusical and ill bred. Above all, he wrote great sounds for great buildings. He knew that his most celebrated predecessors had written for large choirs and it irked him to work with small choirs of men and boys who were largely inaudible in the spaces in which they found themselves. In his published tirade about cathedral music of 1849 he wrote:

> Music, as it is now performed in our Cathedrals when compared with well-regulated performances elsewhere, bears to them about the proportion of life and order which an expiring rush-light does to a summer's sun ... Thus it is, that the Choral Service of the Church presents not one feature in its present mode of performance which can interest or affect the well-informed auditor.[42]

Wesley went to Leeds because he believed that there he would find better conditions and the choral service valued as it had not been at either of his two previous posts; and he was right. But by then he had virtually given up on choristers. He would have much preferred not to have choristers in his choirs at all. Wesley's proposal for a remedy, along with more singers and better remuneration, was to replace choristers by women. Boys' voices, he maintained, 'are a poor substitute for the vastly superior quality and power of those of women'. But he reluctantly accepted that his preferred choice, the substitution of mature sopranos for immature trebles, was likely to be 'inadmissible'; so he fell back on a call for *more* trebles, ten to twelve at minimum, and he delegated the task of training the boys to one of his organ apprentices, believing it to be a task beneath a good organist's dignity. Under no circumstances, he was to write in 1849, should 'the organist, if a man of eminence in his art, be teazed with the tuition of the singing boys. The rudiments of an art may be better taught by those from whom nothing is expected in the higher branches.'[43] Nevertheless he demanded that his Leeds choristers should be taught to sing to the highest standards and he was not disappointed. But he missed the cathedral environment and in 1849 he successfully sought appointment as organist at Winchester. All went well at first, but by 1858 the chapter were recording their complaint that he was failing to teach the choristers (a task he urged should be undertaken by the precentor or a vicar choral). A year later he suffered a chapter admonition for absence from services: they had been counting and he had been absent from half of those he should have attended, leaving the organ in the hands of a fourteen-year-old boy. By 1861 his negligence was causing disasters: choral services falling apart and only two boys capable of singing solos.[44] As Humphrey Clucas has described, in his witty and touching poem, Wesley had been finding the Itchen fish more congenial than the cathedral singers.

> Preferring fishing to the human race,
> I make my way to where the gudgeon bite,
> The wilderness and the solitary place.
>
> I could not look my Maker in the face.
> I crawled across the transept, out of sight,
> Preferring fishing to the human race.
>
> The Dean and Chapter call for my disgrace.
> God's in the Itchen, in the morning light,
> The wilderness and the solitary place ...[45]

Not all the leading church musicians in the early years of Victoria's reign disparaged their choristers. Happily there were cathedral musicians at work at this time for whom the choristers and their training were, as at Tenbury, of first importance. Unquestionably the most remarkable was Zechariah Buck of Norwich.[46] In 1807 the cathedral organist of Norwich was Thomas Garland. He had been appointed to the post in 1749 at the age of eighteen and was to hold the office for fifty-nine years. One day in 1807 he was taking a stroll along the castle embankments when, from the ditch below, he heard the most beautiful voice of a young boy singing.

'My boy, who are you?' he asked.
'Zechariah Buck, sir', came the reply.
'You must come and be my choir-boy', said Garland.

So, with the agreement of his impoverished tradesman father, in September of that year, aged nine, Buck joined the choir. So exquisite was his voice, especially as a soloist, that one of the chapter, Canon Pretyman (not Pretyman, dean of St Paul's), took financial care of him and paid for him to have organ lessons. Seven years on, his voice having changed, he was apprenticed to Garland's successor, John Beckwith, as organist. Beckwith, however, was unwell: from 1817 Buck began to stand in for him and when, in 1819, Beckwith died, Zechariah Buck was appointed in his place, aged not quite twenty.

His first step on appointment was to seek and gain permission to undertake at his own expense a tour of English cathedrals in order to observe the best practitioners of the day at work. Throughout his career – and he was to be organist and choirmaster at Norwich until 1877 – his prime concern was the training of his boys' voices, and at this he was supreme. His fame was nationwide and equally famous were his idiosyncratic means of achieving his results. He based his work on that of the best Italian singers in England from whom he himself, the possessor of a rich alto voice, took lessons; but he added to their techniques his own eccentric methods. A boy who failed to sing the words 'Without Thee all is dark' from Mendelssohn's *Hear My Prayer* was sent to experience the full awfulness of darkness by spending time in a small, windowless cupboard. Hoarse voices were treated with gum arabic. Young soloists were sometimes prepared for their lone venture with a small vial of port. But most remarkable of all were Buck's devices for getting his boys to open their mouths fully. At first he tried filling their mouths as they sang with beans, marbles, acorns, coffee berries and nuts. The nuts proved the least successful because the boys were inclined to crack and eat them. Eventually he designed a small mouthpiece, shaped like an orange segment, hollowed with grooves for the teeth, made out of boxwood by the local ecclesiastical builder, B.W. Spaull, and supplied at sixpence each. (Some of his pupils subsequently had the devices copied in silver and kept as treasures.) He would exercise voices until they could reach C above the treble stave by requiring the boys to sing not only with theirs mouths open but also with closed mouths. One boy who was unable to sing top G open-mouthed found that he could reach the C above G with his mouth closed. Buck was a hard taskmaster, disciplining misbehaviour by canings called 'custards' and taking choristers out of their albeit brief academic lessons for extra practice on solos. But the musical harvest of all this endeavour was exceptionally sweet. As one who experienced the singing of Buck's choristers at first hand was to write, 'from the distinguished lad Smith of 1819 to the little Livelock of 1867, Norwich cathedral enjoyed so brilliant a succession of choir-boys that it maintained a reputation unrivalled for trebles, whose refined and finished style of singing was little short of marvellous'.[47] Perhaps the most notable fruit of Buck's teaching was the chorister Arthur Henry Mann, later to be the creator of the choral renaissance at King's College, Cambridge.

Not only the stars among the cathedral musicians were calling for higher standards. That there was a groundswell of dissatisfaction with the lax Georgian ways was strikingly illustrated by an initiative of about 1840. In the archives of Westminster Abbey there has survived, perhaps uniquely, a copy of a petition, or 'memorial' as it was called, sent from the organists of some twenty cathedral and collegiate foundations, supported by over thirty other professional musicians and 117 clergymen, to the 'Deans and Chapters of Cathedral and Collegiate Churches of England and Wales', bemoaning 'the imperfect manner in which the Service is at present performed in our Cathedral Churches' and offering a series of suggestions for its improvement.[48] It should be the organist who is in charge of a cathedral's music and he should be regarded by all members of the choir as their 'Musical Director'; as such he should attend every service.[49] In particular, he should, as Master of the Boys (as many statutes so term him), be responsible for the boys' musical training, both vocal and instrumental, with the discreet use of a practice room set aside for the purpose, where, at least once a week, the men also should practise with the boys. Lay clerks should be sufficient in number for the singing of antiphonal music, preferably four altos, four tenors and four basses at every service, matched by an adequate number of boys.[50] Among the musicians signing or supporting the memorial were Zechariah Buck, Turle of Westminster Abbey, Professor T.A. Walmisley, of Cambridge, Arthur Corfe of Salisbury, William Hawes of St Paul's and the Chapel Royal, and Sir George Smart, one of the Chapel Royal's organists. Notably but unsurprisingly absent from this company was Samuel Sebastian Wesley. Not one of the supporting clergy was a member of a cathedral chapter, but this may be because members of cathedral chapters, to whom the memorial was addressed, had not been invited to write to themselves. Certainly not all cathedral clergy were antipathetic to reform.

The reforms to the choristers' education at Canterbury and Lichfield have already been noticed. When Wesley's Hampton vicar, John Merewether, arrived at Hereford as dean he was horrified by the conditions he found in the cathedral's acts of worship. They were, he said, 'a disgrace, a blot to the Church – from the insufficiency, the coldness, the meagreness of the choral performances'. So he began fining not just vicars choral but also canons when they were absent from matins or evensong. He would personally castigate choristers when they were absent or slack. But the chapter dug in when faced by this imperious attitude and Merewether and Wesley found themselves facing insistent opposition to their endeavours for reform.[51] Durham was different, a cathedral where the liturgy had never been allowed to sink to the depths, as if the spirit of John Cosin continued to influence 'this sumptuous church'.[52] A very rich foundation, Durham saw to it throughout the eighteenth century that its singing men were of high quality, recruited nationally and generously paid, and that its choristers, though non-resident, were well taught and clothed under the cathedral's care, and given proper apprentice fees when they left. There is evidence intermittently that numbers were maintained by the appointment of probationary choristers in waiting. This care continued into the nineteenth century. When, in 1847, the organist, William Henshaw, complained to the chapter that his boys were neither punctual nor obedient, the chapter proposed boarding them, despite a likely increase in the cost of their maintenance from £236 to £460 a year. That they did not do so was due to a strong line from the parents who, despite the cost to them of night school after daily evensong, preferred to have their boys living at home. Two years later a change of precentor occurred and the Revd John Bacchus Dykes, the writer of notable hymn tunes, was appointed. He was to be resident and to be responsible for the boys' moral and religious development and to keep an oversight of their secular education and progress. Indeed, he was paid additionally for personally providing teaching in classics. From the late 1840's there was steady improvement in Durham's care of its choristers.

It is curious that Durham's exemplary care of its choristers should have attracted little other than local notice while reforms at Salisbury are part of the legend.[53] Walter Kerr Hamilton, precentor of Salisbury from 1843 and bishop from 1854, is rightly seen as one of the most influential reformers to serve the Victorian cathedrals.[54] He successfully attacked pluralism; he did much to restore the fabric of his cathedral; he opened it to the public free of charge at all hours and he founded its theological college. More importantly for the choristers, he made the choral worship orderly and beautiful. No longer did boys and men come into choir in twos or threes, putting their surplices on as they came. No longer was the choice of canticle setting or anthem made at the last minute, with the head chorister whispering the residentiary's choice to singers and organist. The choice became the precentor's (in discussion with the organist for high days and their eves) and anthems were carefully selected to reflect the church's year or the theme of the readings. More significantly, Hamilton as precentor caused the choristers' school to be transformed. He moved it to larger premises and appointed an efficient headmaster. The school was made economically viable by allowing the head to recruit non-choristers alongside the singing boys. Above all, Hamilton returned to Bishop Martival's roots and brought the choristers in as boarders under the care of a resident master. Yet within a decade, once Hamilton had become bishop and so found himself powerless to make orders for the cathedral, and perhaps because his expectations of rising income were not fulfilled, all this fell apart: the excellent headmaster resigned, the boarding of choristers ceased and the school relapsed to its dismal early nineteenth-century conditions. In any case, not all his proposals were practical: the notion that the cathedral chancellor should double as the school headmaster, while certainly giving the chancellor something to do, assumed that a headmastership was merely a part-time office.[55] In fact in many ways, although Hamilton's influence on the quality of the worship in Salisbury Cathedral was to be lasting, his influence as a major improver of the lives of the choristers was ephemeral. Its misleading fame rests on the coincidence that just as everything was at its best the Royal Commission on Cathedral and Collegiate Churches of 1852 was gathering its evidence and picked on Salisbury as its paradigm. So the Commissioners wrote:

> At Salisbury the Choristers' school is endowed with the tithes of Preshute which are expected to produce, in 1856, an income of more than £800. The boys are boarded in the Master's house, instructed gratuitously both in music and in general knowledge; they have a provision for clothes, and an apprentice fee of £30 on quitting the choir. *This is the most complete arrangement we have found existing in the old Cathedrals.* [My italics][56]

This is what Hamilton told them, and of course it was true. But they also received (though they may not all have read) a submission from the headmaster of the choristers' school, J.W. Richards. He pointed out that he was unsalaried, receiving only any fees paid by supernumerary non-chorister pupils and the sum paid by the chapter for the maintenance of the boarding choristers, that he personally had to pay for lodgings for the assistant master because the school house was too small to accommodate him, that one of the classrooms was his family dining room and that the choristers' dormitory, in the roof-space of the house, was unheatable in the winter and unventilatable in the summer. No wonder he resigned.

At this mid-century point the shadow of the Georgian nadir was still lying over the choristers of many of the choral foundations. Yet it is clear that calls for reform were becoming widespread and the essential elements for major transformation of the life, worship, education and music of the English chorister were all, here or there, already in place: brilliant treble training at Norwich; transformed and worshipful choral liturgy at Salisbury; wonderfully singable anthems and canticles from the pen of S.S. Wesley; a school dedicated to the serious academic as well as musical education of choristers at Tenbury. In the second half of the century these strands were to come together in foundation after foundation.

12

The Fruits of Reform

Sir Frederick Ouseley, designing his model choral foundation, sought excellence in four particular areas: in the worship, in the music, in the performers of that music and in the pastoral care and education of the boys. Paramount was the quality of the worship: that was the purpose of the Tenbury enterprise. The heart of the Georgian problem had been that, in most of the choral foundations in which boys sang, the quality of the worship was regarded with indifference by many of the clergy responsible for it. Yet without a desire for excellence in choral worship there was likely to be little concern for the welfare of the boys and men who undertook it. And if the maintenance of a daily round of exemplary worship was not the prime function of choral foundations, and especially of cathedrals, what was their purpose? From the 1830s this question was insistently and repeatedly asked, by individuals, by groups and, not least importantly, by government.

It had been in the 1830s that the then Whig ministry began to take an interest in the cathedrals. This interest was a response to widespread public outrage at the obscene contrast between the huge accumulated wealth that enabled many of the bishops and cathedral chapter members to lead affluent and seemingly idle lives and the failure of the Established Church to provide places of worship for the rapidly growing number of artisan families in new, churchless urban areas. The most direct consequence of the early parliamentary interest – the Dean and Chapter Act of 1840 – took no cognisance of, and was of no benefit to, choristers. On the contrary, by transferring from the cathedrals to the Church Commissioners great swathes of income-generating property and radically reducing the cathedrals' staffs of clergy, the Act might be thought to have made more difficult, and ultimately did make more difficult, the task of any cathedral chapter looking to improve provision for their choristers. Nevertheless, governments, having intervened once, developed a taste for reforming the Established Church. In 1852 and 1879 Royal Commissions were set up to enquire into the state and condition of the cathedrals and of collegiate churches such as Westminster Abbey and St George's Chapel, Windsor, and to assess how well these establishments were fulfilling their purposes. (The choral foundations of schools, universities and parish churches were outside the Commissions' remit.)

The reports of the Commissioners in the 1850s and 1880s are documents of the first importance for any study of the Victorian chorister. They identify exactly how many choristers were maintained at each cathedral and the selected collegiate foundations in the mid and late nineteenth century and can be compared directly with Maria Hackett's figures of 1837. They show us the pace of development at the choral establishments through the century, clearly identifying those foundations that gathered large bodies of trebles and those that remained static. In Table 2 are shown the numbers of choristers and probationers, sometimes called supernumeraries (designated 'P' in the table), reported by Maria Hackett for 1837[1] and by the Commissioners in 1853/4[2] and in 1882–4.[3] Numbers from other sources are given in square brackets.

TABLE 2

	1837	1854	Change	1884	Change
English Cathedrals					
Bristol	8	6+2P	–	18	+10
Canterbury	10	10	–	10	–
Carlisle	6	8+2P	+2+2P	?16	?+6
Chester	8	8+?P	+?P	12+?P	+4+?P
Chichester	6	10	+4	?	?
Durham	10	10+4 to 8P	+4 to 8P[4]	10+10P	+2 to 6P
Ely	8	12	+4	16	+4
Exeter	10	10+6P	+6P	12	+2
Gloucester	8	8+2P	+2P	8+2P	–
Hereford	8	8+2P	+2P	8+4P	+2P
Lichfield	8	8+4 to 6P	+4 to 6P	14 to 16	+6 to 8P
Lincoln	10	10	–	8+4	+2
London, St Paul's	8	8+4P	+4P	40(incl. P)	+2
Norwich	8	10+2P	2+2P	12	+2
Oxford, Christ Church	8	8	–	8[+5P][5]+5P	
Peterborough	6	6 or 8+4P	?+2+4P	?	?
Rochester	8	8+4P	+4P	8+4P	–
Salisbury	8	8+2P	+2P	14	+6
Wells	6	8	+2	8+4P	+2P
Winchester	8	8+2P	+2P	16+?P	+8
Worcester	10	10	–	16	+6
York	8	10	+2	?13	?+3

	1837	1854	Change	1884	Change
Welsh Cathedrals					
Bangor	14	?14	?–	14[6]	–
Llandaff	0	0	–	10+6P 'soon'	+10+6P
St Asaph	4	0	–4	14	+14
St David's	6	6	–	?	?
Collegiate Foundations					
Cambridge, King's	16	[16]	–		
Cambridge, St John's	6 from Trinity [8]	+2			
Cambridge, Trinity	10	[?]	?		
Eton College	10 from Windsor	[?]	–	[16+12P] from 1868	
London, Chapel Royal	[10]	[12]	+2		
London, Westminster Abbey	8	2+4P	4+4P		
Manchester Collegiate Church	4	10	+6		
Newark Parish Church	[5]	[5]	–	[5] until 1901	
Oxford, Magdalen	16	[16]	–		
Oxford, New	16	[16]	–		
Southwell Minster	6	6+4P	+4P		
Winchester College	12	[?]	?		
Windsor, St George's	10	12[7]	+2		

Two points of interest emerge from this table. The first is the identification of probationers as a specific category. Of course almost all choristers must have needed probationary periods, that is to say, there was almost always an initial period during which they could not usefully contribute to the choir. The exceptions will have been those boys recruited by impressment to privileged foundations, most especially the Chapel Royal. In those cases the master of the choristers had toured the country and picked out proven singers. But impressment had disappeared by the eighteenth century. There will of course have been boys who, as happens nowadays, joined foundation choirs after training elsewhere. It is unimaginable that Arthur Sullivan would have needed any probationary period on joining the Chapel Royal choir at the age of twelve. But those apart, right back to the days of monastic oblates new boys required a period of time in which to become useful. Also, it had been common for boys to be paid differentially according to seniority. Nevertheless, until the 1850s no figures have survived distinguishing between those boys who were professed choristers and those who were still more or less probationary. The distinction now clearly drawn by the Commissioners is a helpful one: probationers and choristers were to be categories universally adopted henceforward, though it is a pity that in 1879 the Commissioners did not ask specifically for probationer numbers.

The second striking point revealed by the table is that in the decade and a half between 1837 and 1854 numbers had begun to rise after the long doldrums of the Georgian years. Here is the start of a trend that was to become dramatic as the century progressed. One cannot from these tables produce unchallengeable figures for increased chorister numbers because one does not know whether Maria Hackett's census of 1837 included or excluded probationary boys in waiting. But it is incontrovertible that numbers were increasing almost everywhere. Even ignoring the probationers, the foundations were reporting over thirty more singing boys in 1854 than there had been in 1837. There is no mystery as to why this should be. The petition from the organists of 1840 will have come before every English and Welsh cathedral chapter and it specifically called for boys' numbers sufficient to balance the twelve men that they regarded as minimally adequate.[8] So it is that Maria Hackett, on an undatable asterisked page supplementary to her main 1827 report, after praising the 'indefatigable exertions' of Zechariah Buck, went on to commend the Norwich chapter for generously increasing the statutable number of their choristers.[9] By 1850 national musical standards, and indeed choral standards in parish churches such as St Peter's, Leeds, and the Margaret Chapel, were making the music of the cathedrals sound insipid by comparison. This was to be the tenor of S.S. Wesley's broadside to the Commissioners. The accession of canons influenced by the Oxford Movement to cathedral staffs, most famously at Salisbury, led a growing number of chapters to want their sung offices to be more musically adequate acts of worship. Confirmation that this was so comes from the Commissioners' report itself. They record that bishops and chapters had been calling for an increase in numbers of quire personnel 'in order that the choral services may be conducted with augmented power and effect', especially having regard to 'the vast dimensions of the noble fabrics' that call for the services of 'a full and efficient choir'. Ely, for example, had reported their recruitment of four additional boys (and by 1860, under the reforming Dean Harvey Goodwin, they were to add a further four) because of the inability of their eight men and eight boys adequately to perform choral music in so large a building.[10]

When, in 1879, the second Royal Commission was set up, inquiring into the condition of cathedral churches in England and Wales, its reports,[11] published between 1882 and 1884, reveal the accelerated pace of increase over these next three decades. To quote some examples: Bristol had doubled their chorister numbers and had increased their probationers from two to six; Ripon, made a cathedral in 1836, had increased from eight to twelve; the former eight choristers of Wells had become fourteen as had those at York; Lichfield had leapt from eight to fourteen or in good years sixteen. Sixteen was also the complement now at Winchester and Worcester. Chapter intentions to increase their chorister numbers can be seen in the frequent incorporation of minimum chorister strengths into the new statutes that the Commission invited each chapter to draft, such as 'no fewer than ten' (Canterbury), 'no fewer than twelve' to which number probationers were to be additional (Chester) and 'such number as the dean and chapter deem necessary' (Wells). The most dramatic increase of all was at St Paul's, and this hugely influential development we shall consider in detail later in the chapter. Overall numbers were further increased with the revival of Welsh choral foundations in the 1870s: twelve or more boys appointed to sing at St Asaph and fourteen at Bangor (but these two cathedrals had choral services only on Sundays and festivals); more significant was the recovery of a full choral establishment with a choir school opened at Llandaff in 1880, inspired by an article in the *Guardian* of 1871 about Hamilton's school for boarding choristers at Salisbury.[12] With the building of an Episcopal cathedral at Edinburgh there was provided from the start a Scottish choral foundation with a school for its boy choristers.[13] And in England, at Truro, in the first post-Reformation cathedral to be newly built, a statutory choir with choristers was determined upon from an early stage.

The year 1868 saw the achievement of something for which Maria Hackett had fought furiously and fruitlessly in the 1820s: the restoration of the Eton choristers and their school.[14] We have seen how the college had, at some uncertain post-Restoration date, replaced their own discreet choral foundation by sharing the use of the Windsor choristers and lay clerks. A parliamentary select committee in 1818 had observed that this was a deviation from the founder's intentions and Maria Hackett had brought this deviation to public notice in an article in the *Gentleman's Magazine* the following year and done paper battle with the provost thereafter. But the nearest the college came to changing their arrangements had been, during the middle decades of the century, to bring in a few boys from the Porny School, the little elementary school in Eton High Street, to sing at morning chapel.[15] Then in 1861 the Clarendon Commission was appointed to investigate the 'nine great schools'. Their report on Eton, published in 1864, condemned the abandonment of the college's choral foundation:

> We can discover no justification at all of the total neglect ... on the part of Eton College, of the statutable provisions that require the College to maintain a proper choir and choral

service in their own Chapel. [The] choristers were actual members of the College ... wholly maintained by it and enjoyed a right of preference in the election of Scholars. [So] the general model of existing cathedral establishments ought to be followed at Eton.[16]

Eton might ignore Miss Hackett: but it could not ignore the Parliamentary Commissioners. The sharing of choristers with St George's Chapel was abandoned following a final Christmas Day service at Eton in 1867. In the next year an elementary day school for sixteen choristers and twelve probationers was opened in a building close to College Hall. To widen recruitment, boarding the choristers was briefly tried in the 1870s but soon abandoned, the local singing boys reverting to the benefits of free education and a free lunch. In musical terms the refoundation was a success: within a few years, the boys, along with six lay clerks, were singing a repertoire of sixty canticle settings and approaching two hundred anthems.[17]

The late Victorian decades were also the high point of the parish church choral foundations with boy choristers. Some were of considerable distinction, notably Leeds Parish Church and, in London, All Saints, Margaret Street (formerly the Margaret Chapel), and St Andrew's, Wells Street.[18] Provincial churches with choir schools and weekday choral services included St John the Evangelist, Torquay (1861), All Saints, Clifton, Bristol (1868), St Michael's, Croydon (1871), St James's, Grimsby (1880), and St John the Evangelist, Upper St Leonard's (1881). Samuel Reay claimed to have established at Newcastle in 1843 'the first surpliced and regular antiphonal choir formed in the north of England outside a cathedral, with choral service and choral celebration performed by an efficient staff of men and boys from the parish school'. Reay went on to become the endowed schoolmaster and organist of that anomalous survival of the medieval parochial choral foundations, Newark parish church, with its five choristers singing daily matins and its diminutive 'song school' that survived until 1901.[19] But the twentieth-century emphasis on congregational participation in parochial singing, along with the unsatisfactory nature and high maintenance costs of a school for a few boys, were to doom all these choral foundations except for the unique survivor, St James's, Grimsby.

To return to the cathedrals, it is clear from the reports both of the 1850s and the 1880s that choristers were required to sing matins and evensong every day of the week in all cathedrals in England except newly-founded Ripon.[20] Choral communion was quite otherwise. At Bristol, Carlisle, Chester, Ely, Gloucester, Hereford, Lincoln, Manchester, Norwich, Peterborough and Wells in the early 1850s the sacrament was celebrated only once a month and on high festivals, and then never or scarcely ever chorally. Often, as had been widespread in the eighteenth century, communion was an appendage to matins, the 'second service'.

If the choir sang at all, it was restricted to the *Sanctus*, sung as a link between matins and communion, with Cranmer's threefold *Kyries* and the *Gloria* at the end, all of course in Prayer Book English. In some places this appendage to matins was evidently a nuisance. In the 1840s, as a young man, Frederick Temple, later to be archbishop of Canterbury, attended Sunday matins at St Paul's with the intention of remaining to make his communion. But a verger approached him and pointed out that if he stayed he alone would be causing a minor canon the 'bother' of celebrating.[21] When, in 1866, the dynamic and reforming Dean Duncome of York introduced a full choral celebration at the Minster he was ordered by his archbishop to discontinue it. Not until 1874 was it restored as a regular part of Sunday worship. By then Chester, Chichester, Ely, Exeter and Hereford had already adopted the initiative.[22] Thereafter the gathering frequency of choral communion as an independent service on Sundays and festivals was to be one of the major developments of the second half of the nineteenth century. Choral communion, entailing as it did an entirely new repertoire, added significantly to the demands on the choristers, not only in the services themselves but also in the additional rehearsal necessary.

Rehearsal time depended very much upon the current regime. While Chichester in the 1830s had managed on just three rehearsals a week, Exeter at the same time, Buck at Norwich throughout his long tenure and precentor J.B. Dykes at Durham in the 1850s and 1860s expected their boys to rehearse for some two hours a day.[23] F.E. Gladstone, Buck's successor as organist of Norwich, writing to the Commissioners in 1880, stated that his boys were engaged in the cathedral or song school for four hours every day, so that 'they certainly devote more time to the cathedral than any other member of the cathedral establishment (clerical or lay)'.[24]

It needs to be recalled that some cathedrals required the attendance of their choristers twice on almost every day of the year. Clearly this was not sensible. The headmaster of Bristol Cathedral School wrote to the Commissioners in 1854 that the boys' attendance 'at Divine Service twice every day the whole year without intermission is injurious to their health, education and morals'.[25] At Chichester, Maria Hackett recorded in her 'Recent Alterations' of the late 1860s that the choristers were given leave of absence for *one* week of the year (her italics), or a second week occasionally allowed if requested. A later addition, undated but almost certainly from the early 1870s, and perhaps a direct result of her pleading on the boys' behalf, notes that leave has been extended for all to four weeks a year.[26] In her later years the need for boys to have holidays became one of the principal elements of Miss Hackett's campaigns. At Westminster Abbey, she recorded in her additions of the 1870s, choral services were maintained by giving choristers holidays 'alternately', that is to say, by using half the chorister force by rota during holiday periods. At Windsor, during the school's summer vacation, the boys were given breaks from singing, two boys at a time for a fortnight, again by rota.[27] A decade later the Bristol chapter adopted a similar rotational scheme – it had been proposed by the headmaster in 1854 – for what might seem to be the opposite purpose. They reported to the Cathedral Commissioners in 1882 that 'all the choristers have to attend both [daily] services if required; but we increased our number of choristers for one reason among others, that we may be able through a system of relays to afford more time for the younger boys of attending school'.[28]

An important aspect of reform was the recognition that hours spent in the choir stalls could be of little spiritual value to choristers unless the nature and importance of what they were about was borne in on them. Dignity and decorum were to be of the essence. Georgian choristers had wandered in before the service in twos and threes; gradually from the mid-nineteenth century processional entry and recession became the custom. The choir of Wells, for instance, adopted the practice from Whitsun 1847.[29] In the 1860s Hereford was regarded as unusual in preceding the introit procession with vestry prayers. But from then on the practice spread, and vestry prayers were adopted at Chester from 1869, at Lincoln from 1871 and at St Paul's from 1872. Dignity of worship could be aided by decorum in dress. In 1861 Dean Duncombe at York put the choristers into cassocks and surplices in place of their former fur-trimmed coats. Initially, in the nineteenth century choristers wore open-fronted (and often unwashed) surplices, flapping open over secular clothes, as in the 1852 pen and ink sketch from St George's, Windsor, or indeed as is still the custom today (though well laundered) for non-choir members of some Oxbridge colleges on Sundays, feasts and their eves. The change, in the second half of the century, was initially into unslit surplices but still over day clothes (with trouser legs visible). Then cassocks were introduced beneath the unslit surplices in a quire garb that left unseen all hint of secular clothing, as at Lincoln from 1886 and at Westminster Abbey from 1897. St George's, Windsor, replaced their trouser-revealing, open-front surplices with cassocks and unslit surplices early in the twentieth century. By then this was the standard quire dress for most groups of choristers – though not everywhere: Winchester college quiristers continued to wear surplices over secular clothes without cassocks until 1939.[30]

Most significant of all, however, was an overt recognition that choristers were ministers of the church and members of the collegiate body and should perceive themselves as living out a vocation. The Commissioners in the early 1880s, recognising perhaps for the first time that no two cathedrals were the same, and that many, if not all, were hamstrung by anachronistic statutes, invited each chapter to submit to them its own new draft statutes. And just as the Henrician statutes for the New Foundation cathedrals following the Dissolution of the monasteries invariably included a statute about the choristers, so most of the chapters in 1882 and 1883 had a stab at defining the role of their choristers in their draft statutes. Some were heartlessly minimal. At Hereford:

> The Choristers shall hold their offices at the pleasure of the Dean and Chapter, and on such terms as shall be fixed from time to time by the Dean and Chapter. [Draft statute 17][31]

Some were less dismissive and more thoughtful, none more so than that drafted for the new cathedral foundation at Truro, doubtless by its bishop, who was also uniquely its dean, Edward White Benson (formerly master, that is, headmaster, of Wellington College and subsequently to become archbishop of Canterbury), a statute that combined an over-riding pastoral concern with an eye for practical detail.

> The choristers, being younger ministers of the Divine Worship, are to be cared for sincerely as to their good morals and manners, their good teaching and advancement in life. The choir scholarships are to be strictly bestowed and payments made to or for the boys, as good as may be, with some insurance set aside through the hands of Mr Treasurer, and pains taken for their well placing when they leave the choir. Let them be taught music well and without severity. The explanation of the Psalms to have ever a place in their teaching. The two elder to follow the Canon in the course of procession, and two by turns to put books in order and to find places for the Canons, vicars and singers in the music books before service, so that they all may read the Lessons and pray the prayers without distraction. All to have Bibles in their places and read therein; one or two to go before preachers to the pulpit if bidden. [Draft statute 25][32]

Serious attention to the spiritual role and training of the choristers seems to have been little considered since medieval times. Now it was to become a major concern of those responsible for the upbringing of choristers, as will be evident, subsequently, from the frequent discussions of the matter at early meetings of the Choir Schools' Association headmasters. Benson's requirements that the boys should understand the psalms and follow the lessons and prayers in their books were symptomatic of this new emphasis. The concern also led to consideration of how new choristers should be admitted. Throughout the nineteenth century, admission could be very casual. Herbert Brewer, later to be organist of Gloucester, as a boy desperately wanted to become a chorister of that cathedral. But he had wilfully given up singing in his parish church choir and, when examined by the Gloucester organist, C.H. Lloyd, was found not to be a very good singer, though a promising pianist. He was given a place, nevertheless, so that he could keep an eye on his younger brother who was also admitted at the same time. Lloyd's judgement was poor. The younger boy's voice never developed but Herbert's blossomed brilliantly and within a year he had begun a four-year stint as head chorister and principal soloist.[33] At Magdalen College, Oxford, we can catch the point at which the selection and occasion were still casual but the actual admission was taken seriously. On 25 October 1847, L.S. Tuckwell, orphan son of a medical practitioner, was told to report to the college's dean of divinity at 3 p.m. The dean took him to the president's lodging where the president, Dr Routh, could just be discerned, 'hidden, gowned in a deep armchair'.

> 'My boy', Dr Routh said, 'your father by his skill brought me through a very serious accident, and when I heard of his death I was glad to have a choristership to offer to you … God bless the lad, be a good boy, and do what the Organist tells you.'

Then, addressing the dean of divinity, Dr Routh added, 'See that he is properly admitted'. So young Tuckwell was taken back to the dean's rooms, had a surplice formally put on him, was given an apple and an orange and thus was admitted.[34] Then, after evensong, the master of the choristers took Tuckwell to his room in college, impressed upon him the solemnity of what had happened and gave him a volume of prayers and instructions that he had compiled.[35] So mid-century Magdalen was a place where choristerships were taken seriously, though admission itself was still informal. But it began to be seen that such a mode of admission to five or more years of duty in quire was too casual. The introduction of a simple rite of admission in quire for new choristers, with prayers and investiture into the surplice, was perhaps first introduced at Norwich about 1871, and subsequently was adopted widely, though not universally.[36] Here, incorporating, it may be noted, Dr Routh's two admonitions and the dean's investititure, but much expanded and coloured by Benson's antiquarian turn of mind and phrase, is his solemn and potent Truro rite.

> Form of Admitting a Chorister
>
>   On the day appointed, after the conclusion of Evensong, the boy to be admitted shall be brought by the precentor (or his deputy) to the stall of the Bishop (or Canon who is to admit him), the senior chorister attending and holding the surplice to be worn by the candidate. The Precentor then says:
>   Reverend Sir, I present to you this boy to be admitted a chorister[37] of this Cathedral church.
>
> Q. Do you desire to be admitted a chorister of this Cathedral church?
> R. I do.
> Q. Do you promise obedience to the Lord Bishop[38] and chapter, and all officers duly set over you?
> R. I do.
>
>   Then shall the candidate for admission kneel down before him and he shall take his hands between his own and say:
>   In the name of the Father, and of the Son, and of the Holy Ghost, I admit thee [here naming him] to be a chorister of this Cathedral church. Then shall he take the surplice

and place it on the boy and thus address him as he stands before him:

Thou art admitted a chorister of this our church. Take thou good heed that what thou singest with thy mouth thou dost believe in thy heart, and what thou believest in thy heart thou dost practise in thy life. Then all kneeling he shall say:

V. Behold now praise the Lord all ye servants of the Lord.

R. Lift up your hands in the sanctuary and praise the Lord.

Let us pray.

Almighty and everlasting God, be Thou merciful unto our sins, and purify this Thy servant from the service of the world; that being clothed with Thy grace for ever, he may by Thy power keep the eternal inheritance in his heart; through Jesus Christ our Lord who liveth and reigneth with Thee and the Holy Ghost, ever one God, world without end. Amen.

Then sitting in his stall he shall say:

My Son, you must know that you have honourable standing in our church: see that you never lose it by fault of yours; and that by all good ways and works you study to please God. May he grant you so to do through his Holy Spirit. Amen.

Then the boy shall take his place in the choir, and Psalm cxxii shall be chanted.[39]

It will have become evident that in the care of choristers the role of individuals, deans in particular, could be paramount. In 1865 the young Mandell Creighton, later to become bishop successively of Peterborough and London, gave up regular worship at the cathedral in his native Carlisle, on account of the general air of slackness, not least 'the small boy choristers amus[ing] themselves all the time by squabbling and pinching each other in the middle of a chant ... while the precentor sits blinking above, looking down on all this irreverence, which he plainly sees, with an air of abject helplessness'.[40] The dean of Carlisle at the time was Francis Close, who, in his Cheltenham days, had tried to close down the Three Choirs Festival, and who took some time as dean of Carlisle to appreciate the spiritual blessings that well-sung cathedral services could dispense.[41] Increasingly from the late 1850s, however, very able men deeply committed to the liturgy and to the welfare of its singers were being appointed to influential cathedral posts. When Augustus Duncombe became dean of York in 1858 he was dismayed at the state of the Minster, its structure mouldering and its services 'cold, flat, meaningless and without life'. Four years later he took on additionally the office of precentor in order that he would have authority to improve the standard of the services. He personally donated £2000 to increase the Minster's choral forces.[42] Chester Cathedral's physical restoration and the revival of its worship stemmed from the appointment of John Howson as dean in 1867. Everything he touched was said to have been transformed by his unaffected and straightforward vision and vigour. Vestry prayers from 1869 set the tone. He inherited a nave 'used only as a place for loitering'; by 1872 it was packed with worshippers at Sunday evening services.[43] At Ely, under Harvey Goodwin, dean from 1858 to 1869, the choral worship came to be regarded by some as the finest in England. The musicians, of course, were also important: Duncombe attracted E.G. Monk to York and Howson appointed J.F. Bridge who, after Chester, was to transform the music of Westminster Abbey and earn himself a knighthood.

Most influential of all was the cluster of great men gathered together at St Paul's Cathedral. Robert Gregory was appointed a canon in 1868, later to become dean; H. P. Liddon, the finest preacher of the age, came from Oxford in 1870; the following year they were joined by the Cambridge theologian J.B. Lightfoot and the Gladstone-nominated Richard Church as the new dean. They were four visionary and determined men who, unusually for such a circumstance, formed what has been widely recognised as an outstandingly harmonious and effective chapter. Together they turned St Paul's from being a byword for dismal slovenliness into a worshipping community that drew thousands to it and became – what it should always have been – a beacon to the whole nation.

We have seen the dire conditions in which the St Paul's choristers existed, despite the best efforts of Maria Hackett. Even after the termination in 1846 of William Hawes's negligent oversight of the boys their circumstances went on being unsatisfactory. A brief attempt at boarding all the boys ended in 1848. Thereafter they slept at home but, between 9.30 a.m. and 6 p.m. each day, they were to attend the cathedral and its school. They sang two services, were taught singing for ninety minutes and given schooling by a grammar master for three hours. Their only food and refreshment throughout these more than eight hours was such as they brought with them from home. They had some respite from school lessons at Christmas, Easter, Midsummer and Michaelmas but were still required to come and sing the services. The services were all too often distressing occasions: notwithstanding the high musical standing of Sir John Goss, organist from 1838, the men of the choir were irresponsible, the chapter showed little interest, and Goss, from his eyrie in the organ loft, had no control over the boys who were slovenly and ill-disciplined.[44] Maria Hackett reported an occasion in September 1834 when she suffered hearing the anthem *O Never Bow Me Down* 'never so ill performed'.

Shortly after his appointment in 1868 Robert Gregory was told by a minor canon, 'Do not imagine that you can make any changes or improvements … this is an Augean stable that nobody on earth can sweep'.[45] Gregory was determined to prove him wrong. On All Saints Day 1869 he was appalled by the slovenliness of the two services. The following morning, after matins, instead of following the verger into the canons' vestry he accompanied the choir into the south aisle and there, under his authority as canon in residence, told the singers that there had got to be improvement: meticulous attendance; dignified processional entrances and exits; no secular reading or chattering during the service, and care for their quire dress. Part of the trouble, of course, was Goss's lack of authority. He was by then almost seventy and in indifferent health. As late as 1871 it was reported of a Sunday evensong: 'At no time did there appear to be more than an irregular confused hum of children's voices, trying to sing something of which the majority seemed incapable'.[46] In 1872 Goss was persuaded, with the offer of a pension, to retire. Liddon knew, from his Oxford years, that there was one man who could transform the music, the former St Paul's chorister, now organist of Magdalen College, John Stainer. The chapter offered him the post and persuaded him, not without some difficulty, to accept. He knew the mess he was inheriting and asked for two years free of criticism in which to put things right. Within that time, with his combination of personal devotion, drive and efficiency, and above all his kindly and irresistible charm, he had a responsible team of willing singing men, regular in attendance, enthusiastic, respectful in quire.

Improvement for the choristers was to be even more dramatic. Two years before Stainer's arrival the chapter had determined that there must be a new choir school, providing for more choristers, all boarding. Stainer was able to bring to their discussions and plans his experience of St Michael's, Tenbury, and of the benefits boarding had brought to the Magdalen boys. As for numbers, Stainer wanted not the eight choristers and four probationers that he inherited but *forty*. The chapter agreed. A site for a new school had been secured just to the south west of the cathedral in Carter Lane, and £20,000 was committed to the new building. It was to have state of the art facilities: a large dining room and kitchens, proper ablutions adjacent to the dormitories, studies, a song-room where Stainer could conduct his practices and, on the roof, a playground, caged in with wire mesh, where the boys could play football. There was to be a minor canon as headmaster with assistant teachers who could teach a full preparatory school curriculum. Candidates, recruited nationwide, were, of necessity, to be musical but were also expected to possess a good educational foundation. Board and education were to be free, with the parents paying for specified clothing, travel and pocket money. In 1873 twelve additional choristers were elected, all as boarders, accommodated temporarily at 1 Amen Court, where Stainer and his family were later to live. Building began in January 1874 and on 26 January 1875 the new school opened. Not long before the opening Stainer was able to bring Maria Hackett, now in her ninetieth year, to see and look round the fulfilment of her dreams, guided by the man whose earliest organ lessons she had charitably funded, now in charge of the music of her beloved St Paul's.[47] By 1880 the choir had forty boys, matched by twenty men, of whom never less than twelve were to be present on every weekday. The choral sound, that hitherto had been just audible in the quire on a good day, could now fill the nave, as was necessary on Sundays for the crowds who came to hear Liddon preach, the choir sing and Stainer send them home with a thrilling voluntary. Each year in Holy Week from 1873 Stainer's choristers had the incomparable experience of singing in Bach's

St Matthew Passion to full orchestral accompaniment, the work in whose first English performance (but without orchestra) Stainer had sung in the Hanover Rooms in April 1854 as a treble.

Twenty years before the chapter of St Paul's had resolved the seemingly intractable problem of how to give a proper education to boys whose first priority and most time-demanding requirement was singing the praises of God in quire, the Cathedral Commissioners had grappled with this very matter. Impressed by what W.K. Hamilton had achieved at Salisbury, they recommended in their 1855 report:

> That there should be connected with every cathedral a school in which the choristers should receive a sound, religious, liberal and useful education, in addition to their musical training; and that they should receive an apprentice fee on leaving the choir, with the approbation of the Chapter, except in the case of their receiving an exhibition to the University, and that new choristers should be boys likely later to be apt for the Grammar School.[48]

Here we see government chastising those few foundations at which they had found no schooling whatsoever provided for the choristers; suggesting an alternative to those foundations where the grammar school struggled to educate choristers as part-time pupils in special junior classes; and chiding those foundations that threw their broken-voiced boys out into the world without any financial aid. Perhaps most surprisingly the Commissioners addressed the issue of the *kind* of boy the foundations should be recruiting, showing a strong preference for boys who, like the medieval choristers, would be apt for grammar schooling and, hopefully thereafter, for university, rather than for those who would go on at fourteen or fifteen to apprenticeships.

What the Royal Commissioners were calling for was the best kind of discrete elementary school, such as had worked satisfactorily at least from time to time at St George's, Windsor, Durham (despite the appallingly inadequate premises),[49] Exeter and Wells. Other foundations in the 1840s and early 1850s had already been seeing this as the way forward for the education of their choristers. First, perhaps, had been Winchester Cathedral, where a chorister school was opened in the early 1840s. In 1845 at Canterbury, as we have seen, a grammar master to the choristers was appointed, followed in 1847 by a choristers' schoolmaster at Westminster Abbey. In 1850 both Chester and Chichester opened chorister schools and Lincoln was set on tidying the messy arrangements they had hitherto tolerated. Worcester ran such a school from 1852 for ten years, then closed it, then tried again in 1881. The Commissioners, dazzled by what might nowadays be called the 'spin' of W.K. Hamilton, thought they had found the perfect exemplar at Salisbury, and indeed so it might have been had it not proved ephemeral.

They were just too early to be able to learn from Ouseley's ground-breaking establishment at Tenbury.

Yet the discrete elementary schools were to prove a false lead. The elementary schools took boys in at the age of seven or eight and kept them until their voices broke, which might, in the nineteenth century, be at any age between thirteen and eighteen. At that point – with, if they were lucky, a 'good commercial education' – the boys would be sent out into the world, armed with a modest golden handshake towards an apprenticeship. These little schools of perhaps a dozen pupils with a wide age range were utterly dependent on the quality of the lay clerk, vicar choral or minor canon who for the time being had been chosen by the chapter to teach the boys. The education could be just about adequate or, in rare happy cases, really rather good, or scandalously useless. Toward the end of the century we find the inspectors being scathing about many of them. In the course of the nineteenth century chapters desperately and often blindly felt around for a solution to the seemingly intractable problem of the innate inadequacy of these elementary schools; of the problem of how adequately to educate boys who were obliged to spend their best hours learning or performing church music. York and Winchester provide case studies of two chapters mired in distressing attempts to find a solution to the problem.

The York choristers were almost certainly being educated at St Peter's School in Minster Yard until that school moved out in 1844 to Clifton, too distant from the Minster for the choristers. So the boys were sent to be guinea pig pupils in the newly-opened Diocesan Teacher Training School nearby until, after very few years, the chapter decided that it was too expensive and sent them to the Manor School where the cost was a penny a boy per week. This too would not do and in 1850 they tried 'Mr Ashworth's School'. By 1858 they were back to having the boys taught in the Zouch Chapel and its vestry by a vicar choral and then by a rapid succession of short-lived lay clerks. Dean Duncombe saw that this was not good enough and had a house in Minster Yard converted to provide a schoolroom and residential accommodation for a master and boarders. This brave experiment, perhaps modelled on that of Salisbury, lasted from 1874 to 1887, but then 'for divers good causes' – unspecified – it was closed and the boys were sent to Archbishop Holgate's Grammar School, desperately short of pupils at the time. By 1903, however, that school was flourishing and their part-time chorister pupils were a bother. The chapter was requested to remove them.[50] It is a desperate saga, but not unique.

Winchester, both cathedral and college, also saw the establishment of a diocesan training school as a way of avoiding the limitations of a tiny elementary school. The cathedral boys had been thrown out of the local Central School in 1818, 'all measures hitherto taken in the regard to the Choristers having proved totally ineffectual' in trying to cure their 'irregular example'. For six months they were taught with the college quiristers, then separated from them and put in the charge of a lay vicar, William Garrett. But, as at York, a diocesan training school was established and in 1840 took over the premises of the quiristers' school for its model school and enrolled the two sets of singing boys as its guinea pigs. Garrett became a simple lay clerk once more. Then, as at York, the model school was found not to be the best arrangement. In 1843 the quiristers were withdrawn and put under the care of a young man of seventeen who had been one of their student teachers, William Whiting, best known today as the author of *Eternal Father, strong to save.* He was to prove an admirable choice and remained their much-loved schoolmaster until his death in 1878, a case of a small elementary school that really worked well.[51] (So it was not necessarily scandalous that the Exeter choristers in the 1850s had their education at the hands of a pupil of the Diocesan Training School.)[52] Meanwhile the cathedral choristers had been withdrawn from the training college's model school a year after the quiristers and returned to the care of lay clerk Garrett, with whom they remained until 1856. A few years previously a training college lecturer had opened in the town the Mathematical and Commercial School with boarding facilities. It was to this school that the chapter decided to move their choristers in 1857, enabling them, on Wesley's urging, to recruit 'from any locality' and board some at least of their boys. By the 1870s, however, parents were complaining that the Commercial School was unsatisfactory and the Commercial School was complaining that the part-time pupil choristers 'materially interfered with the general work of the school'. So the chapter found a house in the Close (later to become the judges' lodgings), once more abandoned boarding and appointed another lay clerk to be schoolmaster to the now fourteen choristers, along with up to a dozen 'prospective choristers' from the town. On Whiting's death in 1878 the sixteen college quiristers joined the school yet again, and yet again abandoned the experiment after a short time, in part owing to rivalry and animosity between the two sets of unangelic singing boys.[53]

The alternative favoured by most of the former monastic foundations was to educate their choristers in their Henrician grammar schools, alongside their more numerous non-chorister pupils. But with the curriculum in the grammar schools becoming increasingly demanding, so long as the choristers were required to sing matins mid-morning, evensong mid-afternoon and be taught their music once or twice a day, the singing boys were at a severe disadvantage. As was reported to the Commissioners by T.B. Power, the headmaster of Hereford Cathedral School in 1854, the choristers suffered from 'a comparatively small portion of time allotted to school', so most left between the ages of twelve and fifteen in order to go into trade, with little more than 'a fair knowledge of their own language'.[54] We find headmasters wringing their hands about what to do with these pupils who were in effect part-timers, and the chapters responding by taking the boys out of the grammar school and, as urged by the commissioners, opening an elementary school. Such was the case at Ely in 1857, where in the early 1850s the cathedral grammar school had been 'in the lowest stages of decay' and the chorister pupils had 'no notion of school work or school discipline'. At Worcester, as we have seen, by 1882 'the inconvenience of having a large proportion of the school absent for a considerable portion of every day' had become so obvious that a discrete chorister school was re-established.[55] At Bristol the cathedral school, supposedly a grammar school, had by the early nineteenth century effectively become an elementary school.[56] The cathedral school at Carlisle, where the eight choristers were supposed to be educated, had twice prior to 1850 nearly ceased to exist and in 1843 had no pupils on roll at all.

Not all the grammar schools educating choristers were disastrous. The King's School at Peterborough seems to have managed to provide satisfactorily for its choristers throughout the period. And there was one foundation with an academic secondary school where, thanks to specific provision for its choristers, all the reforming elements came together to produce something like ideal circumstances: Magdalen College, Oxford.

Magdalen had never suffered the worst aberrations of Georgian negligence, but in the mid-nineteenth century two individuals with a deep commitment to choral worship and the welfare of choristers brought a pervading influence for good to that foundation. One was the choristers' schoolmaster, Mr Millard, himself a former Magdalen chorister. He was part of a larger school, yet specifically responsible for the choristers. He was deeply committed to the choristers' primary purpose: 'nothing angered him so much as slovenly behaviour at prayer and irreverent treatment of holy places and things'.[57] He it was who had presented the young Tuckwell with a book of prayers and instructions following his admission as a chorister. Two examples of his care for his boys were the high quality of the food and beer – vouched for by the boys themselves – and his insistence, in a school hard by a river, that every boy should from his earliest days be a competent swimmer.[58] It was on his initiative that in 1849 the college made a property, 58 High Street, available in which to board all the choristers together after a long period of their living at home or in lodgings. Two years later the college was to provide the boys with a new and much improved schoolroom. Millard could not have achieved these advances without committed college backing. The most influential of the fellows was John Rouse Bloxam, sixth son of the under-master of Rugby School during the legendary headship of Thomas Arnold. At Oxford, where Bloxam came under the spell of John Henry Newman,[59] he was elected to a fellowship at Magdalen College in 1836 and was resident there until 1862. Sometime dean of divinity, bursar, vice-president and librarian of the college, he had a passionate concern for its choral tradition and took a personal interest in the welfare of the singing boys. Thanks to his initiatives certain days of the year became indelibly planted in the memories of former choristers as imbued with a golden glow.

Gaudy Day was one such, when the choristers waited at tables, the senior chorister attending personally on the president, the boys competing as to who could make the loudest 'pop' as the soda bottles were opened. Later, when the diners were 'in a comfortable condition and inclined to be generous' the boys went round for tips. The four senior choristers each received a bottle of port. (L.S. Tuckwell used to sell his to the organist, Dr Corfe, for 4s. 6d.) More memorable still was Christmas Eve. School term had ended four or five days earlier, the choristers continuing in residence, being left to enjoy themselves and indulged with a round of parties by members of the fellowship. On the morning of Christmas Eve they sang 10 a.m. matins, followed by a rehearsal of the evening's festive programme. In the afternoon the boys went out to the Civet Cat, a favourite Oxford shop, where they bought presents that were put into silk bags and hung from the Christmas tree. Then, that evening, came the party. In the early years it was held in the set of rooms of its initiator and host, Dr Bloxam, but growing numbers of guests led to its move into college hall. At 9 p.m. there was a performance of part 1 of Handel's *Messiah*. Then, with the choristers seated at high table, waited upon by adults, came the supper of frumenty (wheat cakes boiled in milk with sugar, cinnamon and other rich spices), mince pies and the mulled wine called negus. Carols were sung and presents were exchanged. Precisely at 11.57 p.m. there was silence. Then at midnight the college bells sounded the hour and Pergolesi's *Gloria in Excelsis* 'rose like an exhalation'.[60] Finally a loving cup sent them home ready for the morning's choral celebrations. Unsurprisingly, one fellow complained that the party outshone Christmas Day itself.[61]

John Bloxam was responsible for another and more lasting initiative. We have seen how the custom at Magdalen of having the choir sing from the top of the 144 foot tower may well have begun with the 'topping out' celebration in 1509 or thereabouts.[62] The earliest specific reference to the ceremony is found in a late seventeenth-century Bodleian Library manuscript,[63] recording the annual payment of £10 by the rector of Slimbridge to Magdalen College, Oxford, 'to keep up ye ancient Custome there on May Day, when ye Quire entertain the place with musick vocall and Instrumentall from the top of ye Coll Tower'. John Pointer in 1749 referred to 'a Concert of Music upon the Top of the Tower, every May-day, at 4 o'clock in the Morning', and, improbably, thought it originated from a requiem mass for Henry VII, 'the founder of the tower'. Wade's guidebook of 1817 first mentions the singing of a hymn, the *Te Deum Patrem Colimus*, written as a college grace by Benjamin Rogers (*informator choristarum*, 1665–86). All explanation as to how a secular concert became the singing of a Latin hymn are of dubious reliability, most dubious of all being the story that *informator* Philip Hayes (1777–97) was so stout – 'as big as six ordinary men' – that had he tried to mount the tower 'he would have been stuck fast, like [a sweep] in a tight chimney', so the choir went up without him and sang the simplest thing they knew. What is certain is that by the early nineteenth century the occasion had become a bit of a riot. Men and boys ascended the tower in their secular clothes and sang the hymn with their hats on. Down below the town boys gathered, trying to drown the singing by banging cans and blowing tin trumpets, to which the choristers responded by throwing down rotten eggs upon them. There is a reliable report that on 1 May 1840 some hundred eggs were rained down. John Bloxam was deeply offended by this. In 1844 he decided to impose changes. Using his authority as dean of divinity (later confirmed by the president) he ordered the choir to ascend the tower in their surplices and, for the singing of *Te Deum Patrem Colimus*, to uncover their heads and turn east toward the rising sun. This intervention proved to be transforming. Fellows of the college and dons from other colleges began to attend in growing numbers; hundreds, later thousands, of the populace would come, in orderly manner to witness the dawn hymn of praise. It became deeply affecting, as this account from the Magdalen schoolboy and later distinguished historian, J.R. Green shows:

> May morning was a burst of poetry every year of my boyhood ... At first we used to spring out of bed, and gather in the grey of dawn on the top of the College Tower, where choristers and singing men were already grouped in their surplices. Beneath us, all wrapped in the dim mists of the Spring morning lay the city [and] the silent reaches of the Cherwell ... There was a long hush of waiting just before five, and then the first bright point of sunlight gleamed out over the horizon ... and, above, in the stillness, rose the soft pathetic air of the hymn *Te Deum Patrem Colimus*. As it closed the sun was fully up, surplices were thrown off, and with a burst of gay laughter the choristers rushed down the little tower stair and flung themselves on the bell-ropes, 'jangling' the bells in rough medieval fashion till the tower shook from side to side. And then, as they were tired, came the ringers; and the 'jangle' changed into one of those 'peals', change after change, which used to cast such a spell over my boyhood.

Perhaps the weakest element during this period of reform at Magdalen College was the actual quality of the chapel music. As is apparent from L.S. Tuckwell's election, little in the way of a voice trial for choristers took place. Tuckwell himself recalls that 'a considerable proportion [of his chorister colleagues] were unable to sing at all', only four men (lay clerks – not yet choral scholars) regularly sang and, although there were always several boys with beautiful voices, the choir as a whole was 'not over-efficient'. All this was to change from 1860 with the appointment as *informator choristarum* of Sir Frederick Ouseley's twenty-year-old protégé and St Michael's, Tenbury, organist, John Stainer. He was to be a third powerful influence for good over the choristers. Within four months of his appointment he had persuaded the college to require and, with his extraordinary charm of personality, had persuaded the lay clerks to be willing to attend choir practices. As for the boys, one of his former Magdalen choristers wrote 'Directly we choristers saw him and heard him we adored him and did so ever after. Over and above his unapproachable playing, he was one of the very few touched with the radiance of the inner life of sacred music'.[64] This two-year coincidence of Bloxam, Millard and Stainer was to be immortalised twenty years later by William Holman Hunt in his *May Morning on Magdalen Tower* in which all three can be identified. The angelic singing boys, however, are not portraits of the actual choristers: one of Holman Hunt's sons modelled the boy with the lily.[65]

Despite the innate inadequacies of both the elementary and the grammar school models, inspired schoolmasters such as William Whiting and inspired foundations such as Magdalen could rise above the difficulties. But these were the exceptions. Had the Commissioners done their research just five years later they might have found that St Michael's, Tenbury, produced a better model than the Salisbury school. But even Tenbury had two deficiencies that prevented it from being a paradigm: it was financially unsustainable without Ouseley's capital injections, and it lay in the hidden fastnesses of the borders of Herefordshire and Worcestershire. St Paul's was a lighthouse, known to everybody and visible to everybody. But St Paul's too had one untypical feature: it educated a huge complement of forty choristers. Nevertheless, St Michael's, and perhaps more so St Paul's, were to became models for other choral foundations determined to escape from the Scylla of the tiny unacademic elementary school and the Charybdis of the unaccommodating grammar school.

The first to follow St Paul's, determined to improve its music and, to that end, determined upon a change of site and enhancement of scope for its chorister school, was King's College, Cambridge. The fellowship had become impatient with the often ill-behaved local boys who, after begging their scanty supper from the college kitchens, would then produce 'frequent disturbances and mischief in the Old Court from their noisy irregular behaviour ... without any proper control'.[66] As at Magdalen, so at King's, the chapel had until the mid-1870s suffered from indifferent choral music. Part of the problem was the poor quality of the singers, lay clerks and boys; part was the inadequacy of the organist, William Amps. The college had, when rewriting its statutes in the 1850s, separated the office of organist from that of 'master over the choristers', and that was to prove a useful step. But it was in the 1870s that the college set out seriously to reform its choral foundation. In a process that was not to be complete until 1928, as lay clerks retired they were to be replaced by undergraduate choral scholars. In 1876 William Amps was pensioned off, to be replaced by an organist of outstanding calibre, Zachariah Buck's sometime Norwich chorister, Arthur Henry Mann. Most significant of all, as at St Paul's and closely modelled on that initiative, the college determined upon the building of a completely new school for their choristers, with not only far better teaching facilities – for the new school was to be a preparatory school – but with accommodation for an entirely boarding community of boys. At first negotiations took place with Trinity College with a view to the two foundations sharing a chorister school; but Trinity did not want boarders. St John's at this time, though they had their own set of choristers, was scarcely a choral foundation, choral services being sung only on Sundays, Red Letter Days and their eves.[67] So King's proceeded on their own, and, as at St Paul's, appointed a new headmaster: a graduate, indeed with a doctorate and with excellent teaching experience. Like St Paul's, they set about recruiting boarders from outside Cambridge while the new school was being built. An advertisement in the *Guardian* during 1876 produced twenty-four candidates, of whom three were selected, all clergy sons. For two years they were lodged in a house on the southern outskirts of the town. Meanwhile a tender for £3997 from a local builder was accepted, and on a site across the river to the west of the college, where the fellows' stables had been, the new choir school went up, being completed in December 1878. The building consisted of a house for a married headmaster, a classroom and, partitioned off it, a dining room. Upstairs was a single dormitory with sixteen partitioned cubicles, each with its own washbasin. The headmaster's house had the luxury of a bath, which the boys were occasionally allowed to use, presumably when their state of filth had become intolerable. The only lavatories were in an outdoor shed. Nevertheless, this was a highly attractive school by most choir school standards. By 1880 all sixteen choristers were boarders. In the following year the headmaster was permitted to take in his own accommodation additional non-chorister boarders, from whose fees he was able himself to pay an assistant teacher; three years later the college agreed to pay the assistant, who was to be always an undergraduate of King's, the cost to be covered by the admission of day pupils. In the course of the next five years a playing field with a cricket square was laid down and a recreation room doubling as a second classroom and a sanatorium were added. The choristers were no longer waged: on the contrary, the parents were to pay £12 a year towards the estimated £100 cost of their boarding education. The college provided their surplices (but not yet cassocks) and academic gowns, but the cost of providing three Eton suits and sixteen collars fell upon the parents. Here then was the true template: a preparatory boarding school, specifically for the education of choristers who were to sing daily matins and evensong, but with a stiffening of non-chorister pupils for the financial and educational benefit of the school. The boys would, after their voices changed, go on to good public schools and, in due course, proceed to university.

Meanwhile, in the chapel, wonderful things were happening to the music. The jovial 'Daddy' Mann with his twinkling eyes was adored by his choristers with whom he had an excellent relationship. They enjoyed shared jokes. He would collect the choristers each day for morning practice. As breakfast was coming to a close his face would appear at a dining-room window. He would lift up his watch and tap it meaningfully; in chorus the boys would lift up their watches and tap them in imitation. Practices were often hilarious. Yet he demanded the highest standards. For Mann, as for Stainer, flawless music was an essential element in Christian worship. As a consequence the chapel became a magnet for congregations who would come to hear such wonders as Walmisley's D minor evening service in which the quartet phrases 'He rememb'ring, rememb'ring his mercy ...' would be repeated by the full choir in the ultimate *pianissimo* of *pianissimos*. The singing of the King's College choir became legendary.[68]

In the decade following the opening of the new schools at St Paul's and King's a trio of ardent reformers came together at St George's Chapel, Windsor. The new dean was the thirty-five-year-old Randall Davidson, later to be archbishop of Canterbury, the organist was Stainer's Magdalen successor, Walter Parratt, later to be Master of the Queen's Music and knighted, and the impatient motivator was the precentor, Canon C. L. Courtenay. Since the 1850s the education of the Windsor choristers in cramped premises in the castle had been, as two pupils later described it, 'of a rough and ready kind, not as good as a village school of today' where 'lessons did not seem to matter, there were no examinations and no prizes'. In 1885 Canon Courtney sent questionnaires to a number of choral foundations whose chorister education had been reformed, King's, Cambridge, amongst them. The following year one of Her Majesty's school inspectors was called in and deemed the boys' education no better than 'satisfactory' (a code for scarcely tolerable) and suggested that it was time they were taught to write on paper and not just on slates. In 1892, coincidentally, the unsatisfactory schoolmaster resigned and the Admiralty announced their intention to close down Travers College, a substantial almshouse for retired naval officers just below the castle's northern ramparts. The chapter determined to try to acquire it and establish a proper King's-style preparatory choir school in the college premises. Negotiations were tedious, but eventually in October 1893 the chapter bought the building. A Cambridge M.A. from the staff of Summer Fields, Oxford, was selected from eighty-three applicants to be headmaster, chorister numbers were increased and non-choristers were recruited to create a school of forty boys, drawn from the families of 'clergymen, officers and other professional men'.[69]

St Michael's, St Paul's, King's, St George's: it was a trickle, but it was to become a tide, as one after another the choral foundations appreciated that a preparatory school was the ideal environment for the formation of able choristers, and that boarding could enhance recruitment both in numbers and calibre. In the course of the next half-century almost every choir school in the country would become 'preparatory' – either free-standing or as the junior department of a predominantly secondary school.

Before we leave the nineteenth century, the music that formed the choristers' stock-in-trade needs to be considered. At the heart of every matins and evensong was the psalter. E.W. Benson, in defining the work of his Truro choristers, had insisted that an explanation of the psalms must have a major role in their liturgical education. Earlier, we noted that not until the mid-eighteenth century did organists begin to try to create cohesion in the singing of psalms to Anglican chants by producing, for local use, pointed psalters. These certainly helped to hold a choir together, but at a price in a rigidity that ignored natural verbal stress. It was not until 1875 that something like a standard psalter appeared, edited by a group of leading church musicians that included James Turle of Westminster Abbey and Stainer of St Paul's. Their *Cathedral Psalter* became the almost universal choice. Much used, not to say battered, copies must have been familiar to every late Victorian chorister. The psalm singing may have been orderly but, by today's standards, it was offensively insensitive to the emphases of the language.[70] Another change from earlier times was the arrival of the hymn. Originally spurned as a Nonconformist aberration, then adopted in the parish churches, hymns crept into the cathedral repertoire by three routes: the great Sunday evening non-liturgical services that were introduced first at St Paul's and Worcester, and soon became almost universal; the Anglo-Catholic love of the office hymn; and the growth of choral eucharists with something like a necessity for hymns at the gradual and offertory. Hymn books for Anglican use had been appearing since the late 1820s, but it was not until 1861 that *Hymns Ancient and Modern* appeared, rapidly to become ubiquitous, with four and a half million copies sold in seven years. Alongside hymns came carols. It was in 1880 that the Truro choristers found themselves leading the singing in a form of service devised by their young succentor, the Rev. G.H.S. Walpole, that in the course of the following century was adopted world-wide as a favourite vehicle for the celebration of approaching Christmas – the ceremony of nine lessons and carols.

Of course the daily meat of the chorister's musical diet remained the canticles and anthems. The Victorian cathedral repertoire has not been generally well regarded. Most cathedral organists were unadventurous, limiting themselves to music from the eighteenth century, supplemented by compositions from the organist's own day, often from his own pen. Bernarr Rainbow, in his *Choral Revival in the Anglican Church*,[71] reproduced the service lists for May 1857 from fourteen English cathedrals and four other well-regarded choral foundations. To take the matins canticles as examples: Travers (d. 1758) in F scores highest at nine times (but three of these were on successive Sundays at Lincoln's Inn Chapel); settings by Boyce (d. 1779) appear six times; Attwood (d. 1838) and 'Serviceable' King (d. 1748) score five each; Aldrich (d. 1710) and Nares (d. 1783) four each, Nares because his canticles in F were sung two Sundays running at

St Paul's. The only evidence of seventeenth-century music is the listing once each (from eighteen foundations over five Sundays) of Child in G at Southwell Minster, Rogers in D at St George's, Windsor, Gibbons in F at Lincoln's Inn and, at Lichfield, 'Purcell in B' (sic). The mysterious 'Mendelssohn in A' appears at several cathedrals. These come from a single month at mid-century, but the service lists that have survived at Lincoln between 1820 and 1900 show an almost unchanging repertoire. As late as 1905 King's canticles in F were still being sung almost once a month.[72] Very little of the cathedral music from the eighteenth and earlier nineteenth centuries has proved itself to be of lasting worth. Stanford wrote of church music in 1914 that 'sugary sentimentalism is the order of the day … turned out by the bushel'.[73] Recent revaluations continue to take this view. Toward the end of his life Stainer, perhaps the most prolific church composer, walking with Edmund Fellowes in the grounds of Magdalen College, Oxford, said that he wished he had not allowed most of what he had written to be published: he was ashamed of it. Then he went on to explain that as a young man he had been encouraged by the popular demand for his anthems and had been in need of the handsome fees. 'Who can blame him?' asks Fellowes in his *Memoirs*.[74]

Before the end of the nineteenth century two things occurred that were to change hugely for the better the music that English choristers were called upon to sing in their daily work of worship. The first was the recovery by scholars of the church music of the great sixteenth- and seventeenth-century masters, and its publication, mostly by Vincent Novello. The second was the emergence, largely under the influence of the London music academies, of a number of composers, not primarily church musicians, but willing to undertake church commissions and able to do so with a new cleanness of melody and harmony, a new honesty and truth of emotional expression and a strikingly effective deployment and combination of vocal lines. One has to think only of the highly characteristic and individual series of canticle settings by Charles Villiers Stanford to appreciate the bright, clean air into which church music was moving. After nine years as director of music at Trinity College, Cambridge, Stanford was to move out of chapel employment, but he continued to offer fine compositions for the liturgical use of chapel and cathedral choirs. Hence it was that at one evensong in 1904 a solo chorister was privileged to be the very first to sing this then unknown, now so familiar, incomparable opening verse.[75]

Stanford, *Magnificat in G*

13

The Twentieth-Century Framework: Foundations, Liturgy, Music

The twentieth century saw the loss of only one ancient and one Victorian English choral foundation and the significant addition of not a few new foundations.[1] Chorister numbers continued to increase throughout the century. By 2004 there were some 900 boys (and over 250 girls) enrolled as choristers or probationers in cathedral and collegiate choirs where daily services are sung. This means that there are perhaps twice the number of boys singing in quires today than there were even in the great choral decades of the early sixteenth century.[2]

In the fifty years between 1877 and 1927 the Church of England established eighteen new dioceses, each with its own cathedral. At Truro, Liverpool and Guildford the cathedrals were built from new. Elsewhere, existing churches were adopted, adapted and, in most cases, enlarged. One of these new cathedrals, Southwell Minster, had been a choral foundation with weekday sung services since medieval times.[3] Of the others, only Truro and Guildford made immediate plans to provide weekday choral services.[4] Truro, as has been noted, determined upon a choral foundation with provision for the education of its twenty singing boys from the start. Guildford in 1959 reached agreement with a local preparatory school, Lanesborough, for the education of its choristers.[5] The other new cathedrals gradually introduced weekday choral services. Chelmsford, Coventry, Newcastle, Portsmouth, Southwark and Wakefield in time came to arrangements with designated local schools for the education of all or most of their singing boys.[6] Others drew and continue to draw boys from a range of local schools, placing on their parents significant and sometimes heroic logistical demands in fetching and carrying. It has been estimated that at Guildford in 1994 parents drove their chorister sons 50,980 miles between home, cathedral and school for singing purposes – twice round the world.[7]

Some, notably Liverpool and St Albans, achieve miracles of regular choral liturgy without the aid of a choir school. Others began strongly but have been unable to maintain the momentum. In 1934 evensong was being sung daily at Derby and almost daily at Newcastle: in 2005 both manage choral services on only three weekday evenings with boys singing on only two of these. At Birmingham in 1934 they were singing weekday evensongs five times a week; by 1958 this was down to two; today they have a highly contemporary pattern:

Monday is the 'dumb day', on Tuesdays the men sing, on Wednesday the boys, on Thursday the girls, on Friday the full choir; on Saturdays, as also at Blackburn, Bradford, Coventry, Guildford, Peterborough (and occasionally at Rochester and Wakefield) evensong is sung by visiting choirs, giving their home team a touch of weekend break ahead of the demands of Sunday.

Not all the new cathedrals have yet achieved a choral establishment such as can properly enable their choirboys and choirgirls to fall within the scope of this book. Birmingham sing five evensongs each week, but their boys or girls are involved in only three of these. Coventry did not have any weekday choral evensongs until 1962: now their boys and their girls sing on just one day a week each, as they do at Leicester. At Bradford either the boys or the girls sing on Mondays, and that is all. Seven of the new English Anglican cathedrals, however, may be judged to qualify themselves for inclusion on grounds of current weekday choral services. Liverpool sing full-choir evensong on every evening except Wednesdays. That is more than a few of the ancient cathedrals manage. St Albans sing on every weekday evening, but the pattern is: boys on three evenings, girls on two evenings and the full choir only on Saturdays. It is an admirable solution to the problems of having no historic endowment and no choir school. Chelmsford sing five weekday evensongs, three full, one for boys only and one for girls only. Guildford also sing five evensongs but, despite having a choir school, the boys are used on only three evenings. At Southwell Minster and Truro the boys sing four evensongs a week, always with the men at Truro and three times a week with the men at Southwell. Southwark offer four weekday choral evensongs, two by the boys and men and two by the girls alone. This illustrates how the introduction of a girls' choir can enable a cathedral to fulfil a programme of weekday choral evensongs that would probably be impossible for its boys and men.

The choir of St Michael's College, Tenbury, sang choral matins and evensong on every day of the week except one until the foundation was forced to close in 1985. It was the last place in England where daily choral matins, or indeed any weekday choral matins, could be heard.[8] It must be added that generally it was heard only by God. A St Michael's chorister between 1899 and 1904, later to become organist of the college and later still organist of Norwich Cathedral, Heathcote Statham, recalled in the 1960s how the main business of his schooldays had been to sing the daily services in a chapel with no congregation:

> That was, and still is, the charm of St Michael's – this singing of the daily offices in an empty church in the very depths of the country. I suppose there is nothing else quite like it in the world.[9]

There is, of course, something exactly like it apart from the absence of boys: the Cistercian tradition. But, in reality, 'the daily offices in an empty church in the depths of the country' were to be not only the glory but also the undoing of

St Michael's. Even in Ouseley's day it had been financially unviable and he had plugged the fiscal gaps. For some decades after his death there were reserves that could be raided. Half-successful appeals in the 1960s and 1970s kept St Michael's afloat and enabled brave improvements to the buildings to be made and staff salaries to be brought up to something approaching national scales. In its final decade, in the hope of increasing or even maintaining pupil numbers, girls and pre-prep children were introduced. But prospective parents, including even old boy fathers, were deterred by the conviction that St Michael's was fundamentally a place where a few boys and fewer men sang the daily offices in an empty church, and hence was not a proper school. Coincidentally, rich trusts and corporations that might have responded (indeed did respond) to similar appeals from viable choir schools could see at a glance that at Tenbury they would be pouring money down a hole. In 1985 the trustees acknowledged the inevitable and, with honourably ample notice given to parents, the school was closed. Virtually every St Michael's chorister was found a place in some other, more viable, choir school and its choir. Ouseley's unique library was donated to the far more accessible Bodleian. The capital raised from the eventual sale of the property was put into an 'Ouseley Trust' to be used for 'maintaining to a high standard the choral services of the Church of England' and assisting the education of pupils in Anglican choir schools – a purpose the trust continues generously to fulfil.[10]

The twentieth century proved to be an equally difficult time for the parish churches that during the nineteenth century, under the stimulus of the Oxford Movement, equipped themselves with a choral foundation and undertook cathedral-style services. The little choir schools serving such churches as All Saints, Margaret Street, and St Andrew's, Wells Street, in London, or St Saviour's, Eastbourne, and St John's, Torquay, on the south coast were educationally inefficient and a drain on their churches' funds, a drain increasingly difficult to justify when the theology of the age strongly favoured congregational participation rather than meditative listening. One after the other these churches abandoned the attempt to be pseudo-cathedrals and gave up the daily choral office until, today, only St James's parish church, Grimsby, retains its commitment to its more than a century-old Victorian choral tradition.

One other choral foundation came to an unsurprising end in the twentieth century. In 1968 Eton College, for the second time in its history, determined that the provision of a daily choral service with a professional choir of boys and men, attended by a diminutive congregation, was an anachronism and the maintenance of twenty-six choristers and probationers paying no fees for their education an unjustifiable financial burden. To the dismay of its intensely loyal former choristers, the college closed its educationally effective but physically 'shoddy' little choir school. Some of the money saved went to fund newly introduced music scholarships, two of the first year's awards going to an Eton chorister and to the head chorister from St George's. Before closing its choir school Eton had given consideration to trying again some form of amalgamation with St George's, Windsor, but St George's was not keen. Closure was the only rational alternative.[11] Ten years later amalgamation was to save the college quiristers at Winchester, where, in place of the tiny college choir school, the singing boys would receive scholarships for their education alongside the cathedral choristers at the Pilgrims' School, even though their college chapel singing commitment became limited to services on Sundays, high days and Tuesday evenings.

Four new Anglican choral foundations were established in England during the twentieth century. Today, only one of them still flourishes. Each of the four is or was in its own way idiosyncratic. The earliest of them was undoubtedly the most extraordinary of any choral foundation to be considered and was, indeed, only briefly a choral foundation as defined in this history.

St Mary's, Somers Town, close by Euston Station, was one of those heroic Anglo-Catholic churches planted in the nineteenth century in the heart of a destitute slum district. It was staffed by a vicar and five curates, virtually all recruited from that most Tractarian of theological colleges, St Stephen's House, Oxford. Their mission combined dedicated high-ritual worship with a passionate social ministry that led, especially under the inspiration of the saintly curate, Basil Jellicoe, to the formation of a housing association that replaced appalling slums by the handsome blocks of flats that still grace Eversholt Street today. In 1919 Desmond Morse-Boycott was appointed to the team of curates. His *curriculum vitae* read: expulsion from school, brief career as shorthand typist, two years at Lichfield Theological College and two curacies from both of which he had been dismissed.

He was given responsibility for the boys of the parish. They readily joined his boys' club and played in his football team, but came only with reluctance to his church. So he determined to form a boys' choir and in 1928 turned a basement under Eversholt Street into a primitive schoolroom. Two years later, in the course of a train journey, he had a mystical experience that inspired him to establish a choir school. His wife, having noticed a pair of adjacent properties for sale in Cholmeley Park, Highgate, sacrificed her life savings as a mortgage security, while Father Desmond set about fund-raising with incomparable skill and passion. As an officer from the Board of Education was to put it in 1932, 'He was a good beggar'. (He also had a brilliant and lucrative sideline as a journalist.) In July 1932 St-Mary-of-the-Angels Song School was dedicated by the bishop of London with some two dozen boarding choristers on the roll. No fees were charged. Each day, except Wednesdays and Saturdays, the boys were driven between Highgate and Somers Town to sing evensong and, on Sundays, the whole gamut of matins, sung mass, evensong and benediction. Morse-Boycott had appointed himself headmaster ('My knowledge of schoolmastering was nil'); his wife, a Red Cross nurse, became matron. Amazingly, pupils came and were indeed educated, standards of worship and manners were established, 'mothers were kept at bay', some boys won bursaries to public schools and even went on to ordination.

It did not, however, please the vicar and curates of St Mary's, to whom, in contrast to their social work, it seemed a risky and indulgent sideshow. The school's finances were in a constant state of crisis. Both in school and in church Morse-Boycott liked to do things his own way. Lines of communication were bad. He was the stone in the oyster whose unwanted pearls came to be resented. In February 1935 the vicar resigned as a trustee of the school and, following the Candlemas services, announced that his church would no longer be using the boys' choir. So Morse-Boycott advertised his choir as available to sing at weddings, funerals, concerts and parties. Briefly they sang regularly at St Martin-in-the-Fields.

In 1938, with war threatening, Morse-Boycott decided to go green. The Highgate property was sold and a lease taken on a large house with grounds at Addlestone near Weybridge. From here they began to specialise in film work – *Tom Brown's Schooldays, The Guinea Pig, Never Take No for an Answer* – and (a circumstance hardly proper to divulge in a book such as this), in a film about the coronation, while the viewers saw the choristers of Westminster Abbey singing, the dubbed sound was provided by the boys of St Mary-of-the-Angels Song School. They also began a series of extended concert tours. It was during one of these tours in Devon in 1940 that they learned that their school had been burnt down. For two months the boys were dispersed; then a neighbouring property was rented and the boys were brought back to a dormitory in a cellar and a classroom in a garage. Unsurprisingly, it alarmed the Ministry of Education. They saw Morse-Boycott as an exploiter of children: he found the ministry 'as threatening as Hitler'. By 1942 their burnt shell had been restored and they returned to it. After the war they took to continental touring and began to liken themselves to the Vienna Boys' Choir. It was at this point that they parted company with the Choir Schools' Association. They had for some years not been fulfilling the Association's criteria in that they did not 'sing daily services in quire'. More financial problems forced them to leave Addlestone in 1952. For six years the school was continued in a smaller property, Three Gables, at Beaconsfield. From here, Morse-Boycott claimed, they were the first choir (or did he mean the first boys' choir?) to appear on television. Then in 1958, pressed by 'a credit squeeze', the Song School was forced to close. Yet this was not the end. Morse-Boycott opened a boarding house and for ten years, aged sixty-eight to seventy-eight and a widower, he recruited boys from local schools to come into weekend residence, five boys at first, more later, to sing for weddings, funerals and the local film studios, but no longer in any serious sense a church choral foundation.

In retirement at Worthing, in his eighty-eighth year, he wrote of his extra-ordinary venture:

> I survived uncrushed between the upper and the nether millstone, my work unwanted and unhelped by the Establishment, and regarded, if thought of at all, as the eccentric 'hobby' of an embarrassing parson.

Whether it was a dubious hobby or a devoted vocation, his vision has survived his life, because at the last he set up a charitable trust (still active) to provide funds for the education of needy choristers.[12]

The second of these independent foundations was less risky but shorter-lived. Sydney Nicholson had, as organist successively of Manchester Cathedral and Westminster Abbey, become increasingly interested in the state of Church of England music as a whole. He was deeply involved in the work of the archbishops' committee on church music – it was to be the first of a series – that published *Music in Worship* in 1922. Six years later he resigned from the Abbey in order to become first director of his brainchild, the English School of Church Music (later renamed the Royal School of Church Music). In the following year the ESCM was able to establish at Chislehurst the College of St Nicholas where not only could training courses be held but where, in its chapel, a resident choir with ten boy choristers could maintain a daily exemplary evensong. They lived and had instrumental tuition free at the college and were educated at neighbouring Bickley Hall Preparatory School at 10 guineas a term. But just as the Second World War dislocated Morse-Boycott's song school, so it brought to an end the College of St Nicholas. Evacuation to St Michael's, Tenbury, secured the future of ESCM but not of its choral force, and, when, in the 1950s, the Royal School of Church Music was re-established for two decades at Addington Palace, it was without any resident choir.

At Reigate a parish church choir with boys had existed before the twentieth century, but it was in 1918 that Godfrey Searle, an enthusiastic layman, funded choral scholarships for boys who at first were drawn from Reigate Grammar School. Some twelve years later he opened a boarding house for them, of which he appointed himself honorary superintendent. Then, in 1950, Searle negotiated with the grammar school a merger of their preparatory department with his sixteen choristers and four probationers, thereby founding the Reigate St Mary's Choir School. But, just as St Mary's, Somers Town, parted company from Morse-Boycott's song school, so, after Searle's death, St Mary's church, Reigate, dispensed with the services of the choristers, dissociating itself from its eponymous choir school. The school, however, with increasing numbers of non-chorister pupils, flourished, its choral tradition surviving without the support of St Mary's. In 2003 Reigate Grammar School itself reacquired the choir school and today, as Reigate St Mary's Preparatory and Choir School, it forms the grammar school's kindergarten and preparatory department. Meanwhile, St Mary's church has welcomed the choir back on weekdays in term time, the choir singing matins or evensong on four days a week, most often in St Mary's but also in other local churches, in cathedrals and their own school chapel.[13]

The most recent Anglican foundation was at Tewkesbury. Miles Amherst, a teacher at the King's School, Ely, and lay clerk at the cathedral, for some years cherished an ambition to found a choir school. His opportunity came when he discovered in the early 1970s that the Girls' High School hard by Tewkesbury Abbey had been closed and was for sale and that the vicar of Tewkesbury would welcome the singing of daily evensongs in his great church. Amherst was in a position to buy the school property and in 1973 opened the Abbey Choir School for prep school age boys. There were just five at first, but numbers steadily grew, including up to fourteen with benefit of chorister scholarships. Altos, tenors and basses were recruited, some to the school staff, and in due course a choir of twenty-six was singing weekday evensongs on five evenings a week during school terms, leaving, as at Reigate, the parish choir to lead the congregational singing on Sundays, and high days out of term. This arrangement put the boys and men into a position similar to that of the Oxbridge college choirs, that is, with freedom to undertake extended choral tours at times when cathedral choirs were required for Christmas and Holy Week services. Recordings and broadcasts have vouched for the quality of the choir in recent years. The school grew in numbers of boys and girls aged three to thirteen and about the turn of the millennium became a charitable trust with a board of governors. But private choir school ventures from St Michael's, Tenbury, onwards have rarely been financially robust. Tewkesbury has been no exception, and in the spring of 2006 it was announced that the school would close at the end of the academic year. Happily, Dean Close School has secured the future of the choristers and their singing.

So far, that is since the Reformation, all the choral foundations we have considered have been Anglican and their choristers have sung the Anglican liturgy. The twentieth century, however, saw the establishment of the first post-Reformation Roman Catholic choral foundations in this country.[14] Not surprisingly the earliest was at Westminster.[15] Cardinal Vaughan was determined that his great new cathedral off Victoria Street should have the full choral liturgy of sung mass and offices from the start. When he opened his new choir school in October 1901 he welcomed thirteen new choristers as 'the foundations of the cathedral'. Despite periods of considerable financial difficulty, Vaughan's vision has been maintained without a break. Indeed, Westminster Cathedral is almost certainly the only Catholic cathedral in the world to sustain daily sung mass and vespers with a choir of men and boys. What is more remarkable, Westminster Cathedral choir attained a reputation for singing of outstanding distinction from a very early time, thanks to the appointment of R.R. (later Sir Richard) Terry as the founding master of music. Terry introduced a ground-breaking repertoire that included rediscovered Renaissance music, edited by Terry himself, twentieth-century continental masses unheard in Anglican cathedrals at that time, and exciting commissions from contemporary composers. As early as 1906 the *Daily Telegraph* described Terry's choir as 'one of the most beautiful choirs in Europe' and in 1923 Gustav Holst observed that every music-lover in London would find his way to Westminster Cathedral at some time during Holy Week. Daily services were maintained throughout the First World War; but the dangers of bombing from 1939 saw first the boys evacuated to Uckfield, then the choir school closed altogether, with choral services sustained by men. The choir school reopened in 1946 and under George Malcolm, master of music from the following year, fifteen choral services each week were sung. A major crisis was faced in the inflation-ridden early 1970s when it looked for a time as if the cathedral could not both run a costly choir school and maintain its leaking buildings. The ailing Cardinal Heenan struggled to solve a seemingly intractable dilemma. But his successor from 1976, Basil Hume, abbot of Ampleforth, made clear his conviction that the cathedral's purpose was the daily worship of God and that to fulfil this purpose worthily a choir school was not an option but a necessity. Aided by an outstandingly supportive parents' committee, he was ready to seek help from well beyond the Catholic constituency.[16] A world-wide appeal for funds was supported by the archbishop of Canterbury and the moderator of the General Assembly of the United Reform Church, as well as Benjamin Britten, Colin Davis, Ralph Richardson and Alec Guinness. The Duke of Gloucester joined the architectural advisory committee. An outstanding headmaster, Peter Hannigan, was appointed and under him the premises available to the choir school were extended, non-choristers were introduced and the cathedral was able to boast a school well able to match those run by their friendly neighbours at the Abbey and St Paul's. In recent decades the cathedral's music has again earned international renown, including the winning of a 'golden disc'.

More recently the Roman Catholic cathedrals at Cardiff and Liverpool have developed choral foundations. Liverpool's architecturally innovative Roman Catholic cathedral of Christ the King was completed in 1967. From the start its choristers have been drawn from St Edward's College, a large and distinguished Voluntary Assisted Catholic comprehensive school with its own junior school where the probationers and younger choristers are educated. Cardiff has the older cathedral but the younger choral foundation. The De la Salle College at Cardiff had been founded in 1935, but in 1987 it was taken over by a board of lay trustees, renamed St John's College, and established as the choir school for the Metropolitan Cathedral. In less than twenty years, under the redoubtable headship of David Neville, the cathedral organist, the school has grown phenomenally from ninety-five pupils to over five hundred boys and girls. Plans for a girls' choir are now in hand. As yet, however, at neither Liverpool nor Cardiff are daily choral services sung.

It is in the great pre-nineteenth-century Anglican choral foundations that daily choral services were maintained throughout the twentieth century, in face of considerable difficulties. Table 3 indicates the consistency with which this duty of choral worship has been upheld.[17] The service that has been determinedly maintained is evensong. Daily matins was doomed. For most of the nineteenth century both matins and evensong were sung daily in almost all the choral foundations listed in the table. Already by the later decades of that century the challenges presented by the singing of two daily offices had begun to be evident. One difficulty was the conflict that arose, in those foundations whose choir school was not exclusively for choristers, between the demands of the quire and the demands of the classroom. Here are Herbert Brewer's observations of this conflict insofar as they affected him (and his brother) when they were choristers at Gloucester in the late nineteenth century.[18]

> The choristers were educated at the College School (now known as the King's School), but they had not the advantages that the present boys enjoy [c.1930]. The education was of the scantiest on account of the time spent in the Cathedral at practices and morning and afternoon services, all of which came out of school hours.
>
> In spite of this the choristers competed and more than held their own with the ordinary schoolboy. They not only passed the Oxford and Cambridge local examinations but won open scholarships at the Universities direct from the school. Some achieved still further renown, a notable instance being the present distinguished headmaster of Westminster School, Dr Costley-White.

Herbert Brewer's complacency was evidently justified in his case, as in Dr Costley-White's. But Brewer and Costley-White were both, in their different ways, outstandingly gifted students. As educational demands increased, headmasters, parents, inspectors of schools and eventually deans and organists became unwilling to tolerate such inroads into schooling as were made by daily practice and two services. An even greater problem afflicted the lower voices. Organists wanted their men to be drawn from more cultured and educated classes than had generally been the case in the eighteenth and nineteenth centuries. But men in demanding fields of work, other than the self-employed, simply could not make themselves free for an hour every morning at 10 a.m. and every afternoon at 3 p.m., the favoured hours of matins and evensong. Recruitment of good lay clerks became very difficult. Table 3 charts the pace at which choral matins gave way and indeed shows how, in England, its demise has been absolute. (That the daily choral matins still to be heard in St Patrick's Cathedral, Dublin, is sung only by the boys provides a clear indication that of the two problems the men's was the more pressing.)

The Church Music Society, noting that in 1934 only St Paul's, Lichfield and Wells maintained daily matins and evensong, believed this to be evidence that the choral service was facing elimination. They saw a long tradition of daily sung offices, unique to England, productive of 'the noblest heritage of English art', facing extinction, as they 'watched with apprehension the gradual crumbling of the tradition of daily choral worship in Cathedrals'.[19] Happily the CMS authors were wrong. Choral matins indeed was doomed: it was simply impractical to try to maintain it. But the choral tradition itself was not at risk and, as the table shows, weekday choral evensong has been everywhere treasured and preserved.

The matins choral repertoire, or at least parts of it, is still sung on all Sundays by boys (or in some places occasionally by girls) and men at the cathedrals of Canterbury, Chichester, Durham, Exeter, Guildford, Hereford, Lincoln, London (St Paul's), Oxford, Peterborough, Salisbury, Wells and Winchester, and at St George's Chapel, Windsor, and Westminster Abbey in London. Matins is sung on three out of four Sundays at Bury St Edmunds and York Minster and on alternate Sundays at Chelmsford, Chester, St Albans and (in term time) King's College, Cambridge.

Against the widespread loss of matins must be set the gain of the almost universal spread of the choral eucharist on Sundays and high days since the last few decades of the nineteenth century. By 1938 nineteen choral foundations were singing a eucharist every Sunday and every Anglican cathedral except Liverpool had a choral celebration at least once a month.[25] Now, virtually all the cathedrals have a choral celebration every Sunday. This reflects a fundamental theological and liturgical shift in the Church of England (and to some extent in other reformed churches) back to the conviction of the pre-Reformation church that the central act of worship must be that which stems from Christ's commission 'Do this in remembrance of me'. Not only do most Anglican cathedrals now celebrate holy communion at least daily, but in most choral foundations the choristers cannot fail to perceive that Sunday's choral eucharist is the high point of the liturgical week. This service in many places brings the choir down from the quire to portable stalls behind a nave altar, to sing with and to an often very large congregation. Confirmed choristers make their communion weekly; others receive a laying on of benedictional hands. As we shall see, the musical consequence, the vast broadening of the repertoire, has been transforming.

In the past few decades of the twentieth century there has been a further major change to the choral eucharist. Matins and evensong continue, universally, to be sung to the 1662 office, using, in most places, Coverdale's incomparable (if not wholly accurate) English psalter.[26] But Cranmer's communion service is now a rarity in the choral eucharist. The rites found in *Common Worship* return

TABLE 3

Weekday Choral Services In The Historic Foundations
(*M = Matins; E = Evensong*)

	1934		1958		2005	
	M	E	M	E	M	E
'Old Foundation' and 'New Foundation' Cathedrals						
Bristol	–	5	–	5	–	6
Canterbury	2	6	1	6	–	6
Carlisle	–	5	–	5	–	5
Chester	3	5	2	5	–	4
Chichester	2	5	–	5	–	5
Durham	2	6	2	6	–	6
Ely	6	5	–	6	–	5
Exeter	4	5	–	5	–	5
Gloucester	3	5	–	5	–	5
Hereford	5	4	–	5	–	5
Lichfield	6	6	?[20]	?	–	5
Lincoln	3	5	2	5	–	5
London (St Paul's)	6	6	5	6	–	6
Manchester	4	6	–	5	–	4
Norwich	5	5	–	5	–	5[21]
Oxford (Christ Church)	–	5	–	5	–	5[22]
Peterborough	–	5	1	5	–	6[23]
Ripon	5	5	–	5	–	5
Rochester	–	5	–	5	–	4[24]
Salisbury	4	5	–	5	–	6
Wells	6	6	–	5	–	6
Winchester	4	5	3	5	–	5
Worcester	5	5	2	5	–	6
York	4	5	2	5	–	5
Royal Peculiars						
London (Chapel Royal)	–	–	–	–	–	–
London (Westminster Abbey)	3	6	2	6	–	5
Windsor (St George's)	4	5	3	5	–	5

the sacrament to the ancient shape of the liturgy. At once the pre-Reformation mass settings of such as Byrd and Lassus, the masses of Palestrina and Victoria, of the Austrian classical masters and the modern French school can be sung exactly as set – and in Latin. Also, the worship of many choral foundations has been enriched by the use of the recently published liturgies for special occasions and most notably for Holy Week. Once again, Maundy Thursday and Good Friday can be occasions of special resonance for the choristers as they were for their medieval predecessors, as feet are washed or as the *Reproaches* are sung. And on Palm Sunday they may have the entertaining and sometimes hazardous thrill of processing behind a real live donkey or, as at Salisbury, of singing to the congregation still outside, through the nine medieval apertures above the west doors:

> All glory, laud and honour, to Thee, Redeemer, King,
> To whom the lips of children made sweet hosannas ring.

Perhaps most remarkable of all, the Boy Bishop has risen from his puritan grave. Today at Hereford (the first cathedral to reinstate their Boy Bishop), at Salisbury and doubtless elsewhere, at evensong on or close to the feast of St Nicholas, during *Magnificat*, the mighty bishop is put down from his seat and the humble and meek senior chorister, episcopally robed, is exalted to the bishop's throne. Later the Boy Bishop preaches a sermon – no longer written for him by one of the canons, but of his own making (though perhaps not without some guidance). Boy Bishops can make exemplary preachers. It is a special occasion, rich in the spirit of worship, entirely serious, yet full of delight.

Since the seventeenth century, choristers have been called upon to sing at special, non-liturgical services such as that for the Corporation of the Sons of the Clergy at St Paul's, for thanksgivings for special blessings – Harvest Festival was a late-nineteenth-century initiative – and for combined celebrations such as the Three Choirs Festival. The twentieth century has added many further special occasions. Some bring to the cathedral civic dignitaries such as the judges and the mayoralty or major charitable organisations; some teach them to be patient with hordes of little children who (unlike choristers) may not know how to behave. Local regiments have their cathedral services, not always attended by the choir, but the sound of the bugle and solemn silence are familiar everywhere on Remembrance Sunday. Festivals in which choristers sing with and get to know their fellows from neighbouring foundations now occur. Alongside the historic Three Choirs Festival at Gloucester, Hereford and Worcester there are now the annual Southern Cathedrals Festival by rotation at Chichester, Salisbury and Winchester; the Border Cathedrals Festival bringing together for two days each year the choirs of Carlisle, St Mary's Edinburgh and Newcastle; and Ripon sings in festivals both with Durham and York and with Leeds Parish Church and Wakefield. These provide new musical experiences for the boys in two senses: they open the repertoire to works too long to use in the liturgy and they enable familiar grand-scale works, such as the coronation anthems of Handel and Parry, to be sung by unfamiliar grand-scale numbers of singers. They even make possible the singing of Tallis's great forty-part motet. The Corporation of the Sons of the Clergy now invite not just their traditional London choirs but, by rotation, cathedral choirs from the provinces to join the home team in their annual festival. The Queen distributes her Maundy about the country and choristers far from London or Windsor have a chance of seeing their monarch at close quarters, sometimes even of meeting her. They may also find themselves meeting royalty from other countries. In 1989 one St John's, Cambridge, chorister, singing at the Queen of the Netherlands' Birthday Concert on his own birthday, was amazed, on being introduced to Her Majesty, to find her opening her handbag and handing *him* a birthday present.

Above all, the twentieth century witnessed a huge transformation in and extension of the repertoire of music sung by choristers in the ordinary course of the liturgy. The best of the staple diet of eighteenth- and nineteenth-century works sung by the Victorian choirs is still there. (Christopher Dearnley, in his time as organist of St Paul's, was also noted for keeping in the repertoire Georgian works long and comprehensively expunged from other cathedrals' lists.) Now the work of the great high Tudor and early Stuart composers, of Tallis and Byrd, of Weelkes, Tomkins and Gibbons, is universally sung. In adventurous foundations the repertoire is pushed back to include some of the earliest church polyphony, not only from this country but from schools such as that of Flanders, frequently to the dismay of the choristers who, having to adjust to not having 'the tune', can find early sixteenth-century polyphony trying. In the Roman Catholic foundations plainsong is again part of the boys' stock-in-trade, less often in Anglican foundations, where there is a tendency to make plainsong the speciality of offices sung only by the men. It is curious that hardly anywhere can one hear plainsong sung by boys and men an octave apart as it would have been sung for centuries in every non-monastic medieval cathedral.

The expansion of the repertoire into contemporary music is even more dramatic. It drew momentum from the admirable practice of commissioning new works for liturgical use. Notable have been the commissions of Walter Hussey when vicar of St Matthew's, Northampton, and dean of Chichester (Britten's *Rejoice in the Lamb*, Finzi's *Lo, the Full Final Sacrifice*, alongside more extensive non-liturgical works), or those of the collegiate foundations (Tippett's evening canticles for St John's, Cambridge, and the annual Christmas commissions from King's), or the influence of Westminster Cathedral in drawing from Britten his *Missa Brevis* for boys' voices or, right at the start of the century, in inspiring if not actually commissioning Vaughan Williams's incomparable *Mass in G Minor*.

Much of the new music, and often the best, asks of the boys skills in a wide range of unfamiliar techniques.[27] Frequent progressions of discords require of them very sophisticated tuning skills. Thus the Tippett canticles challenge the choristers with their atonality and demand of a solo treble a hair-raisingly improbable and exposed *Nunc Dimittis* entry. Less challenging, but perhaps more fun, are the requirements of Bryan Kelly and others for a feeling for jazz rhythms. Happily it is relatively rare for cathedral choristers – at least, in quire – to be asked to adopt the vocal tones and other singularities of the 'pop' music that has made the ephemeral so beloved of the urban parish church, though a commission by Harrison Birtwistle did require the King's boys to stamp and shout. Major, primarily secular, composers have been inspired to write liturgy-enriching pieces: Walton by royalty and Taverner by Orthodoxy, for example. The ancient tradition of cathedral organists and lay clerks writing for their own choirs or local communities continues and much of the best finds its way into the general repertoire, including the well-loved responses of Humphrey Clucas and anthems of Richard Shephard. Absolutely ubiquitous are the carols of John Rutter. Choristers today are also likely to encounter and relish the unique sounds of Poulenc and the profundities of Vierne, Duruflé and Langlais from France. Or, from farther afield, to discover the exotic musical languages of Kodály, Pärt and Rachmaninov. If anyone doubts that the tradition of composing for the liturgy is other than vibrantly alive today, it is only necessary to listen to the recent anthology of twelve such works written between 2000 and 2005, sung by (and nine of them specially commissioned for) the Vasari Singers under Jeremy Backhouse.[28] Here is thrilling music in a great variety of wholly contemporary styles, set to profound and moving texts. The Vasari Singers are, of course, adult singers of the highest calibre. But this very competition, as it were, between adult groups and choral foundation choirs with children providing the top lines is widely deemed to have been a major stimulus in driving up standards of performance in cathedrals and collegiate chapels in the second half of the twentieth century. Few doubt that those standards have never been higher. When the archbishops' commissioners on cathedrals (1992–94) asked individuals what was specially good about their cathedral 'the first answer was invariably the music'.[29] And, one can add without fear of contradiction, never in the entire history of the English chorister has the repertoire of music sung in the liturgy of the choral foundations been so wide and varied as can be heard in the first decade of the twenty-first century.

14

The Twentieth-Century Choir School

In the early decades of the twentieth century the education of choristers was often unsatisfactory. In October 1914 the Rev. R.M. Tuke, Master of Manchester Cathedral Choir School, contributed an article to a short-lived journal, *Cathedrals Quarterly*, on the subject of 'The Education of Cathedral Choristers'.[1] He emphasised two particular difficulties: the oft-repeated one of how to fit education around three hours of singing each day, and the necessity of a chorister leaving the school not when he had completed a suitable stage of education but the moment his voice broke, in order that a successor could be instantly brought in: 'At the first convenient moment off he goes, whatever stage of mental attainment he may have reached'. So high educational ideals were pursued in often very trying circumstances, with irritating, albeit necessary, interruptions so that frequently 'the strand of human patience [was] stretched at times almost to the point of breaking' and the ideals 'seem to fade farther and farther away'. Tuke knew what was needed for his boys' proper education; and he knew that the circumstances of chorister education, in which 'from the Cathedral point of view the Choir is the first consideration, the School only the second' made their educational needs impossible of attainment. The history of twentieth-century chorister education is the story of how Tuke's frustrating mastership and his pupils' frustrated schooling were to give way – everywhere – to chorister education of a very high order, at its best among the finest in the world.

We can look first at the two particular problems identified by Tuke. The interruptions occasioned by musical and liturgical demands have, over the course of the twentieth century, been greatly diminished if not wholly removed. The biggest single problem had been daily choral matins. It happened right in the middle of prime teaching time, causing intolerable disturbance to educational provision and concentration. Its universal abolition was a major victory for chorister education over liturgical demand. Alongside this went the progressive postponement of evensong. To take Durham as an example, it was moved in 1970 from 3.45 to 4 p.m., in 1979 to 5 p.m. and finally in 1984 to 5.15 p.m.;[2] in other words, to an hour when choristers' schooling and lay clerks' employment would be over. That left rehearsals as the main battleground. Generally it was found possible to fit rehearsals into time before, between and after school hours. Most foundations now rehearse their choristers, whether boarding or non-resident, after an early breakfast before the start of school; and/or in the lunch hour; and (often with the men) between end of afternoon school and the start of evensong. Weekends provide additional opportunity for rehearsal of the more substantial Sunday music and in some foundations for individual singing coaching. The choristers may still be devoting three hours a day to rehearsal and the liturgy, but the school timetable, including sport, is left intact. One telling reform of significant benefit to the choristers of the two Cambridge choral foundations, for example, was the organist coming to the school for morning practice rather than the choristers going to the college with its inevitable half hour or so of walking time lost to lessons.[3]

The point at which a boy chorister should leave his school was a more complex problem. In the early twentieth century its most common aspect was the failure of a boy's voice to change until long after the most suitable age for entry to secondary school. In recent decades it has more often been the loss of treble voice well before the usual age of transfer. In both cases a battle could arise between Tuke's two antagonists: the needs of the choir and the needs of schooling. Some individual cases exemplify the issues. In 1948 a boarding chorister at New College School, in his fourteenth year, won a place at Repton together with a music exhibition. In the July the warden of New College wrote to the headmaster of Repton suggesting that, as the boy's voice was still unchanged and he was at his most valuable stage in the choir, his entry to Repton should be postponed for a year. The headmaster replied by return that, both for him and for the boys' parents, postponement was unacceptable on educational grounds: 13+ was the normal age of entry and the boy would be seriously disadvantaged if he entered at 14+. The Warden grudgingly accepted the decision but added: 'We do not give choristers the long training which enables them to get a [music] scholarship in order that they may leave us when they begin to be useful'.[4] In the 1980s an identical problem could arise over a matter of a single term. At another choral foundation another music award to another public school had been won by a brilliant and still treble-voiced chorister. The public school wanted him in September for the start of the academic year. The organist wanted him to remain, still aged under fourteen, for the Michaelmas Term, culminating in important Christmastide occasions. The boy's contract as a chorister (for by the 1980s most choristers were subject to contractual agreements) stipulated that the parents would not remove the boy before his fourteenth birthday. But the parents were determined to remove him and indeed did so. The organist urged that the parents be sued for breach of contract; the school governors knew that to sue would probably be unsuccessful and would certainly attract bad publicity. Once again education and a boy's best interest had defeated choral music and a choir's best interest.

Today the more common *early* voice-break can pose a different problem. In the 1990s one of the cathedral choral foundations was drawing up a series of new contracts between cathedral, choir school and chorister parents and their various obligations to each other. The question arose as to whether a chorister scholarship should continue to be paid to parents of a pupil who might need to remain in his choir school when he was no longer able to sing treble, which might be for a year or more. Just such a case was at issue at that moment. The organist needed to fill his vacant place; but the cathedral's budget had an absolute and necessary limit on the scholarships it could fund at any one time; the school's budget did not include funding of chorister scholarships; and the parents might not be able, indeed the parents of the boy in question were not able, to afford the full fee for a final year. It is characteristic of the present age that all parties agreed that the welfare of an individual boy was paramount. Nevertheless, it is an expensive virtue when a choir finds that it has lost four or five voices, a year or more before the boys are due to leave their choir school, as can happen with today's well-nurtured young.

Tuke tactfully did not include in his article another problem that went beyond singing hours and breaking voices: the fact that some of the choir schools in 1913 were simply bad schools. What follows is certainly not an attempt to write a history of the twentieth-century choir schools but to consider the principal lines of development that have, in one way or another, affected and improved each of them. It is possible to place every early twentieth-century choir school, albeit sometimes uncertainly, into one of three categories. The 'elementary' schools taught an elementary syllabus most suitable for boys who would leave school once their voices had broken. Sometimes they are found referred to as 'commercial' or 'middle-class' schools. Their pupils often continued until, but rarely beyond, their sixteenth year. 'Preparatory' schools dealt with an often similar age range, though the upper age dropped down to fourteen as the century progressed. Their purpose was, as their name implies, to prepare boys for the secondary Public Schools (and, a little later, the Royal Navy). Their syllabus was, consequentially, 'classical', that is, Latin was at its heart. Elementary and preparatory schools were distinct from secondary or grammar or 'public' schools in that secondary schools prepared for university entrance; nevertheless most secondary schools, especially secondary choir schools, also contained junior classes that could accommodate young choristers. In the course of the century many secondary schools developed their junior class or classes into discrete junior or preparatory departments. Well into the century, however, many of the schools defied categorisation, partly because such categories were hardly yet established, partly because many schools were of uncertain structure or in states of change and flux.

The weakest of the early twentieth-century choir schools were chiefly (though not solely) the little schools serving either choristers only or the choristers with a handful of non-chorister pupils. Manchester Cathedral Choir School itself, educating twenty choristers and four probationers in the early decades, was largely 'elementary', yet pupils were encouraged to stay on after their voices had changed in order to take Manchester University matriculation and some pupils even attended the university's extra-mural classes in history and geography. In the early 1930s pupils remaining after voice-break were studying Greek and Spanish and were able to go to the technical college for classes in chemistry and physics.[5] Clearly Tuke wrought miracles against the odds. But there is a doubtful future for any school whose continuing efficiency depends upon miracles. The salvation of the Manchester choristers' education came with the decision in 1952 to close the choir school and enrol the choristers in the nearby ancient bluecoat school, Chetham's.

New College School, like the Manchester school, was supposedly 'elementary' or 'preparatory' at the start of the century yet retained – or tried to retain – its pupils for as long as they could sing treble, sometimes into their later teens. E.T. Campagnac, Professor of Education at Liverpool University, was invited to inspect the school in 1912. He found plenty to criticise: untrained staff, just three men teaching a nine-year age range, consequently a standard of work no better than moderate. Above all he berated a school that was trying to be, but was incapable effectively of being, a sort of quasi-grammar school. No doubt as a consequence of his report, the college council came to an arrangement with Magdalen College that New College boys still singing in quire after the age of fourteen could be educated at Magdalen College School.[6] But these secondary-age boys, no longer New College School pupils, continued to board with New College's younger choristers up to the age of seventeen if their treble voices held, as some still did in the 1930s.[7] The academic age-limit of fourteen, however, categorically established the school as 'preparatory', and so it has remained. Under the headship of Alan Butterworth, from 1955 to 1988, the school developed a famous reputation for the winning of academic and musical scholarships to very good senior schools. Recent developments have included the admission of girls to the school and increasing use of the choristers in recording work, notably, for a time, with the King's Consort.

Another example of the preparatory choir school that taught some secondary age boys was Exeter Cathedral Choristers' School. Between the wars it was professedly preparing its twenty-six choristers and probationers for the public schools, yet 'they usually leave about the age of 16'.[8] So some of the public schools were generous about admitting pupils at an educationally very awkward age. By contrast, Bristol Cathedral School, where shorthand typing had been added to the curriculum in 1885 to provide a 'commercial' rather than a classical education, struggled to retain pupils beyond the age of fourteen. In 1919 only three of the school's 113 pupils were fifteen or over. Only from the 1920s did the school steadily return to its original status as the cathedral grammar school.[9] Likewise, Wells Cathedral School was historically and by intention a grammar school, yet the school photograph of 1923 seems to display no boy of more than preparatory school age.[10]

One after another the small elementary choir schools were found to be unsatisfactory. Ripon may have been the first to abandon its choir school and recruit boys from local schools, as it was to continue to do until 1961 when the present preparatory choir school was founded. Another early casualty was Lincoln. In 1918 the chapter were heavily in debt and faced a daunting repair programme. So they sold urban property, including the school where their choristers had been taught. For four decades from 1919 they provided no education for their choristers.[11] Then in 1961 the chapter opened a new preparatory choir school. Although this grew steadily, the lasting solution was not found until 1996 when the Church Schools Company took over the choir school in amalgamation with two other schools, establishing the co-educational Lincoln Minster School with 276 children aged two to eighteen. Ten years later, so successful has it been, there are now over 800 pupils, including, in its preparatory department, the cathedral's boy and girl choristers.[12] Closure of the Chapel Royal School in Streatham Common occurred in 1923, by which time it had only eight pupils; education for the choristers thereafter was provided by the City of London School; but the Children of the Chapel had long since ceased singing regular weekday services and its school was absolutely an anachronism. The Cathedral School at Carlisle was closed in 1935. Since then the Carlisle choristers have been educated in various local schools. Early in the century Canterbury Cathedral was still maintaining its tiny elementary choir school. The number of ten choristers remained constant until the 1930s, but the 'probationers' had been increased from six to twenty by 1932, many of them presumably singing regularly in quire. It offered a curriculum that, like Bristol, included Pitman's shorthand, taught by the headmaster, John 'Bogey' Reid. In the late 1930s the prospects for Canterbury's choir school looked bright. The old schoolroom in the precincts was transferred to the King's School and a larger house with boarding facilities was made available for the choir school. Here the chapter developed a preparatory school of some sixty boys, with boarding (from 1937) and day non-choristers added to the choristers and probationers. Here the school returned after Second World War evacuation to Cornwall. Yet by 1971 this too was deemed to be unviable; it was closed, and the chapter came to an arrangement whereby their choristers continued to be boarded in a precinctual Choir House but were bussed up and down St Thomas's Hill to be educated at St Edmund's Junior (that is, preparatory) School, as they are, entirely satisfactorily, today.[13] Truro adopted a similar strategy when, in

1983, they transferred their choristers, most successfully, to Polwhele House, a private preparatory school just outside the city. Chester clung to their tiny choir school until 1977 but since then have drawn their singing boys from local schools.[14] A year later Newcastle closed the choir school they had established in 1947. No wonder there was a feeling in the 1970s that choir schools were an endangered species.

More constructive than closure was the turning of an unsatisfactory elementary school into a viable preparatory school. St Paul's, King's, Cambridge, and St George's, Windsor, had made such a change in the last quarter of the nineteenth century, in every case with the aid of a new building on a new site. For decades St Paul's was deemed to have a large enough chorister strength to flourish without bringing in non-choristers, and this continued to be the case when the 1875 Carter Lane choir house was abandoned in 1967 to be replaced by an uncompromisingly modern building immediately east of the cathedral. In the late 1980s, however, the almost inevitable decision was taken to strengthen the school's viability and competitive challenge by bringing in non-chorister day-boys and in 2002 the first girls were admitted. The thirty-eight pupils, then all choristers, of 1967 are now two hundred.

King's College's expanding number of non-choristers helped it, notably during the headship of Charles Jelf (1912–27),[15] to establish dauntingly high academic standards that it has never lost. The school's development since the 1870s has seen steady growth in numbers, broadening of curriculum, the introduction of girls (but not as choristers), and fine new buildings culminating in the recent provision of state-of-the-art music facilities. St George's, too, went through a long period of steady growth as a well-regarded boys' preparatory school. Then, after a crisis in the early 1990s which left pupil numbers at less than seventy, a phenomenally successful appeal for £2,000,000 enabled the school to transform its buildings, open a pre-prep, bring in girls and assure its future by adding almost three hundred pupils in five years. Christ Church Cathedral School at Oxford also transformed itself from a tiny elementary school educating only sixteen choristers and probationers into a preparatory school for twice that number by introducing fourteen 'candidates' for choristerships, made possible by adding to its 1892 building additional facilities in 1927.[16] Since then it has achieved miracles of development on its modest site. It has remained a boys-only preparatory school, but today, amongst its 150 pupils, and alongside its twenty boarding choristers, are the day boys who sing with the undergraduates in the choir of Worcester College.

Elsewhere the change from 'elementary' to 'preparatory' waited for the retirement of a long-serving elementary school head. George Arthur Scaife was head of York Minster Choir School for almost half a century, from 1903 until 1951. For many years alone, then – reluctantly – with the help of a junior mistress, he transmitted to his pupils skills and facts in English, arithmetic, geography (capes and bays), history (battles and monarchs), scripture, a little basic Latin and, at the very end, a gesture towards science. In 1927 the pupils, twenty-one choristers and seven probationers, were described as 'of the elementary school type of boy'; inspectors in 1949 noted twenty-nine boys aged from nine to fifteen benefiting from 'a sound general education' that had recently included biology but with little opportunity for sport. After Scaife's retirement things changed. His successor, the Rev. Donald Hewitt, had been a choral scholar at King's, Cambridge. He knew what a proper choir school should be like. Numbers were doubled by the admission of non-choristers and the curriculum was broadened to prepare boys for entry to Public Schools. Since his time it has steadily development into a fine day preparatory school, with the admission of girls and the opening of a pre-preparatory department in the late 1980s.[17]

A similar pattern was seen at St John's College, Cambridge. Sam (*sic*) Senior, later to be ordained, was appointed master of the college's little elementary day choir school in his final year as a Cambridge undergraduate in 1912. He remained in post, successful and much loved despite formidable skill with the cane, until retirement in 1955, that is, for his entire working career. The school occupied cramped premises close to the college. Figures from 1931 list fourteen choristers, up to eight probationers and some twenty non-singing boys, as many as could be crammed into the one room, later divided, climbing over others' desks as the only way to get to their own. The curriculum consisted of religious knowledge, maths, 'English subjects', French and art. No boy could remain beyond the age of sixteen; some choristers went on to secondary schools when their voices broke; many left to go straight into 'business'. Sam Senior's retirement in 1955 was a watershed. A college committee was formed to consider the future of the choir school and at first a majority was in favour of doing without one. Boys for the choir, some thought, could be recruited from local schools. But George Guest, organist since 1951, and his predecessor, Robin Orr, were adamant that a good choir needed a good choir school. Numerous leading musicians were urged to write in support, culminating in a telegram from Italy reading 'Save Saint John's Choir School at all costs', signed Ralph Vaughan Williams. The college was convinced and a fine college house was made available in Grange Road, close by the college playing fields. The new school was preparatory from the start and was able in 1973 to absorb an adjacent girls' preparatory school thereby making possible, as at York, co-education and a pre-preparatory starter department. 'This wonderful school' now educates 460 children on four sites along Grange Road.[18]

The lack of clear distinction between elementary and preparatory schools can be strikingly found in entries in the *Choir Schools Directories* of the period around 1930. Durham and Lichfield cathedrals continued to run choir schools for choristers and probationers only: twenty-four boys at Durham, and thirty-six, an exceptionally large number, at Lichfield. Durham had decided in 1902 that for proper education alongside proper liturgy boarding was a necessity. To accommodate the additional residents, No. 3 The College was released by the chapter to be the boarding house. Four years later Nos 4 and 5 were turned into the 'Chorister School' (a new name to distinguish it from the 'Song School' where choral practice took place). In the Directory of 1928 Durham was specific that their school offered 'the curriculum of an ordinary preparatory school'; but of their leavers, their voices having broken, whilst 'many' were said to proceed to public schools, principally Durham School, 'others go direct to banks, etc.'[19] By contrast, Lichfield Cathedral Choir School, at the same period, advertised itself as furnishing 'a good commercial education', and then adding 'but a few boys proceed to Public Schools'.[20] Here then were two schools in a state of transition. Durham by 1930 was virtually a preparatory school and had a new headmaster who declared his intention specifically to make it one. In the following decade non-choristers were introduced and the maximum leaving age brought down to that normal in preparatory schools. By the 1950s there were over a hundred pupils. Later expansion saw a pre-prep, formally opened by non-chorister alumnus Tony Blair in 1993. Co-education followed two years later.[21] Meanwhile, Lichfield in the 1930s had remained 'elementary' but aware that increasingly its choristers looked for preparation for entry to public schools. (Incidentally, of Lichfield's twenty-six full choristers six only were boarded, 'chosen with a view to solo work'. The resident soloists enjoyed holidays twice as long as those allowed to the day boys.) In 1942, however, still with just choristers on the roll, the unexpected availability of the bishop's palace made it possible for Lichfield to take the plunge and, in those more spacious premises, become specifically a preparatory school with non-chorister pupils. Today they number some 275 boys and girls. Recently Lichfield has made radical major decisions about future development. In 2005 they began to meet the local demand for the education of older children, at least to GCSE; simultaneously they are in negotiation to acquire another local preparatory school to run in parallel with the cathedral school.[22] As a preparatory choir school meeting demand for upward expansion Lichfield is not alone. In Wales, Llandaff Cathedral had moved its choir school into its bishop's palace in 1955, enabling expansion within three years to almost two hundred pupils. Two decades on girls were admitted, from amongst whom a 'top line' has been formed who now sing cathedral evensong three times a fortnight. More recently classes for secondary-age pupils were added. Llandaff Cathedral School now educates six hundred pupils, an astonishing success story. Llandaff's neighbour, St John's College in Cardiff, founded as recently as 1987, now educates over 500 pupils across the whole educational age span, and recently headed the A-level league-tables in Wales.

At Salisbury, where the school's status and purpose had varied widely during the nineteenth century, it was the Rev. Arthur Robertson, headmaster between 1900 and 1930, who determinedly created a preparatory school over that period. He was, despite having no formal training as an educationalist, an extraordinarily forward-looking man. Already by 1928 the boys had the use of two playing fields, a carpentry shop, a photographic dark room, and access to two billiard tables, a cinematograph and a wireless set.[23] After the Second World War the bishop decided that a former canonry would be more suitable for his home than the palace and, as at Lichfield, the palace was offered to the school. There, in an ideal location, the bishops' Great Room has become the Big School Room and park-like episcopal lawns have been turned into on-site playing fields.

> Grubby and trivial though our schoolboy lives
> Were as all are, we found in singing
> That liberation and delight result from lessons
> Under the ageless aegis of the spire ...
> Choristers in that Close lead lucky lives [24]

Despite every imaginable hindrance from the planning authorities, fine new school buildings have been added, the school has become co-educational and acquired one, indeed for a few years two, pre-preparatory departments.

Winchester Cathedral certainly had a 'preparatory' choir school in the early decades of the century. But it was dreary and attempts to strengthen it by the admission of non-choristers proved unsuccessful. A report by inspectors from the Board of Education in 1931 was highly critical. A new dean, Gordon Selwyn, had been installed in that year. He had been a student at King's College, Cambridge, and, like Donald Hewitt of York, he knew what a proper choir school should be like. Selwyn was determined, and persuaded his chapter to agree that Winchester too should have a model choir school. A man with good prep school experience, Humphrey Salwey, was appointed headmaster and sent off to see how they did things at King's. A more ample site in the Close was found and, although the premises were hardly sufficient when the transferred school opened that September, major building work proceeded very soon. Inspired by the adjacent medieval pilgrims' hall, it was decided that the new school should have a new name: the Pilgrims' School. The transformation proved so successful that thirty-five years later, with over a hundred boys in the school, the fifteen quiristers of Winchester College were enrolled experimentally as 'Pilgrims'. The arrangement was not to be reversed and, indeed, was to be sealed in 1978 when the headmaster of Winchester and one other representative of the college became members of the governing body of the Pilgrims' School alongside the dean and chapter.[25] Partnership with the college has done much to help the school establish its notable reputation. The college now makes available to the Pilgrim's School high-calibre facilities that few preparatory schools are likely to be able to provide for themselves. Meanwhile the quiristers, albeit singing in quire on only Tuesdays, Sundays, high days and their eves, distinguish themselves in public performance and on CD.

Perhaps the most surprising transformation occurred at Chichester. Here, in order to rescue his cathedral's two schools – the Prebendal School and the Choristers' school – from a state of dire crisis in 1929, the dean, Arthur Duncan-Jones, appointed himself headmaster, at first nominally and two years later actually. The Prebendal School was the city's ancient grammar school, close by the cathedral in West Street. It was there that for centuries the choristers had been educated. But in 1914, presumably in despair at the state of the Prebendal School, the chapter had moved their twelve choristers and twelve probationers to the premises of a former dame school some distance from the cathedral in North Street. Thereafter the grammar school continued to decline until by 1931 it had no pupils. So the Prebendal School building, and its name, were taken over to be the new home for the choristers' school and Dean Duncan-Jones set out – successfully as its later history has proved – to create a viable preparatory choir school on the lines of King's, Cambridge, and St George's, Windsor.[26]

Today, the only English choir school that continues to educate just choristers and probationers – the only true choir school, some would say – and in doing so flourishes, is Westminster Abbey Choir School. Little more than an 'elementary' school at the start of the century, the impetus for change came from the dynamic headmastership of Rev. R.D. Blackmore (1898–1908). Aspirations were raised and the curriculum was changed to match those aspirations. Latin replaced German, boys began to go on to good public schools, Westminster School itself introducing a closed exhibition for able Abbey choristers. In 1915 the present fine Choir House was opened in Dean's Yard and 'it became the custom rather than the exception' for boys to go on to 'famous' senior schools.[27] Under the mercurial Rev. William Morgan, head briefly from 1918 to 1921, it was one of only two choir schools to be taken into membership of the Association of Preparatory Schools (as IAPS then was). Like St Paul's, the Abbey's school educated a large complement of choristers, some forty boys, large enough to have them for many years, in two divisions, singing on alternate weeks and holidaying at different times from each other. Today, having a choir school exclusively for choristers enables the Abbey to be the only choral foundation to maintain full choral services for the whole octave of Christmas, in a week when everywhere else choristers are on holiday.

Bristol, Chichester, Wells and, for a time in the nineteenth century, Salisbury maintained schools that might have been, could have been, perhaps should have been, predominantly senior. Chichester by default, Salisbury by choice, settled for being preparatory. Bristol and Wells recovered their senior classes and became predominantly secondary with junior classes amongst whose pupils were all or most of their choristers. In the course of the nineteenth century four predominantly secondary cathedral schools, Ely, Norwich, Rochester and Worcester, succumbed to the recommendations of the Parliamentary Commissioners and separated off the education of their choristers from their cathedral grammar schools into newly created free-standing choir schools. This may for some decades have best served the needs of their singing boys, but it was not to be a lasting solution. The little choir schools thereby created could not hope to provide adequately for the twentieth century's more sophisticated educational demands. The King's School, Rochester, had opened a Junior House in 1925, but the choristers were not among its pupils. The choristers, all day boys, were educated along with a few non-choristers at a separate choir school in Minor Canon Row within the cathedral precincts. It was originally an elementary school, despite being described in *Kelly's Directory* of 1912 as 'for the sons of gentlemen and professional men'. In 1927 the headmaster of the King's School persuaded the dean and chapter to modify their choir school so that it could teach a preparatory-type curriculum. Within a decade, however, it became evident that better education and a more efficient use of resources could be provided by drawing the choir school pupils into the King's Junior School and this was effected in 1937. Now formally known as the King's Preparatory School, it has, like its senior school, been co-educational since the 1980s.[28]

With regard to the education of the choristers at Ely, the Schools Enquiry Commission had reported in 1867/8 that prior to 1857 the choristers had been taught in the grammar school, but that their attendance at cathedral services 'interrupted the school work of the other boys, and rendered more conspicuous the social differences which separated the choristers from their schoolfellows'. So, in an act of what would today be termed 'political correctness', the Ely chapter duly established a separate choir school for choristers only in 1857, teaching 'the rudiments of Latin' in addition to 'the simpler subjects'. Occasionally, the report says of the 1860s, a chorister passes into the grammar school, but more usually they simply leave school when their treble voice fails.[29] By 1931 this little choir school still educated just its twenty-four singing boys, with additionally three non-singing pupils who needed somehow to be occupied during the time of matins every weekday morning. Not until 1948 was the absurdity of the situation recognised and the choristers were returned to the King's School, within a clearly defined preparatory department, which, in 1970, like so many others became co-educational.

The Norwich choristers may never, prior to recent times, have been educated in the cathedral grammar school, possibly because Norwich had not been statutorily provided with a cathedral grammar school until some years after the Dissolution. Meanwhile the choristers had needed education, hence the

continuance at Norwich of a little choristers' school. By 1928 it is described as
providing a 'secondary type' of education, including drawing and shorthand,
for its twenty-one singing boys, often recruited as late as the age of eleven, some
continuing their education there after their voice-change. Canon E.A. Parr had
been appointed headmaster in 1922 and it was not until his retirement in 1951
that the chapter grasped the nettle of a hopelessly inadequate choir school,
urged on by the Ministry of Education who had counted square feet and found
them wanting. Ten years earlier its premises, occupying the eleventh-century
monastic locutory along with some rooms over the cloisters, had been described
as 'unfit for human habitation'. So in 1951 the choristers were welcomed into the
appropriate classes of Norwich School, which had its own junior department for
the younger ones; a suitable 'funeral' service for the old choir school was held
in the cathedral; and the headmaster of Norwich School was rewarded with the
choir school headmaster's stall in quire; and his school with a free gift of property
and land. The choristers were, and have subsequently been, rewarded with the
opportunity to be educated in a school that regularly stands at the top of its
county's academic league tables.

Worcester Cathedral, as we have seen, had had two shots at educating its choristers
separately from its cathedral grammar school. The second attempt, in 1882, was
the more successful. In 1911 the buildings on College Green were largely rebuilt
and further extended in 1928. On the closure of the Chapel Royal school in 1923,
its efficient and enlightened headmaster, P.F. Davis, was wooed by the Worcester
chapter to take on their own choir school, whose headship had become vacant.
By 1933 there were approaching fifty pupils, boarding and day, including the
generous total of twenty probationary choristers. All were expected to proceed
to public schools when their voices broke. They had a broad curriculum that
included preparation for academic scholarships. The facilities included tennis
courts, swimming instruction and cricket and football on the prestigious County
Cricket Ground. The choristers enjoyed exceptionally generous holidays for
the time: three weeks after Christmas, three weeks after Easter and six in the
summer. At the outbreak of the Second World War the King's School buildings
were commandeered by the government for twelve months and the school was
evacuated to Criccieth for that period. But the choir school stayed put and the
choristers sang on throughout the hostilities, sheltering in the central room of the
house which 'Pa' Davis had had specially strengthened with blast walls. In 1943,
when the headmaster's time for retirement was reached,[30] the occasion was seized
on by the chapter to transfer the property, assets and liabilities of the choir school,
educationally successful but financially unviable, to the governors of the King's
School, and a member of the King's School staff moved into the choir house as
master in charge of the choristers and other young boys there.[31]

There are seven secondary schools that have educated choristers from early days: the medieval secular cathedral schools at Hereford and Wells; the post-Dissolution Henrician cathedral schools of Bristol, Gloucester and Peterborough; Southwell Minster Grammar School (but with a four-decade gap in the mid-sixteenth century); and William Wayneflete's foundation of Magdalen College, Oxford. It should at this point be recalled that at times Bristol, Gloucester and Wells cathedral schools all struggled to find secondary-age pupils.

Had the Commissioners in the 1850s looked more carefully at how Hereford, Peterborough, Southwell and Magdalen College educated their choristers they might not have been so swift to advocate dismemberment of the 'secondary' choir schools. All four seem to have managed skilfully the care of their singing boys through the huge educational transformations that have characterised the twentieth century and, in the case of Peterborough, through the removal of the school in 1884 from the precincts to the suburbs. The danger for such schools is that the choristers can become an almost invisible sub-species of pupil within a huge 'normal' community. A hint of this risk can be detected at Oxford. Magdalen College School's move to a spacious site across the Cherwell in 1928 led to steady expansion in numbers and buildings. In headmaster Robert Stanier's fine history of Magdalen School the choristers feature very significantly in the centuries before the twentieth, though they fade from the later chapters. What is more, in the school's supplementary history, published in 1980, the choristers actually do disappear from the text, proof perhaps of their seamless integration into the everyday life of this outstanding school.[32]

Hereford Cathedral educated their choristers in their grammar school until 1976. In 1898 a school had been founded by one of the prebendaries in an iron shed in the garden of a house behind the Deanery, as a feeder to the grammar school. Over the years it had moved to more salubrious and spacious premises but had been sold to a schoolmaster as a private venture school in 1947. Despite being called the Cathedral Preparatory School, the choristers had never been educated there until, in 1976, it was decided that the 'prep' would be a better option for the choristers than the junior forms of the grammar school and they were moved there. Ten years later the cathedral school bought the goodwill of the preparatory school, renting its premises and calling it Hereford Cathedral Junior School. In 1994 they recovered the freehold. By then, following the practice of the senior school, it had become co-educational and today the junior school educates well over two hundred pupils. Expansion has helped to make it possible to achieve more secure funding for the choristers.[33]

The cathedral schools of Bristol and Wells were both languishing in the early years of the twentieth century, as was Gloucester Cathedral School. Bristol's recovery from its 'commercial' doldrums can be dated to the years following the First World War. In 1919, with 119 pupils on roll, the governors asked the Board of Education for an inspection in order that the school might be 'recognised' under the terms of the 1918 Education Act. The inspectors were gravely critical: unqualified, underpaid staff, insufficient classrooms and no laboratory or workshop were some of their concerns. In summary, the school was not efficient. With the energy that panic can inspire an appeal was launched, plans were made for provision of the necessary facilities and new building swiftly went ahead. Formal recognition was received in 1921. Thereafter progress was not unbroken – the school suffered bombing in 1940 – but the graph was broadly upwards, with Direct Grant status aiding the school between 1945 and 1975, followed by a successful move to full independence. New buildings kept pace with increasing pupil numbers: over 400 by 1970. Ten years later the first girl joined the sixth form. The Bristol choristers have been well provided for throughout, helped by funds from the chapter's Choral Foundation since 1983.[34]

There had been times in the nineteenth century when the variously named King's School or Cathedral School at Gloucester found it difficult to maintain secondary age pupils, particularly when its neighbour and rival, the Crypt School, was going through a good patch. Indeed, there is a suggestion in the report of inspectors as late as 1919 that the King's School might consider becoming a preparatory school for the Crypt School, and the school's prospectus for 1920 states, 'Boys are prepared for the Public Schools and for business'. Although there was a recovery in the 1920s, with new facilities built, it was to be ephemeral. By 1942 there were only some twenty choristers and six commoners on the roll. That was to be the nadir. The true recovery came after the war under successive headmasters E.H.J. Nott and Tom Brown. Numbers soared, there were new buildings and acquisition of old ones, most notably the bishop's palace which became the heart of the school. There has been no setback and the school's quality has recently been acknowledged by the election of the present head to the Headmasters' and Headmistresses' Conference.

Wells, likewise, has always had a firm commitment to educating its choristers at its cathedral school. Indeed, during the Wells doldrums, at their worst in 1870, the school educated only the choristers and three other boys. By 1899 chorister numbers had increased to fourteen, and non-chorister numbers had doubled – to six! The turning point came with the appointment as head of the Rev. A.F. Ritchie in 1924. He inherited a school of forty boys and bequeathed to his successor at his death in 1954 over 300 pupils. To cope with this expansion he persuaded the chapter to lease houses to the school and successfully begged buildings from the Church Commissioners. When the city's Girls' Grammar School closed their boarding house, Ritchie himself bought it and from it ran a parallel feeder preparatory department, which the governors subsequently had to buy from him. An even more remarkable period of growth and transformation was to follow under the twenty-two-year headship of the dynamic Alan Quilter from

1964.[35] In 1969 the school became co-educational; as numbers grew they built classrooms and laboratories, a sports hall, a swimming pool, a dining hall and, most significant of all in the light of what follows, a notable music centre.[36]

A unique arrangement is found at Chelmsford, where the cathedral draws its choristers from both its own voluntary aided cathedral primary school and from St Cedd's independent preparatory school. Three cathedrals, however, draw their choristers entirely from associated state schools. Two are schools with long histories as choral foundations: the King's School, Peterborough, and the Minster School, Southwell. A more recent choral school is St Edward's College, Liverpool. They are all voluntary aided, non-fee-charging, secondary comprehensive schools with associated junior departments or schools. All have fine academic as well as musical traditions. In addition, King's, Peterborough, was awarded Specialist Science School status in 2005. Truly dramatic change is afoot at Southwell where a £34 million development programme will see virtually a new school completed in 2007, including (as befits a Specialist School for Music and the Humanities) a 500-seat hall, a 150-seat theatre, a recital room, as well as lavish teaching and sports facilities. Its junior department makes particular provision for choristers and gifted instrumentalists.[37]

Three British choir schools have acquired specialist music school status: Chetham's, Wells and St Mary's Episcopal School, Edinburgh. The earliest specialist music school in the country, inspired by examples in Russia, was the Purcell School, founded in 1962. The following year Yehudi Menuhin opened his boarding school for young gifted musicians at Stoke d'Abernon. Shortly afterwards the Public Schools Commission included in its report a recommendation that further academies for specialist music teaching were needed,[38] and a similar recommendation was made in a report of the Calouste Gulbenkian Foundation in 1964. In the wake of all this, three existing independent schools, all cathedral choir schools, decided to develop a specialist music function. Since 1981 the government has undertaken to provide fee-support for gifted children admitted for specialist musical training at any of these designated schools.[39]

The first choir school to determine to become a specialist music academy was Chetham's at Manchester. The cathedral's choristers had already been educated there since 1952, so the school already had a musical bias. In the later 1960s the governors gave consideration to strengthening this emphasis and in 1969 announced their intention of becoming a school exclusively for gifted musical children between the ages of eight and eighteen. Today just short of three hundred boys and girls, mostly boarders, half of them in the sixth form, undertake a general education but with substantial time devoted to instrumental and vocal music, taught by a galaxy of specialist tutors. This environment and range of expertise is of outstanding benefit to Manchester's boy and girl choristers who, uniquely in England, together form the cathedral's top choral line.[40]

Coincidentally Wells was considering a similar development. In the middle 1960s the Earl Waldegrave had become a governor of the school. At one of his early meetings he had asked the headmaster, 'For what is this school particularly renowned? Some produce doctors, some intellectuals, some criminals! What do you produce here?' Alan Quilter responded that probably the school's greatest distinction was its music. So in 1970, the donation of funds for scholarships having been agreed in anticipation by a number of generous trusts, the governors determined on the appointment of a team of distinguished instrumental teachers and the recruitment of musically gifted children. When, shortly after this, it was decided to move Wells Theological College, by amalgamation, to Salisbury, it was agreed to acquire their beautiful medieval library and convert it into a music school. Wells differs from Chetham's in two major respects. It has from the start placed a particular emphasis on string playing. More significantly, the specialist musicians at Wells are part of a larger community of children: it is not a school for specialist musicians only. Here too the environment and facilities are highly beneficial for the boy and girl choristers (who do *not* sing together, except on high festivals).[41]

The third and most recent choir school to seek specialist music status was St Mary's Episcopal Choir School at Edinburgh. In the 1950s and 1960s there had been much debate about the future of this small school of some fifty pupils. There were thoughts of amalgamation, even of closure. About 1970 a concern at the lack of good musical education in Scotland began to be articulated. Yet that was precisely what the Episcopal Choir School was already providing. Consultation with the authorities in Edinburgh, Glasgow and Aberdeen, and visits to the Yehudi Menuhin School, led to the decision to raise the upper age limit, and begin to recruit talented young instrumentalists who would be taught by specialists from the Royal Scottish Academy of Music and Drama and elsewhere. That was in 1972 and the venture has proved hugely successful, not least in securing the future of the education, at what is now called St Mary's Music School, of Edinburgh's boy and (since 1977) girl choristers, who, as at Manchester, *do* sing alongside each other.[42] But the choristers of these three foundations are not the only ones to benefit from the advanced level of instrumental and vocal teaching that these specialist schools provide. Gifted choristers from other choir schools often move on to develop their musical talents further at Chetham's, Wells and St Mary's.

There have been many astonishing things in this fourteen-hundred-year history of the English chorister, but surely none more astonishing than the transformation in the quality of chorister education that the twentieth century has witnessed. Less than a hundred years ago many, perhaps a majority, of the English choristers were being brought up and taught in small, failing grammar schools such as those at Bristol, Chichester, Gloucester and Wells, or in tiny, hopelessly inadequate elementary schools, as at Canterbury, Chester, Durham, Ely, Lichfield, Norwich and Rochester. For good measure one might add the little choir school of St Saviour's, Eastbourne, where, in the 1920s, its two dozen boys were taught divinity, maths, English and (very enlightened, this) French, along with some games and the fashionable 'drill' three times a week, under their doubtless aptly named headmaster, Mr Thrasher.[43] Of the twenty-four cathedral schools at this time, sixteen had ordained headmasters, few with any identifiable training as teachers, many with no previous teaching experience before a vacancy had occurred and the chapter had searched among their minor canons and vicars choral to find a man who might also take on the burden of educating their choristers, thereby saving the chapter a teacher's salary. (To give just one example from many: when a minor canon, the Rev. H.Y. Ganderton, took on the additional responsibilities of being head of the choristers' school at Durham, the chapter added only £100 to his annual salary of £250.) From such schools, even in the eighteenth-century nadir of the choristers' days, successful and cultivated men did sometimes emerge. But more often the singing boys were likely to find themselves sent out, fit only for a life of modest, undemanding, unprofessional work. Some chapters or governors went on tolerating this until mid-century, lacking the finance and the vision to do better, until, as at Carlisle and Chester – and Eastbourne – they accepted closure as the only solution. And they were right. It was what the inspectors were to recommend at Norwich as late as 1951.

Already, however, in the early decades of the twentieth century, there were schools that maintained a creditable quality of care and education, as at Magdalen College, Oxford, and Peterborough and Eton, or that supported reforming headmasters, as at Salisbury and Worcester and Westminster Abbey, or that had transformed their chorister education for the better, as at St Paul's and King's, Cambridge, and St George's, Windsor. One striking example can do service for many. In 1921 the war-invalided father of a six-year-old son died. His widowed mother was left impoverished so two years later she entered their son, Charles, already a choirboy at his local church, for a voice trial at St Paul's. He was successful and became one of two probationers elected to join the choir in January 1924. The following year his mother also died. The choir school headmaster, Reginald Couchman, and his wife took Charles in as if he were their own son. So the choir school became, in his own words, 'home and family to me' and provided him in addition with 'a liberal education both academic and musical' and, it might be added, with a lasting Christian faith. On that foundation was to be built the career of the renowned conductor Sir Charles Groves. It had been Couchman, together with heads of two others of these exemplary schools, who, by founding the Choir Schools' Association in 1918, set about trying to light the torch of general reform. But reform in any case was in the air, government led, and inspectors became increasingly critical at unsatisfactory places such as Bristol and Gloucester, where the schools were clearly not efficient and so suffered the indignity of being 'unrecognised'.[44]

Today, the picture of an association of fine schools, educating some 25,000 pupils and over a thousand choristers and probationers is little less than thrilling. Read the academic results tables of the country's secondary schools published annually and there at or close to the top of their respective lists stand the secondary choir schools, whether independent and selective or Voluntary Aided and comprehensive. Go to the internet and read the latest inspection report of any choir school and one can find a picture of enlightened schooling and attentive pastoral care, the best reports outstandingly, even movingly, good. Further, the pace of development in several of the choir schools over the past twenty years is little less than a marvel. Of course not every school suits every child, nor does every child suit every school, and of course even the best schools can suffer a bad patch; but to send a son or a daughter to a choir school today is close to a guarantee of a first-class education.

15

Threats and Support

Notwithstanding the great progress made in the choir schools, there were, during the twentieth century, times when the very survival of the English chorister seemed to be in jeopardy. The late Victorians had categorically cured the disease of cathedral lassitude. They had rediscovered both the old purposes of the cathedrals as places of exemplary choral worship and found new purposes that placed the cathedral at the heart of its diocese and its city. Cathedrals were once again busy and people came, even flocked, to them. But the drastic financial surgery that had been effected by Parliament in the legislation of the 1830s and 1840s, when cathedrals seemed to be doing next to nothing with obscenely vast resources, had been replaced by a situation that saw chapters struggling to preserve their ancient buildings, extend their diocesan mission, and maintain, let alone enhance, their choral resources. Sometimes it seemed impossible for all three to be sustained together. Unsurprisingly, some foundations deemed the least painful arena for economy to be their choir. The pressures became particularly intense between the two world wars, when national and international financial crises and depression worsened the cathedrals' existing straits. Sydney Nicholson, the founder of the Royal School of Church Music, wrote in 1932: 'Calls on cathedral revenues … are heavy, and in nearly all cases the music is starved … choir schools are too often run in the least expensive way compatible with the bare requirements of the educational authorities'.[1] Against this background must be seen the reduction and ultimate elimination of weekday matins, with the consequential saving of lay clerk and other expenses. More drastic was the closure of the choir schools and abandonment of dedicated chorister education between the wars at Lincoln, Ripon, Carlisle and the Chapel Royal.

The chapters' problems were increased by government pressure, this time not directly on the cathedrals but on their schools. In the closing months of the nineteenth century government had taken a significant step in monitoring standards in independent schools by the creation of an inspection-verified category of schools deemed 'efficient'. This left a consequential assumption that those not so categorised must be inefficient. The Fisher Education Act of 1918 tightened the knot on the 'inefficient' schools by requiring all schools to be registered, and by making available to efficient schools free inspections and (through a later amendment) the government superannuation scheme for teachers.[2] From 1919 what came to be known as the Burnham Committee was to keep teachers' salaries under review, which meant, once the depression of the 1920s and 1930s was over, mostly rising.[3] These pieces of legislation were, of course, beneficial, but they made more vulnerable than ever schools that were 'inefficient' or paid their unsuperannuated teachers a pittance. Around this time we find associations of independent schools discussing, in near panic, what to do about the problems of their weaker members. Indeed, a short-lived federation of the Private Schools Association (now ISA), the College of Preceptors and the Preparatory Schools Association (now IAPS) was formed to face the challenge and monitor future educational legislation. The PSA's magazine, *Secondary Education*, in May 1918 contained an editorial that put the choice facing the proprietors of an unrecognised school very bluntly: 'it must be helped to become efficient or it must be closed down'. Very few choir schools by 1918 had sought and gained the cachet, 'recognised as efficient': almost certainly only Hereford and Peterborough.[4] Some, as has been seen, had sought inspection but been refused recognition as a consequence; others took no such step because they well knew what the consequence would be. Many of the choir schools were doubly vulnerable: they were poor schools in both senses of the adjective. Closure seemed unavoidable and imminent.

There had been one clause in the draft legislation of 1918 of particular concern to choral foundations. It appeared to make choristerships illegal. It forbad any child under the age of twelve and restricted any child under the age of fourteen from being employed for singing, playing or performing. Choristers sang and, in 1918, many of them were waged for doing so. Of course the legislation had its eyes fixed on other forms of children's musical performance but, as drafted, choristers were caught in the net. Happily, representation from the cathedrals clarified the position and allowed the employment of boys singing in choral foundations to continue. But the carelessly drafted clause had caused great alarm.

One consequence of all this was to be of lasting benefit to the choir schools and their choristers. Late in 1918 a meeting took place at Westminster Abbey Choir School between its headmaster, the Rev. W.E. Morgan, the headmaster of St Paul's Cathedral Choir School, the Rev. R.H. Couchman, and the headmaster of King's College Choir School, Cambridge, Mr C.R. Jelf. By the conclusion of the meeting they had agreed a simple resolution: 'that in view of the urgent educational requirements of the present time a Choir Schools' Association be formed at once'. Reginald Couchman, at his speech day soon after, on 2 January 1919, said that 'in the era of Reconstruction that lay before us [following the First World War], Choir Schools would have to look to their laurels. He did not think St Paul's had much to fear; but it was a sign of the times that an Association of Choir Schools had recently been formed'.[5] In particular, the association would be 'watching the effect of the new Education Act on the special position of choir schools'. The concern of these three founder members was an act of altruism. It is unlikely that any of them had worries about the standing of his own establishment: all three ran good schools. Their concerns were for the choir schools as a whole and in particular for the weaker ones, above all for the future of the English chorister. In the cases of Couchman and Morgan there was also an underlying concern for the future of the Anglican choral liturgy. But probably not so for Jelf: one of his several curiosities was that, although head of King's College Choir School, he could not abide the worship of King's College Chapel.[6] The association, duly established, held certainly one and possibly two meetings in 1919. Morgan was to leave the choir school world in 1921; lack of records prevents us from knowing whether Jelf played a significant role in the association during his eight further years at King's; but Couchman clearly became the association's mainstay as honorary secretary, and continued so to serve until his retirement in 1937. He, more than anybody, ensured that the association developed strongly. The assumption must be that from 1919 the heads of the majority of the country's Church of England choir schools met annually, although this is an assumption and not a certainty, due to the unhappy circumstance that in 1942 all the association's records were lost. So we have no way of knowing whether CSA reacted directly to the legislation of the time, what steps it took, if any, to support the weaker schools or what its chief areas of concern were in the inter-war years. All subsequent documentation, however, makes clear that the primary concern of the association has always been the welfare of the choristers. The happy discovery of two annual directories from 1928 (a revised version of the original 1925 edition) and 1931 does enable us to know which schools were represented, that is, which heads were in membership. Of the predominantly senior schools only Hereford, Southwell and Wells had joined CSA by 1925; but almost all the junior schools were in membership, including the parochial choir schools of All Saints, Margaret Street, St Saviour's, Eastbourne, and St Mary's, Reigate.

Twelve years earlier than the foundation of CSA, but less directly concerned with the welfare of choristers, the Church Music Society had been established, or, strictly speaking, re-established.[7] The society's primary focus was on the quality, that is, the often poor quality, of music performed in church. But they began publishing occasional papers and some of these concerned themselves with the choral foundations and their choristers. It was CMS that, in 1922, requested the archbishops of Canterbury and York to convene a committee to report on the place of music in worship and on the training of church musicians and the musical education of the clergy. The report of that committee, *Music in Worship*, addressed, among much else, the problems being faced by the cathedrals in the maintenance of their choral liturgy. Although the committee were clear that parish churches should not attempt to emulate the musical practices of cathedrals, a very strong note in support of cathedral music was sounded. The music of the daily office, they urged, 'represents some of the highest ideals both of art and of worship; and expresses in a unique form some of the best of Christian devotions. On all grounds this inheritance must be maintained and developed.'[8] The committee then addressed the practicalities and the problems. 'The maintenance of choral establishments on an adequate footing' was among a cathedral's chief obligations and that obligation included the maintenance of discrete chorister education. If funds were insufficient for this purpose and new sources of funds could not be found, the cathedral should undertake 'the suppression of one or more clerical offices'. In other words, the proper education of a team of choristers should be seen to be more important than the continued employment of one or more canons. Despite this unambiguous statement of priorities from the two metropolitans, choristers were robbed of choir school education in the weakest foundations during this period, albeit in very few.

The next major threat was the Second World War. Between 1914 and 1918 England had not been in any significant sense a theatre of war. No choral foundation had been so much as damaged. It is true that on 7 July 1917 St Paul's Cathedral's service of matins, sung, as often during that war, by the boys only, began to be disturbed by the sound of anti-aircraft fire until, 'with volleying and thundering' a bomb fell 150 yards from the cathedral. The boys, as the *Church Times* was to put it, 'showed themselves English boys, and English boys at their best', and went on singing regardless, with the happy consequence that the king's private secretary came later to present them with a cricket catching cradle 'in recognition of their calmness under fire'. Perhaps even more surprising: Dean Inge, for almost the only time in his life, actually visited the choir school to thank the boys. The chief impact of that war was to be the high toll of ex-chorister combatants who were to lose their lives.

The war of 1939–45 was different. Many choral foundations suffered disruption. All three London choirs sent their boys into evacuation. St Paul's shared duties with Truro for the duration, each choir singing the offices on alternate days. Westminster Cathedral evacuated their boys in 1939 to a country house near Uckfield, subsequently disbanding them. The recruitment of a new team in 1946 proved a difficult task. Westminster Abbey sent their choristers to live, study and sing with the boys of Christ's Hospital at Horsham until December 1940 when even that was deemed too risky, and the chorister body was disbanded. Their removal from London saved their lives. In May 1941 the abbey choir school suffered a direct hit and the premises were not fit for occupation again until 1947. When the choir was re-formed in that year it included some of the boys who, from 1943, had come in on Sundays to keep the flame of choral liturgy alight. Another choir school to be severely blitzed, effectively destroyed, in the war was Exeter, tragically killing the daughter of the headmaster, Edward Langhorne. Even choir schools that were not evacuated were touched by the war. Stuart Pearson became a Lichfield chorister a week after war had been declared in 1939. He recalls reductions in teaching staff and frugality of rationed food; then, from 1940, the noise of the bombing of Birmingham and the fearsome red glow in the sky as Coventry blazed caused the dormitory to be moved from the top floor of the choristers' house to the cavernous cellars of one of the canonries.[9] Canterbury was among the choral foundations whose boys had to be evacuated in this period, to Cornwall in conjunction with the King's and St Edmund's schools. If an excuse was wanted for the permanent disbandment of a choral foundation this was it. But, on the contrary, ironically the war can be seen to have strengthened the perception that the cathedral choral tradition was part of the heritage that the country was fighting to defend. By 1947 all were back in place.

The war over and the choral foundations again in full song, the archbishops of Canterbury and York convened a second committee to consider all aspects of the role of music in the worship of the Church of England. Their report, published in 1951 and reissued with revisions in 1957, was entitled *Music in Church*.[10] Once again a consideration of the choral worship of the cathedrals formed part of the committee's remit. And once again they urged that 'the maintenance of the choir on a sound basis should be regarded as a first charge on the financial resources of a cathedral'. Specifically the report called for 'the preservation of choir schools as independent schools'. Unlike the 1922 report, that of 1951 contains a section specifically concerned with the choristers. It stresses the importance of the boarding choir school:

> Of the value of choir schools it is impossible to speak too highly. The carefully-balanced life of a boarding school enables the boy to take his singing in his stride, alongside his work, games and other recreations. Experience of many years in many choir schools has demonstrated that the training in intelligence and character, demanded by the singing of beautiful and often complicated music in the religious atmosphere of a cathedral, gives the boy immense advantages. Cathedral choir boys as a class do well at their subsequent schools, and in later life.

It is significant that neither in the 1951 report nor in its 1957 revision is there any sense of crisis, any perception that new storm clouds might be looming on the horizon for the choir schools. In fact, by the middle decades of the second half of the twentieth century three strands had combined to put the choral foundations yet again under threat. One was the familiar problem of financial straits. In the 1970s in particular, due to inflationary pressures on school fees, chorister education was becoming rapidly more expensive. Cathedrals had absolutely no support out of public funds for the maintenance of their buildings and faced growing demands on their slender financial resources. Additional sources of income commonplace in today's cathedrals, such as 'voluntary' donations for entry, were as yet untried. At the same time there was a burgeoning theological movement that cast doubt on the value of the choral service. The trend was all for congregational participation, plebification of church language, lay ministry, the move from the chancel to the nave. It was a parochial movement but it threatened to be passed up to the cathedrals. The Scouse poet Roger McGough had celebrated the opening of Liverpool's Metropolitan Cathedral as a place

> Where lovers meet after work
> For kind words and kisses
> Where dockers go of a Saturday night
> To get away from the missus
> Tramps let kip there through till morning
> Kids let rip there every evening ...

and where

> Koppites teach us how to sing
> God's 'Top of the Pops' with feeling.[11]

Here, with all the clarity of the poet, was a debased theology that subsumes the first commandment in the second, robs Christianity of the mysteries of incarnation, atonement and resurrection, and reduces the cathedral to a fusion of social services refuge and roaring disco. McGough clearly approved; but another poet, lay clerk Humphrey Clucas, writing fourteen years later, expressed his abhorrence of cheap music and demotic language with angry vehemence:

> We mouth a godless dialect –
> Farewell to timeless prose;
> It's pick'n'mix, each church a sect,
> Anything goes.
>
> So let the pop-hymn fret the air,
> Pallid and out of date;
> And you may wince, but we don't care
> That's progress, mate.[12]

In 1980 the then dean of St Paul's could write a fine essay on the contemporary role of cathedrals that is full of ecumenism, exhibitions, Taizé services, tourism, pilgrimage, the role of lay people – but with not a mention of the daily office.[13] There was a real perception about in the 1970s that a costly choral foundation might be an anachronistic luxury.

On top of these problems came a political threat. At that time all but two of the choir schools were independent, that is, as the left liked to call them, 'private schools'. Private schools were believed by many to be the root cause of Britain's class-ridden and divided society. In September 1973 Roy Hattersley, shadow education spokesman for the Labour Party then in opposition, addressed the annual conference of the Incorporated Association of Preparatory Schools. As he himself put it, he came to deliver their death sentence. He warned categorically that when next in power it would be a Labour government's intention 'initially to reduce and eventually to abolish private education in this country'. If this was an alarming threat for all independent schools it was especially alarming for the choir schools. 'Initial reduction' could most easily be effected through financial measures, including removal of charitable benefits and the charging of VAT on school fees and such like. Most choir schools in 1973 ran tight budgets. Impecunious chapters funded expensive chorister scholarships. Neither chorister parents nor chapters could afford to fund astronomically increased school costs. If, under attack, private schools started to close, choir schools would surely be in the first *tranche*. One dean actually told a meeting of choir school parents that he doubted whether the chapter could go on maintaining their expensive musical foundation. But not just this. Some cathedral chapters and doubtless all college senior common rooms included people who believed that private schools were 'socially divisive bastions of privilege' or, in the words of Eric James, a residentiary canon successively of Southwark and St Albans, 'exclusive structures of commercial privilege which run counter to the very heart of the gospel.'[14] Fellows of Oxbridge colleges were asking why they were running a private, fee-charging school just for the purpose of maintaining an elitist choir. Shirley Williams, the liberal-minded wife of the Provost of King's College, Cambridge, affirmed that 'freedom to send one's children to an independent school is bought at too high a price for the rest of society'.[15]

At this time a number of local authorities were willing to assist with the payment of fees, sometimes in full, for the education of choristers. In 1974 a Labour government was indeed formed. Their first step in implementing Roy Hattersley's threat was to announce an intention to prevent local authorities from paying fees for any pupils attending independent schools. This step rang alarm bells. People and groups who cherished the cathedral choral tradition began, not before time, to marshal their defences. Eric Kemp, then dean of Worcester, later to be bishop of Chichester, a man of huge energy and a wide network of influential contacts, set up a Choral Foundations Working Party whose representations to government and contacts with the Association of Chief Education officers swiftly achieved exemption from the proposed regulation for the choir schools, specialist music schools and ballet schools. Thus religion saved the arts and the arts saved religion, or at least its choristers. But only for a time. The threat to independent schools as a whole remained. Gradually the other bodies, the heads and governors of choir schools, the cathedral organists through their own association, began to formulate and coordinate a response. Largely under the impetus of Lionel Dakers, Director of the Royal School of Church Music, through the medium of a

committee representing deans, precentors, organists and headmasters, the threat
to the choir schools began to be articulated. Individuals did what they could.
With Labour once again in opposition in the 1980s, George Guest, the organist
of St John's, and his choir school headmaster had a meeting with Neil Kinnock,
then shadow education spokesman, at which they were able to spell out the risk
to the country's musical heritage unwittingly implicit in Labour's plans. Kinnock
was in favour of music. He, like Guest, was Welsh. Welshmen sing. Causing the
closure of forty good choirs was not on his agenda.

This combination of threats had a transforming effect upon the Choir Schools'
Association. In the earliest years from which its records have survived, that is in
the 1940s and 1950s, with many of the heads still drawn from the minor cathedral
clergy, the association, through its annual meeting, very strikingly concerned
itself with the welfare of its boys, not least with their spiritual welfare. In 1947
the bishop of Stafford spoke to the heads on the need for choristers to have a
religious rule of life; two years later at Eton the conduct [chaplain] spoke of
the unique opportunity heads had for deepening a boy's religious convictions.
Then in the 1950s and 1960s CSA dropped into a sort of doldrums. There was
just one non-residential meeting each year. Chairmen changed annually by a
semi-automatic rotation. It is difficult to conclude from the cryptic minutes that
anything of importance was discussed, other than keeping the Roman Catholic
schools out. It drifted into being little more than a luncheon club for like-
minded friends with common interests. 1972 marked the depths of this languor:
Canterbury had closed the choir school and there was nothing anybody could
do about it; the annual Directory was discontinued because it was loss-making;
and the association's bank balance stood at £4. 33p. The following year came
the realisation that their schools (and with them their jobs) were under threat
and that, to their shame, the deans and chapters were starting to do something
about it and had invited CSA to nominate representatives to their working
party. But not until 1974 did a prophet speak: Alan Quilter of Wells uttered a
passionate call for the association to change its purposeless nature, to become
a professional body and to take action to save the choral heritage of which they
were custodians.

The transformation over the following decade was astonishing. In 1981,
under what was to be the decisive two-year chairmanship of Michael Barcroft
of Peterborough, the committee met with Robert Holtby, the passionately
pro-choir school dean of Chichester, with Lionel Dakers, the Director of RSCM,
with Barry Rose, the BBC's producer of choral evensong broadcasts, and Jane
Capon, the press officer of the Independent Schools Information Service. The
committee emerged bursting with initiatives. By 1984 not only were the Roman
Catholics in, but the head of Westminster Cathedral School was chairman; the
association had an annual magazine that made a four-figure profit; there was

an annual choristers' composition competition with a fine silver salver donated by the Friends of Cathedral Music; the few choir schools not in membership were nagged into joining; there was a very active publicity sub-committee; the Gulbenkian Foundation was underwriting the costs of a choir schools' brochure; an annual questionnaire and census had been launched; a bursary trust to help towards school fees was founded with a £200,000 legacy under offer; and 75 per cent of the choir schools were reporting rising numbers of candidates at voice trials. By 1986 the association had reserves of £10,000. In 1989, after ten years of Conservative government under Margaret Thatcher, the Labour Party had been persuaded to love the choir schools. Jack Straw, their shadow education spokesman, was guest at the CSA's AGM at Ely. He told the heads that their schools played 'an important part' in 'our national, cultural, as well as educational life' and that he looked for 'constructive discussion about future support from public funds for the work of your schools'.[16]

This transformation had not been achieved by the Choir Schools' Association alone. Another body that passionately lent its support was the Federation of Cathedral Old Choristers' Associations. Being one of a team of choristers is among life's most bonding activities. Cohesion in a choir is as necessary as in a rugby scrum – choristers, of course, would say more so; both are generative of lifelong friendship. From the later decades of the nineteenth century alumni clubs began to be founded whereby former choristers could meet, reminisce and relish again the music of the choir in which they had once sung. Sometimes men who had sung in other choirs were brought along as guests at such gatherings. In 1910, ex-choristers from York and Lincoln were guests at the Peterborough Old Choristers' Association gathering. In conversation it seemed to them that it would be good if there could be formed a federation of all such associations. A letter was sent to every cathedral precentor in England and Wales. So enthusiastic were the responses that a provisional committee was formed. On 29 June 1911 the inaugural meeting of what came to be called the Federation of Cathedral Old Choristers' Associations was held, again at Peterborough. Associations initially in membership were Bristol, Canterbury, Carlisle, Durham, Lichfield, Lincoln, Manchester, Norwich, Peterborough, Rochester, Salisbury, Truro, Winchester, Worcester, York and Melbourne, Australia. The following year the first Federation festival was held, at York. Since 1914, the war years excepted, gatherings have been held almost annually. The associations represent a large body of former choristers, and often their relatives, who hold the choral liturgy in deep affection. In the threatening years of the 1980s their voice was heard and was important. In 1982 the Federation lobbied the leaders of all the main political parties on behalf of the choral foundations and their schools.[17]

Not only did former choristers rally in support. In 1954 the Rev. Ronald Sibthorp, the then succentor of Truro, read a paper to the Association of Minor

Canons that sounded warning bells about the reduction in the number of choral services in the cathedrals. Two years later he and thirty-eight like-minded people met to discuss the matter and from that meeting the Friends of Cathedral Music was born. Steadily and undramatically the organisation has grown so that today it has approaching four thousand members, lively diocesan branches, national and regional gatherings and two fine publications: a twice-yearly journal, *Cathedral Music*, and an annual schedule of times of the regular services in the choral foundations called *Singing in Cathedrals*. With assets in excess of £1.5 million the association is able to make grants of upwards of £100,000 a year principally to endow choristerships, thereby reducing the costs to cathedrals of their choral force and ensuring that choristers do not come only from the families of the well to do.[18] They too, in the 1970s and 1980s, were another body active in the defence of the choir schools at a time when they appeared to be, and indeed were, at hazard.

Today there is not the same sense of threat, or at least the threats are different. The condemnatory voice of the political left, if not quite silent, is very much a minority one. There seems no longer any serious likelihood of independent education being initially reduced and ultimately abolished by government diktat. On the contrary, the quality and importance of the choir schools is clearly recognised and admired in high places. As anticipated by Jack Straw in 1989, a Labour government has continued to maintain and enhance the provision of funds to help boys and girls from poorer families sing in cathedral and collegiate choirs and benefit from choir school education under the provisions of the Education (Grants)(Music, Ballet and Choir Schools) Regulations (1995),[19] later empowered by the 1996 Education Act.[20] The governors of choir schools for their part are going to great lengths to try to ensure that funds are available so that choristership is not a socially exclusive opportunity. Nor do the financial pressures on the cathedrals – or at least on some cathedrals – seem so parlous as they were thirty years ago. The preservation and repair of buildings has been facilitated by successful appeals, substantial funds from sources such as the National Heritage Fund have been made available, growing cathedral congregations have learnt to make their offertories by tax-efficient direct debits and for some cathedrals cultural tourism has been a pot of gold. Even the ancient Benedictine duty of hospitality has helped by way of profits from welcoming refectories. Indeed, somehow funds have been found not only to maintain the levels of boy choristerships but also to pay, if usually less generously, for a top line of girls. There is no ground for complacency. Some foundations remain very pressed and have indeed abolished canonries to preserve choristers; and a terrorist attack can for a time almost eliminate tourism.

The most remarkable change, however, seems to be the liturgical one. Where now is there a choral foundation that reveals any serious theological doubt that the central role of a cathedral is the offering of the finest possible gifts of worship within the liturgy, with beautiful music its chief embellishment? On the contrary, by the introduction of girls, choral evensong has in some places been restored to a daily occurrence. Cathedral choirs are proudly sent around the diocese, to help the parishes, to show what really fine church music can be like, and quietly to do a little gentle chorister recruitment. Where the musical force is now a cathedral's major expense, that is accepted as being how it should be. And of course the choir school is an essential asset, partly because it provides such fine education not only for the choristers, partly because (apart from the cost of chorister scholarships) it is unlikely to be any drain on the cathedral's finance; on the contrary, as a tenant it is likely to be an important source of cathedral income. The central role of music was again confirmed in the most recent commission on church music set up by the archbishops in 1988 with its report, *In Tune With Heaven*, published in 1992.[21] This, in its section on the cathedrals, was more challenging than its two predecessors had been. It called for musical experiment, both in style and in resources, and strongly encouraged the introduction of girls, whilst acknowledging the irreplaceability of the traditional boys. One recommendation that has been widely adopted is the appointment of a cathedral's chief musician as Director of Music rather than, as formerly, Organist, particularly since one great change that has occurred during the twentieth century has been the descent of the 'organist' from the organ loft to the conductor's stand beside the singers. In the decade since the publication of the report, however, cathedrals have been less keen to replace the music of Byrd and Purcell, Stanford and Wood, by worship songs and Negro spirituals. Whilst urging that lay clerks should be better paid and that means should be found for the recruitment of choristers from 'less wealthy' backgrounds (but how many chorister parents are, in fact, 'wealthy'?), the report seems unaware that the greatest problem in the provision of fine music in cathedrals today is almost certainly the recruitment of the choral force. Organists will tell one that the main future threat to fine choral liturgy is likely to be the difficulty of finding musically trained men with good voices ready to take on lay clerkships that require them to be in church on almost every evening of the week and for three services on Sundays for most the year.[22] Similar, but less pressing, is the difficulty of recruitment of choristers.

It is probably impossible to form any estimate of the nationwide proportion of candidates to vacancies at early twentieth-century voice trials. There is reference to eight candidates for four places being average at Windsor; but in 1938 fifteen boys competed for just two places. At Durham in 1913 there were ninety-nine candidates. This vast crowd was reduced to some two dozen, then these survivors were required to sing in groups to test for the blend of their voices. After an academic test nine were chosen, to be called up as voices broke and consequent vacancies arose. Parents would then get a message asking for their boy to report to school and choir in three days' time.[23] But this itself was an improvement on the more usual earlier practice when a boy might undertake a voice trial for an existing vacancy and be enrolled immediately. Records suggest that in the 1960s and 1970s demand was usually buoyant, the more celebrated foundations attracting seven, even ten boys for every vacancy. However, since the 1980s, not everywhere and not in any consistent pattern, recruitment of boys has been cause for concern. As a consequence schools and choirmasters have varied their modes of recruitment. Some regularly hold two voice trials a year; some have almost abandoned formal voice trials and simply test applicants as they appear; and some tour the primary schools. In 2000 Salisbury invented the 'Be a Chorister for a Day' initiative, inviting anything up to a hundred young boys and girls to come and meet the choristers, experience a choir practice, the cathedral and the school, eat a sumptuous free school lunch and join with the choir in a simple item at evensong. It has proved an effective aid to recruitment and has been copied elsewhere.

Difficulty in recruitment does not apply so much to girls, partly because they are still only to be found in less than half of the choral foundations, partly because there is still a 'novelty' element about girl choristerships, and partly because at many foundations they are required to sing less often than the boys. The problem with the boys is not (as is sometimes suggested) that boys do not want to be in choirs where there are also girls: there is absolutely no evidence to show that boy recruitment is more difficult in foundations where a girls' choir has been established. The problem is more to do with the attractions of family weekend activities in an affluent society, and with the deep reluctance of some parents, especially many mothers (who make the educational decisions these days), to part with young sons to boarding school, even to the modern open-house boarding school with generous opportunities for family contact and pupil leave-out. Yet the benefits and the fun of a choristership, and particularly of a boarding choristership, have never been greater.

16

Choristership

A choristership in the early decades of the twentieth century could be a hard life and indeed was so in all but a few foundations. Matins was sung on most mornings and evensong almost every day in all but five of the cathedrals well into the 1930s. This should be borne in mind when today's choristers complain, justifiably, that there is not a minute in the day to catch breath, or when their teachers say, though rarely as wittily as Geoffrey Howell of Durham Choristers' School: 'The trouble with the choristers is that they are always supposed to be somewhere else five minutes ago'.[1]

Horrors recalled from the early decades at St George's, Windsor, include the cold and draughty dormitories and the struggles, well before 7 a.m., with an Eton collar, obligatory for choristers in those days at most foundations – 'a devilish device, whose upper edge chafes the tender skin of the neck, and whose lower edge digs into the collar bone'. (Eton collars were not abandoned at Durham until 1975, and are still to be seen at King's, Cambridge.) Then, at Windsor in 1913, came a Scripture lesson before a breakfast of porridge without sugar and, in the afternoon, clearing up the cowpats before the football field was fit to play on. Lunch might include the curious experience of reading on the day's slice of meat, in printer's ink back to front, a news item indelibly implanted by the newspaper in which the meat had been wrapped by the butcher.[2] Almost all chorister recollections from this period refer to the terrible food. At New College bread and dripping at breakfast and again before bed at night was preferable to the alternative, bread and margarine that tasted like candle fat. Some of the New College boys would anyway not have fancied breakfast, having fainted at the pre-breakfast chapel service.[3] A special treat on Saturday morning breakfast at St George's in the 1930s was an allowance of one and a half bananas to spread on one's bread and margarine. One boy managed to create a record by eking it out over thirteen slices. On Sundays there was a warm chipolata for each boy, while the master at the head of the table ate his bacon and eggs.[4] Today, of course, Health and Safety regulations would ring alarm bells at newspaper-wrapped comestibles. Heads and governors know that high on the list of quality criteria come good meals. Today's standards demand choice, 'five portions of fruit and veg', and availability of second helpings for generally hungry choristers.

In almost all schools at the start of the century discipline was harsh. The cane, or in Scotland the taws, was an ever-present threat, and continued to be a normal weapon of retribution for sins of commission and omission, even administered *en masse* when the culprit was too frightened to own up and could not be identified. At St George's in the 1930s the punishment, no matter what time the crime had been committed, was delayed until bedtime, when pyjamas provided minimum protection and surrounding boys were an appalled, or, worse, eager, audience. Yet ex-chorister J.R. Poole, writing long afterwards, could remember this having happened only once in his time at St George's.[5] Enlightened heads were abandoning their canes in the 1950s and 1960s. Graham Kalton's 1966 survey of the public schools (twelve educated choristers) recorded that, out of 166 schools, 145 permitted masters to use the cane and 103 allowed senior boys to do so.[6] But by this time public opinion was turning against corporal punishment. Only two years after Kalton's report the Public Schools Commission noted that 'a marked change [had] taken place in the last decade, and beating is on the decline'. The report contains a strong recommendation that corporal punishment of any kind should cease and made clear that the government-funded assisted places that were under consideration would not be awarded in any school that maintained the practice.[7] Ten years later it was illegal.

Outside the classroom, throughout the first half of the century, in many schools bullying was not only commonplace but tolerated by authority as part of the toughening-up regime. This is so much the stuff of the fiction and autobiography of the time that elaboration would be gratuitous. But it must be said that it was not universal, even in the early decades. While a former St George's chorister John Barkham writes of bullying as 'rife', his near-contemporary, Myron Kok, recalls his time at St George's as having been blissfully happy: 'I could not have been cared for by nicer people'.[8] At King's, Cambridge, there was a sort of golden age from 1927 to 1950 under headmaster Cedric Fiddian. Happy informality took over from the tight regime of his predecessor, Jelf. What former choristers remembered was – long before Design Technology had been invented – building canoes in the carpentry shop, only to discover on the first outing to the river that they were not watertight; or – long before the Health and Safety Executive existed – repairing a gas leak with chewing gum; or plays in which – long before the days of Manuel, the *Fawlty Towers* waiter – 'Fid' would take the part of an incompetent butler, with constant opportunity for dropping of plates and spilling of soup. In the summer, lessons went outside onto the lawns. All this provided release from the strict discipline maintained and high standards demanded by 'Daddy' Mann's successor, Boris Ord, in chapel.[9]

Today the strictures of the Children Act protect choristers from both the harshnesses and, in some ways regrettably, the risk-taking, of earlier decades, when there were obvious opportunities for bullying and abuse. Inspectors of boarding choir schools write reports that express incomprehension at the pace of life lived by cathedral and collegiate choristers, and even sometimes attempt (without success) to rein them in. But there cannot be any doubt that in the twenty-first century choristers, surrounded as they are by high quality pastoral care, are protected from the brutalities and privations of earlier decades. Among these were the rough initiation rites for new probationers. At Winchester Cathedral there was an old iron-bound chest in the south transept. Into this prison a new probationer would be incarcerated; then, on release, he was made to crawl between six sculpted angels supporting an episcopal tomb. 'Lifting the crown' involved removing the top of one of the cathedral's ancient stoves, the probationer consequencially being covered in ash. And there was 'Stephening', that is, stoning the young boy with hymn books. Vestiges of these harsh rites can still be found, but wholly sanitised, such as the 'bumping' of a new chorister at Salisbury, nowadays painless and bruiseless. Today's regulations also do everything they can to protect choristers from sexual abuse. There is no reason to believe that choristers have been more subject to this appalling offence than any other class of children, but in the nature of the case instances have rightly captured the headlines. Until the most recent decades there were obvious opportunities for bullying and abuse. Choristers were frequently out and about unchaperoned. The walk from choir school to song school would be under the head chorister's charge, not an adult's, even when it involved the crossing of a dangerously busy road and hazards from tourists, as at Cambridge. The child protection legislation of the 1980s has stopped this. Formerly, adults had ample opportunity to be alone with boys, as for example in giving an individual music lesson in a remote and enclosed music room. The Children Act requires such rooms to have clear glass in door or wall. And, if bullying and home-sickness cannot ever be wholly eliminated, great efforts are made to prevent them and, if they happen, to deal sensitively with them. All choir schools today have written pastoral care policies and written anti-bullying policies.

Holidays used to be short. In 1928 Canterbury closed its classrooms for eight weeks in the summer, but 'for the greater part of [this period] choristers do their full work in the choir'. At York there was no schoolwork for twelve weeks of the year, but for seven of these the boys were required to be there to sing. Chichester allowed its choristers just twenty days off singing duties in August and nothing else. Lichfield's day boy choristers were excused choir for only a fortnight in the summer and the inside of a week after Epiphany and Low Sunday. Dates of holidays could even be at the whim of the boys: a St George's chorister recalled that, at the close of the nineteenth century, holidays were given to one or two boys at a time, the dates being selected by the boys themselves in order of seniority.[10] In 1900 boarders saw their parents only in these brief holidays. Even non-boarding choristers were away from home for long hours. There were no half terms. Nor, of course, was there contact by telephone, let alone e-mail. Choristers wrote letters home, often censored to ensure that the picture painted was rosy, and good parents replied. But the parents almost never came to the school, except, perhaps, for speech day, held usually at the end of the then school year after the feast of the Epiphany, just before the short post-Christmas break, and, in a growing number of schools, for a sports day in the summer. Parent/teacher days had not been invented, still less parent/teacher associations. Today, even the boarding schools see parents as part of the community, assets rather than threats. Most governing bodies include one or two present, or – as some prefer it – recent chorister parents. Many foundations have annual or even termly opportunities for parents to meet the cathedral or college director of music. As for those choral foundations without dedicated choir schools, the choir could not function without devoted parental involvement. Meanwhile, in the cathedrals, chorister families are likely to form a significant part of the congregation and are often found among the cathedral's army of volunteers: as eucharistic administrators, stewards, guides, coffee-makers and members of the voluntary choirs that keep things going when the choir is on holiday.[11] The parents may even be canons and deans.

Today's chorister is likely to have holidays almost as long as those of non-choristers. The chorister, of course, will stay on for Christmas, Holy Week and Easter. He or she will, in most foundations, sing the weekend services after a term or half a term has ended on a Friday and come back to sing the Sunday services before term resumes on the Monday. In fact the 'stay-ons' are often deemed the best part of a chorister's life. Read any edition of *Choir Schools Today* to enjoy accounts of the Christmas parties, outings, high-jinks and low life that enliven these weeks at school but without schooling. And instead of a Christmas Day cruelly away from the family, the family is likely today to be invited to school to join in the turkey, the mince pies and the fun. (Christmas evensongs, as a consequence, are not always the most polished of services.) But choral foundations accept that it is in the interest of their choristers that there should be in any year perhaps fifteen or sixteen weeks of holidays and half-term breaks when their domestic choral force will not be singing, and when choral services will be maintained by their own 'Congregational Choir' or by other local groups or by visiting choirs from the universities, the RSCM, or touring choirs from this country or overseas.

Meanwhile, for the choristers not all the holidays will be holiday, as they would have been at the start of the century. Royal foundations will, of course, always have been alert to the call for a special service at any time and often at short notice. Royal weddings and funerals and above all coronations live forever in choristers' memories. When Queen Victoria died the top six Windsor choristers were rushed to Osborne for the lying-in-state in such haste that their choir practice with Sir Walter Parratt took place on the train. The private chapel at Osborne gave one chorister his first experience of electric lighting.[12] But then it is usual for chorister memories to retain the strangest things. For Basil Houle at the coronation of George V in 1911 it was the frightening sight of the Begum of Bhopal in her muslim headdress with just 'two slits for her eyes'. At the funeral of George VI in 1952 the lasting memories for more than one chorister were the sombre mingled sounds as the coffin was brought from the station, the tolling funeral bell, the dull thud of the cannons' rounds and the distant lament of wailing bagpipes. Another boy, at the coronation that followed in 1953, appreciated how extraordinary it was for him and his fellow choristers to be sitting there 'in the centre of practically the whole world's thoughts'.[13]

These were special occasions for privileged boys. The more frequent interruptions to the normal alternations of term-time school and liturgy and vacation-time holidaying for most choristers are concerts, choir tours and recordings. Moral people such as Maria Hackett regarded the singing of concerts by choristers as a reprehensible prostitution of their sacred calling. So far as singing in taverns for the choirmaster's financial benefit is concerned all would agree with her. But today it is readily expected that part of a chorister's singing life will be the giving of public concerts, most often of sacred music, but not invariably so. To give just a single example – though concerts by choristers are so universal that example is unnecessary – no BBC Promenade Concert season would be culturally complete without performances by one, and more often several, groups of choristers. Such concerts are important in bringing the riches of the country's heritage of church music to that multitude who cherish a sense of the transcendent but have no confessional faith and never cross the threshold of a church. Similarly, choristers playing their part in concerts within their cathedral or collegiate chapel draw people into a place of worship that they might not otherwise enter. Some of the 8.8 million tourists who visited the English cathedrals in 2003 will have chanced upon the beauty of a choral office in progress, the sacrament of 'sacred music on sacred ground'.[14] In such ways choristers are part of the church's missionary outreach.

Explicit 'outreach' by choristers has developed in the twenty-first century in response to the widespread lack of singing or, indeed, of music at all, in state primary schools. Few primary schools have teachers trained to teach singing, and head teachers, conscious of the need to be 'inclusive', often steer clear of specifically Christian music in school assemblies. In many primary schools no child sings; in others the singing is done with a chesty, 'pop' style voice. There had, of course, been occasional joint musical ventures between choir schools and neighbouring maintained schools, such as the Saturday morning music courses run in the 1980s at King's College School, Cambridge, under the initiative of the headmaster, Gerald Peacocke. Then at Truro, in 2000, headmaster Richard White, with funding assisted by government, formed a partnership with a cluster of local primary schools. Truro choristers and Cornish primary school children were to have joint singing classes that would culminate in a concert given in the cathedral. A similar scheme was launched at Liverpool Metropolitan Cathedral. This form of outreach has since been taken up at Hereford, Durham, Lichfield, Salisbury and at Ampleforth Abbey, under the overall direction of Richard White, and supported by government money. In 2006 Ely, Gloucester, Winchester and York were also seeking to set up partnerships under the Outreach programme. Through the Outreach programme, children otherwise starved of musical education are able to hear how splendid 'proper' singing by ordinary but trained children can be, and are then thrilled to discover they too can make the same fine sounds. Children who have lived for all their early years within sight of great cathedrals have experienced the wonder of entering these breathtaking spaces and then singing in a generous acoustic. Choir schools have released their music specialists to visit selected maintained schools regularly each week, to hold singing classes and to nurture musical members of the primary school staff in order that they can themselves expand the work. The Durham Cathedral choristers have sung to over 2500 children in schools within the Sunderland LEA, and 800 of those children have been brought to sing in that 'sumptuous' cathedral. At Cambridge a similar venture, though with an emphasis on fundraising, has been growing through the participation of King's College School in 'Future Talent', the charity founded by the Duchess of Kent to ensure that 'those with the most opportunities in music share with those who have the least'. Other schemes have been initiated elsewhere. Of course the benefit of these ventures works in both directions, enriching for the choristers as it is for those with or for whom they go out to work. The Outreach programme is one of the most exciting initiatives of the Choir Schools' Association since its foundation.[15]

Missionary again, in the sense of disseminating Christian culture, and far more exciting for choristers than domestic music-making, are overseas tours. Singing abroad has an ancient history. The Chapel Royal Children were doing it in the fifteenth century. One of the earliest modern choir tours – half abroad – was made by the choir of Winchester Cathedral in the summer vacation of 1935 to that southernmost part of the Winchester diocese, the Channel Islands. Concerts were given and services sung on Jersey and Guernsey and an anthem sung at an infant baptism on the diminutive island of Herm. It was while bathing off Herm that one of the choristers would certainly have drowned had he not been rescued by a courageous colleague. Before the next choir tour of the Channel Islands in 1949 the dean wisely drew up a table of fines for misbehaviour that included 'For being late: 6d.' and 'For being drowned: £5'.[16] In 1936, the year after Winchester had first ventured to the Channel Islands, the dean of King's College, Cambridge, was asked by the Foreign Office on behalf of the British Council, whether his choir would be willing to sing in Amsterdam, Copenhagen, Stockholm and 'not more than one or two other places'. The college was in favour. In writing to the parents for permission the dean stressed that it would be 'a holiday with a little singing'. In the event, in what one presumes to have been the first such choral venture into continental Europe, they sang seven concerts or services in six locations, including Hamburg, with long and tiring train and boat journeys in between. They met warm receptions everywhere, but were especially struck by the appreciation of English church music by the Dutch audiences. The people of the Netherlands have, indeed, continued to show a voracious appetite for the singing of English cathedral and collegiate choirs.[17]

Perhaps the most famous overseas tour of modern times was the great visit by the choir of St Paul's Cathedral to the USA and Canada in the autumn of 1953, marking the building of an American Memorial Chapel in the cathedral in honour of the 28,000 US servicemen who had lost their lives in the Second World War. Forty-one concerts were given in places within the rectangle formed by New York, New Orleans, Chicago and Montreal. It was the first time in eight hundred years of history that the choir of St Paul's had sung outside London. In recent decades tours such as this – though usually not so demanding – have become essential parts of every chorister's life. For them, the enriching experiences of these tours are among the most beneficial developments of the twentieth century. Lasting memories? Trying to smuggle a deadly black widow spider, live in a glass jar, onto a Quantas flight home. The passionate fan club of ever-present teenage Japanese girls, outside the hotel at dawn and dusk daily, and lying in wait at Tokyo airport on departure, in tears and oblivious of a famous pop group leaving on the same flight. Heroic Hal Vernon, walking through a plate glass door in an unfamiliar Australian concert hall and having the guts and commitment to be on stage two nights later to sing a solo, in a body patched with sixty-nine stitches. Meetings with kings and queens, princes and princesses, presidents and premiers, archbishops and popes, not to mention world famous 'celebrities'. Cultures wholly different from one's own. Welcoming hosts; generous gifts; lifelong international friendships. Above all, perhaps, standing ovations from audiences world-wide for this uniquely British chorister-dependent form of music making.

Recording sessions also burgeoned in the course of the century. The earliest surviving vocal record, preserved at Menlo Park, New Jersey, has *Mary Had a Little Lamb* scratchily engraved on tinfoil by Thomas Edison in December 1877. The earliest flat disc recordings date from 1894.[18] Probably the first recording of a boy 'soprano' took place in August 1898 in the Cockburn Hotel, London, when John Buffery's voice was captured on a two-minute 7-inch zinc disc by a recording company soon to become HMV.[19] Twenty-eight years later a fourteen-year-old Temple Church chorister, Ernest Lough, using the Gramophone Record Company's first-ever mobile recording van, was to record Mendelssohn's *Hear My Prayer* and thereby attain instant international fame. This 'most sublime

The Most Sublime Record
Ever Made

Boy Soloist and Choir of the

Temple Church
London

EXCLUSIVELY ON

"**His Master's Voice**"

ELECTRICAL RECORDING

His master's voice (Ernest Lough)

record ever made' sold 650,000 copies in the first six months. For some time Lough's father insisted that Ernest should acknowledge every piece of fan-mail individually, until the task became impossible. Later it was to become the world's first million-selling disc. Lough received his golden disc to prove it in 1963.[20] In the 1920s a number of the choral foundation choirs were making 78 r.p.m. discs: for example, St George's, Windsor, for the Columbia Gramophone Company in 1926 and Salisbury for HMV in 1928. In those days, when the recording was made directly onto the master disc, it was a long and tedious business. Today there is no cathedral choir that cannot be heard on CD and the leading choirs expect to make two or three discs a year. What is striking is the number of these CDs that achieve 'Record of the Month' status or better. Alongside the recordings go the broadcasts. The radio airways are filled with, and the TV channels are no strangers to, the sound (and sight) of English cathedral and collegiate choirs. Christmas is only the peak of this year-round exposure. Perhaps as remarkable as the cult status of Christmas carols from King's is the fact that the BBC's weekly live relay of Choral Evensong, first heard on 7 October 1926, is the longest running programme on British broadcasting.

One modest benefit to the English chorister of all this touring, concert giving, recording and broadcasting, is that he may, at the end of four or five years, find that he has built up a not inconsiderable savings account. In the nineteenth century, of course, almost every chorister had the compensation of being waged, but the twentieth century saw that being phased out. By 1928 only at Rochester (£5 a year on leaving), St John's, Cambridge (£2.50 to £6 a year plus bonuses for good service), and Salisbury (£5 and £2 a year for the top two boys respectively), along with unspecified payments or 'small traditional fees' at Norwich, Southwell, Wells and St George's, Windsor, had payment survived. Indeed in place of wages had come the charging of school fees, almost universally for boarding. Gradually the happy chorister has seen performance fees go some way to make up for the loss of wages.

As long as choristers have sung there have been some with outstanding voices. Ernest Lough's voice was merely the first to be captured for posterity. This has ensured that there is a sort of roll of honour of famous trebles, all the more poignant because the treble voice, especially the treble voice in its last months before change, is both distinctively beautiful and yet ephemeral. Far from being blamed for producing teenage celebrities, choirmasters are to be thanked for ensuring the preservation on tape and vinyl of treble voices like those of Aled Jones, Paul Phoenix or Anthony Way. It may be that the risks for the outstanding girl chorister are greater: certainly the opportunities and temptations of the glamorous world of pop music are very great.

If we put aside the cathedral choirs that draw their choristers from the specialist music foundations of St Mary's, Edinburgh and Manchester, where girls and boys sing together in the choir's top line, and if we discount the singing of girl oblates in the quires of medieval nunneries, the history of the English chorister over fourteen hundred years until the 1990s has been the history of singing boys. Coupled with the universal use of male altos in these foundations, the choirs have been exclusively male-voice. When in 1990, choirmaster Richard Seal of Salisbury, supported by his dean and chapter, decided that it would be right to recruit a 'choir' – strictly speaking a 'top line' – of girls, and when, in the years that followed, one foundation after another decided to follow suit, it caused bitter dismay in the hearts of many for whom the all-male choir was a unique treasure. When the Friends of Cathedral Music debated the matter at Lichfield in 1997 defenders of the male tradition were virtually in tears, some shaking with anger, and Richard Seal must have wondered whether he would escape from the hall unscathed.

Why had he done it? In 1989 Seal had been attending a meeting of the Choral Foundations Working Party at Church House, Westminster, and someone in the course of discussion – it had not been on the agenda – had said 'One of these days we're going to have to think about the girls'. Seal spent the hour and a half on the train from Waterloo doing just that. By the time he reached Salisbury he knew he should have girl choristers in parallel to his boys. In the months that followed he found the already co-educational school keen on the idea and the dean and chapter supportive. What had moved Richard Seal so deeply was the realisation that the opportunity of a choristership, with its riches of liturgical and musical experience and its uniquely formative education, was utterly closed to half the country's children, simply because they happened to have been born female. He thought of his sister, 'more musical than I am', and how much she would have benefited from what he himself had received as a chorister at New College that had 'sowed in me something that was with me for life'.

Salisbury went into the scheme with no funds and no scholarships to offer. Yet over thirty girls applied and sixteen were elected and all accepted. Since then there has been a major appeal and gradually the scholarship fund has built up. At first the girls were to sing with the men on Mondays, by themselves on Wednesdays, formerly the 'dumb' day, and to relieve the boys of one of their three Sunday services, still leaving the generously scholarship-aided boys to carry the major burden of the liturgy. By 2006 they were at the point when boys and girls could bear absolutely equal shares and receive equal scholarships. Wakefield and York are aiming for a similar equality. Since 1991 girls' top lines have been recruited for the cathedral choirs at Birmingham, Bradford, Bristol, Chelmsford, Chester, Coventry, Derby, Exeter, Leicester, Lincoln, Llandaff, Norwich, Peterborough, Rochester, St Albans, Sheffield, Southwark, Wakefield, Wells, Winchester and York.[21] Gloucester has a Cathedral Youth Choir that includes girls aged eleven to eighteen. Other foundations are making preparations. To date, none of the

Royal Peculiars and none of the Oxbridge foundations has taken the plunge (for perhaps obvious reasons) but at King's a mixed undergraduate choir sings Monday evensongs. At Wells, largely for financial reasons, there were problems that caused temporary disbandment of the girls' choir, but the problems have been resolved. Winchester's decision to recruit a team of rather older girls (aged twelve to sixteen) was despite and not because of threats of court action under the equal opportunities legislation. Not all girls' groups as yet sing a very onerous schedule: at Norwich just once a week, at Llandaff three times a fortnight. But there can be no doubt that the girls are here to stay.

Opposition to this development is based on several grounds. One, of course, is simply the wish to preserve exclusively a cultural tradition. There is no answer to that: either one holds that view or one does not. A variant of this view suggests that once the girls are brought in the boys will disappear and then the supply of male altos, tenors and basses will wither. This has not happened, nor is there a shred of evidence to suggest that it will. Indeed, the lightening the boys' load as a consequence of the girls' singing schedule may actually increase boy recruitment. A third ground is that the sound produced by a group of girls is so different from that produced by a group of boys that it is unacceptable as an alternative. It is certainly true that nobody would confuse the voices of solo boy-treble Aled Jones with that of solo girl-treble Charlotte Church. But put the boys and girls into their same-sex teams and the differences fade, indeed they can fade so greatly that groups of cathedral organists and groups of choir school heads have been largely unable to distinguish the sounds by gender when put to carefully devised tests.[22] What was found easier to distinguish was the sound of a particular foundation, the sound reflective of a particular choirmaster's style. The argument that most English church music was written with boys' voices in mind is irrefutable in part; but in that case boys should stop singing the Byrd masses which, in the composer's time, if sung at all, would almost certainly have been sung by mixed-gender groups of recusants. It is true that a second body of choristers puts additional burdens on cathedral finances, in the funding of scholarships and frequently in the appointment of additional musical staff. And it has added complexities, like knowing which items in the repertoire (including what psalms) are under which group's belts. But set against all this is the fact that there are now some two hundred and fifty girls enjoying a very specially beneficial kind of childhood.[23]

One undoubted benefit to the boy choristers in foundations where there are also girls is the lightening of the boys' load. Of course, a chorister today (other than in Dublin) spends less time in choir than did his predecessor a century ago. But he may spend more time in rehearsals. A survey conducted in 1996 revealed an average weekly choral commitment by boy choristers – rehearsals and services – of eighteen hours a week with six choirs calling for over twenty hours.[24] A third of the choirs had no day in the week when there was not either a rehearsal or at least one service. On top of this, the demands made by a chorister's academic education, with broadened curriculum and raised expectations, are far greater than they were, let us say, in 1900, when many of the schools were still providing a minimal elementary education that prepared choristers for nothing other than apprenticeships into trades or clerkships after their chorister days were over. Today's choristers work a curriculum that has university entry as its aim, and in the interstices between classwork and singing they will virtually all be learning two instruments, necessary if the chorister, no matter how gifted a singer, is to win one of the music scholarships that will enable independent senior schooling to be affordable. Nobody will be surprised to read that from among chorister bodies there emerge, from time to time, astonishing instrumental prodigies. So let one boy be exemplar for many: on 22 June 2003, in the St Paul's Cathedral Sunday recital series, a series that features internationally famous organists, the recitalist was Ben Sheen, a thirteen-year-old chorister. His organ playing had gained him Associated Board distinctions at grades 6, 7 and 8 in three consecutive terms and, subsequently, with a little help from his cello, piano and voice, a music scholarship to Eton.[25] How choristers so frequently gain high Associated Board grades on top of demanding academic programmes, sports, up to twenty hours of services and practices a week, together with concerts and recordings that may bite into thirty days a year in the most prestigious choirs, is a mystery, particularly it seems to school inspectors.

Choristers have, of course, been carefully selected for both talent and promise. Quality of voice is not the prime criterion. Nowadays much professional expertise is brought to the development of boys' and girls' voices. A number of foundations employ professional voice trainers as a matter of course, calling on specialists such as those in Alexander Technique if a voice seems to need particular attention.[26] A good ear and musical feel are more important. Secondly, a chorister must have the intellectual potential to cope with an academic curriculum without strain. This is not simply a matter of IQ: commitment and ability to concentrate come into it. A boy with average ability and high stickability may well make a better chorister than an idle brainbox. Above all, what choirmasters look for is sparkle, a bright eye, confidence and initiative. Here are three examples of initiative from a seventy-year span. Two were brilliantly successful, one brilliantly disastrous.

In 1935 chorister Guy Kemp Robinson found himself alone, locked in Winchester Cathedral after evensong. What should he do? Make as much noise as possible seemed the best course. He was an organ pupil so knew where the greatest noise in the cathedral could be made. He went up into the loft, switched on the organ and began playing pieces he had been taught. Conventional organ music, however, raised no alarms outside: organists often practised in the evenings. So Kemp Robinson changed to *The Isle of Capri*, *fortissimo*, and in no time there was the dean, anxious to know who was profaning his cathedral.[27]

A decade later, on 8 May 1945, VE Day had been declared. The Canterbury choristers had expected some sort of fun and games but, apart from a special evensong, the day had turned out to be very ordinary. So the two head choristers, Donald Grayston Burgess and Anthony Curry, decided that after 'lights out' they would organise their own celebration. When all was dark and quiet they got the whole dormitory up in pyjamas and dressing gowns and led the choristers down the iron fire escape, across the precincts and up the cathedral firewatchers' ladder onto the north end of the quire roof, then round the Corona to the south side, along the (hazardous) two planks that skirted the Bell Harry tower, until they were on the nave roof south parapet. What they did not know was that the mayor, who happened to be also their headmaster, had ordered a celebratory (post-blackout) flood-lighting of the cathedral's south face. At the stroke of ten the chorister body found themselves brightly illuminated in full view of the entire city council and their wives. Getting back was alarming because the lights had not only revealed them but had also blinded them. In the event, nobody fell off. But as they reached the bottom of the ladder there was their headmaster, Clive Pare, furious that the entire council had seen how little authority he had over his own boys. As they passed him, each boy heard the dreaded words, 'My study'. In the nineteen-forties that meant only one thing: and in pyjamas, and without opportunity to pad them with newspaper.[28]

In 2003 the head girl chorister at Salisbury was Grace Newcombe, a girl who knows her history. At a service with a military presence Grace spotted a senior officer in full dress uniform complete with spurs. Setting out on a course no female in the world had previously trodden she accosted him and demanded spur money. So generous was the soldierly response (and so generous is Grace's nature) that all the girl choristers found themselves suddenly enriched.

Choirmasters and choir school heads welcome initiative, up to a point. Above all choirmasters look for enthusiasm and an appetite for a choristership. One director of music recalls how, at a recent voice trial, he was blessed with an exceptionally brilliant candidate. As the boy was leaving the room he fired a parting question:

> 'Tell me, why do you want to be a chorister?'
> 'I don't', was the reply.
> 'You don't?'
> 'No, not at all. I'd hate it.'
> 'Well, why are you here?'
> 'My parents want me to be a chorister.'

The boy was not elected.

Even with the most careful selection a choristership is never going to be a bed of roses. The newsman, Jon Snow's, recollections of the Pilgrims' School when he was a Winchester Cathedral chorister in the 1950s are of a Dickensian nightmare. Cold showers and beatings by butter pat on the hand or seat from an ex-Guards officer headmaster.[29] In the 1970s, by which time there were no beatings and showers were warm, boarding from the age of eight at St John's, Cambridge, left predominantly unhappy memories for baritone Simon Keenlyside.[30] Even today, when pupils' happiness is a prime objective in schools, there can be tricky years when a young chorister is nine and ten and very likely has not mastered the competing demands of choir-stall and classroom desk. After a day's work, two rehearsals and evensong on the 15th evening,[31] an hour's prep will be the straw that does the breaking. What is then most needed is patience from the teachers and an understanding that this prep or that bit of work do not, in the long term, matter. Because miraculously, when he is eleven or twelve, the chorister discovers that he can cope; that he can actually learn quite quickly, that preps can be fitted into fragments of time, that days' schedules can be organised. A good thirteen-year-old chorister has mastered all the necessary skills of a managing director, and without benefit of an MBA, along with the knowledge of how to make friends and influence people. He has, as former Christ Church, Oxford, chorister, the late Sir David Calcutt, QC, put it 'done a man's job at a boy's age'.[32] At the same time he may well be a Grade 8 cellist and have learnt a love of beautiful things, taste, the discrimination that knows the difference between the excellent and the merely good, and, distinctively, that love of a cathedral and its music that Jon Snow took away with him from Winchester, a feeling for choral worship that will never be lost. In Simon Keenlyside's case the legacy was a deep admiration for a choirmaster for whom nothing less than the very best would do and the undying thrill of singing in a choir animated by George Guest. Howard Goodall recalls from his time as a New College chorister that the great experience was being part of a team.

> We were miles better as an ensemble than any of us could have hoped to be individually. We sang as a group, we played and worked and joked and fought and caught 'flu as a group. Collectively we soared, there's no other word for it. The sound of sixteen trained boys or girls scaling some great musical height in the echoing grandeur of a cathedral, abbey or college chapel is thrilling. It's one of the things we do as a nation that is quite unique, musically outstanding and culturally without price.[33]

No wonder so many choristers subsequently win choral or organ scholarships at the most selective universities. No wonder so many then go on to achieve distinction in a great variety of spheres.

This is not biased exaggeration, conjured up for the book's peroration: it is fact. There are chairmen of companies, top civil servants, members of government and Parliament from across the political spectrum; bishops, priests, monks;

there are actors, comics, producers, directors, broadcasters; novelists, poets, journalists and their editors; chefs and wine experts; doctors and surgeons; leaders of charitable causes, sportsmen; leading educationalists and academics. Unsurprisingly there are entrepreneurs, including the founder of Pizza Express, whose products sustain hungry choristers and their mums on 'dumb' Wednesday afternoons. Above all, in their multitudes, there are distinguished musicians. Here are a few, by way of illustration, with apologies to the many equally distinguished not here included: Jeremy Backhouse, Howard Goodall and Simon Keenlyside already mentioned; Stephen Barlow, Michael Berkeley, James Bowman, Bob Chilcot, Nicholas and Stephen Cleobury, Charles Daniels, Stephen Darlington, Mark Elder, Roy Goodman, Harry Gregson-Williams, David Hill, Ralph Holmes, Grayston Ives, Francis Jackson, Andrew Kennedy, James Lancelot, Ian Partridge, Simon Preston, Christopher Robinson, Christopher Seaman, Roger Vignolles, David Willcocks ...

Behind these leaders of today's national, spiritual and cultural life lie generations of choristers who, in their time, kept alive a fourteen-hundred-year tradition of boys being educated to sing in the choirs of our choral foundations. The opportunity to be a part of that heritage as a chorister today, and to enjoy its unique quality of education, is available to any boy or girl with the necessary talents, irrespective of parental income or background. The heritage of choral music in liturgy that choristers maintain is a cultural glory unique in the world. That heritage, of which this book is both a history and a celebration, was often hard won and is still vulnerable. But it has never been more splendid and it has never been more widely valued, both by the growing congregations in our cathedrals and by millions of admirers in every continent.

Appendix 1

The Tale of Sister Margaret and Sister Gertrude

Caesarius of Heisterbach, who was a great medieval collector of gossip, claimed to have had this tale of two child oblates directly from their abbess. The story is quoted by Power, *English Nunneries*, pp. 28 and 29 n. 3, and can be found directly in M. M. Banks (ed.), *An Alphabet of Tales: An English Fifteenth-Century Translation of Alphabetum Narrationum of Etienne de Besançon* (London, 1904/5), pp. 249f. The two versions differ in some details. One, for instance, has the story set in Germany, the other in 'an abbay of Saynt Saluaturs'. I have skimmed the cream from both and made a conflation. The story is no doubt continental and is strictly an illegitimate interpolation in this history. Yet here if anywhere are the mind-set, the very voice even, of a ten-year-old nun in a medieval monastic quire, with its conflict between the monastic discipline imposed by the habit and the natural giggly girl within, egged on by her best friend. The story, with some text directly from the fifteenth-century *Alphabet of Tales*, goes thus.

Sister Margaret and Sister Gertrude were very dear friends. Day by day they stood and sang beside each other in quire. Then one day little Gertrude died. One can imagine Margaret's grief. A day or so after, while the evening office was being sung, Sister Margaret turned in her place in quire and to her astonishment saw Sister Gertrude standing beside her. Margaret was filled with terror, so much so that the other nuns noticed her distress and told the abbess. So Margaret recounted her vision. The abbess, clearly a woman of some wisdom, said to her, 'Sister Margaret, if Sister Gertude appears to you again, say to her "*Benedicite*", and, if she replies "*Domino*", question her as to where she comes from and why she is here in quire.' The following day Sister Gertrude appeared again. Margaret did as the abbess had advised, turned to the ghost and said, '*Benedicite*'; and Gertrude indeed replied, '*Domino*'. So, it being now clear that Gertrude was not a spirit from the devil, Margaret asked her why she was there with them. Gertrude explained. 'I come here to make satisfaction. Because I willingly whispered with thee in the choir, gossiping in half tones,[1] therefore am I ordered to make satisfaction in that place where it befell me to sin. And unless thou beware of the same vice, dying thou shalt suffer the same penance.'

When she had for four days come to the Office and made satisfaction in the same way by prostrating herself, she said to Sister Margaret, 'Now have I completed the satisfaction; henceforth thou shalt see me no more.' And thus it was done. In the sight of her friend, Gertrude's ghost floated out of the chapel and over the wall into the nuns' cemetery. 'And thus she was taken into Heaven with angel-song.'

Appendix 2

A Day at Christ Church, Oxford, in November 1573

In 1938 an account of an imagined typical day in November 1573 spent by a chorister was published in *Music and Letters*.[1] The author, Ernest Brennecke, Jun., claimed that, although it is fiction, 'every statement that it contains is made with some foundation of fact, authority or logical inference'. It is not quite so: there are a few demonstrable errors. But the whole effect is so charming, rather in the fashion of a *novella* such as Mörike's *Mozart's Journey to Prague*, that the few slips can be overlooked. The foundation is Christ Church, Oxford; the boy is ten-year-old John Milton, later to be father of his eponymous son, the celebrated poet.

It is a long day. John is up in his breeches and shirt at dawn, eating his porridge with his fellow-choristers in time to don surplice and be in quire for 5 a.m. matins. Only after evensong, late in the afternoon, does he relax over supper and retire to bed about 9 p.m. Between those two offices he has had two sessions of formal schooling. First there were passages of the catechism to be recited from memory, the master's birch rod at hand for any who failed. Then Latin exercises followed from the *Sententiae Pueriles* and passages from Virgil, Horace and Cicero: these, be it noted, the classical authors beloved of the Renaissance, not the syllabus of the medieval chorister. After two hours of this there is instrumental work with the distinguished *Informator*, William Blitheman, on organ, lute, viol and recorder. That brings John to lunch in hall, a substantial meal of meats, begun and ended by a sung grace. After that, it is back to the second two-hour session of Latin. Then follows what we would call music theory under Blitheman, mastering the Gamut, an essential item for those occasions when a chorister, having demanded spur money from a worshipper foolish enough to come to the cathedral wearing his spurs, might be challenged by the wearer to recite his Gamut, the slightest slip on the boy's part disqualifying him from claiming the fine. Only now are the boys joined by the lay clerks, so that music for evensong and the following day's matins can be learned and practised. Still there is time for rehearsal of a play that the boys are to perform at Christmastide. That would be fun, as was the breather they had for outdoor exercise and games before evensong. Matins and evensong were the purpose of it all, with high standards demanded and expected. The morning service had entailed singing Tallis's responses, polyphonic canticles by Causton and the Tallis anthem, *If Ye Love Me*. Sixteenth-century Christ Church sang a wide repertoire of music.

Here then, albeit in the clothing of historical fiction, is evidence that not everywhere in the late sixteenth century were cathedral music and the condition of the choristers in a state of 'decay'. John Milton's school day was clearly very fulfilling, but it must equally be the case that the music of Christ Church Cathedral, Oxford, at least during the years when William Blitheman was in charge, was well chosen and seriously performed.

Endnotes

Notes to Chapter 1: Beginnings

1   *New Grove Dictionary of Music and Musicians*, 20 vols (London, 2nd ed., 1980), 'Chorus (i),1', p. 342.

2   At Colossians 3:16 and Ephesians 5:19; and examples of possible liturgical elements are found at Colossians 1: 15–20; Ephesians 5: 14; Philippians 2: 6–11 and I Timothy 3:16.

3   See Robert F. Hayburn, *Papal Legislation on Sacred Music, 95 AD to 1977 AD* (Collegeville, MA, 1979), pp. 1f.

4   Closely similar views are reached by J.A. Smith, 'The Ancient Synagogue: the Early Church and Singing', *Music and Letters*, 65 (Jan. 1984), pp. 1–16, and J.W. McKinnon, 'On the Question of Psalmody in the Ancient Synagogue', *Early Music History*, 6 (1986), pp. 159–93. For the early Christians see David Hiley, *Western Plainchant* (Oxford, 1993), pp. 484–87.

5   Dom Gregory Dix, *The Shape of the Liturgy* (2nd edn, Westminster, 1945), p. 303.

6   Paul F. Bradshaw, 'Continuity and Change in Early Eucharistic Practice', in R.N. Swanson (ed), *Continuity and Change in Christian Worship* (Oxford, 1999), p. 1.

7   Bede, *Historia Ecclesiastica*, bk i, c. 25. I use Leo Sherley Price's Penguin Classics translation, *A History of the English Church and People* (1955), throughout. His use of 'in unison' here must not be understood to imply, anachronistically, 'as opposed to harmony'. For Augustine's mission see Bede, bk i passim.

8   Nicholas Brooks, *The Early History of the Church of Canterbury* (Leicester, 1984), pp. 91f.

9   For Augustine's *familia* at Canterbury, see Margaret Deanesly, 'The Familia at Christchurch, Canterbury, 597–832', *Essays in Medieval History presented to T.F. Tout* (Manchester, 1925), pp. 1–13; and J. Armitage Robinson, 'The Early Community at Christ Church, Canterbury', *Journal of Theological Studies*, xxvii (1926), pp. 35–42.

10 Rule of St Benedict, c. 59. See Chapter 2, n. 4.

11 Bede, *Historia Ecclesiastica*, bk iii, c. 24.

12 Whilst seven, when infancy gave way to childhood, was the normal minimum age for acceptance of child oblates, earlier oblation at this period was clearly provided for, and it would be difficult for any nunnery to turn down the gift of a royal princess. Bede is precise about the dates and the assumption has to be that Elfleda went to Hilda soon after weaning was complete.

13 W. Levinson (ed.), *Alcuinus, Vita Willibrordi* (MGH Scriptores rerum merovingicarum, Hannover and Leipzig, 1919), pp. 177–78.

14 For Hildemar see below. I draw this reference from Mayke de Jong, 'Growing up in a Carolingian Monastery: Magister Hildemar and his Oblates', *Journal of Medieval History*, 9/2, March 1983, pp. 99–126.

15 Bede, *Historia Ecclesiastica*, bk i, c. 27.

16 Hence the King's School, Rochester, dates its foundation to 604, whilst conceding precedence in antiquity by seven years to the King's School, Canterbury, which claims to be 'as old as English Christianity'. King's, Canterbury, however, cannot claim to be the oldest English 'choir school', having educated no cathedral choristers at least since the Dissolution of the Monasteries. Even King's, Rochester, which *is* now a cathedral choir school, fails on continuity of chorister education.

17 Bede, *Historia Ecclesiastica*, bk ii, c. 20.

18 Bede, *Historia Ecclesiastica*, bk iv, c. 2.

19 The York Minster Song School and St Peter's School, York, both make claim to have been founded in 627 in their entries in the *Independent Schools Yearbook*. Robert Holtby, in *The Minster School York: A Retrospect* (York, 1994), pp. 1–5, demolishes this claim with some vigour: what Paulinus and James the Deacon established and maintained were not 'schools' in any modern sense of the word, and continuity has been repeatedly broken. That accepted, there can be no serious doubt that in the seventh century boys were being taught chant and liturgy at York or that these boys were, in some sense, 'choristers' and hence the distant predecessors of those choristers educated at the Minster School today.

20 F.M. Stenton writes of it as 'absolutely obscure', see *Anglo-Saxon England* (3rd edn, Oxford, 1971), cap. 6, passim.

21 Guido of Arrezzo, *Prologus antiphonarii sui*, of *c*. 1025, quoted in Oliver Strunk, *Source Readings in Music History* (London, 1952), p. 117.

22 Bede, *Historia Ecclesiastica* bk i, c. 27, response 2.

23 But Timothy McGee, in *The Sound of Medieval Song* (Oxford, 1998), works valiantly on the near-impossible.

24 Bede, *Historia Ecclesiastica*, bk iv, c. 18.

25 This is a field for excited dispute amongst musicologists and palaeographers. Hiley, *Western Plainchant*, pp. 362ff, has a full and balanced discussion of the issue, judging the earliest western notation to derive from Byzantine models and naming a treatise by Aurelian of Reome, *c*. 850, as the western prototype. Susan Rankin, 'From Memory to Record: Musical Notations in Manuscripts from Exeter', *Anglo-Saxon England*, 13 (1984), pp. 97–112, cautiously proposed a northern French provenance of *c*. 830.

26 But see Rankin, *Memory to Record*, p. 97, n. 3. For the 'Winchester Tropers', see below pp. 18.

27 In his *Dialogus ecclesiasticus institutionis*.

28 Hiley, *Western Plainchant*, pp. 297ff.

29 Recorded in the Laud and Parker Chronicles as 787, due to transcription errors which run from 756 to 845. I have taken my Chronicle references from G.N. Garmonsway's edition (London, 1960).

30 Quotations are from H.T. Riley, *Ingulph's History of the Abbey of Croyland* (London, 1854), pp. 42–47. Ingulf was secretary to William I and from 1086 abbot of Crowland, a man 'full of energy though much afflicted with gout'. Whether the chronicle is actually Ingulf's has

been matter for lengthy academic dispute. The debate is summarised (up to *c.* 1920) by R.W. Hunt in his article on Ingulf in DNB, x, pp. 453ff. Whilst the language and vocabulary seem to be fourteenth rather then eleventh century, and whilst 'the book contains many curious and evidently untrue stories', it is reasonable to accept that much about the abbey's early years (including the sack by the Danes) incorporates material written by a late tenth-century monk which may well be based on reliable local tradition.

31   Dom David Knowles, *The Monastic Order in England* (Cambridge, 1940), pp. 21–25. Knowles summarised his view in D. Knowles and R.N. Hadcock, *Medieval Religious Houses: England and Wales* (London, 1953), p. 4: 'at the beginning of the tenth century regular monastic life was wholly extinct in England, and the ancient sites were either desolate, or in lay hands, or at best in the possession of a family of clerics'.

32   Brooks, *Canterbury*, p. 174, states that 'the Christ Church community was struggling throughout the ninth century to achieve even a basic literacy in Latin'.

33   For a recent discussion see Barbara Yorke, *Wessex in the Early Middle Ages* (Leicester, 1995), pp. 192ff.

Notes to Chapter 2: *Anglo-Saxon Choir Children*

1   Charlemagne had determined, to quote his own metaphor, that the imperial church should no longer drink from the Frankish river but should go back to the Roman fountain-head itself. So Amalar of Metz was sent to Rome to consult Pope Gregory IV and, if possible, borrow the pope's own liturgical texts, only to find that they had already been lent to the abbey of Corbie on the Somme. There Amalar found what he was seeking. From this model he produced an 'antiphoner' which was to become the imperial template.

2   But the monastic transformation of York did not survive Oswald's death.

3   See Adalbert de Vogue and Charles Philippi, ed. Luke Eberle, *The Rule of the Master: Regula Magistri* (Kalamazoo, Michigan, 1977).

4   I have throughout used Abbot Justin McCann's edition, *The Rule of St Benedict in Latin and English* (London, 1951).

5   I have not had access to Hildemar's text, information on which I have taken from Mayke de Jong, 'Growing up in a Carolingian monastery: Magister Hildemar and his oblates', *Journal of Medieval History*, 9/2 (March 1983), pp. 99–128.

6   For the *Regularis Concordia* see the text, introduction and commentary by Dom Thomas Symons (London, 1951). All details that follow are taken from and enumerated as in that edition.

7   I have used the trilingual version of the *Colloquy* to be found in the still invaluable A.F. Leach, *Educational Charters and Documents, 598–1909* (Cambridge, 1911). Aelfric's *Colloquy*, edited by his pupil Aelfric Bata, is at pp. 36ff.

8   David Knowles and R.N. Hadcock, *Medieval Religious Houses: England and Wales* (London, 1953), p. 7.

9   Ibid., p. 61 for Canterbury, p. 218 for Shaftesbury and p. 63 for Cranborne.

10   See de Jong, *Growing up*, p. 99, and the bibliographical references given there, all to German language texts.

11   de Jong, ibid., p. 102. 'Oblate' from *oblatus*, the past participle of *offerre*, to give or to present.
12   *Regula Magistri*, 91.
13   See above, p. 5, and below, p. 42.
14   Power, *Medieval English Nunneries*, p. 39.
15   Cf. Knowles, *The Monastic Order*, p. 418.
16   There has, for more than a century, been a substantial literature on child oblation, much of it continental. John Doran, 'Oblation or Obligation? A Canonical Ambiguity', *The Church and Childhood*, Studies in Church History, 31 (Oxford, 1994), pp. 127–41, is a good recent discussion with comprehensive references to earlier books and articles. A substantial study of the subject by Mayke de Jong has been promised for some years and must be eagerly awaited. Other texts are distressing. Patricia Quinn (in the book detailed at note 21 below) devotes forty pages to the oblates' supposed sexual development yet hardly makes reference to their role in quire. The chapter on children in ecclesiastical foundations in Shulamith Shahar, *Childhood in the Middle Ages* (London and New York, NY, 1990) makes similarly little reference to their primary role of performing the liturgy and is in other ways unreliable. (The New York school of psychohistory it seems is thin on the sources and has a distinctly idiosyncratic view of the middle ages.)
17   The prior tonsuring appears in Lanfranc's *Constitutions*: Dom David Knowles (ed), *The Monastic Constitutions of Lanfranc* (London, 1951), p. 110.
18   *Regula Magistri*, 91, where poverty is justified by numerous biblical quotations.
19   *Rule of Benedict*, 59.
20   *Rule of Benedict*, 54.
21   Patricia A. Quinn, *Better than the Sons of Kings* (New York, NY, 1989), writes of monastic oblates as living, worshipping and being educated in an area of the monastic precinct quite separate from that of the monks, as indeed they did in the time of the fourth-century St Basil. Her thesis is based on the St Gall Plan, an extraordinary drawing on parchment, probably of the ninth century, discovered in the Swiss monastery of St Gall in 1604. It is a blueprint for the ultimate monastery, a veritable monastic utopia, which shows every imaginable facility that an abbot in his wildest dreams might hope for: fireplaces, drains, breweries and bake-houses, with every tree and plant botanically identified. It includes a school and a subsidiary church. In its complexity it bears no resemblance to any known European monastery, certainly not to Christ Church, Canterbury, for which Gunter Noll, 'The origin of the so-called plan of St Gall', *Journal of Medieval History*, 18/3 (Amsterdam, 1982), pp. 191–240, deems it to be a model. Yet almost solely on the basis of this phantasmagoria Patricia Quinn has all monastic oblates living and worshipping separately from the monks.
22   *Regularis Concordia*, x, 62.
23   de Jong, *Growing up*, p. 116.
24   Quoted by Margaret Deanesly, *History of the Medieval Church* (6th edn., London, 1950), p. 96.
25   Here the word *schola* unambiguously means the school or group or even choir of boys. But elsewhere in *Regularis Concordia*, as in other documents, *schola* can and does mean the *schola cantorum* or semi-chorus of monks, which had, and today still has, a significant role in the Benedictine sung mass.

26 *Regularis Concordia*, Proem, 11.

27 *Rule of Benedict*, 39.

28 *Rule of Benedict*, 37.

29 Quoted in Knowles, *Monastic Order*, p. 434, from *Chronicon Monasterii de Abingdon*, i. 461.

30 Ekwall, *Oxford Dictionary of English Place-Names* (4th ed., Oxford, 1960): see Childwick, Chilton and wic.

31 *Regularis Concordia*, *i*, 20.

32 de Jong, *Growing up*, p. 103.

33 *Regularis Concordia*, iv, 47.

34 *Rule of Benedict*, 36. It will be noted in Chapter 12 that when King's College, Cambridge, built a new boarding school for their choristers in the late 1870s no baths were provided.

35 E.g. *Regularis Concordia*, *i*, 19.

36 de Jong, *Growing up*, p. 113.

37 Oliver Strunk, *Source Readings in Music History* (London, 1952) identifies Odo as the famous abbot of Cluny (922–942). I have taken my quotation from p. 103. New Grove challenges the identification and provides full detail on the monochord, Odo, *NGD*, 17, pp. 2–3.

38 *Regularis Concordia*, *i*, 24.

39 de Jong, *Growing up*, p. 113.

40 *Rule of Benedict*, 30.

41 *Rule of Benedict*, 45.

42 *Regularis Concordia*, *i*, 22.

43 Lanfranc is detailed about how the boys must be accompanied to the dormitory by masters who may not leave the boys until they are settled for the night. Lanfranc (ed. Knowles), *Monastic Constitutions*, p. 117.

44 *Regularis Concordia*, *i*, 17. The *trina oratio* were three groups of psalms and prayers, one group said privately before each of Matins and Terce and the third aloud following Compline. See Dom Thomas Symons, 'A Note on the *Trina Oratio*', *Downside Review* xlii (January 1924), pp. 67ff.

45 The manuscripts are Oxford, Bodleian 775 and Cambridge, Corpus Christi College 473. For a comprehensive discussion of the Tropers see J. Handschin, 'The two Winchester Tropers', *Journal of Theological Studies*, 37 (1936), pp. 34–49 and 156–72.

46 For early music notation at Exeter see Susan Rankin, 'From Memory to Record', *Anglo-Saxon England*, pp. 97–112, from which these details come.

47 Not quite his original translation, which began: 'Glory and laud and honour'.

48 *Regularis Concordia*, iv, 37. For later development of the Palm Sunday procession see pp. 34f.

49 I have cheated here. *Regularis Concordia*, iv, 37 actually states that all the lights are put out from the start; but a letter from Aelfric to the monks of Eynsham describes the progressive extinguishing of candles and Dom Thomas Symons believes it to have been the widespread English custom, Symons, *Regularis Concordia*, p. 36, n. 6. Certainly the Use of Sarum specifies the extinguishing of one candle after each of twenty-four antiphons, W.H. Frere (ed.), *The Sarum Ordinal* (Cambridge, 1898), p. 66.

50 *Regularis Concordia*, v, 52.

51 *Regularis Concordia*, x, 62.

52 Knowles, *The Monastic Order*, pp. 212 and 420–22. As will be seen in Chapter 4 below, the nunneries were less assiduous than the monasteries in observing the ban on oblation. Knowles (p. 421) makes reference to a decree of 1215 banning infant oblation (*Corpus Juris Canonici*, Decret. Lib. 3, tit. xxxi, c. 8). John Doran, 'Oblation or Obligation', in *The Church and Childhood* (Oxford, 1994), challenges this: p. 141, note 81. I have been unable to resolve the matter.

Notes to Chapter 3: Choristers of the High Middle Ages

1   Quoted from Eadmer's *Miracula Sancti Dunstani* in Frank Barlow, *The English Church, 1000–1066* (London, 2nd ed. 1979), p. 210.

2   Kathleen Edwards identifies Monreale in Sicily and Downpatrick in Ireland as two rare examples of medieval monastic cathedrals outside England: K. Edwards, *The English Secular Cathedrals in the Middle Ages* (Manchester, 2nd edn, 1967), p. 10.

3   W.R. Matthews and W.M. Atkins (eds), *A History of St Paul's Cathedral* (London, 1957), pp. 13f.

4   By Rosalind Hill and Christopher Brooke in G. Aylmer and R. Cant (eds), *A History of York Minster* (Oxford, 1977), pp. 25–28.

5   But with the episcopal *cathedra* variously at Benedictine Chester and Coventry between 1075 and 1228.

6   The see was moved a mile downhill from Old Sarum to what is now Salisbury in the 1120s.

7   The bishops of Wells between 1090 and 1140 intermittently located their *cathedra* in the Benedictine abbey at Bath, hence the full episcopal title, Bishop of Bath and Wells.

8   Details to be found under 'The Succession of Bishops' in F.M. Powicke, Charles Johnson and W.J. Harte (eds), *Handbook of British Chronology* (London, 1939), pp. 132ff.

9   The rule of Chrodegang, eighth-century bishop of Metz, was the most commonly used rule for canons.

10 A modern edition of the surviving copy of the Exeter rule, with parallel texts in Latin and Old English, now in the library of Corpus Christi College, Cambridge, is: A.S. Napier (ed.), *The Enlarged Rule of Chrodegang* (London, 1916), see especially ch. 46. The critical phrase regarding their residence, not without ambiguity, is '*omnes in uno conclaui atrii commorentur*' (p. 82).

11 For an exhaustive and convincing analysis, with text, of Osmund's foundation charter and *Institutio* see Diana Greenway, 'The False *Institutio* of St Osmund', in D. Greenway, C. Holdsworth and J. Sayers (eds), *Tradition and Change* (Cambridge, 1985), pp. 77–101.

12 For instance, boys are mentioned in the statutes of Wells, dating certainly from 1159, perhaps as early as 1153: see L.S. Colchester, D.Tudway Quilter and A.Quilter, *A History of Wells Cathedral School* (Wells, 1985), pp. 3 and 12; and in the mid-thirteenth-century statutes of Hereford: see John Caldwell, 'Music before 1300', in Gerald Aylmer and John Tiller (eds), *Hereford Cathedral: A History* (London, 2000), p. 369. For other references to boys in the secular cathedrals see Edwards, *English Secular Cathedrals*, p. 307, n. 9.

13 See Craig Wright, *Music and Ceremony at Notre Dame of Paris, 500–1550* (Cambridge, 1989), p. 165.

14 Edwards, *English Secular Cathedrals*, p. 307.

15 A table can be found in Greenway, 'False *Institutio*', at p. 84.

16 Julia Barrow in Aylmer and Tiller, *Hereford Cathedral*, p. 22.

17 Aylmer and Cant, *York Minster*, p. 22.

18 Indeed, in the eleventh century, before Rome began to be fierce about such matters, chastity seems to have been no more than an option. In 1055 canon Eilmer of Hereford was killed with his *four* sons, defending Hereford cathedral from the Welsh. Anskar, a canon of Bayeux, came over to be a canon of St Paul's, bringing with him his wife, Popelina: of their two sons one was to become bishop of Evreux and the other archbishop of York. At St Paul's in 1127 certainly nine and more probably twelve of the canons were sons of former canons: see Matthews and Atkins, *A History of St Paul's*, p. 23.

19 Robert of Lotharingia, bishop of Hereford, 1079–1095, made grants of land to the canonical body but also 'small personal tenancies for members of the cathedral community – embryonic prebends': Aylmer and Tiller (eds), *Hereford Cathedral*, p. 25.

20 Quoting from Aylmer and Cant, *York Minster*, p. 28.

21 Dora Robertson, *Sarum Close* (London, 1938), p. 35.

22 Matthews and Atkins, *A History of St Paul's*, p. 21.

23 Edwards, *English Secular Cathedrals*, p. 87.

24 Ibid., p. 165.

25 For Lincoln: ibid. pp. 326–48; for Salisbury: Christopher Ross, *The Canons of Salisbury* (Salisbury, 2000), pp. 111f. For a pair of unsavoury papally provided precentors of Salisbury, the Saluzzo brothers, see Robertson, *Sarum Close*, p. 42.

26 The vicars choral were to establish themselves as corporations with definite rights and splendid tied houses, as, most memorably, at the Vicars' Close, Wells.

27 Edwards, *English Secular Cathedrals*, p. 169.

28 Translation taken from Robertson, *Sarum Close*, p. 41.

29 C.W. Foster and K. Major, *The Registrum Antiquissimum of the Cathedral Church of Lincoln* (Lincoln, 1931–), ii, pp. 429–30. A grant in 1254 by the prior and community of Caldwell to the twelve Lincoln boys of two marks a year (approximately a shilling a boy) perhaps underlines their hand-to-mouth existence. See H. Bradshaw and C. Wordsworth, *Lincoln Cathedral Statutes*, ii (Cambridge, 1897), p. 161.

30 Details from *The Place-Names of Lincolnshire*. There is another similar place-name on the Wirral peninsula: Childer Thornton. This was 'Thorinton' about 1200 but by 1288 had become 'Childrethornton', the manor being owned by the abbey of St Werbergh in Chester, for whose almonry boys its income was evidently an endowment.

31 F. C. Hingeston-Randolph (ed.), *Register of Walter Bronescombe, Bishop of Exeter* (London, 1889), pp. 77–78. See Nicholas Orme, 'Early Musicians of Exeter Cathedral', *Music and Letters*, 59 (London, 1978), pp. 395–410. For York: Edwards, *English Secular Cathedrals*, p. 311.

32 There is no documentary evidence about the building of the Salisbury spire, but the architecture, archaeology and dendrochronology point unanimously to the two decades 1300–1320.

33   For this and what follows, see Robertson, *Sarum Close,* pp. 39–43.

34   The *Medieval Latin Word-List* gives 1267 as the earliest occurrence of the word *chorista,* but does not identify its source.

35   Edwards, *English Secular Cathedrals,* pp. 240 and 310, quoting Dean Baldock's statutes of about 1300.

36   See below, ch. 3, p. 39ff.

37   Edwards, *English Secular Cathedrals,* p. 314, and T.N. Cooper, 'Children, the Liturgy, and the Reformation: the Evidence of the Lichfield Cathedral Choristers', in D. Wood (ed.), *The Church and Childhood* (Oxford, 1994), pp. 261–74. The Lichfield choristers' house served as such for only half a century: by the 1580s it was let, and the boys were once more boarded out about the town.

38   Nicholas Orme in Aylmer and Tiller, *Hereford Cathedral,* p. 568.

39   Such documents as the foundation statutes at Winchester and Eton and, above all, the very detailed rules for the choristers and their masters issued at Wells in 1461, *vide infra* pp. 55–9.

40   Edwards, *English Secular Cathedrals,* p. 185.

41   Ibid., p. 188.

42   Roger Bowers, 'Cathedral Worship to 1640', in D. Owen (ed.), *A History of Lincoln Minster* (Cambridge, 1994), p. 55.

43   Nicholas Orme, *English Schools in the Middle Ages* (London, 1973), p. 64, refers to this generally; Dora Robertson, *Sarum Close,* pp. 64–66, is specific that from about 1340 the older Salisbury choristers went for their lessons to the cathedral's grammar school just outside the Close; and when in 1448 John Lane was appointed master of the grammar school his contract obliged him to teach 'the choristers and altarists'.

44   Edwards, *English Secular Cathedrals,* p. 315.

45   N. Ollerenshaw, *A History of the Prebendal School* (Chichester, 1984), p. 4.

46   See D. W. Sylvester, *Educational Documents, 800–1816* (London, 1970), p. 31.

47   The *Ars Minor* of the fourth-century Donatus was the ubiquitous elementary grammar text book until the later middle ages.

48   A. F. Leach, *History of Warwick School* (London, 1906), pp. 65–6.

49   For this and what follows: Orme, *English Schools in the Middle Ages,* pp. 60–62.

50   The Eton College statutes referring to choristers are xv, xvi, xxix and xxxvi.

51   For the development of the daily Lady mass see below, pp. 38ff.

52   It is very striking that shortly after the Anglo-Norman conquest of Ireland in 1170 a council of the Irish bishops summoned by Henry II should have accepted that Sarum practice ought to be adopted throughout Ireland. F.Ll. Harrison, *Music in Medieval Britain,* 2nd ed. (London, 1963), p. 16.

53   But it must not be assumed that 'adoption' of the Sarum Use meant that it was invariably *used.* Many of its prescriptions implied human resources well beyond the availability of, for example, modest collegiate churches. Hereford obediently records that *Gloria laus* is to be sung on Palm Sunday by seven boys – 'or five', the alternative acknowledging that Hereford had only five boys! Richard Pfaff, *Liturgical Calendars, Saints and Services in Medieval England* (Aldershot, 1998), p. 202, emphasises that for the smaller establishments '[most] of the rubric is likely to have been honoured only in the breach'.

54 C. Wordsworth and D. Macleane (eds), *Statuta et Consuetudines Ecclesiae Cathedralis Beatae Mariae Virginis Sarisberiensis* (London, 1915), p. 88.

55 Walter Howard Frere, bishop of Truro from 1923 to 1935, produced between 1894 and 1924 a series of scholarly (Latin) editions of the Sarum Gradual, Antiphonal, Consuetudinary and Customary, with magisterial introductions and unusually detailed English indices. They are: W.H. Frere, *Graduale Sarisburiense* (London, 1894); W.H. Frere, *Antiphonale Sarisburiense* (London 1901–1924); W.H. Frere, *The Use of Sarum*, i and ii (Cambridge, 1898–1901). A recent brief introduction to the Use is Philip Baxter, *Sarum Use* (Salisbury, 1994). Nick Sandon is engaged in producing a performing edition of the whole Sarum rite, drawn from what he judges to be the best of the many surviving forms. He has completed the mass: N. Sandon, *The Use of Salisbury* (Antico Church Music, LCM 1–6, 1989–1999). He is now working on the office. The Latin texts are supported by (authentic) rubrics in English and there is, introductory to vol. 1, a Historical Summary that includes a full table of feasts categorised into their ten liturgical grades, and a comprehensive bibliography. What follows in my text is drawn from these sources, and it would be tedious and unhelpful, in a general history such as this, to give detailed pagination, other than at points of particular interest.

56 The Customary and Consuetudinary are virtually two versions of the same text, the one probably meant for use at the cathedral itself and the other for churches within the Sarum diocese, especially for such large collegiate churches as Wimborne.

57 'Notandum quod pueri tenentur in omni dupplici festo et in omnibus dominicis et in festis nouem leccionum, que habent inuitatorium triplex, interesse uesperis completorio matutinis prime hore diei et misse, uigiliis quoque mortuorum quociens fuerit pro corpore presenti et in trigintalibus et in anniuersariis.' Frere, *Use of Sarum*, i, p. 93, from the Customary.

58 Boy canonries were an abuse that could be strikingly used by the powerful: in 1366 Queen Philippa, wife of Edward III, secured papal dispensation for the appointment to a Southwell canonry of Philip Beachamp 'who is nearly six'; over the next eight years the queen secured thirteen further preferments for him. See H.B. Workman, *John Wyclif* (Oxford, 1926), ii, p. 112.

59 But an octave higher, of course.

60 Except in Advent and Lent.

61 Frere, *Use of Sarum*, i, p. 51.

62 Ibid., i., p. 16.

63 See Karl Young, *The Drama of the Medieval Church*, 2 vols (Oxford, 1933), i, p. 90.

64 G.E. Gingras (ed. and trs.), *Egeria: Diary of a Pilgrimage* (New York, NY, 1970): see the introduction at pp. 35f.; Egeria's text is at p. 105, and see also p. 156, n. 167. The text of Egeria's diary, with translation, can also be found in L. Duchesne, trs. M.L. McClure, *Christian Worship, its Origin and Evolution* (London, 1927), pp. 490–523 and 541–71. Gregory Dix, *The Shape of the Liturgy*, 2nd ed. (Westminster, 1945), pp. 348f., gives a brief summary, adopting the name 'Etheria' and dating the diary to 385. I accept Gingras's careful argument for a date rather more than a century later.

65 The Sarum Palm Sunday mass and its procession are dealt with in Frere, *Use of Sarum*, i, at pp. 41f. and 161f.; and in J. Wickham Legg (ed.), *The Sarum Missal edited from three early manuscripts* (Oxford, 1916, reprint 1969), at pp. 92–96. A broader view can be found in the

chapter, 'Holy Week Rites of Sarum, Hereford and Rouen compared' in E. Bishop, *Liturgica Historica* (Oxford, 1918), pp. 276–300, and in Craig Wright, 'The Palm Sunday Procession in Medieval Chartres' in M.E. Fassler and R.A. Baltzer, *The Divine Office in the Latin Middle Ages* (Oxford, 2000), pp. 344–371. The matter of the specific route is considered in detail by N. Davison, 'So which way round did they go?', *Music and Letters*, 61/1 (1980), pp. 1–14. Sandon, *Use of Salisbury*, follows Davison. In Pamela Z. Blum, 'Liturgical Influences on the design of the West Front at Wells and Salisbury', *Gesta*, 25 (1986), pp. 145ff., an essay that at some points is in contradiction to both the documentary and the architectural evidence, assumptions about the third station, no doubt correct for Wells, are applied, contrary to all evidence, to Salisbury. The whole question of the route (or perhaps chronologically successive routes) of the Sarum Palm Sunday procession, and exactly what happened at its first three stations, calls for further and comprehensive research.

66   Bishop, *Liturgica Historica*, pp. 279–81.

67   W. G. Henderson (ed.), *Processionale ad usum insignis et praeclare Ecclesiae Sarum* (Leeds, 1882), p. 94. One hopes that he vanishes safely: the only possible 'high places' are very high indeed and not a little dangerous.

68   Details can be found in E. Duffy, *The Stripping of the Altars* (New Haven, Connecticut, and London, 1992), p. 24.

69   So suggest Davidson and Sandon. It is indeed the only high place close to the canons' cemetery that would have been other than puericidal* for seven boys. (*The neologism I owe to Roger Bowers.)

70   It is these west front apertures about which Pamela Blum writes in her 'Liturgical Influences on the Design of the West Fronts at Wells and Salisbury'. She says there are eight at Salisbury: there are nine.

71   The Sarum Customary records the *Benedicamus* to be sung *dupliciter*, that is, in two parts, on Christmas Day and on three other feasts: see Harrison, *Music in Medieval Britain*, p. 109.

72   See especially, Roger Bowers, 'To Chorus from Quartet', in *English Church Polyphony* (Aldershot, 1999), ii, p. 1. For fuller bibliographical references to the development of polyphony see the notes to the following chapter.

Notes to Chapter 4: The Great Flowering

1   The standard work on the music of these centuries in Britain remains F.Ll. Harrison, *Music in Medieval Britain*, 2nd ed. (London, 1963). Two decades of research of the first importance by Roger Bowers has been gathered together, but keeping its original journal paginations, in R. Bowers, *English Church Polyphony* (Aldershot, 1999). The development of the four-timbre chorus is described by Bowers (ibid. ii, p. 1) as 'perhaps the most enduring of all vehicles for the performance of art music'.

2   See Bowers, *English Church Polyphony*, v, pp. 210–11.

3   See especially: 'To Chorus from Quartet', paper ii in Bowers, *English Church Polyphony*. The only reference I have found to choral part-singing as early as the thirteenth century, presumably early faburden, is a requirement in the *Customary of Norwich* of *c.* 1250, for the whole choir to sing in three parts (*triplici cantu ab omnibus*) during the procession to

St Stephen's altar after Vespers on Christmas Day, quoted in Harrison, *Music in Medieval Britain*, pp. 113–14. But the Customary may well be referring to past practice, see note 17 below.

4　See B.R. Gaventa, *Mary* (Edinburgh, 1999), pp. 102–07.

5　See Hilda Graef, *Mary: A History of Doctrine and Devotion* London (1963), pp. 12ff. Averil Cameron, 'The Cult of the Virgin in Late Antiquity' in R.N. Swanson (ed.), *The Church and Mary* (Studies in Church History, 39) (Woodbridge, 2004), pp. 1–21, is a comprehensive survey of the early development of the Marian cult.

6　See F. Arnold Forster, *Studies in Church Dedications*, 3 vols (London, 1899), i, pp. 41ff.

7　D. Knowles, *The Monastic Order in England* (Cambridge, 1941), pp. 510f.

8　H.T. Riley (ed.) *Gesta Abbatum Sancti Albani* (London, 1863–76), i, pp. 284–85. The practice was not confined to monasteries: as early as 1210 one priest and six clerks were celebrating a daily Lady Mass at St Paul's Cathedral; it is found at Salisbury from 1225 and a special endowment funded it at Exeter shortly after that. See Harrison, *Music in Medieval Britain*, pp. 77–78.

9　Subsequently to become one of the Henrician cathedrals.

10　For a detailed consideration of his Prioress's Tale, see below, p. 60–2

11　Knowles, *Monastic Order*, p. 540.

12　'For more than a century there is no record of a boys' school in a Benedictine house.' S.J.A. Evans, 'Ely Almonry Boys and Choristers in the Later Middle Ages', in J.Conway Davies (ed.), *Studies Presented to Sir Hilary Jenkinson* (Oxford, 1957), p. 155.

13　For the almonries see Knowles, *Monastic Order*, pp. 482–86.

14　The almonry schools have received scant attention from historians. Leach comprehensively belittled them. In 1994 Roger Bowers read a paper to the 6th Harlaxton Symposium, published as 'The Almonry Schools of the English Monasteries', B. Thompson (ed.), *Monasteries and society in medieval Britain* (Stamford, 1999), pp. 177–222. This is the only reliable work on the subject: to it this and the following paragraph are comprehensively indebted.

15　The Ely evidence comes from an ordinance of 1314 for the almonry school, published in S.J.A. Evans, *Ely Chapter Ordinances* (Camden Miscellany xvii, 1940), pp. 38f. Ely is quoted as the first in David Robertson's *King's School, Gloucester* (Chichester, 1974), p. 24, and in D.L. Edwards, *History of the King's School, Canterbury* (London, 1957), where the claim is attributed to Knowles.

16　Bowers, 'Almonry Schools', p. 188.

17　Joan Greatrex, 'The Almonry School of Norwich Cathedral Priory in the Thirteenth and Fourteenth Centuries', in D. Wood (ed.), *The Church and Childhood* (Oxford, 1994), pp. 169–181. The document in question is Worcester Cathedral Muniment B. 680. It was common for one foundation to seek guidance from another. The presence of this document at Worcester might suggest that Norwich was known to be at the leading edge of Benedictine thirteenth-century liturgical practice. The situation at Norwich is further complicated by the existence in the library of Corpus Christi College, Cambridge, of a Norwich *Consuetudinarium* (MS 465), dating from around 1260, that describes duties of boys, duties that draw heavily on the *Regularis Concordia* and give every appearance of referring to the oblates of an earlier century, duties probably later transferred to young novices. See J.B.L. Tolhurst, *The Customary of the Cathedral Priory of Norwich* (London, 1948).

18 Bowers, 'Almonry Schools', p. 191 and Evans, 'Ely Almonry Boys', p. 155.

19 Indeed, there is evidence from the dawn of the thirteenth century of two or three country boys being boarded in the almonries of Bury St Edmunds and Durham in order that they could attend the abbey grammar school: Bowers, 'Almonry Schools', p. 181. For Worcester, ibid., p. 191.

20 Robertson, *King's School, Gloucester*, p. 21, suggests that this is 'the almonry school lying to the west of the cathedral'. Roger Bowers, however, understands 'the schoolroom of the monastery' to be more likely the novices' schoolroom.

21 A characteristic statement to this effect is, 'about the year 1320 … boys were introduced into the monastic churches, to sing the services in the lady chapel': W.A. James, *An Account of the Grammar and Song Schools of … Southwell* (Southwell, 1927), p. xiii.

22 There is a telling reference from Norwich where, in 1308, bishop Salmon stipulated that, when monks celebrating private masses had no monastic acolyte available, the almoner was to draw up a weekly schedule of three suitable almonry clerks (i.e. boys), apt for altar service, who were to be available as acolytes at side altars in the mornings no later than the end of high mass, after which they were to return to their schoolroom. Greatrex, *The Almonry School of Norwich*, p. 174, referring to Norwich Record Office, DCN 92/1. In the early 1430s Bishop Gray of Lincoln ordered two small Bedfordshire priories to take into their almonries and educate three or four boys specifically in order that the monks could be served when celebrating mass. The whole matter of serving at altars by almonry boys is covered thoroughly in Bowers, 'Almonry Schools', pp. 189–93.

23 Bowers, *English Church Polyphony*, v, p. 215.

24 Caroline Roslington (ed.), *The King's School, Worcester* (Worcester, 1994) p. 16; and Harrison, *Music in Medieval Britain*, p. 40.

25 Bowers, *English Church Polyphony*, v, pp. 216f.

26 Worcester Cathedral Muniment B680.

27 Or, Roger Bowers has suggested, the boys may at this stage have been only serving the celebrant at mass.

28 John Crook, *A History of the Pilgrims' School* (Chichester, 1981), pp. 5 and 134, n. 9, referring to G.W. Kitchin (ed.), *Obedientiary Rolls of St Swithun* (London, 1892), p. 398, cites payments to almonry boys in connection with the Boy Bishop ceremony (for which, see Chapter 5 below): four dishes of meat and a special issue of wine and beer in 1312. But Roger Bowers identifies these boys as more probably young novices, who would have taken over the oblates' liturgical roles in quire after the ending of child oblation.

29 Crook, *Pilgrims' School*, p. 5.

30 Bowers, *English Church Polyphony*, iv, pp. 414–26.

31 Examples given in Magnus Williamson, '*Pictura et Scriptura*', *Early Music*, August 2000, pp. 360f.

32 On the nunneries I have again drawn heavily on Eileen Power, *Medieval English Nunneries* (Cambridge, 1922).

33 The tables in D. Knowles and R.N. Hadcock, *Medieval Religious Houses in England and Wales* (London, rev. ed. 1971), give useful statistical details.

34　Power, *English Nunneries*, pp. 569 and 572 for this and the following example.

35　Ibid., pp. 25f.

36　Ibid., pp. 35 and 30 for this and the following case.

37　This is not to say that girls were unable to sing. The great English madrigal tradition shows that there was much domestic mixed-gender music-making in Tudor and Stuart times. And after the Restoration girls are sometimes found singing in parish gallery choirs. What girls could no longer do was sing the liturgy in choral foundations.

38　See Christopher Wordsworth (ed.), *Horae Eboracenses: The Prymer or Hours of the Blessed Virgin Mary*, Surtees Society, cxxxii (Durham and London, 1920), pp. xxx–xxxi. The Hours of the Virgin were a set of short offices, based on the monastic hours, but with hymns, lessons, responses and prayers devotionally focused on the Virgin Mary.

39　Chapter 16 of Margaret Wood, *The English Medieval House* (London, 1950; pagination taken from 1983 ed.), pp. 227–246, includes reference to eighty-nine surviving medieval domestic chapels.

40　For the details that follow, see Harrison, *Music in Medieval Britain*, pp. 24–26; Kate Mertes, *The English Noble Household, 1250–1600* (Oxford, 1988), pp. 139–160; and Andrew Wathey's published D. Phil. Thesis, *Music in the Royal and Noble Households in Late Medieval England* (New York, NY, and London, 1989), passim.

41　Fiona Kisby, 'A Mirror of Monarchy', *Early Music History*, 16 (Cambridge, 1997), pp. 203–231.

42　Percy, Thomas (ed.), *The Regulations and Establishments of the Household of Henry Algernon Percy, Fifth Earl of Northumberland* (privately printed, 1770, 1827 and 1905).

43　1 Peter, 3:19 and 1 Corinthians, 3: 10–15. For a comprehensive history of the doctrine of Purgatory see J. Le Goff (trs. A. Goldhammer), *The Birth of Purgatory* (London, 1984). Eamon Duffy, in *The Stripping of the Altars* (Yale, New Hampshire, and London, 1992), p. 8, argues that 'there is a case for saying that *the* defining doctrine of late medieval Catholicism was Purgatory'. In chapters 9 and 10 he deals fully with the impact of the doctrine of Purgatory on late medieval piety.

44　In the *Mystagogical Catacheses* attributed to Cyril, see Paul F. Bradshaw, 'Continuity and Change in Eucharistic Practice', in R.N. Swanson (ed.), *Continuity and Change in Christian Worship* (Woodbridge, 1999), pp. 1–17.

45　Chantry chapels and votive masses have had a bad press from the largely Protestant English historians. The most thorough study of chantries is K.L. Wood-Legh, *Perpetual Chantries in Britain* (Cambridge, 1965), whose author found deeply unacceptable the notion of a God who was 'a being of infinite severity ... who prefers the endless repetition of the sacrifice [of the mass] to any manifestation of Christian character' (ibid. p. 313). G.H. Cook, in *Medieval Chantries and Chantry Chapels* (London, 2nd ed., 1963), takes a more sympathetic stance. Clive Burgess, in '"A fond thing vainly invented": an essay on Purgatory and pious motive in late medieval England', in Susan Wright (ed.), *Parish, Church and People* (London, 1988), pp. 56–84, sets out to put the matter in the context of late medieval piety and belief.

46　For the Burghersh Chantry see D. Owen (ed.), *A History of Lincoln Minster* (Cambridge, 1994), p. 151.

47　For which, see T. Tatton-Brown and R. Mortimer (eds), *Westminster Abbey: the Lady Chapel of King Henry VII* (Woodbridge, 2003).

48   The full passage from More's *Supplication of Souls* is given in A.G. Dickens, *The English Reformation* (London, rev. ed., 1967), p. 19.

49   Article xxii: *Of Purgatory*.

50   For the Newarke, see A. Hamilton Thompson, *The History of the Hospital and the New College of the Annunciation of St Mary in the Newarke, Leicester* (Leicester, 1937) and for chantries generally, Harrison, *Music in Medieval Britain*, pp. 26–30.

51   'Almost none of the new schools of the fifteenth century was founded as a school alone.' Nicholas Orme, *English Schools in the Middle Ages* (London, 1973), p. 155.

52   For New College and its choir school see J. Buxton and P. Williams (ed.), *New College, Oxford, 1379–1979* (Oxford, 1979) and Jonathan Edmonds, *New College Brats* (Oxford, 1996); for Winchester College as a choral foundation see Alan Rannie, *The Story of Music at Winchester College* (Winchester, 1970).

53   Neville Wridgway, *The Choristers of St George's Chapel* (Windsor, 1980), p. 1.

54   For King's College, Cambridge, and its choir school see John Saltmarsh, *King's College and its Chapel* (Cambridge, 1969) and R.J. Henderson, *A History of King's College Choir School, Cambridge* (Cambridge, 1981). For Eton College the most comprehensive history remains Sir H.C. Maxwell Lyte, *A History of Eton College, 1440–1910*, 4th ed. (London, 1911). See also Albert Mellor, *Music and Musicians of Eton College* (Eton, 1929). Tim Card's recent histories have little to say on the choristers.

55   Wayneflete founded at the same time another associated grammar school at his eponymous birthplace, Wainfleet in Lincolnshire. For Wayneflete's educational work and foundations see Virginia Davis, *William Wayneflete: Bishop and Educationalist* (Woodbridge, 1993).

56   Roger Bowers convincingly surmises that it enhanced the educational provision of the foundation. Significantly, in 1860, when the Public Schools Commission criticised Eton for having abandoned their choristers, it was the discontinuance of the founder's intended educational provision that concerned them.

57   Bowers, *English Church Polyphony*, ii, p. 17. For a detailed study of the Westminster Abbey Lady Chapel choir see R. Bowers, 'The Musicians and Liturgy of the Lady Chapels of the Monastery Church, c. 1235–1540', in Tatton-Brown and Mortimer, *The Lady Chapel of King Henry VII*.

58   The figures from the *Northumberland Household Book* are discussed in S.R. Westfall, *Patrons and Performance: Early Tudor Revels* (Oxford, 1990), p. 15, see especially n. 7; and the earl of Oxford's figures are quoted from p. 16.

59   Fiona Kisby, 'Music and Musicians in Early Tudor Westminster', *Early Music*, 23/2 (1995), p. 226.

60   Fiona Kisby, 'A Mirror of Monarchy', *Early Music History*, 16 (1997), pp. 212 and 214.

61   David Baldwin, *The Chapel Royal Ancient and Modern* (London, 1990), p. 313. For the link between the Chapel Royal and the King's Hall, Cambridge, see below p. 54ff. The lane leading to King's Hall was actually called 'King's Childers Lane'.

62   I have taken the Chapel Royal numbers from Tables 1 and 2 in Wathey, *Music in the Royal and Noble Households*, pp. 124–27. Baldwin, *The Chapel Royal*, p. 315, gives sixteen choristers in 1421/2. Wathey's figure of fourteen is taken from the Wardrobe accounts (TNA, E 361/6) where provision of surplices is recorded 'for William Rote and thirteen

other boys'. But figures drawn from records of supplies need to be read with caution. Did all boys need new surplices at the same time? Does this explain the seemingly very low numbers on occasion? The Earl of Oxford's household accounts mention 'shoryng and dyeing of ix gounnys for the chylderyn off the chappell', yet coincidentally there is a list of twelve such children. See Westfall, *Patrons and Performance*, p. 16, n. 8.

63 Ouseley's foundation of St Michael's College at Tenbury in the 1850s had eight choristers and eight probationers.

64 Bowers, *English Church Polyphony*, i, p. 185, note 56.

65 See especially Bowers, *English Church Polyphony*, ii, passim.

66 Ibid.,ii, p. 32. Bowers gives a list of 'likely' polyphonic choirs in *English Church Polyphony*, ii, p. 11.

67 L.S Colchester, D. Tudway Quilter and A. Quilter (eds.), *A History of Wells Cathedral School* (Wells, 1985), pp. 22f., as corrected, with regard to the tabulars, by Roger Bowers.

68 'Faburden' was, at least originally, a style of polyphony improvised to a formula above and below the tenor plainchant. 'Counter' was a sixteenth-century English term used, in this context, to designate a melody improvised below a given tune; descant, improvisation above a given tune.

69 Brian Crosby, *Come on, Choristers!* (Durham, 1999), p. 9.

70 Baldwin, *The Chapel Royal*, p. 300.

71 Bowers, *English Church Polyphony*, vi, p. 57.

72 A table of eleven such appointments is given by Jane Flynn in her chapter 'The Education of Choristers in England during the Sixteenth Century' in J. Morehen (ed.), *English Choral Practice, 1400–1650* (Cambridge, 1995), p. 182. However, her inclusion of Aberdeen in the list is misleading since the requirements there were for trained *priests*, not trained choristers. I have not been able to check all her sources. Dates from Salisbury and Worcester provided by Roger Bowers.

73 3 & 4 Edw. VI, c.10: Statutes of the Realm, iv, 110.

74 Harrison favoured the Chapel Royal (*Music in Medieval Britain*, p. 170); Bowers (*English Church Polyphony*, ii, p. 18) proposes the Clarence chapel as the source; Margaret Bent (*NGD*, xiii, pp. 526–9) suggests different sources for the Old Hall Manuscript's two identifiable layers, the second layer revealing at least four Chapel Royal scribes. So far as the first layer is concerned, certainty is elusive.

75 Eton College Library MS 178.

76 Magnus Williamson, 'Pictura et Scriptura', *Early Music*, August 2000, p. 361.

77 The ranges of meanes and trebles are comprehensively discussed in David Wulstan, *Tudor Music* (London, 1985), especially pp. 210–14 and 237–42, and I have here quoted his opinions. Converting medieval musical texts into modern notation is never other than problematical, and it has to be said that today few musicologists accept Wulstan's theses. See, in particular, Peter Phillips, *Early Music*, August 2005. Nevertheless, that English polyphonic trebles sang close to the upper limits of a modern boy treble's range, producing a thrilling sound, seems beyond dispute.

78 Much of the Eton Choirbook music, recorded between 1991 and 1995 by The Sixteen under Harry Christophers, can be heard on a five-disc boxed set: Collins 70472. Davy's *Passion* and two shorter pieces from the Choirbook were recorded by the Eton College Chapel

Choir under their precentor, Ralph Allwood, in 1994: Future Classics, FCM 1004, giving an all-male sound within the Eton College chapel acoustic.

79   David Wulstan, *Tudor Music*, Ex. 119, p. 240. The Cornysh *Magnificat* can be heard, along with all Cornysh's surviving church music, on CDGIMO 14, sung by the Tallis Scholars.

80   TNA C 66 402 m11v, and *Calendar of Patent Rolls, 1416–22*, p. 272.

81   TNA C 66 447 m14v, and *CPR, 1436–41*, p. 452.

82   Brown, R. (ed.), *Calendar of State Papers (Venetian)*, ii (London, 1869–), p. 247.

83   From Bowers, *English Church Polyphony*, vii, p. 205 and Baldwin, *The Chapel Royal*, pp. 45f.

84   Wulstan, *Tudor Music*, pp. 238f.

85   For the Windsor cases see Wridgway, *Choristers of St George's Chapel*, pp. 12 and 21.

86   J. Stevens, *Music and Poetry in the Early Tudor Court* (Cambridge, corrected ed., 1979), p. 304.

87   For Bramston, see Colchester, Tudway Quilter and Quilter, *A History of Wells Cathedral School*, p. 23, and J. Collard, D. Ogden and R. Burgess, *A History of Bristol Cathedral School* (Bristol, 1992), pp. 8f. Bramston gave up his mastership of the Wells chorister in 1531 and turned his hand to commerce, with considerable success. Ultimately he left generous charitable bequests in his will, none of them to musical causes.

Notes to Chapter 5: At Work and Play

1   Joan Greatrex, 'The Almonry School of Norwich Cathedral in the Thirteenth and Fourteenth Centuries', in *The Church and Childhood* (Oxford, 1994), p. 176.

2   L.S. Colchester, D. Tudway Quilter and A. Quilter, *A History of Wells Cathedral School* (Wells, 1986), p. 15. This list contradicts the conventional understanding that the only surviving lists of medieval pupils are those of the scholars at Winchester and Eton.

3   David Baldwin, *The Chapel Royal, Ancient and Modern* (London, 1990), p. 321, sources there quoted.

4   Seiriol Evans, 'Ely Almonry Boys' in J. Conway Davies (ed), *Studies Presented to Sir Hilary Jenkinson* (London and Oxford, 1957), p. 159.

5   Nicholas Orme, Education and Society in Medieval and Renaissance England (London 1989), p. 191.

6   A.F. Leach, *A History of Winchester College* (London, 1899), pp. 94ff.

7   'Respectable birth' may simply have meant 'not illegitimate'.

8   R.S. Stanier, *Magdalen School* (2nd ed., Oxford, 1958), p. 25.

9   R.J. Henderson, *A History of King's College Choir School, Cambridge* (Cambridge, 1981), p. 9.

10   A. Wathey, *Music in the Royal and Noble Households of Late Medieval England* (New York, NY, and London, 1989), pp. 87f.; and H.N. Hillebrand, 'The Child Actors', in *University of Illinois Studies in Language and Literature*, xi/1, February 1926 (Urbana, Illinois, 1926), p. 42.

11   Roger Bowers suggests a mis-spelling of the nearby village, Croscombe. The author wonders whether, if so, the mis-spelling might have been wittily intentional.

12   Taken from the Salisbury *Accounts of Choristers' Collectors*, as quoted by Dora Robertson, *Sarum Close* (London, 1938), pp. 120f.

13   Ibid., pp. 15 and 17–21, from which I here quote extensively.

14   These are fifteenth-century ligatures, note-clusters indicative of both pitch and rhythm. See Dom Anselm Hughes, 'The Painted Music in No. 25 The Cloisters', *Report of the Friends of St George's*, 4 (1965), p. 282, and N. Wridgway, *The Choristers of St George's Chapel* (Windsor, 1980), pp. 13f.

15   A. Hamilton Thompson, *History of the New College in the Newarke, Leicester* (Leicester, 1937), pp. 115 and 184.

16   W.A. James, *An Account of the Southwell Grammar and Song Schools* (Southwell, 1927), pp. 51f.

17   Wridgway, *Choristers of St George's Chapel*, pp. 4f.

18   John Plummer, master of the choristers, was owed £20 for boys' expenses in the early 1440s. Instead of payment he was given a series of bills of assignment, promising payment from identifiable future royal income: from the Ely diocesan tithe in 1445, but it was not forthcoming; then from the customs income of Sandwich and Dover in 1449 and again in 1450 – but still no payment reached him; eventually it was paid out of taxes from the sheriff of Shropshire. Wathey, *Music in the Royal and Noble Households*, p. 154.

19   Henderson, *King's College Choir School*, p. 5.

20   Robertson, *Sarum Close*, pp. 118f.

21   Ibid., p. 120, where one, Crede, the bell-ringer, is paid 8d. 'for calling the choristers to Mattins this term'.

22   See above, pp. 16f.

23   J.T.Fowler (ed.), *The Rites of Durham*, Surtees Society, cvii (London, 1903), pp. 51f.

24   For these developments see Orme, *English Schools in the Middle Ages* (London, 1973), pp. 42ff and 96–101.

25   Now in the library of Lincoln College, Oxford. For this early *Vulgaria* see J. Collard, D. Ogden and R. Burgess, 'Where the Fat, Black Canons Dined': a History of Bristol Cathedral School (Bristol, 1992), pp. 10–13, drawing on N. Orme, 'Grammatical Miscellany of 1427–65 from Bristol and Wiltshire', *Traditio*, 1982.

26   For the influence of Magdalen, see Orme, *English Schools in the Middle Ages*, pp. 107 ff. and Stanier, *Magdalen School*, *passim*.

27   'Clergeon' is taken from L.D. Benson (ed.), *The Riverside Chaucer* (3rd ed., Oxford, 1988), and I have used pp. 209–12 of this edition for all quotations that follow, except for words in square brackets. W.W. Skeat, *Chaucer: The Prioresses Tale* (Oxford, 1916), has a still valuable introduction. 'Chorister' was used by Neville Coghill in his edition of *The Canterbury Tales* (Harmondsworth, 1951), pp. 192–99, a usage supported by the *Oxford English Dictionary*.

28   E.K.Chambers, *The Medieval Stage*, 2 vols (Oxford, 1903), remains the standard history of this remarkable development. Both Chambers and Karl Young, *The Drama of the Medieval Church*, 2 vols (Oxford 1933), were in no doubt that an unbroken line could be traced from the late Anglo-Saxon liturgical drama, by way of the mystery plays, to the sixteenth-century 'Children of Pawles'. 'The growth of drama within the heart of the ecclesiastical liturgy, which began in the tenth century ... [ultimately] broke the bonds of ecclesiastical control, became laicised and culminated in such dramas as the guild Corpus Christi cycles.' (Chambers, *Medieval Stage*, ii, p. 180) That is now in question, with an influential body of

opinion believing that vernacular market place drama had its own originals independent of the Latin drama of the liturgy. Several contributors to Eckehard Simon (ed.), *The Theatre of Medieval Europe: New Research in Early Drama* (Cambridge, 1991), refute such continuity, e.g. 'Continued belief in some logical, evolutionary pattern of organic development ... became impossible to sustain.' (p. 16); and 'the mystery plays were not developments from liturgical drama but had their own separate genesis.' (p. 86)

29   See Timothy J. McGee, *The Sound of Medieval Song* (Oxford, 1998), p. 2, n. 3.

30   Dom Thomas Symons (ed.), *Regularis Concordia* (London, 1953), pp. 49f.

31   The Easter sepulchre, a feature of virtually every medieval church, though most often a temporary structure.

32   For the *Visitatio sepulchri* text, with the original neumes and modern notation see William L. Smoldon, *The Music of the Medieval Church Dramas* (Oxford University Press, 1980), pp. 94f.

33   In thus describing the Winchester *Visitatio sepulchri* I am not nailing my colours to any of the multitude of scholarly masts that illuminate this topic. The principal issues are whether the rite as found at the monastery of St Martial, Limoges, is the earliest surviving manuscript, and if so whether it was the progenitor of all others; whether (as at Limoges) the *Visitatio* was meant to be an addition to the introit antiphon of the Mass or (as at Winchester) a trope preceding *Te Deum* at the close of matins; whether the three-sentence form is more primitive than the five-sentence form found at Winchester and elsewhere; and so on. But none of these issues has significant bearing on the history of the English chorister: to give detailed references to the extensive literature would be otiose.

34   S.R. Westfall, *Patrons and Performance: Early Tudor Household Revels* (Oxford, 1990), p. 30.

35   Young, *Drama of the Medieval Church*, i, pp. 323ff.

36   Ibid., ii, pp. 1–14 for the continental examples; F. Ll. Harrison, *Music in Medieval Britain* (London, 2nd ed., 1963), p. 107, for Salisbury.

37   Harrison, p. 107, quoting in translation from *Ordinale Exon*, i, p. 64.

38   Young, ii, p. 522.

39   Ibid., ii, Appendix D, p. 539.

40   Evans, 'Ely Almonry Boys', p. 160.

41   Examples taken from Hillebrand, 'The Child Actors', pp. 10f.

42   Chambers, *Medieval Stage*, ii, pp. 54f. (The biblical reference is to Numbers, 22: 28–30.)

43   The main source for what follows is Hillebrand, 'The Child Actors', pp. 40–59. Sydney Anglo, *Spectacle, Pageantry and Early Tudor Policy* (Oxford, 2nd ed., 1997), is disappointingly thin on chorister roles in court revels.

44   Hillebrand believes this to be 'the first play of romantic source on record in England'. Ibid., p. 55.

45   For a succinct general background to the Field of the Cloth of Gold: J.J. Scarisbrick, *Henry VIII* (London, 1968), pp. 74–80. For more detail: Anglo, *Spectacle, Pageantry and Early Tudor Policy*, ch. 4. By far the fullest recent study is J.G. Russell, *The Field of the Cloth of Gold* (London, 1969): notably, even indulgently, rich in detail on the banquets. Two surviving eye-witness accounts, calendared, are especially rewarding: Brewer, Gairdner and Brodie (eds.), *Letters and Papers (Foreign and Domestic): Henry VIII*, iii pt 1 (1519–1521) (London, 1862–1910), pp. 303–312; and R. Brown (ed.), *Calendar of State Papers (Venetian)*, iii

(1520–1526) (London, 1869–), pp. 20–30, 40f, 55 and 73f. On the other hand, Edward Hall, ed. Charles Whibley, *Chronicle of the Reign of Henry VIII*, i (London, 1904), pp. 181–192, perhaps as an anti-Catholic, has little to say about the great concluding mass.

46 All this can be seen in the splendid contemporary painting of the event by an unknown artist that hangs at Hampton Court Palace. For this, see S. Anglo, 'The Hampton Court Painting of the Field of the Cloth of Gold considered as an Historical Document', *The Antiquaries Journal*, xlvi (1966), pp. 287–307.

47 Anglo, *Spectacle, Pageantry and Early Tudor Policy*, p. 156, states that 'it had been arranged … that the French organist, Pierre Mouton, should accompany the English singers [and] that the English organist should accompany the French.' But the contemporary French account (*L & P, HVIII, iii, i*), p. 311, makes it absolutely clear that such an impractical arrangement did not happen. In any case, the organists merely *introduced* the Mass ordinaries, which were then sung unaccompanied (with the exception of the *Patrem*, as described in my text).

48 Anglo, *Spectacle, Pageantry and Early Tudor Policy*, p. 157, on the evidence of a payment (TNA, SP, 1/20, fol. 80) referring to 'a canvas to be used for covering a dragon', believes the apparition to have been a firework, built by the English and intended for the evening's pyrotechnic display, set off by accident at the wrong time. On this strange incident we are all reduced to guesses.

49 Chambers, *Medieval Stage*, i, p. 369, for these titles.

50 Ibid., i, p. 344.

51 Ibid., I, p. 325.

52 Quoted, using a translation by Chambers, in Craig Wright, *Music and Ceremony at Notre Dame of Paris, 500–1550* (Cambridge, 1989), p. 240.

53 Matt. 18:2–4 and 19:13–15.

54 Noted by A.F. Leach in *Archaeologia*, lxii, pt. 1, p. 218.

55 There is a considerable literature on this subject. E.K. Chambers is, as ever, an invaluable source. Vol i, chapter 9 of *The Medieval Stage* is devoted to the Boy Bishop. In vol. ii, Appendix M, Chambers gives the text of the offices at which the *Episcopus Puerorum* presided. This text can also be found, with scholarly apparatus, in Christopher Wordsworth (ed.), *Ceremonies and Processions of the Cathedral Church of Salisbury* (Cambridge, 1901), pp. 52–57. Chambers also quotes from E. F. Rimbault, *Camden Miscellany VII* (1875) the text of the York Computus of 1396, which lists all the gifts and expenses of the famous Visitation by the Boy Bishop of that year. Rimbault has an invaluable introduction and prints in full the texts of two sixteenth-century Boy Bishops' sermons. A.F. Leach published a much-cited article, 'The Schoolboys' Feast' in *The Fortnightly Review*, lix, 1916, pp. 128ff. I know of no recent study that throws significant new light on the matter, but I give references for local sources where I have used them.

56 Robertson, *Sarum Close*, pp. 86f.

57 Chambers, *Medieval Stage*, i, p. 356.

58 Various suggestions have been mooted as to why these royal foundations should have been thus out of line. The wording at King's (given by Henderson at p. 5) is curious: 'On the feast of St Nicholas, but by no means on the feast of the Holy Innocents, we *allow* that the choristers may be *permitted* [my italics] to say and perform vespers, matins and other of-

fices by reading and singing.' This sounds like a concession: the ceremony is a nuisance but is too popular to ban, so we shall see that it is all over and done with as soon as possible.

59   Chambers, *Medieval Stage*, i, pp. 346 and 354.

60   There are two certain reasons for the omission. In nearly all surviving manuscripts passages making reference to the Boy Bishop have been removed, doubtless following the banning of the ceremony in 1541. But also, the documents that do make reference, on which Christopher Wordsworth's edition is built, deal only in what might be termed 'propers', texts of the office particular to the specific day. The text for matins, for example, makes reference only to the third nocturn. At vespers *Magnificat* was part of the 'ordinary', sung daily, hence it goes unmentioned.

61   E.F. Rimbault, *Two Sermons Preached by the Boy Bishop* (Camden Miscellany vii, London, 1875), pp. 24f. The other sermon, on the text *Laudate pueri, dominum*, is from St Paul's, written by the almoner, dating from the reign of Henry VII.

62   These details, and the York menu in the following paragraph, from Robertson, *Sarum Close*, pp. 84–86.

63   The text, from which I have quoted, has been widely published; D. Wilkins, *Concilia* (London, 1737), has it in vol. iii at p. 864.

Notes to Chapter 6: Turmoil

1   For a bravura discussion as to whether, and, if so, to what extent, any event or development might be regarded as 'inevitable', see the 1953 Auguste Comte Memorial Trust Lecture: Isaiah Berlin, *Historical Inevitability* (Oxford, 1954). In the course of a passionate attack on determinism and determinist historicism, Platonic, Hegelian, Marxist, Comtian or whatever, Berlin defends the use of 'inevitable' by non-determinist general historians (pp. 51f.) as conveying a meaning 'much the same as that which it has is ordinary, non-technical thought and speech'.

2   For general background to Chapters 6 and 7 I have drawn on A.G. Dickens, *The English Reformation* (London, rev. edn, 1967) and, specifically for liturgical changes, on Horton Davies, *Worship and Theology in England*, Bk.1,i (Grand Rapids, Michigan, and Cambridge, 1996). For an exposition of the faith of the reformers, largely in their own words but embedded in a committedly supportive modern text, see P.E. Hughes, *Theology of the English Reformers* (London, 1965); and for a defence of what the reformers expunged, Eamon Duffy, *The Stripping of the Altars* (New Haven, Connecticut, and London, 1992) is a passionate valediction to late medieval Catholic piety.

3   Since the eighteenth century it has been widely believed that to puritans music was an unchristian activity. In Calvin's Geneva, Charles Burney, wrote, 'Not a musical instrument was suffered within the walls of Geneva for more than a hundred years after the Reformation; and all Music, except ... Metrical Psalmody, was proscribed wherever the doctrines of this reformer were received', *General History of Music*, i (1776). In the 1930s Percy Scholes set out with 'active purpose' to refute the 'calumny' that puritans had no music, and in his *The Puritans and Music* (Oxford, 1934) did so to the seeming satisfaction of all serious music scholars subsequently. Nevertheless Calvinists had no time for choristers.

4   26 Henry VIII, c.1. The Act of 1534 was, of course, the culmination of a series of anti-papal measures that had been enacted over the previous four or five years.

5   J.J. Scarisbrick, *Henry VIII* (London, 1968), p. 337.

6   27 Henry VIII, c. 28; and 31 Henry VIII, c. 13.

7   Eileen Power, *Medieval English Nunneries* (Cambridge, 1922), p. 579.

8   A.F. Leach, *Educational Charters and Documents, 598–1909* (Cambridge, 1911), p. xxxii.

9   J.J. Scarisbrick, *Henry VIII*, pp. 512f.

10 Other former monastic churches were subsequently to become episcopal sees, especially in the nineteenth and twentieth centuries. Westminster was to become monastic (but not episcopal) again during the brief reign of Mary.

11 At the same time (1546) Henry established, on a lavish scale, Trinity College at Cambridge: there was, however, no statutory choral foundation there before Mary's reign.

12 Details of the houses subject to dissolution can be found in D. Knowles and K.N. Hadcock, *Medieval Religious Houses* (London, rev. ed., 1971). Unfortunately the authors show no interest in numbers of singing children. A convenient list of the chief monastic houses in order of wealth is given in Peter le Huray, *Music and the Reformation in England* (London, 1967), p. 3.

13 Shakespeare, *Sonnet* lxxiii.

14 Dr Roger Bowers tells me (e-mail, September 2003) that 'at some of the greatest monastic churches', of which St Albans and Winchester were two, 'the full team of Cantor, secular singing-men and boys was also required to attend certain of the most important of the monks' services held in the monastic quire: commonly High Mass and second vespers on the greater feasts and also first vespers on the eve'. On the other hand, at Westminster, than which no abbey was grander, 'there is no indication that the boys ever joined the singing-men at services in the monks' quire on the ten principal feasts'. R. Bowers, 'The Musicians and Liturgy of the Lady Chapels' in T. Tatton-Brown and R. Mortimer (eds), *Westminster Abbey: the Lady Chapel of Henry VII* (Woodbridge, 2003), p. 51.

15 Not quite the mere pocket money it sounds, at a time when eight pence paid for a sick Salisbury chorister to be boarded and nursed and fed for a week. The Nocton reference comes from V.C.H., Lincolnshire, ii, p. 168.

16 For Durham, here and in the following paragraph, see Brian Crosby, *Come on, Choristers!* (Durham, 1999), pp. 13f.

17 C.J. Stranks, *This Sumptuous Church* (London, 1972), p. 39, drawing on W. Hutchinson, *History and Antiquities of Durham* (Durham, 1823), ii, p. 133.

18 B. Crosby, *Come on, Choristers!*, p. 13.

19 Ian Payne, *The Provision and Practice of Sacred Music at Cambridge Colleges and Selected Cathedrals, c. 1547 to c. 1646* (New York and London, 1993), p. 201.

20 The guess is supported by Bowers, in Tatton-Brown and Mortimer (eds), *Westminster Abbey: the Lady Chapel of Henry VII*, p. 57: 'The government of Henry VIII appreciated the value of the Lady chapel choirs sufficiently strongly to instruct that in the case of any re-founded institution its choir was not to be dissolved along with the parent monastery'. (No source given.)

21 R. Harries, P. Cattermole and P. Mackintosh, *A History of Norwich School* (Norwich, 1991), pp. 24 and 26.

22   R.G. Ikin, *Notes on the History of Ely Cathedral Grammar School* (Cambridge, 1931), p. 16.

23   John Crook, *A History of the Pilgrims' School* (Chichester, 1981), p. 7.

24   Caroline Roslington (ed.), *The King's School, Worcester* (Worcester, 1994), p. 19, and facsimile and translation, p. 20.

25   R. Bowers in Tatton-Brown and Mortimer (eds), *Westminster Abbey: the Lady Chapel of Henry VII*, p. 57.

26   R.V.H. Burne, *Chester Cathedral* (London, 1958), p. 10. The abbot, Thomas Clarke, died shortly before he was due to be consecrated. Ibid., pp. 1f, with an exceptionally interesting list of his personal property.

27   D. Robertson, *The King's School, Gloucester* (Chichester, 1974), pp. 23ff. Robertson, like Maria Hackett, records the statutes as providing for eight choristers; but le Huray, *Music and the Reformation*, p. 14, records the figure as six. Some of Robertson's dates, however, are unreliable.

28   Geoffrey Baskerville's confident assertion, in his *English Monks and the Suppression of the Monasteries* (London, 1937), p. 282, that 'those [almonry boys] in the choir schools of the cathedrals, old, like Canterbury and new, like Westminster, remained undisturbed' is probably too sweeping.

29   J. Collard, D. Ogden and R. Burgess, *'Where the Fat, Black Canons Dined'* (Bristol, 1992), p. 15 and, for what follows, p. 20.

30   This would have been intended to be the grammar school room, almost certainly not the room where the choristers were taught by their *Informator Choristarum*.

31   At Gloucester there was a grammar school, but there were no king's scholarships so no free places, and no subsequent exhibitions to the universities.

32   No grammar school was provided at Winchester, where William of Wykeham was deemed already to have met the need, or at Oxford.

33   At Canterbury, priority for places at the King's School was to be shown not only to Canterbury choristers but also to those of the Chapel Royal. But the stipulation was almost wholly ignored.

34   W.H. Frere and W. McC. Kennedy (eds), *Visitation Articles and Injunctions of the Period of the Reformation* (London, 1910), ii, pp. 138f.

35   The use of the verb *'pulsare'* implies keyboard rather than bowed instruments.

36   For Henry VIII's Canterbury statutes, as amended and confirmed in 1636, I have used the first printed edition with supporting English translation: *The Statutes of the Cathedral and Metropolitical Church of Christ, Canterbury* (Canterbury, 1926).

37   See above, cap. 3, p. 32f.

38   F. Ll. Harrison, *Music in Medieval Britain* (London, 2nd edn, 1963), p. 196.

39   Precisely that view is stated by David Wulstan, *Tudor Music* (London, 1985), p. 277. There are, of course, great difficulties in dating much (but not all) of Tallis's music.

40   No copy survives.

41   Dickens, *The English Reformation*, p. 255.

42   N. Wridgway, *The Choristers of St George's Chapel* (Windsor, 1980), p. 24.

43   Thomas Becon, 'Jewel of Joy', in *The Seconde Parte of the Bokes which Thomas Beacon hath made* (London, 1560), ii, pt ii, fo. xiii.

44 Quoted from *The Catechism of Thomas Becon* in Horton Davies, *Worship and Theology*, 1, i, p. 382, n. 15.

45 2 and 3 Edward VI, c.1.

46 Frere and Kennedy, *Visitation Articles*, ii, p. 145 for Canterbury and pp. 148f for Winchester.

47 E.F. Carpenter in W.R. Matthews and W.M. Atkins (eds), *A History of St Paul's Cathedral* (London, 1957), p. 122.

48 Act for the Dissolution of the Chantries, 1 Edward VI, c. 14. A large part of the endowments of the 2374 chantries dissolved 'eventually went to the harpies who surrounded the young king', J.R. Tanner, *Tudor Constitutional Documents* (Cambridge, 1948), p. 103. The exceptions permitted to continue (clause xv) are found at pp. 106f.

49 Ottery St Mary and Tattersall had in fact been been suppressed in 1545. For a useful list, see le Huray, *Music and the Reformation*, pp. 12f.

50 The work was originally published in 1557 as *A Hundreth Good Pointes of Husbandrie*, but the verses I quote are drawn from the extended edition of 1573, as found in W. Payne and Sidney J. Herrtage (eds), *Thomas Tusser's Five Hundred Pointes of Good Husbandrie* (London, 1878), pp. 205f.

51 At Newark, Robert Kyrkebe had been appointed Master of Song at the foundation of the choral establishment in 1531 and remained in post throughout all the upheavals until his death in 1573. Cornelius Brown, *A History of Newark-on-Trent*, 2 vols (Newark, 1904 and 1907), ii, pp. 190 and 205f.

52 le Huray, *Music and the Reformation*, p. 17.

53 R. S. Stanier, *Magdalen School* (Oxford, 2nd ed., 1958), pp. 86–88; and Joan Simon, *Education and Society in Tudor England* (Cambridge, 1966), p. 258.

54 Cranmer seems to have been reporting to a committee of Convocation, but all its records were burned in the Great Fire of London, 1666.

55 D. Baldwin, *The Chapel Royal, Ancient and Modern* (London, 1990), pp. 147f.

56 For this, and the second Prayer Book of 1552, see the Everyman edition, anonymously edited: *The First and Second Prayer Books of Edward VI* (London, 1910).

57 Act against Superstitious Books and Images, 3 and 4 Edward VI, c. 10. My italics.

58 These are found in the Wanley part-books, see note 60 below.

59 Frere and Kennedy, *Visitation Articles*, ii, p. 168. The final phrase, of course, paraphrases Cranmer.

60 Bodleian Library, Wanley MS, Mus. Sch. e. 420–22. There is a very full discussion of the Wanley books in le Huray, *Music and the Reformation*, pp. 172–76, with a complete list of contents (table 15). There were originally four sets, two alto, a tenor and a bass; but the tenor has long been missing, though some reconstruction is possible and some of the music is known from other sources.

61 *The First and Second Prayer Books of Edward VI*, p. 390.

62 See, for instance, le Huray, *Music and the Reformation*, p. 29.

63 1 Mary, st 2, c. 2.

64 Gyffard part-books: British Library, Add. MSS 17802–5. They contain twelve mass cycles, numerous pieces for mass propers, five magnificats and forty-six motets, mostly dated to the mid-1530s. See NGD, 17, Sources, MS ix, 19.

65 See D. Wulston, *Tudor Music*, p. 294. There is an extended discussion of these Chapel Royal developments in Baldwin, *The Chapel Royal*, pp. 146–52.

66 Frere and Kennedy, *Visitation Articles*, ii, p. 224.

67 The college's finances were in a parlous state.

68 Dora Robertson, *Sarum Close* (London, 1938), p. 127.

69 Payne, *The Provision and Practice of Sacred Music*, pp. 28 and 214.

70 Ibid., pp. 32, 214 and 268.

71 Roger Bowers, 'The Liturgy of the Cathedral and its Music, *c.* 1075–1642', in P. Collinson, N. Ramsay and M. Sparks (eds), *A History of Canterbury Cathedral* (Oxford, 1995), p. 431.

72 Payne, *The Provision and Practice of Sacred Music*, p. 40. See also pp. 32–42 for the Marian revival generally.

73 Wulstan, *Tudor Music*, p. 297.

74 The judgement is that of Paul Doe, *Tallis* (Oxford, 2nd edn, 1976), pp. 24f.

75 Patrick Collinson, 'The Protestant Cathedral', in Collinson, Ramsay and Sparks (eds), *A History of Canterbury Cathedral*, pp. 164f.

Notes to Chapter 7: From Elizabeth I to Cromwell

1 P. le Huray, *Music and the Reformation in England* (London, 1967), p. 29.

2 See, for example, Norman Sykes, in his introduction to the reprint of W.H. Frere and C.E. Douglas, *Puritan Manifestoes* (London, 1954), p. vi.

3 The few points of difference were significant, but do not have direct bearing on this history.

4 All cathedrals were collegiate, along with other choral foundations.

5 W.H. Frere and W. McC. Kennedy (eds), *Visitation Articles and Injunctions of the Period of the Reformation* (London, 1910), iii, pp. 22f. The word 'hymns' clearly embraced anthems, motets etc. It will be noted that the queen's original intention was to have these sung at the beginning and end of services. It was not until the 1662 Prayer Book, following the Restoration, that the preferred location for the anthem was stipulated as after the third collect 'in Quires and Places where they sing'.

6 The basis of the table is Peter le Huray's Tables 3, 4 and 5 in *Music and the Reformation* at pp. 14–17. I have excluded St John's College, Oxford, whose choral establishment with six choristers ran only from 1555 to 1577; also Ripon, a collegiate church where there was no post-Reformation choral foundation before 1604; and Ludlow parish church where a choral establishment was maintained only intermittently.

7 Chichester Act Books, 1128. For this practice 'according to the old laudable custom', see Thurstan Dart, 'Music and Musicians at Chichester Cathedral, 1545–1642', *Music and Letters*, 42 (1961), pp. 221ff.

8 There is evidence, however, that at Magdalen College choristerships between 1564 and 1591 were being awarded to youths aged from fifteen to twenty on admission, in other words the choristerships were being used to fund additional undergraduates. This policy was formally rescinded in 1592 under a new president. See R.S. Stanier, *Magdalen School* (Oxford, 2nd ed., 1958), p. 94. A similar situation was occurring at Trinity, Cambridge, see n. 9, below.

9   For the complexities and uncertainties of the Trinity College choral foundation at this period, in particular the occurrence of 'dry' choristers who were not in fact boy trebles, see Ian Payne, *The Provision and Practice of Sacred Music at Cambridge Colleges and Selected Cathedrals, c. 1547–c. 1646* (New York, and London, 1993), pp. 217–221. There is an implication from Laud's visitation report that at latest by the 1620s there was choral music at Trinity only on Sundays and Feast Days: ibid. p. 121.

10 BL, Royal MS 18.B.xix.

11 'An admirable refuge from clarity of thought', Christopher Hill, *Society and Puritanism in Pre-Revolutionary England* (London, 1964), p. 13. A handy aid to clarification is the Historical Association pamphlet G106: Patrick Collinson, *English Puritanism* (London, 1983).

12 A. Peel (ed.), *The Seconde Parte of a Register* (Cambridge, 1915), i, pp. 284f.

13 Sykes in Frere and Douglas (eds), *Puritan Manifestoes*, clause 17, p. 32.

14 Amos v, 23 – the whole passage an example of superb Hebrew poetry.

15 See le Huray, *Music and the Reformation*, p. 37, and, for the abolition of organs or organists, Payne, *Provision and Practice of Sacred Music*, pp. 54ff.

16 As examples from just one not uncharacteristic foundation: at Chester Edward Hawford, prebendary from 1561–82, also held rectories in Leicestershire, Northamptonshire and Suffolk and was master of Christ's College, Cambridge. A colleague complained that he had been seen in Chester 'not once in ten years'. Meanwhile, it was reported at the 1578 Visitation, the dean, Dr Longworth, had visited Chester only twice in five years. R.V.H. Burne, *Chester Cathedral* (London, 1958), pp. 37 and 56. Less directly relevant, but symptomatic of the marginalization of cathedrals in Elizabethan church life, is the circumstance that archbishops Grindal and Bancroft never set foot inside their cathedral at Canterbury.

17 Gerald Aylmer and John Tiller (eds), *Hereford Cathedral: a History* (London, 2000), p. 94.

18 R.J. Henderson, *A History of King's College Choir School Cambridge* (Cambridge, 1981), p. 11.

19 Quoted, but with no source given, by W.L. Woodfill, *Musicians in English Society from Elizabeth to Charles I* (Princeton, New Jersey, 1953), p. 136.

20 Dora Robertson, *Sarum Close* (London, 1938), p. 127.

21 BL, Royal MS 18Bxix, folio 7 verso, quoted in Woodfill, *Musicians in English Society*, p. 140, note 8.

22 R. Holtby, *The Minster School, York* (York, 1994), p. 19.

23 A.P. Norton, 'Tudor Reforms in the Royal Household', R.W. Seton Watson (ed.), *Tudor Studies* (London, 1924), pp. 250f.

24 T.N. Cooper, 'Children, the Liturgy, and the Reformation: the Evidence of the Lichfield Cathedral Choristers', D. Wood (ed.), *The Church and Childhood* (Oxford, 1994), p. 272.

25 For Lincoln: R. Bowers, 'Lincoln Cathedral: Music and Worship to 1640', D. Owen (ed.), *A History of Lincoln Minster* (Cambridge, 1994), p. 64; for Carlisle: S.E. Lehmberg, *Cathedrals under Siege* (Exeter, 1996), p. 162; for Salisbury: P. Smith, *900 Years of Song* (Salisbury, c. 1992), p. 11.

26 For Canterbury: R. Bowers in P. Collinson, N. Ramsay and M. Sparks (eds.), *A History of Canterbury Cathedral* (Oxford, 1995), p. 438; for Exeter, Lehmberg, *Cathedrals under Siege*,

p. 162; for King's, Cambridge: Henderson, *A History of King's College Choir School*, p. 9; for Windsor: a facsimile of the Chapter Act of 1633 appears as Plate 3 in N. Wridgway, *The Choristers of St George's Chapel* (Windsor, 1980), facing p. 38.

27 Jonathan Edmunds, *New College Brats* (Oxford, 1996), pp. 18 and 79.

28 For the situation at Chichester both before and during the choirmastership of Thomas Weelkes, see David Brown, *Thomas Weelkes* (London, 1969), pp. 26–46.

29 Thurston Dart, 'Music and Musicians at Chichester Cathedral, 1545–1642', p. 222.

30 The organ had been restored to duty soon after the puritan Horne ceased to be bishop in 1680.

31 Despite which, he was soon after reinstated as organist and singing man *but not informator choristarum*, and continued to come into service drunk and disorderly from the alehouse until a few months before his death in 1623.

32 le Huray, *Music and the Reformation*, pp. 41ff. gives the whole sorry story.

33 For the Salisbury saga: Dora Robertson, *Sarum Close*, pp. 136–140 on Smythe; chapter 9 *passim* on John Farrant.

34 Woodfill, *Musicians in English Society*, p. 143.

35 A brilliant narrative of this extraordinary circumstance is given in Robertson, *Sarum Close*, pp. 175–85.

36 For Durham see Brian Crosby, *Come on, Choristers!* (Durham, 1999), pp. 17–26.

37 E.A. Horsman (ed.), *Dobsons Drie Bobbes* (Durham, 1953).

38 Wridgway, *Choristers of St George's Chapel*, p. 32.

39 For a full discussion of these possibilities see John Harvey, *William Byrd, Gentleman of the Chapel Royal* (Aldershot, 1997), pp. 18–22 and Appendix E, pp. 397–400.

40 Details of these composers are most readily found in NGD.

41 John Harley, *Orlando Gibbons* (Aldershot, 1999), p. 27.

42 I have made some abbreviations to Hunnis's petition and used the spelling and punctuation given in David Baldwin, *The Chapel Royal Ancient and Modern* (London, 1990), pp. 156ff.

43 The story can be put together from Baldwin, ibid., pp. 119f. and le Huray, *Music and the Reformation*, pp. 63–65.

44 Charles Butler, *The Principles of Musik* (London, 1641), p. 41, quoted in Harley, *Orlando Gibbons*, p. 171.

45 K.R. Long, *Music of the English Church* (London, 1972), p. 66 holds that '… it is impossible to give a straight-forward answer to such an obvious question as "Who wrote the first verse anthem?" It could have been Mundy, Farrant or Byrd – or perhaps some other composer whose pioneering effort was subsequently lost.'

46 The latter today never sung to its unusable original words but widely found in cathedral repertoires as *O Thou, the Central Orb*, words adapted by the Rev. H.R. Bramley for Ouseley's edition of 1873 from an overblown Victorian sonnet.

47 Long, *Music of the English Church*, p. 129 (with detailed analysis in the following two pages).

48 The Gibbons work may have been written for a celebratory royal occasion or as an Oxford doctorate exercise rather than for liturgical use. See Harley, *Orlando Gibbons*, pp. 168f.

49 '[Notwithstanding] the rosy accounts of emotional visitors, the vast mass of evidence makes it obvious that in most provincial cathedrals and choral foundations the general

standard of singing must have been deplorably low and the organ would have been essential to keep body and soul together.' (Long, *Music of the English Church*, p. 56.)

50 For St Paul's: R. Gair, *The Children of Paul's* (Cambridge, 1982), pp. 25ff., 31 and 35.

51 Robertson, *Sarum Close*, pp. 185–88.

52 The question is raised by Kenneth Long, ibid., pp. 154f.

53 All that follows can be found in the anonymous *Breife Descriptions* of Hammond's 'northern' tour of 1634 and 'western' tour of 1635: Camden Miscellany, xvi, London. 1936.

54 Rates of pay given in le Huray, *Music and the Reformation*, p. 41.

55 Hammond's use of the word 'Quiristers' to describe cathedral singers is annoyingly imprecise. In general it seems to refer to the boys, as specifically at Canterbury, York and Winchester; but at Hereford he undoubtedly uses the word to refer to the whole choir.

56 He says there were 'forty singing boys'. The possible explanation is that he was including a party of scholars from the King's School who will certainly have attended the office in surplices.

57 It would be interesting to know when at Winchester 'quirister' came exclusively to refer to college singing boys.

58 L.S. Colchester, D. Tudway Quilter and A. Quilter (eds), *A History of Wells Cathedral School* (Wells, 1985), p. 22.

59 Aylmer and Tiller, *Hereford Cathedral*, p. 399.

60 Payne, *Provision and Practice of Sacred Music*, p. 142.

61 Ian Woodfield, *The Early History of the Viol* (Cambridge, 1984), p. 216.

62 Butler, *The Principles of Musik*, p. 103, quoted in Harley, *Orlando Gibbons*, p. 204.

63 For instruments in church, see Andrew Parratt, '"Grett and solompne singing": Instruments and English Church Music', *Early Music* 6/2 (1978), pp. 182–87.

64 Ibid., p. 183.

65 C.E. Woodruff and W. Danks, *Memorials of Canterbury Cathedral* (London, 1912), p. 452.

66 Woodfield, *Early History of the Viol*, p. 213.

67 Izaak Walton (ed. S.B. Carter), 'Life of George Herbert', *Walton's Lives* (Everyman, London, 1951), p. 303.

68 Wridgway, *Choristers of St George's Chapel*, pp. 22 and 40.

69 Robertson, *Sarum Close*, p. 143.

70 E. Brennecke Jr., 'A Day at Christ Church, 1573', *Music and Letters*, 19 (1938), pp. 22–35.

71 Richard Hooker (ed. R. Bayne), *On the Laws of Ecclesiastical Polity* (London, 1902), bk. v, pp. 168ff.

72 Sources for this paragraph are: Collinson (ed.), *Canterbury Cathedral*, p. 195; Wridgway, *Choristers of St George's Chapel*, p. 42; J. Crook, *A History of the Pilgrims' School, Winchester* (Chichester, 1981), p. 9; Phillip Barratt in Mary Hobbs (ed.), *Chichester Cathedral: an Historical Survey* (Chichester, 1994), p. 252; N. Boston, *The Musical History of Norwich Cathedral* (Norwich, 1963), p. 59; Henderson, *King's College Choir School*, p. 13; and Payne, *Provision and Practice of Sacred Music*, pp. 166 and 168 for Cambridge, Exeter and Peterborough.

73 Payne, *Provision and Practice of Sacred Music*, p. 164.

74 Jocelyn Perkins, *Westminster Abbey: Its Worship and Ornaments* (London, 1952), p. 111.

75   The *coup de grâce* was the parliamentary order of January 1645 banning use of the *Book of Common Prayer*; but most of the chapters and choirs had been driven out of their cathedrals well before then.

Notes to Chapter 8: *Chorister Actors*

1   Chapter 5, pp. 63–6.
2   On Elizabethan drama there is a vast literature. Of general surveys the finest remains the monumental E.K. Chambers, *The Elizabethan Stage*, 4 vols (London, 1923), still essential reading. J.D. Cox and D.S. Kastan (eds), *A New History of Early English Drama* (New York, NY, 1997) is not quite what its title implies. In any case, references to children or choristers in its text are minimal, and in its index non-existent. For the children's companies the best and most comprehensive work remains H.N. Hillebrand, 'The Child Actors', inconveniently buried in *University of Illinois Studies in Language and Literature*, xi, 1 (Urbana, Illinois, Feb. 1926). Russell and Russell of New York published a reprint in 1964. David Baldwin's chapter on the Chapel Royal Theatre in *The Chapel Royal, Ancient and Modern* (London, 1990), pp. 112–126, seems to lack acquaintance with Hillebrand's work, but Baldwin's lists of personnel are invaluable. For the St Paul's choristers as actors, see Reavley Gair, *The Children of Paul's* (Cambridge, 1982). Gair's painstaking location of the theatre adjacent to the cathedral is challenged by H. Berry in 'Where Was the Playhouse in Which the Boy Choristers of St Paul's Cathedral Performed Plays?', *Medieval and Renaissance Drama in England* (Cranbury, New Jersey, and London, xiii, 2001), pp. 101ff. (See note 26, below.) I have been unable to consult Linda P. Austern, *Music in English Children's Drama in the Later Renaissance* (Philadelphia, Pennsylvania, 1992). For texts of the plays performed by the boys, the Manchester University Press is currently engaged in a series of scholarly publications under the general title *The Revels Plays* that already includes much from the St Paul's and Chapel Royal repertoires.
3   For this and what follows, see Hillebrand, *Child Actors*, pp. 58ff. and p. 324.
4   R. Brown (ed.) *Calendar of State Papers (Venetian)*, iv, London (1869–)pp. 57f.
5   For court entertainments during Edward VI's reign see S. Anglo, *Spectacle, Pageantry and Early Tudor Policy* (Oxford, 2nd ed. 1997), chapter 8.
6   See J.E. Jackson, 'Wulfhall and the Seymours', *Wiltshire Archeological and Natural History Magazine*, 15 (1875), p. 174, where a charge of five shillings is recorded 'to the queristers of Poules for playing before my Lord' at New Yeartide 1540. At the same festivities Lord Derby's (adult) Players received 6s 4d.
7   There was also the palace of Sheen at Richmond (where Henry VII and Elizabeth I died), demolished during the Commonwealth, but I have found no evidence of chorister plays being performed there.
8   I have taken the passage from Peter le Huray, *Music and the Reformation in England, 1549–1660* (London, 1967), p. 220. The author is unknown and the original is lost; but the broadside from which it is an extract, '*The Children of the Chapel Stripped and Whipt*', formerly in the Bodleian Library, appeared in T. Warton (ed. W.C. Hazlitt), *The History of English Poetry*, iv (London, 1871), p. 217.

9   Plautus's *Aulularia*, Halliwell's *Dido* and Nicholas Udall's *Ezechias*.

10   See Paul Whitefield White, 'Drama in the Church', *Medieval and Renaissance Drama in England*, vi, 1993 (New York, NY), pp. 15–35.

11   P. Cunningham, *Extracts from the Accounts of the Revels at Court, in the reigns of Queen Elizabeth and King James I, from the original office books of the Masters and Yeomen* (London, 1842).

12   Baldwin, *The Chapel Royal*, p. 119.

13   Shapiro, *Children of the Revels*, lists, in appendix B, all these groups, along with boys from Hitchen (sic) Grammar School. Shapiro's reference (p. 267) to the Westminster choristers is uncertain and ambiguous.

14   N. Wridgway, *The Choristers of St George's Chapel* (Windsor, 1980), p. 28.

15   A contemporary engraving of the wharf with the cathedral (south view) behind can be seen in Baldwin, *The Chapel Royal*, p. 118.

16   Quoted in Gair, *The Children of Paul's*, p. 75.

17   Hillebrand, *Child Actors*, p. 107.

18   R. Gair, *The Children of Paul's*, p. 76.

19   The phrase 'fundamentally of choristers' is discussed below.

20   Hatfield Palace (not Hatfield House, as stated by Gair), was a former property of the bishops of Ely, sequestrated by the Crown at the Dissolution. The performance must have taken place in the great hall, still standing, and illustrated at plate 38 in N. Pevsner (rev. Bridget Cherry), *The Buildings of England: Hertfordshire* (Harmondsworth, 2nd ed., 1977).

21   For the seeming gap between January 1582 and December 1583 see Gair, *The Children of Paul's*, p. 97.

22   A.L. Rowse, *The England of Elizabeth* (London, 1950), p. 531.

23   As in Shakespeare, *A Midsummer Night's Dream*, V, i.

24   This was, of course, the medieval gothic cathedral, to be destroyed by fire in 1666.

25   Two examples may illustrate the range of occupation: a major trunkmaker's business was there; and an 'excavation' into a buttress had been made by a baker to house his oven: J.P. Malcolm, *Londinium Redevivum* (London, 1803), iii, p. 73.

26   Reavley Gair, in *The Children of Paul's*, made a powerful case for locating a rehearsal theatre, developed first by Westcott, as lying within the cloisters, in the protective undercroft of the chapter house. At p. 59, Gair offers a detailed putative plan of how the theatre might have been. However, Berry, 'Where Was the Playhouse …?', pp. 101ff., challenges Gair's siting. Chiefly on the basis of a document seen and described by J. P. Malcolm in 1803, but since lost, Berry locates the playhouse as being part of the almonry, directly against the south wall of the cathedral, eastward of St Gregory's church, directly west of the cloisters and adjacent to the cathedral's lesser south door. (Plan at p. 110.) What cannot be disputed is that people went to the theatre 'at Paul's church'.

27   Gair, in his edition of Marston's *Antonio and Mellida*, p. 41 (see n. 45, below), quotes Richard Flecknoe writing in his *Short Discourse on the English Stage*, of 1664, that 'on weekdays after vespers … the Children of … St Paul's acted plays'.

28   Not to be confused with William Lilye (or Lily), first headmaster of Colet's refounded St Paul's School.

29   For Westcott's will and the above discussion see Gair, *The Children of Paul's*, pp. 95f. For the Chapel Royal non-chorister actors, see the 'Clifton suit' below, pp. 122f.

30   John Lyly, *Endymion* (ed. David Bevington) (Manchester, 1996), Act I, sc. iii, from lines 20–35.

31   John Lyly, *Galatea* (ed. G.K. Hunter) (Manchester, 2000), Act II, sc. *i*, passim.

32   John Lyly, *Midas* (ed. D. Bevington) (Manchester, 2000). (Bevington's edition of *Midas* is published in the same volume as Hunter's edition of *Galatea*.)

33   The *Marprelate Tracts* of 1588 and 1589 were edited and published by William Pierce (London, 1911), preceded by his own *Historical Introduction* (London, 1908). The flavour of the tracts can be sampled in J.R. Tanner, *Tudor Constitutional Documents, 1486–1603* (Cambridge, 2nd ed., 1930), pp. 194ff.

34   Gair, *The Children of Paul's*, pp. 109ff.

35   For Farrant see NGD, 8, pp. 578–9.

36   Hillebrand, *Child Actors*, p. 90, gives 1576 as the date for Farrant's return to Whitehall. But NGD (Peter le Huray and John Morehen), Baldwin's list of Masters of the Children, and Wridgway, *The Choristers of St George's Chapel*, quoting E.F. Rimbault, *The Old Cheque Book of the Chapel Royal* (reprint New York, 1966), p. 2, are specific that the date is November 1569. There is then a further problem. Richard Farrant described himself as 'Master of the Children of the Chapel Royal'. le Huray and Morehen in NGD (and other sources) accept this. But William Hunnis had been appointed Master in 1566 and there is no evidence of his resigning the post before his death in 1597. Michael Smith, in his article on William Hunnis in NGD, accepts that Hunnis was continuously Master from 1566 to 1597. Baldwin offers the quite probable solution that Farrant was in fact under-master at Whitehall and [titular but largely absentee] master at Windsor.

37   Hillebrand, ibid., p. 90.

38   Bevington (ed.), *Midas*, Introduction, p. 121. The text can be found in D. J. White, *Richard Edwards' Damon and Pithias* (New York, 1980).

39   The City authorities were willingly persuaded that plays and the clientele who attended them were unwholesome. The performances at Blackfriars were preserved only by a request from the Privy Council, no doubt speaking for the Queen herself, urging the lord mayor that the boys' performances were important in preparing them for their performances before Her Majesty at court. Hillebrand, ibid., p. 102.

40   Wridgway, *Choristers of St George's Chapel*, p. 31. Wridgway assumes, no doubt correctly, that the Chapel Royal boys would have been resident at Windsor for the Christmas period.

41   There must be a possibility that the alarms associated with the Throckmorton plot put paid to post-Christmas court performances that year. The plot was uncovered in November 1583 and Francis Throckmorton executed in January 1584. That the boys had a play in preparation is evident from their January performances at Blackfriars.

42   A. L. Rowse, *The England of Elizabeth*, p. 257.

43   Gair, *The Children of Paul's*, pp. 98f. and 104; and Elbert N.S. Thompson, 'The Controversy between the Puritans and the Stage', *Yale Studies*, 20, pp. 21f.

44   For this paragraph, see Gair, ibid., pp. 143 and 151ff.

45   John Marston (ed. Reavley Gair), *Antonio and Mellida* (Manchester, 1991), Prologue.

46   Ibid., II, i, 2.

47   For these and the whole development of views on Marston's *oeuvre*, see T.F. Wharton, *The Critical Fall and Rise of John Marston* (Columbia, South Carolina, 1994), especially pp. 62ff.

48   The passionately puritan father of the metaphysical poet, Richard Crashaw, who, ironically, became a Catholic.

49   Gair, *The Children of Paul's*, pp. 162ff. Patrick Collinson, in his 1985 Stenton Lecture, *From Iconoclasm to Iconophobia* (Reading, 1986), pp. 11–14, traces in detail the puritan attack on stage plays, particularly those that dealt in subjects from Scripture, starting with the pamphlet war of 1577 and culminating in the 1605 statute prohibiting stage blasphemy.

50   My account of 'the Clifton suit' is heavily indebted to David Baldwin's lively narrative in *The Chapel Royal*, pp. 120f.

51   The surviving record of the case does not conclude with any judgement regarding the boy.

52   See R. F. Brinkley, *Nathan Field, the Actor-Playwright* (Yale, New Hampshire, and Oxford, 1928). Nathan Field was the youngest child of the Rev. John Field, a leading puritan who had a hand in drafting the text of the Marprelate pamphlet. Had the father lived to find his son impressed for the theatre, the Clifton Suit would have paled into insignificance beside the fury and invective of which John Field was capable. It is clear that Giles, Evans and company were impressing very gifted boys from educated and even influential families.

53   Saloman Pavey had acted at Blackfriars in Jonson's play, *Cynthia's Revels*.

54   Hillebrand, *Child Actors*, pp 197f. Although Gyles lived until 1633, Baldwin's date of August 1626 for a revised commission must either be an error or reference to a confirming document. However, notwithstanding the apparent ban in the commission, there is evidence that the Chapel Royal boys continued to provide entertainments at court in the course of the seventeenth century. In 1612 and 1613 three plays were given there by the Chapel Royal boys (John Harley, *Orlando Gibbons* (Aldershot, 1999), p. 39, quoting TNA, E351/544, m.14r).

55   A lecture was given by Katharine Eggar to the Royal Musical Association in 1961 in which she paints Farrant and Oxford as devoted heroes. The lecture, 'The Blackfriars Plays and their Music: 1576–1610', Proceedings of the Royal Musical Association, lxxxvii 1961, which, incidentally, says *nothing* about the music of its title, is to a very large degree inaccurate and misleading.

56   Shakespeare, *Hamlet*, II, ii, 344–46 and 351.

Notes to Chapter 9: Restoration

1   For music during the Commonwealth, see Percy Scholes, *The Puritans and Music* (Oxford, 1934).

2   Ibid, p. 142, quoting Anthony à Wood.

3   Dora Robertson, *Sarum Close* (London, 1938), pp. 188 and 212.

4   Nicholas Thistlethwaite, 'Music and worship, 1660–1980', in Dorothy Owen (ed.), *A History of Lincoln Minster* (Cambridge, 1994), pp. 77f.

5   Suzanne Eward, *No Fine but a Glass of Wine* (Wilton, 1985), pp. 127f. and 337f.

6   R.J. Henderson, *A History of King's College Choir School, Cambridge* (Cambridge, 1981), p. 14.

7   Eward, *No Fine*, pp. 122 and 135.

8   Quoted in G. Aylmer and R. Cant (eds), *A History of York Minster* (Oxford, 1977), p. 409.

9   Brian Crosby, *Come on, Choristers!* (Durham, 1999), pp. 27f.

10 Wridgway, *Choristers of St George's Chapel*, pp. 46–48.

11 For Henry Cooke see NGD, vi, pp. 385–87 with bibliography; also the Lord Chamberlain's records edited by L.C. de Lafontaine, *The King's Musick* (London, 1909; reprint New York, 1973), pp. 113–246.

12 Cooke's patent of appointment is dated 21 January 1661 NS, but his £40 annual fee as Master of the Children was payable from Michaelmas 1660. Andrew Ashbee, *Lists of Payments to the King's Musick in the Reign of Charles II* (Snodland, 1981), i, p. 109.

13 The age-range, with boys of nine, eleven and thirteen, suggests that Captain Cooke was aware of the dangers of recruiting boys who might all leave coincidentally. As a consequence, even his brilliant boys had through the earliest months to be supported by cornets and men singing *falsetto*. The first voice-change seems to have been in 1663; by then Cooke had already appointed, as a precaution, a thirteenth chorister (ibid. pp. 162, 154 and 157).

14 The careers of these musicians can be followed under their named articles in NGD; their achievements as composers are analysed in Kenneth R. Long, *The Music of the English Church* (London, 1972): Humfrey at pp. 251ff.; Wise at pp. 255ff.; Tudway at pp. 255f.; Turner at pp. 256f.; and Blow at pp. 258–68. The compositions of Cooke himself, much sung in the Chapel Royal in his time, are discussed at pp. 246f.

15 Ibid, p. 170.

16 Samuel Pepys, *Diary*: 16 August 1660; 31 May, 7, 17, 27 Aug., 2, 4, 9 Sept., 26 Oct., 9 Nov. 1664; 27 March, 1669.

17 Andrew Ashbee and John Harley, *The Cheque Books of the Chapel Royal* (Aldershot, 2000), i, pp. 132f. The Cheque Book reference is to a warrant dated 20 September 1665 instructing the Cofferer to make appropriate payments, as required by the earlier letters patent.

18 N. Wridgway, *Choristers of St George's Chapel* (Windsor, 1980), p. 45.

19 David Baldwin, *The Chapel Royal* (London, 1990), p. 192. John Harvey, on the other hand, takes for granted that the master of the children 'was responsible for boarding them': John Harvey, *William Byrd, Gentleman of the Chapel Royal* (Aldershot, 1997), p. 20.

20 In 1674 (Lafontaine, *King's Musick*, p. 280) the four private musick boys are named as Jack, Waters, Coningsby and Smith. John Waters appears regularly from February 1677 NS as a child 'gone off', maintained by John Blow (pp. 215 etc.) and from December 1679 payments for Coningsby 'gone off' appear (pp. 346 etc.).

21 Ibid., pp. 117, 132f, 137, 149, 194 etc.

22 Greatorex's survey is TNA Works 5/15. An accessible version (described as Fisher's) is to be found on the website 'www.londonancester.com/maps/whitehall-palace.htm', where Captain Cooke's House is marked as '35', a u-shaped building on three sides of the tennis court. In considering the position of Cooke's accommodation and the status of the several versions of Greatorex's plan, attributed variously to Vertue, Fisher and others, I have received generous and enlightening help from David Baldwin; but assumptions as to the

location of the choristers' accommodation are mine.

23 Robert King, *Henry Purcell* (London, 1994), p. 67, cites this critical reference from Andrew Ashbee, *Records of English Court Music* (Aldershot, 5 vols, 1986-91), i, p. 51. I am assuming that, then as now, 'tied' accommodation passed from office holder to office holder and that Humfrey's house was the same as that formerly occupied by Captain Cooke. 'A door out of the dwelling house into the bowling green' poses problems, since the only house shown on any contemporary plan as adjacent to the bowling green is that of Lady Villiers. If, however, 'bowling green' is an error for 'tennis court', then the instruction makes great sense, and would decisively confirm the choristers' house as 35 on the 'Fisher' plan.

24 Lafontaine, *King's Musick*, p. 214 (Hampton Court repairs) and pp 245f (Cooke's will and death). See also NGD, 6, p. 385.

25 How these dual responsibilities were managed has not been researched. Often, it has been suggested, 'an uneasy truce was maintained': Ashbee and Harley, *Cheque Books*, i, p. xvi.

26 Cooke did accept office, first as deputy then as marshall, of the musicians of the Corporation of Music (NGD, p. 386).

27 Ashbee and Harley, *Cheque Books*, i, p. 103.

28 Michael Wise's voice had broken in September 1663 (ibid. p. 167); probably by 1665 he was a lay clerk at Windsor and Eton; in 1668, in his very early twenties, he was appointed organist and master of the choristers at Salisbury (*NGD*). For his time at Salisbury, see below, pp. 142f.

29 Lafontaine, *King's Musick*, p. 177.

30 'Cooke, Henry', NGD, pp. 385f.

31 For a grovelling request for payment of arrears from a court musician in dire trouble, May 5th, 1677, see Lafontaine, *King's Musick*, p. 317.

32 Ibid., pp. 374 and 378.

33 20 October 1673, ibid, p. 262.

34 The phrase first appears in March 1669 NS in connection with 'Thomas Tedway' (presumably Tudway) and periodically thereafter (ibid., p. 213).

35 Ashbee, *Lists of Payments*, ii, p. 62.

36 Lafontaine, *King's Musick*, p. 263, for the ending of Purcell's choristership and p. 255 for his court appointment.

37 For Walter Porter see Long, *Music of the English Church*, pp. 238ff.

38 Pepys, *Diary*, 12 August 1660.

39 NGD, Cooke, Henry, p. 386. See also, for Cooke's compositions, Christopher Dearnley, *English Church Music 1650–1750* (London, 1970), pp. 185–90.

40 The list is given in Lafontaine, *King's Musick*, pp. 305ff.

41 Ian Spink, *Restoration Cathedral Music, 1660–1714* (Oxford, 1995), p. 15. See pp. 12–19 for the early development of the Anglican chant.

42 John Wilson (ed.), *Roger North on Music* (London, 1959), p. 269.

43 John Evelyn, *Diary*, 21 December 1662.

44 For the music of James II's coronation see Long, *Music of the English Church*, pp. 262f.

45 Dearnley, *English Church Music*, p. 56, drawing on Rimbault's edition of *The Old Cheque-Book of the Chapel Royal*.

46 Lafontaine, *King's Musick*, p. 407.

47 There was a model for them in the Scottish Prayer Book of 1637.

48 For a full discussion of the drafting of the 1662 Book of Common Prayer see Horton Davies, *Worship and Theology in England* (Grand Rapids, Michigan, and Cambridge, combined edition, 1996), ii, pp. 363–86. The phrase quoted is drawn from p. 386.

49 Thomas Mace, *Musick's Monument* (1676; facsimile, Paris, 1958), pp. 21ff. Thomas Tudway, Introduction to *A Collection of the most celebrated Services and Anthems* (British Library, Harley MSS 7337–42), accessible in Christopher Hogwood, 'Thomas Tudway's History of Music', in C. Hogwood and R. Luckett (eds), *Music in Eighteenth Century England* (Cambridge, 1983), pp. 19–47.

50 Tudway, quoted in Hogwood, ibid., p. 43.

51 From Cartwright's diary for 19 January 1687, quoted in R.V.H. Burne, *Chester Cathedral* (London, 1958), p. 154.

52 Quoted from R. Granville, *Life of Dean Granville*, in Crosby, *Come on, Choristers!*, p. 30.

53 Spink, *Restoration Cathedral Music*, p. 351.

54 Dorothy Own (ed.), *Lincoln Minster*, pp. 80–82 and 195.

55 For Chichester, P. Barrett in Mary Hobbs (ed.), *Chichester Cathedral: an Historical Survey* (Chichester, 1974), pp. 252f.; for Southwell: W.A. James, *An Account of the Southwell Grammar and Song Schools* (Southwell, 1927), p. 62; for Canterbury: C.E. Woodruff and W. Danks, *Memorials of Canterbury Cathedral* (London, 1912), pp. 458f.

56 Leslie Paul, *Music at Bangor Cathedral Church* (Bangor, 1971), pp. 6f.

57 Edward Miller, *Portrait of a College* (Cambridge, 1961), p. 43.

58 Henderson, *King's College Choir School*, pp. 14–16, with illustration.

59 Aldrich's four principles are given in detail, from William Hayes' recollections of 1753, in Dearnley, *English Church Music*, pp. 70f.

60 This practice was becoming widespread and during the eighteenth century (see the following chapter) became the almost universal procedure.

61 The whole Salisbury saga, along with other distinctly unflattering accounts of vicar choral William Powell and organist Michael Wise, can be found in Robertson, *Sarum Close*, pp. 201–09.

Notes to Chapter 10: Georgian Nadir

1 Kenneth Long, *Music of the English Church* (London, 1972), pp. 321f.

2 N. Ollerenshaw, *A History of the Prebendal School* (Chichester, 1984).

3 Neville Wridgway, *The Choristers of St George's Chapel* (Windsor, 1980), p. 50.

4 H. Diack Johnstone and Roger Fiske (eds), *The Eighteenth Century* (Blackwell History of Music, iv, Oxford, 1990).

5 The recollections of Richard Stevens, St Paul's chorister and organ apprentice from 1763 to 1773, are to be found in Mark Argent (ed.), *Recollections of R.J.S. Stevens* (London and Basingstoke, 1992); those of John Harding, Salisbury chorister from 1826 to 1833, feature in Dora Robertson, *Sarum Close* (London, 1938), pp. 269–83.

6 John Byng (ed. C Bruyn Andrews), *The Torrington Diaries* (London, 1938; reprint, New York, and London, 1970), iv vols.

7　The survey of the condition of the country's choristers was undertaken by Maria Hackett, beginning in the second decade of the nineteenth century and continuing almost until her death in 1874. She published her findings as reports seriatim in the *Gentleman's Magazine* between January 1817 and February 1819. In 1827 she gathered these reports, largely unaltered but with some updating, into a single work, her *Brief Account* ..., which she published privately and circulated to those concerned. Revisions and further updatings were added over a long period. For fuller details see p. 317, note 1.

8　See Horton Davies, *Worship and Theology in England* (Grand Rapids, Michigan, and Cambridge, combined pbk. ed., 1996), iii, pp. 52–62.

9　See Jeremy Gregory in P. Collinson, N. Ramsay and M. Sarks, *A History of Canterbury Cathedral* (Oxford, 1995), pp. 232ff.

10　For the background to the Durham tradition see C.J. Stranks, *Anglican Devotion* (London, 1961), pp. 155–58, and C.J. Stranks, *This Sumptuous Church* (London, 1973), p. 76.

11　Even at Canterbury, where Dean Tillotson in 1683 had insisted on a weekly communion service, that practice relapsed in the 1790s to a monthly celebration: Collinson, Ramsay and Sarks, *Canterbury Cathedral*, pp 230ff.

12　*Blessed be the God and Father*. See G. Aylmer and J. Tiller (eds), *Hereford Cathedral, a History* (London, 2000), pp. 417f.

13　'... the prime object of the cathedral ... was to be an instrument of religious, and thereby social and political, stability, by preaching orthodox Anglican doctrine and by supporting the forces of order within provincial society.' Jeremy Gregory, in Collinson, Ramsay and Sarks, *Canterbury Cathedral*, p. 207.

14　*Torrington Diaries*, ii, p. 400 (15 July, 1791).

15　Bernard Bass and John Ingamells (eds), *A Candidate for Praise, William Mason, 1725–97* (York, 1973), esp. pp. x, 11ff and 72ff.

16　*Torrington Diaries*, iii, p. 36 (5 June 1762).

17　Peter Holman, 'Eighteenth-century Music: Past, Present, Future', in David Wynn Jones (ed.), *Music in Eighteenth-century Britain* (Aldershot, 2000), pp. 1–3.

18　See Philip Olleson, 'The London Roman Catholic Embassy Chapels and their Music in the Eighteenth and Early Nineteenth Century', in Wynn Jones, ibid., pp. 101–118.

19　All but two of Handel's anthems required orchestral accompaniment, unavailable for the routine liturgy of any eighteenth-century English cathedral (Holman, ibid., p. 6). For the music of the short-lived chapel at Cannons (dedicated 1720, demolished 1748), see C.H. Collins Baker and Muriel I. Baker, *The Life and Circumstances of James Brydges First Duke of Chandos* (Oxford, 1949), pp. 129ff; and Graydon Beeks, 'The *Chandos Anthems* of Haym, Handel and Pepusch', *Gottinger Handel-Beitrage*, v (1993), pp. 161–193, with details of all anthems written for the 1st Duke of Chandos at pp. 166ff. There is evidence of instruments being used occasionally at the Chapel Royal. A stylised picture of the Chapel Royal in 1712 (BL, Mus. H820) shows an orchestra of some sixteen players in facing balconies; but this is likely to represent a special occasion. An account of probably the 1750s notes only that there were employed for the Chapel an organist, a lutenist and a viol-player (Notebook of William Lovegrove).

20　Brian Crosby, *Come on, Choristers!* (Durham, 1999), p. 33. This was within ten years of the first performance of *Messiah* and forty years earlier than the arrangements made with organ accompaniment by Theodore Ayleward for use in St George's Chapel, Windsor, which Fellowes thought to be a new departure (E.H. Fellowes (ed. J.A. Westrup), *English Cathedral Music* (London, 1969, pbk. ed. 1973), p. 219).

21 See, for instance, H. Watkins Shaw, *Eighteenth Century Cathedral Music* (Church Music Society Occasional Paper 21, Oxford, 1952): 'it is Greene who emerges as the great figure of the period in this special field'; and, most recently, Ian Spink's enthusiasm for Greene's Evening Canticles in C, in up to eight parts – 'a marvellous piece', in D. Keene, A. Burns and A. Saint (eds), *St Paul's: The Cathedral Church of London, 604–2004* (New Haven, Connecticut, and London, 2004), p. 397. But for a more critical view of Greene, see Long, *Music of the English Church*, pp. 296–300.

22 It is difficult to determine how many 'services' King wrote because his compositions include complete morning and evening canticle sets, separate morning sets and evening sets, and isolated items such as a Te deum and a Jubilate. Sets in seven different keys can be identified, 'more … than [by] any other composer of the period', along with eighteen anthems. NGD, 13, pp. 605f.

23 John Hawkins, *A General History of the Science and Practice of Music*, 5 vols. (London, 1776; 2nd ed., 2 vols, London 1875; repr. 1963), ii, p. 798.

24 NGD's amusing entry on King is in vol. xiii at pp. 605f.

25 Christopher Dearnley, *English Church Music, 1650–1750* (London, 1970), p. 260.

26 NGD, xxii, p. 338.

27 G.M. Garrett, 'The Choral Service in Chapel', *The Eagle*, xvi (1891), p. 227.

28 For James Hawkins, see Spink, ibid, pp. 243ff.

29 The practice was recorded by Banks in a Rochester organ-book. See H. Watkins Shaw, *The Succession of Organists of the Chapel Royal and the Cathedrals of England and Wales from c. 1538* (Oxford, 1991), p. 238. There is indication from other foundations that the Sunday repertoire was limited. It may be that chapters wanted their Sunday congregations to be familiar with the music sung, perhaps for ready understanding of the words in echoing buildings without acoustic aids, perhaps even with a view to their joining in the singing with the choir. See, for instance, discussion of the Canterbury regulation of 1696 that 'every Sunday Tallis his Te Deum and Creed be used', in Ian Spink, *Restoration Cathedral Music, 1660–1714* (Oxford, 1985), p. 208.

30 For this paragraph I have drawn on S. J. Curtis, *History of Education in Great Britain* (London, 2nd ed., 1950), pp. 184–229.

31 *Hansard*, 1820, ii, col. 61.

32 R.R. Lewis, *The History of Brentwood School* (Brentwood, 1981), pp. 94ff.

33 For Robert Whiston's extraordinary and tempestuous Rochester headship see Ralph Arnold's brilliant *The Whiston Matter* (London, 1961).

34 *Torrington Diaries*, i, p. 282 (1 August 1787), and Hackett, *Brief Account*, p. 36.

35 H.C. Maxwell Lyte, *A History of Eton College* (London, 4th ed., 1911), p. 327.

36 The Eton/Windsor amalgamation is discussed comprehensively in Wridgway, *Choristers of St George's*, pp. 56–62.

37 The details are from Thomas Wicks, 'An Old Chorister's Reminiscences', as given in Wridgway, ibid., pp. 60ff.

38 By the 1830s chorister numbers had diminished to seven. Ibid., p. 63.

39 *Torrington Diaries*, I, p. 80 (25 August 1782).

40 P.M.J. Crook, 'Fifty Years of Choral Misrule: George Chard', *Winchester Cathedral Record*, lvi (1987), p. 318.

41 Alan Rannie, *The Story of Music at Winchester College, 1394–1969* (Winchester, 1970), pp. 21–27. See also John Crook, *A History of the Pilgrims' School* (Chichester, 1981), pp. 11ff.

42 R.J. Henderson, *A History of King's College Choir School* (Cambridge, 1981), pp. 16f. Not only at Cambridge was the ability to shout loudly deemed a useful criterion for a choristership. Thomas Wicks, whose reminiscences have been referred to above (n. 37), was a very short boy, so much so that at his voice trial for the choir of St George's, Windsor, in 1826 he was made to stand on a stool to sing. Some mischievous choristers, witnesses to the trial, caused the stool 'to assume a position of unstable equilibrium, with the result that I approached earth's centre', the fall accompanied by 'vociferation so violent that Dean Hobart remarked 'It is a good omen; he evidently has good lungs' – and Wicks was elected to a choristership. (Wridgway, *Choristers of St George's*, p. 61.)

43 R.S. Stanier, *Magdalen School* (Oxford, 2nd ed., 1958), p. 126. Details of New College and its choristers from Jonathan Edmunds, *New College Brats* (Oxford, 1996), pp. 30–37.

44 Stanier, *Magdalen School*, pp. 138ff.

45 Jonathan Edmunds, *New College Brats*, pp. 42 and 34, states that the paper was found by one of his predecessor headmasters, he who dubbed his pupils the 'New College brats'. However, the Rev. William Tuckwell, *Reminiscences of Oxford* (London, 1900), claims, pp. 73f, that he himself found the document.

46 *Torrington Diaries*, Christ Church, iii, p. 171 (15 July 1792); Worcester, i, p. 44 (1 July 1781); Hereford, i, p. 314 (10 August 1787); Lincoln, ii, p. 346 (26 June 1791).

47 *Torrington Diaries*, ii, p. 233 (5 July, 1790) for Ely; Hackett, *Brief Account*, Carlisle, p. 13, Chichester, p. 17, Ely, p. 25.

48 Robert Holtby, *The Minster School, York* (York, 1994), pp. 25f.

49 Jeremy Gregory in Collinson, Ramsay and Sarks, *Canterbury Cathedral*, chapter v, *passim*.

50 Stevens (ed. Argent), *Recollections*, esp. pp. 4–12 and 188.

51 A Mr Cotton, who taught them writing and 'Arithmetick'. These two hours in the summer and one hour in the winter were the sum of their daily non-musical education.

52 For a detailed study of Stevens's apprenticeship see Charles Cudworth, 'An 18th-century musical apprenticeship', *Musical Times*, 108 (1967), pp. 602–04, where the articles of apprenticeship are given in full. Quotations that follow are from this account.

53 Widely quoted, for instance in W.R. Matthews and W.M. Atkins (eds), *A History of St Paul's Cathedral* (London, 2nd ed.1964), p. 241; but never, to my knowledge, with attribution.

54 Not dismissal, as stated in Matthews and Atkins's history.

55 Stevens (ed. Argent), *Recollections*, p. 189.

56 Maria Hackett, *Correspondence and Evidences ...* (London, 1832), p. 12.

57 David Baldwin, *The Chapel Royal* (London, 1990), pp. 306, 326f, 330 and 431.

58 E.H. Pearce, *The Sons of the Clergy, 1655–1904* (London, 1904), p. 202.

59 Ibid., p. 205.

60 Ibid., pp. 227f. and 231.

61   For the Three Choirs Festival see A. Boden, *Three Choirs: A History of the Festival* (Gloucester, 1992), and Watkins Shaw, *The Three Choirs Festival* (Worcester and London, 1954). The notices that follow in my text are given in Shaw, ibid. pp. 1f., quoting, for the second, BL Add MS 5811, f. 134.

62   NGD, 25, p. 431, echoing Shaw, ibid., p. 2.

63   From 1838 Francis Close, evangelical vicar of Cheltenham, later to be dean of Carlisle, fought a war against the festival in general and its use of consecrated buildings in particular; and in 1875 the dean and chapter of Worcester refused the use of the cathedral to the festival unless there were no soloists, no orchestra, no platform and no ticket sales; so there were, in that year, just six choral services sung by the combined cathedral choirs. Shaw, *Three Choirs Festival*, p. 55.

64   Ibid., p. 22.

65   Hackett, *Brief Account*, pp. 48 and 51.

66   For the Salisbury choristers' education, including extracts from John Harding's unpublished memoirs, see Dora Robertson, *Sarum Close* (London, 1938), pp. 268–275.

67   Margaret Bowker in Dorothy Owen (ed.), *A History of Lincoln Minster* (Cambridge, 1994), p. 218.

68   N. Thistlethwaite in Owen, ibid., pp. 92–97.

69   The comment came from *The Gentleman's Magazine* (NS, 6, 1836, pp. 562f.), following worship at a Sunday service attended by only three singing-men, of whom two left part-way through.

70   L. S. Colchester, David Tudway Quilter and Alan Quilter, *A History of Wells Cathedral School* (Wells, 1985), p. 37.

71   Lord Liverpool to William Van Mildert, 15 July 1820 (BL MS Add 38286), as quoted in E.A. Varley, *The Last of the Prince Bishops* (Cambridge, 1992), p. 90.

72   Order 6 of 1683, given in W.D. Larrett, *History of the King's School, Peterborough* (Peterborough, 1966), p. 21.

73   Fellowes, *English Cathedral Music*, p. 211.

74   Charles Dibdin, *The professional Life of Mr Dibdin written by Himself* ... (London, 1803), i, p. 20. For an outline of Dibdin's extraordinary life see ODNB, liv, pp. 934ff.

75   A book so influential that it remained a prescribed text-book for the Cambridge Previous Examination until 1919. G.R. Cragg, *The Church and the Age of Reason* (Harmondsworth, 1960), p. 171.

76   M. L. Clarke, *Paley: evidences for the man* (London, 1974), p. 52.

Notes to Chapter 11: The Seeds of Reform

1   Maria Hackett, in her campaign to improve the condition of the English choristers, published privately a series of documents. The most important is her *Brief Account of Cathedral and Collegiate Schools*. This was printed and circulated to interested parties, including the authorities of the schools discussed therein, in 1827. It consists largely of communications that she had submitted for publication in the *Gentleman's Magazine* between January 1817 and February 1819 (Volumes 87 to 89); hence almost all of

its information refers to conditions in the second rather than the third decade of the nineteenth century. Subsequently she circulated two new versions, undated but almost certainly of *c.* 1860 and 1873. In the latter year the precentor of Wells undertook proof-reading for her (GL, MS 10,1089/8). To the unaltered original edition were appended (though at the front) a tabulated account of the choral foundations with chorister numbers and their schools, dated (in her hand) 1837, together with the corrections and additions of *c.* 1860 and further additions from the 1870s haphazardly about the text in a curious italic type. Maria Hackett's own copy, bound together with her later publications and interleaved with manuscript notes and letters, is in the London Guildhall Library, MS 10,189/8. In 1873, in the year before she died, Miss Hackett sent a copy of her *Brief Account* with its additions, also bound together with her other publications, to the Cambridge University Library (Ba.21.38/1): it is chiefly this copy that has been used for researching this chapter. Her correspondence with the bishop, dean and clergy of St Paul's was published by her as *Correspondence, Legal Proceedings and Evidences respecting the Ancient School attached to St Paul's Cathedral* (London, 1832; latest edition, 1916). It is surprising and regrettable that there is no biography of Miss Hackett. Kathleen Garrett published a scholarly essay in *Guildhall Studies in London History*, i/3 (October 1974), pp. 150–63. Briefer tributes are David Gedge, 'Maria Hackett – The Choristers' Friend', *The World of Church Music*, 1983, pp. 41–49, and David Gedge, 'The redoubtable Miss Hackett', *Musical Opinion*, 1297 (Dec. 1985), pp. 441–46; 1298 (Jan. 1986), pp. 11–14 and 1299 (Feb. 1986), pp. 49–53.

2 Dora Robertson, *Sarum Close* (London, 1930), p. 259.

3 Garrett, ibid., pp. 150ff. and ODNB, 24, p. 400.

4 R.J.S. Stevens (ed. Mark Argent), *Recollections of R.J.S. Stevens* (London, 1992), p. 189.

5 The words quoted are Miss Hackett's.

6 For Tomline see ODNB, 54, pp. 934–37.

7 For Miss Hackett's correspondence with the St Paul's clergy see MH, *Correspondence respecting St Paul's, passim.*

8 See n. 1 above.

9 It should also be added that Maria Hackett's concern for what would nowadays be called 'heritage' led her to be instrumental in preserving the last surviving Tudor great hall in the City, Crosby Hall. It had for some years been a packers' warehouse. When in 1831 the lease came on the market she and her relatives purchased it and restored the building, providing there a public library, reading room and concert hall. When, in 1907, radical redevelopment of Crosby Square was proposed, the hall was dismantled, moved to Chelsea and re-erected, where it can be seen today. (Garrett, *Maria Hackett*, p. 158, and Obituary, *City Press*, 7 November 1974 (GL 10189/8).)

10 *Gentleman's Magazine*. 86 (NS 10), Jan. 1817, pp. 11f.

11 Ibid., lxxxviii (NS 11), June 1818, p. 488, the wording repeated without alteration in Maria Hackett, *Brief Account*, p. 32.

12 MH ibid, p. 40.

13 Letter: MH to Samuel Capper, GL MS 10189/4.

14 Ibid, letter to E.F. Rimbault, 16 December 1844.

15 Obituary, *City Press*, Some of her visits were at times other than autumn, cf. undated letter from MH referring to a visit 'as long ago as June' (GL 10189/8).

16   MH to J.W. Burgon, October 1841 (GL 10189/9).

17   MH, *Brief Account*, p. 46, where, at least in the CUL copy, to the printed report is added 'in 1824' in MH's handwriting.

18   See Gedge, 'The Redoubtable Miss Hackett', p. 444. ODNB states that a court order of 1814 required the restoration of certain funds. I have been unable to verify this.

19   MH to H.P. Liddon, 6 May 1870 (GL 10189/8).

20   St John's College Conclusions Book and Rentals, 1819. I am grateful to Mr David Gahan for generously passing to me the notes of his researches in the St John's College archives.

21   MH, *Brief Account, Recent Alterations*, p. 2. Given that St John's and Trinity were sharing organist and schoolmaster in 1827 when the *Brief Account* was published, it is curious that a very favourable report is given of Trinity's choristers – 'the requisitions of the Statute on the subject of the Choir, are in all respects, in spirit, if not to the very letter, liberally fulfilled by the College', whilst of St John's (from whom she had still received no reply) she could say only that the accounts that she had heard from other sources 'are such as I forbear to publish'.

22   For Bristol: J. Collard, D. Ogden and R. Burgess, *'Where the Fat Black Canons Dined'* (Bristol, 1992), pp. 29ff; for Chichester: N.Ollerenshaw, *A History of the Prebendal School* (Chichester, 1984), pp. 14ff.

23   For the Chichester developments see Philip Barrett, 'The Musical History of Chichester Cathedral', in Mary Hobbs (ed.), *Chichester Cathedral: an Historical Survey* (Chichester, 1994), pp. 257f. Barrett must be mistaken in saying that Maria Hackett visited Chichester in 1818.

24   Sir Frederick A. Gore Ouseley, Bart, 'The Education of Choristers in Cathedrals', in J.S. Howson, *Essays on Cathedrals* (London, 1872), p. 234.

25   J. Bumpus, *A History of English Cathedral Music, 1549–1889* (London, 1908; reprint 1972), ii, pp. 426f.

26   The word 'Anglicanism' first appeared, in inverted commas as here, in 1837. Ibid., i, p. 171.

27   From amongst a very large literature the most readable and accessible account of the Oxford Movement remains Geoffrey Faber, *Oxford Apostles* (London 1933, rev. Harmonsworth, 1954).

28   For the development of cathedral-style services in parish churches, the Temple and St Mark's College, Chelsea, see Bernarr Rainbow, *The Choral Revival in the Anglican Church, 1839–1872* (London, 1970, reprint 2005), pp. 15ff. for Margaret Street, pp. 27ff. for Leeds, pp. 38ff. for the Temple Church and pp. 48ff. for St Mark's College.

29   Initially to Anglican chants, later to Oakeley's preferred Gregorian tones.

30   Strictly, re-introduced, because there had been a robed choir earlier in the century, that had never sung cathedral-style services and had disintegrated in the 1830s.

31   Rainbow, *Choral Revival*, p. 50.

32   I have taken the accounts of conditions under Hawes from D. Baldwin, *The Chapel Royal, Ancient and Modern* (London, 1990), pp. 330f.; of his musical activities from NGD, 11, p. 162; and of S.S. Wesley's time under Hawes from NGD, 27, pp. 203ff.

33   Rainbow, *Choral Revival*, pp. 76f.

34   From the late nineteenth century Ouseley and St Michael's have attracted writers. The two most recent works are Watkins Shaw, *Sir Frederick Ouseley and St Michael's, Tenbury* (Birmingham, 1986), scholarly, reliable and informative but published in unattractive

printed typscript; and David Bland, *Ouseley and his Angels* (Eton, 2000), longer, well presented and fully illustrated.

35 Bland, *Ouseley and His Angels*, pp. 25ff. A march for piano from this period can be found in Watkins Shaw, *Ouseley and St Michael's*, p. 18.

36 Ibid., p. 14. For St Barnabas's, Pimlico, and the riots see Bernarr Rainbow, *The Choral Revival in the Anglican Church, 1839–1872* (London, 1970), pp. 153–161.

37 From letters to F.W. Joyce quoted in Bland, *Ouseley and His Angels*, pp. 48f.

38 Watkins Shaw argues that it was a serious mistake on Ouseley's part to allow St Michael's church to be constitutionally independent of St Michael's College, see Shaw, *Ouseley and St Michael's*, p. 31.

39 From M.F. Alderson's reminiscence, ibid., p. 79.

40 Ibid., pp. 28ff.

41 These details from Shaw, ibid., p. 41.

42 S.S. Wesley, *A Few Words on Cathedral Music* (London, 1849; reprint 1975), pp. 27, 12f.

43 Ibid., pp. 72ff.

44 John Crook, *A History of The Pilgrims' School* (Chichester, 1981), pp. 17f. Not a word of Wesley's failings appears in F. Bussby, *Winchester Cathedral, 1079–1979* (Southampton, 1979). For S.S. Wesley generally see Peter Horton in ODNB, 58, pp. 203ff.

45 Humphrey Clucas, 'Wesley by the Itchen', in *Gods and Mortals* (Liskeard, 1983), p. 33.

46 For what follows, see F.G. Kitton, *Zechariah Buck, Mus. D., A Centenary Memoir* (London, 1899).

47 Ibid., p. vii.

48 Westminster Abbey MS 52,823. For a discussion of this petition see David Knight, 'Repertoire and Performance Practice at Westminster Abbey', *Nineteenth-Century British Music Studies*, 2, ed. Jeremy Dibble and Bennett Zon (Aldershot, 2002), pp. 80–98, especially Appendix 1, pp. 90–94.

49 It took the Archbishops' Commission on Cathedrals of 1992–94 to achieve the title Director of Music for those in charge of the music of cathedrals. See *Heritage and Renewal* (London, 1994), pp. 55 and 178. There is no evidence that the commissioners were aware that they were implementing a 154-year-old recommendation of the organists themselves.

50 And provision should be made for their pensioning when illness or the failure of their voices call for retirement.

51 Gerald Aylmer and John Tiller (eds), *Hereford Cathedral: A History* (London, 2000), pp. 156–61 and 416–20; and ODNB, 37, pp. 884f.

52 The phrase is from Robert Hegg, *The Legend of St Cuthbert* (1636) as quoted in C. J. Stranks, *This Sumptuous Church* (London, 1973), to which what follows is indebted, together with Brian Crosby, *Come on, Choristers!* (Durham, 1999).

53 See, for instance, Vivien Brett, *Cathedral Music: the Pitkin Guide* (Norwich, 2003).

54 H.P. Liddon published a short life of Hamilton in 1869. For a recent study see A.E. Bridge, 'The Nineteenth-Century Revivification of Salisbury Cathedral: Walter Kerr Hamilton, 1841–1854', in D. Marcombe and C.S. Knighton (eds), *Close Encounters* (Nottingham, 1991), pp. 137–60.

55 Hamilton was much involved in preparing Salisbury's response to the Cathedral Commission's enquiries. This led him to write a paper to his dean, published in 1853 and

republished two years later under the title *Cathedral Reform* as an address to the diocesan clergy. Here he stresses his concern that residentiary canons had no 'definite duties', so he set about inventing them. W.K. Hamilton, *Cathedral Reform* (London, 1855), see esp. pp. 21 and 33.

56 *Parliamentary Papers: Report of the Commissioners on Cathedral and Collegiate Churches* (London, 1854), xxv, p. 34, and for the headmaster's submission, pp. 749ff. For the dismemberment of Hamilton's choir school reforms see Robertson, *Sarum Close*, pp. 286–292.

Notes to Chapter 12: The Fruits of Reform

1 Maria Hackett, 'Comparative View of the Number and Present State of the Endowed Choristers Educated in the Different Cathedral and Collegiate Schools' included, unpaginated, in M.H. *Brief Account of Cathedral and Collegiate Schools* (London, edition of 1873), dated 1837 in MH's hand in the London Guildhall Library copy.

2 *Parliamentary Papers, Report of the Commissioners on Cathedral and Collegiate Churches* (London, 1854), xxv, pp. 1–39: 'Analysis of Answers'.

3 *Parliamentary Papers, Report of Her Majesty's Commissioners for Enquiring into the Condition of Cathedral Churches in England and Wales* (London, 1882–4), xxi.

4 Three probationers were recorded in 1841 and eight by 1856. Brian Crosby, *Come on, Choristers!* (Durham, 1999), p. 42.

5 Addition of five probationers from 1855 recorded by Rev. E Peake, 'Christ Church Cathedral Choir School' in *Cathedrals Quarterly*, iii, 10 (July 1915).

6 But the boys at Bangor and St Asaph sang only on Sundays and high days.

7 The Royal Commission reported twelve choristers maintained, of whom only six received payment, but the unpaid are not described as probationers, though they may well have been probationary. The statutory number at Windsor was ten.

8 Westminster Abbey MS 52,823.

9 MH, *Brief Account*, p. *41.

10 *PP* (1854), xxv, pp. 934f. and Philip Barrett, *Barchester* (London, 1993), pp. 166 and 383.

11 *PP, Report of Commissioners* (1882, xxi and xxii, 1883, xxi and 1884, xxii), from which the figures that follow are taken.

12 For the Welsh revival see J.J.S. Perowne, 'Welsh Cathedrals', in J.S. Howson, *Essays on Cathedrals* (London, 1870), pp. 185–207; details for Llandaff from anon., *Brief Notes on the History of the Cathedral School, Llandaff* (Llandaff, 2001); and for Bangor, M.L. Clarke, *Bangor Cathedral* (Cardiff, 1969), pp. 52–85.

13 For the establishment of the choral foundation serving St Mary's Episcopal Cathedral, Edinburgh, see Philip Crosfied, *Stones and Songs* (Edinburgh, 1996), pp. 26–33 and 37–40.

14 For the re-establishment of the Eton choral foundation and choir school: Kathleen I. Garrett, 'Maria Hackett and the Choristers of Eton College', parts 1 and 2, *Etoniana*, cxxx (1974) and cxxxi (1975).

15 Albert Mellor, *Music and Musicians at Eton College* (Eton, 1929), p. 83.

16 *Parliamentary Papers, Commissioners on certain Colleges and Schools* (1864), pp. 117f.

17 Mellor, *Music at Eton*, p. 125.

18 For the London churches in particular see Bernarr Rainbow, *The Choral Revival in the Anglican Church, 1839–1872* (London, 1970), pp. 169ff.

19 Cornelius Brown, *A History of Newark-on-Trent* (Newark, 2 vols, 1904 and 1907), ii, pp. 208f.

20 Of the new cathedrals established between 1877 and 1888 – St Albans, Truro, Liverpool, Newcastle, Southwell and Wakefield – only Truro undertook to have a full choral foundation from the start.

21 Barrett, *Barchester*, p. 139.

22 Aston, 'Music since the Reformation', in G. Aylmer and R. Cant, *A History of York Minster* (Oxford, 1977), p. 300 and n. 72; and Barrett, *Barchester*, p. 117.

23 Barrett, *Barchester*, pp. 170ff. and 387, n. 83.

24 *PP, Report of Commissioners* (1884), p. 76.

25 *PP, Report of Commissioners* (1854), Correspondence, Bristol.

26 MH, *Brief Account*, Recent Alterations, p. 5 and italic appendage.

27 Reminiscences of former chorister Dr Hubert Hunt (1931), as given in N. Wridgway, *Choristers of St George's Chapel* (Windsor, 1980), p. 87.

28 *PP, Report of Commissioners* (1883), xxi, p. 200.

29 L.S. Colchester, D. Tudway Quilter and A. Quilter, *A History of Wells Cathedral School* (Wells, 1985), p. 38.

30 A. Rannie, *The Music at Winchester College, 1394–1969* (Winchester, 1970), p. 38.

31 *PP, Report of Commissioners* (1882), xxii, p. 211. Draft statute 17.

32 Ibid. (1882), xxi, p. 65. Draft statute 25.

33 A.H. Brewer, *Memories of Choirs and Cloisters* (London, 1931), p. 3.

34 R.D. Middleton, *Magdalen Studies* (London, 1936), p. 50, states that the boy was given 'a Blenheim orange apple' and this has a convincingly botanical ring. However, L.S. Tuckwell, in his own memoir ('A Former Chorister', *Old Magdalen Days, 1847–1877* (Oxford, 1913), states (p. 5) that he was given 'an apple and an orange'. Oranges are messily memorable. I have given Tuckwell the benefit of the doubt.

35 [L. Tuckwell], *Old Magdalen Days* (Oxford, 1913), pp. 4f.

36 For this development, see Owen Chadwick, *The Victorian Church* (London, pbk edn. 1987), i, p. 376. For the Windsor illustrations: N. Wridgway, *Choristers of St George's Chapel* (Windsor, 1980), facing pp. 72 and 80.

37 The expression throughout, here abbreviated throughout, is 'a choral scholar (or chorister)'.

38 The bishop in his role as dean.

39 *PP, Report of Commissioners* (1882), xxi, p. 75. Capitalisation as in original draft statute 34.

40 L. Creighton, *Life and Letters of Mandell Creighton* (London, 1904), i, p. 25.

41 Francis Close movingly described his conversion to the blessings of the *music* (and not simply the words) of the choral office in his brief tract, Thoughts on the Daily Choral Services in Carlisle Cathedral (London, 3rd edn, 1863), pp. 7 and 10.

42 Chadwick, *Victorian Church*, ii, p. 374, and Anson in Aylmer and Cant, *York Minster*, p. 296. It was said at the time, 'Duncome became the Minster'.

43   *Victoria County History of Cheshire* (London, 1980), iii, p. 188; and ODNB, xxviii, pp. 543f (Edmund Venables, rev. Joanna Hawke). While all this reformation was afoot at Chester, Howson found time during 1869 and 1870 to edit and himself contribute to the collection of *Essays on Cathedrals* that was widely influential at the time and continues to be an invaluable evidential mine of mid-Victorian reforming thought.

44   G.L. Prestige, *St Paul's in its Glory (1831–1911)* (London, 1955), pp. 48–50.

45   W.H. Hutton (ed.), *Autobiography of Robert Gregory* (London, 1912), p. 158.

46   *Musical Standard*, 14 January 1871.

47   For these developments see Prestige, *St Paul's in its Glory, passim*; Penelope J. Cable, 'A New Broom in the Augean Stable', in R.N. Swanson, *Continuity and Change in Christian Worship* (Woodbridge, 1999), pp. 361–373; and Timothy Storey, 'Music, 1800–2002', in D. Keene, A. Burns and A. Saint (eds), *St Paul's: the Cathedral Church of London, 604–2004* (New Haven, Connecticut, and London, 2004), pp. 403ff.

48   *PP, Report of Commissioners* (1855), pp. xviiif.

49   *PP, Report of Commissioners* (1884), xxi, p. 99, letter 17 from the dean: so small and ill-ventilated a room in the crypt that 'the atmosphere after all the boys have been in for some time is most oppressive and repelling'.

50   Robert Holtby, *The Minster School York* (York, 1994), pp. 27–37.

51   For Whiting, see Patricia Hooper, *William Whiting* (Southampton, 1978).

52   *PP, Report of Commissioners* (1854), Correspondence, Exeter.

53   The Winchester saga can be picked out from John Crook, *The Pilgrims' School* (Chichester, 1980), pp. 10–20.

54   *PP, Report of Commissioners*, 1854, p. 16.

55   Caroline Roslington (ed.), *The King's School Worcester* (Worcester, 1994), p. 83.

56   J. Collard, D. Ogden and R. Burgess, *'Where the Fat Black Canons Dined': A History of Bristol Cathedral School, 1140 to 1992* (Bristol, 1993), p. 30.

57   L. Tuckwell, *Old Magdalen Days*, p. 19.

58   R.S. Stanier, *Magdalen School* (Oxford, 2nd edn, 1958), pp. 170f.

59   He was Newman's curate at Littlemore in the late 1830s and caused some scandal by his advanced Tractarian views, later being described as 'the Grandfather of all ritualists' by Lord Blackford (Letter to Bloxam of 1 Nov. 1884, Magd. Ox. MS 304).

60   The phrase is from William Tuckwell, *Reminiscences of Oxford* (London, 1900), p. 171.

61   L. Tuckwell, *Old Magdalen Days*, pp. 14ff.

62   For a comprehensive consideration of the origins and development of the ceremony see Roy Judge, 'May Morning and Magdalen College, Oxford', in *Folk Lore*, xcvii (1986), pp. 15–40.

63   Bodleian Library, Oxford, MS Rawlinson B. 323, f. 86.

64   Quoted in Peter Charlton, *John Stainer* (Newton Abbot, 1984), p. 24.

65   Holman Hunt painted two versions, one now at the Lady Lever Gallery at Port Sunlight, the other at the City of Birmingham Art Gallery. For a discussion of Hunt's painting and its interpretation of the ceremony see Judge, 'May Morning', pp. 25ff.

66   R.J. Henderson, *A History of King's College Choir School, Cambridge* (Cambridge, 1981), p. 20.

67   G.M. Garrett, 'The Choral Services in Chapel', *The Eagle*, xvi (1891), p. 229.

68 Henderson, *King's College Choir School*, pp. 19–32.

69 Neville Wridgway, *Choristers of St George's Chapel* (Windsor, 1980), pp. 92–100.

70 See K.R. Long, *The Music of the English Church* (London, 1972), pp. 396f.

71 Rainbow, *Choral Revival*, Appendix 8, pp. 329–343.

72 N. Thistlethwaite, 'Music and Worship, 1660–1980', in D. Owen, *A History of Lincoln Minster* (Cambridge, 1994), p. 109.

73 C.V. Stanford, *Pages from an Unwritten Diary* (London, 1914), p. 308.

74 Edmund H. Fellowes, *Memoirs of an Amateur Musician* (London, 1946), p. 85. (I owe this reference to the kindness of Barry Ferguson.)

75 C.V. Stanford, 'Magnificat' from his *Evening Canticles in G*, op. 81 (1904).

Notes to Chapter 13: The Twentieth-Century Framework

1 St Michael's College, Tenbury, which was forced to close in 1985: see below, pp. 216f.

2 Figures from the Choir Schools' Association census, May 2004. Early sixteenth-century numbers are incapable of accurate – or even approximate – calculation. 500 is a best guess: see chapter 4.

3 There had been a hiatus during the middle decades of the sixteenth century. The medieval foundation was suppressed in 1547 and, according to Nicholas Temperley, *The Music of the English Parish Church* (Cambridge, 1979, pbk ed. 1983), i, pp. 351f., revived with new statutes by Elizabeth I in 1586. But the list of choristers in W.A. James, *An Account of the Southwell Grammar and Song Schools* (Southwell, 1927), pp. 95ff., lacks any names after 1526 until a single isolated election in 1565, but then shows the full resumption of elections to choristerships from 1570. So Elizabeth's statutes presumably confirmed an already revived choral establishment.

4 At Guildford, according to Simon Carpenter, *The Beat is Irrelevant* (Guildford, 1996), pp. 12, 16 and 17, it was the persuasive new young organist, Barry Rose, who insisted on daily choral services from the start. But in fact (p. 22) there had been Friday and Saturday evensongs at the pro-cathedral before Rose's appointment. Rose, of course, pushed successfully for evensongs throughout the week.

5 In 1978 Lanesborough was to become the junior school of Guildford Royal Grammar School. See: D.M. Sturley, *The Royal Grammar School, Guildford* (Guildford, 1979).

6 A valuable analysis of the cathedrals and the educational provision for their choristers was published in *Cathedrals Quarterly*, i, 1 (January 1913), at pp. 27ff.

7 Carpenter, *The Beat is Irrelevant*, p. 77.

8 St Patrick's Cathedral, Dublin, is the place to go to hear weekday choral matins in 2006 – and even there sung only by the boys. Matins is also one of the services sung on weekdays at varying locations by St Mary's Choir School, Reigate.

9 Quoted from *English Church Music*, xxvi (1966), in Watkins Shaw (ed.), *Sir Frederick Ouseley and St Michael's, Tenbury* (Birmingham, 1986), p. 85.

10 Ibid., pp. 68–77. For the trust, see www.ouseleytrust.org.uk.

11 Information kindly supplied by the last headmaster of the Eton choir school, Mr T.C. Allerton. (His is the word 'shoddy'.)

12 Desmond Morse-Boycott wrote voluminously. Information on his song school can be found in *A Golden Legend of the Slums* (London, 1952), *A Tapestry of Toil* (London, 1970) and *A Pilgrimage of Song* (Leighton Buzzard, 1972). Some of his books borrow entire chapters from others. The illustrations in the *Pilgrimage* show that another of his gifts was taking attractive photographs of his choristers. For the financial circumstances that led to the closure of the Highgate School see the remarkable Board of Education interview memorandum of 22 April 1932: TNA E37/739, T14446 Z/2. The Morse-Boycott Charitable Trust, which welcomes donations, is managed by the Administrator, The Morse-Boycott Bursary Fund, The Royal Chantry, Cathedral Cloisters, Chichester, W. Sussex PO19 1PX.

13 Information on Reigate St Mary's kindly supplied by the school's headmaster and by the master of choristers and from the school's website, www.reigate-stmarys.org.

14 The Catholic London embassy chapels, noticed in earlier chapters, were technically extra-territorial.

15 A comprehensive account of the choral foundation at Westminster Cathedral is to be found in Peter Doyle, *Westminster Cathedral, London, 1895–1995* (London, 1995), pp. 51–69 and 124–137.

16 The author was privileged to be a member of the small committee convened by the archbishop to advise on the future shape and nature of the choir school. Basil Hume's commitment to cathedral choral worship and the choir school were absolute.

17 The figures in this table for 1934 and 1958 are drawn from the Church Music Society's Occasional Paper no. 24, *Sixty Years of Cathedral Music* (London, 1963), and for 2005 from the Friends of Cathedral Music's leaflet, *Singing in Cathedrals, 2005*.

18 H. Brewer, *Memories of Choirs and Cloisters* (Gloucester, 1931), p. 4.

19 Church Music Society Occasional Paper, 11, *The Present State of Cathedral Music* (London, 1934), pp. 5f.

20 Lichfield's statistics were not included in the Church Music Society's Occasional Paper no. 24 of 1958.

21 Norwich: but alternate Thursdays 'dumb'.

22 Oxford (Christ Church): the service on Thursdays is a Sung Eucharist.

23 Peterborough: visiting choirs generally on Saturdays.

24 Rochester: various choirs on Saturdays, including visitors.

25 Church Music Society Occasional Paper, 13, *Forty Years of Cathedral Music, 1898–1938* (London, 1940), p. 7.

26 It is symptomatic of the ephemeral nature of so many 'revised' liturgical texts that Salisbury, where the *Revised Psalter* was virtuously adopted at an early stage, has, from February 2006, reverted to Coverdale.

27 Erik Routley, *Twentieth-Century Church Music* (London, 1964), and more succinctly in his *A Short History of English Church Music* (London, 1977), has distinguished four categories of twentieth-century novelty: atonality, the merging of sacred and secular musical styles, the churches' adoption of folk and 'pop' music and the impact of the new liturgies on compositional demands.

28 Vasari Singers, dir. Jeremy Backhouse, *Anthems for the 21st Century* (Signum Classics, 2005, SIGCD059).

29 *Heritage and Renewal* (London, 1994), p. 21.

Notes to Chapter 14: The Twentieth-Century Choir School

1   R.M. Tuke, 'The Education of Cathedral Choristers', *Cathedrals Quarterly*.

2   Brian Crosby, *Come on, Choristers!* (Durham, 1999), p. 82.

3   At St John's, where the school could provide no suitable facility, a practice room was constructed in 1992 as an extension to the sports pavilion just across the road from the school. King's College School too has a fine practice room at the school.

4   Jonathan Edmunds, *New College Brats* (Oxford, 1996), pp. 68f.

5   *The Choir Schools Directory*, 1931, pp. 30f. (Copies of the no longer published directory are all but non-existent. Quite by chance, a few years ago, the author found copies of the 1928 and 1931 editions in the library of the boys' day room at St Paul's Cathedral Choir School – a discovery comparable in excitement to that of the tomb of Tutenkhamen.)

6   Alternatively a few went on to the City of Oxford School.

7   Ibid., pp. 52f., and Edmunds, *New College Brats*, pp. 59 and 61.

8   *Choir Schools Directory*, 1931, pp. 22f.

9   J. Collard, D. Ogdon and R. Burgess, *'Where the Fat Black Canons Dined': A History of Bristol Cathedral School, 1140 to 1992* (Bristol, 1992), especially pp. 64–66.

10   L.S. Colchester, D. Tudway Quilter and A. Quilter, *A History of Wells Cathedral School* (Wells, 1985), p. 104.

11   Dorothy Owen (ed.), *A History of Lincoln Minster* (Cambridge, 1994), p. 297.

12   *Choir Schools Today*, xix (2005), p. 37.

13   Information largely from Mr David Gahan, former headmaster of St Edmund's College Junior School, supplemented by details from the *Choir Schools Directories* of 1928, pp. 6f and 1931, pp. 6f.

14   *Victoria County History of Cheshire*, iii (London, 1980), p. 232.

15   For Jelf, see the following chapter, pp. 248f.

16   *Choir Schools Directory*, 1928, p. 31.

17   Robert Holtby, *The Minster School York: A Retrospect* (York, 1994), pp. 37–48.

18   For the 1955 events see George Guest, *A Guest at Cambridge* (Brewster, Massachusetts, 1994, rev. ed. 1996), pp. 24–28. *The Good Schools Guide* has described St John's College School as wonderful – or even 'utterly wonderful' – in every edition since 1991.

19   *Choir Schools Directory*, 1928, pp. 11f and 1931, pp. 12f.

20   Ibid., 1928, pp. 24f and 1931 pp. 26f.

21   Crosby, *Come on, Choristers!*, pp. 66f., 70f. and 85–87.

22   For continuing developments see www.lichfieldcathedralschool.com.

23   *Choir Schools Directory*, 1928, pp. 35f.

24   David Gascoyne, *Collected Poems 1988* (Oxford, 1988).

25   John Crook, *A History of the Pilgrims' School* (Chichester, 1981), pp. 36, 39–42, 46f and 80f.

26   Neville Ollerenshaw, *A History of the Prebendal School* (Chichester, 1984), pp. 22–25.

27   Edward Pine, *The Westminster Abbey Singers* (London, 1953), p. 241.

28   R.L.H. Coulson (ed.), *History of the King's School, Rochester* (Rochester, 1989), pp. 15 and 32.

29   Thus far from R.G. Ikin, *Notes on the History of Ely Cathedral Grammar School* (Cambridge, 1931), p. 47. What follows, from R.G. Saunders, *The King's School, Ely, 970–1970* (Ely, 1970), pagination mislaid.

30 Davis's wife, Mary, who had for twenty years 'kept house' at the choir school, lived on in retirement and widowhood to be a centenarian.

31 Sources for this paragraph: Caroline Roslington (ed.), *The King's School Worcester* (Worcester, 1994), pp. 83f., 116, 118 and 138; and *Choir Schools Directory*, 1928, p. 43.

32 R.S. Stanier, *Magdalen School* (Oxford, 2nd ed. 1958) and D.L.L. Clarke, *Magdalen School: Five Hundred Years On* (Oxford, 1980).

33 For Hereford see Jill Howard-Jones, *From Teddy Tail Collars to Itchy Tights* (Almeley, 1998), *passim*, and G. Aylmer and J. Tiller, *Hereford Cathedral: A History* (London, 2000), esp. pp. 597f.

34 Collard, Ogden and Burgess, *'Fat Black Canons'*, pp. 64ff, 80–86, 122, 125 and 135.

35 'I do not usually think before I speak', Alan Quilter wrote of himself. 'I speak in order to know what I think.' Colchester, Tudway Quilter and Quilter, *Wells Cathedral School*, p. 145.

36 Ibid., pp. 44–53 and 152f.

37 For Southwell Minster School see *Choir Schools Today*, xx, 2006, p. 45.

38 *Public Schools Commission, First Report* (London, 1968), I, pp. 134 and 190.

39 It must be made clear that choristers at these schools are not beneficiaries of this government grant, but receive scholarships from the foundations, often supplemented by government-funded bursaries administered by the Choir Schools' Association.

40 Information chiefly derived from Chetham's School's prospectus and website.

41 Colchester, Tudway Quilter and Quilter, *Wells Cathedral School*, pp. 134–140.

42 Philip Crosfield, *Songs and Stones* (Edinburgh, 1996), pp. 31ff. St Mary's enjoys a unique funding scheme, achieved with the help of the Scottish Education Department by way of an exclusive Order in Parliament.

43 *Choir Schools Directory*, 1928, pp. 64f.

44 For Charles Groves, see *The Choir Schools Review* (1982), p. 14f and *ODNB*, 24, pp. 124f.

Notes to Chapter 15: Threats and Support

1 Sydney Nicholson, *Choirs and Places where they Sing* (London, 1932), p. 54.

2 For the 1918 Education Act see Lawrence Andrews, *The Education Act, 1918* (London, 1976). Other sources used for this and the following paragraph are referred to in the text.

3 In the 1920s and 1930s the Burnham Committee actually imposed salary reductions.

4 Early inspection reports in TNA ED 109 indicate that, of schools educating choristers, only Hereford (ref 1975) and Peterborough (ref 4901) had gained approval prior to the Fisher Act. Gloucester had sought approval in 1906 and failed to achieve it. The grammar schools of Worcester and Rochester cathedrals were recognised as efficient in 1905 and 1907 respectively, but neither at that time educated their choristers. The benefits made available by the Fisher Act, most especially the superannuation scheme, greatly stimulated applications for recognition, including in the 1930s by several of the preparatory choir schools.

5 St Paul's Cathedral Choristers' Magazine, February 1919.

6　For Charles Jelf, see R.J.Henderson, *A History of King's College Choir School, Cambridge* (Cambridge, 1981), pp. 55ff.

7　A group of church musicians under the chairmanship of Sir John Stainer had met in 1897, concerned about the poor standard generally of music in the Church of England. This group, that did not reconvene after 1900, was the precursor of the later Church Music Society.

8　*Music in Worship* (Report of the Archbishops' Committee appointed in May 1922, quoted from 4th ed. London, 1947), p. 25.

9　Canon Stuart Pearson kindly supplied me with his 'Memoirs of a Chorister at Lichfield, 1939–41' from the *Lichfield Cathedral School Magazine*, 2004, pp. 1–7.

10　My source has been the second edition: *Music in Church: the Report of the Committee appointed in 1948 by the Archbishops of Canterbury and York* (London, 1957).

11　Roger McGough, *Watchwords* (London, 1969), p. 30.

12　Humphrey Clucas, 'Communion', in *Gods and Mortals* (Liskeard, 1983), p. 30.

13　Alan Webster, 'Cathedrals and Growth', in Alex Wedderspoon, *Grow or Die* (London, 1981), pp. 58–70.

14　The first quotation is from the pen of Horace Dammers, dean of Bristol, himself responsible for a choir school, in the journal *Cathedral*, 1982; the Eric James reference has been mislaid.

15　Shirley Williams, *Politics Is For People* (Harmondsworth, 1981), p. 158. For this and the previous paragraph I have drawn heavily on my essay 'Choirs and Spaces where they Cling', *The World of Church Music, 1982*, pp. 7–17, subsequently republished separately by RSCM.

16　Jack Straw, M.P., House of Commons press notice, embargoed to 17 May 1989. All other details in this paragraph are drawn from the Choir Schools' Association Minutes Book at the relevant dates.

17　The history of the Federation of Cathedral Old Choristers' Associations is recorded in the FCOCA's booklet *Organizing a Festival or AGM* (York, 1996). I owe access to this to the kindness of its author, David F. Horner.

18　Information from the Friends of Cathedral Music's fortieth anniversary leaflet, *The Past the Present the Future* (London, 1996).

19　Statutory Instrument 1995, no. 2018.

20　1996, c. 56.

21　*In Tune with Heaven: The Report of the Archbishops' Commission on Church Music* (London, 1992). The section on cathedral music runs from p. 215 to p. 227.

22　This is what Stephen Cleobury told the author.

23　Crosby, *Come on, Choristers!*, p. 64.

Notes to Chapter 16: Choristership

1　Brian Crosby, *Come On, Choristers!* (Durham, 1999), p. 86.

2　Windsor recollections that follow in this chapter are from an imaginative series of three volumes of archive and invited reminiscences published privately in 2000 and 2001 by the former headmaster of St George's School, Richard Russell, CVO. The titles, 'Carven Arch',

'Soaring Vault' and 'Storied Banner' are taken from a line of the school hymn. For the extracts in this paragraph see Richard Russell, *Carven Arches* (Bray, 2000), pp. 55ff. (Peter Clissold, chorister 1913–17) and p. 71 (F.J. Collins, chorister 1920–25).

3   Jonathan Edmunds, *New College Brats* (Oxford, 1996), p. 57.

4   Russell, *Soaring Vault* (Bray, 2001), p. 8 (recollection of Canon G.G. Griffith) and p. 22 (John Barkham, chorister, 1930–?).

5   Russell, *Carven Arches*, p. 75.

6   Graham Kalton, *The Public Schools: a Factual Survey* (London, 1966), pp. 124–27 and Appendix 1, pp. 143–45.

7   *Public Schools Commission* (London, 1968), i, pp. 115f.

8   Russell, *Soaring Vault*, p. 71 (Myron Kok, chorister, 1939–44).

9   For Fiddian's headship at King's see R.J. Henderson, *A History of King's College Choir School, Cambridge* (Cambridge, 1981), pp. 67–81.

10 Canterbury, York and Lichfield holiday dates from the *Choir Schools Directory*, 1928, *passim*. Windsor arrangements from Russell, *Carven Arches*.

11 See the acknowledgement of this sort of help in *Tradition and Renewal*.

12 Russell, *Carven Arches*, pp. 29 and 33.

13 Richard Russell, *Storied Banner* (Bray, 2001), pp. 16 and 21.

14 The figure was gathered for an English Heritage survey; the quoted phrase is from Grace Davie in Stephen Platten and Christopher Lewis (eds), *Dreaming Spires* (London, 2006), p. 150.

15 Information on the Outreach programme is taken directly from the annual report for 2006 of the Choir Schools' Association's development director, Richard White, supplemented by individual reports in recent editions of *Choir Schools Today*. For 'Future Talent' see *Choir Schools Today*, xix, 2005, pp. 7f.

16 John Crook, *A History of the Pilgrims' School* (Chichester, 1981), pp. 51f.

17 *Choir Schools Today*, i, 1986, pp. 31f.

18 *NGD*, xxi, pp. 7f.

19 Peter Martland, *Since Records Began* (London, 1997), pp. 40f.

20 Ibid., p. 82.

21 The list is derived from the Friends of Cathedral Music pamphlet, *Singing in Cathedrals 2006*.

22 The author was there at one such and failed along with the best.

23 For Richard Seal's decision and views, see R. Seal, 'The Girls in Sarum Green', *Cathedral Music*, 1991, pp. 22–28. For the objections to girl choristers see Roger Bowers, 'The Strangler Fig', *Cathedral Music*, i/2000, pp. 8–11. For the benefits, a decade on, see Lindsay Gray, 'Cathedral Girl Choristers: a Personal View', *Cathedral Music*, ii/2004, pp. 24–26.

24 Choir Schools' Association Survey, May 1996.

25 *Choir Schools Today*, xviii, 2004, p. 37.

26 For this field, see particularly David Hill, Hilary Parfitt and Elizabeth Ash, *Giving Voice* (Rattlesden, 1995).

27 John Crook, *A History of the Pilgrims' School* (Chichester, 1981), p. 50.

28 The story kindly recounted to me by a clearly unrepentant though now reverend Anthony Curry.

29   Jon Snow, *Shooting History* (London, 2004, pbk. edn., 2005), pp. 21–25.

30   Keenlyside in conversation with Ian Burnside, BBC Radio 3, October 2004.

31   The culprit is, of course, wonderful Psalm 78.

32   As quoted in his *Times* obituary.

33   Howard Goodall, 'The Chorister Thing', *Choir Schools Today*, xx, 2006, p. 4.

Note to Appendix 1

1   The Middle English word for what the girls had been up to is 'rouning': whispering or gossiping. [R.E. Lewis (ed), *Middle English Dictionary* (Ann Arbor, Michigan, 1984)]. Chaucer has Pyramus and Thisbe 'rouning' to each other through the chink in the wall.

Note to Appendix 2

1   E. Brennecke Jn., 'A Day at Christ Church, 1573', *Music and Letters*, 19 (1938), pp. 22–35. For John Milton snr see the article by Gordon Campbell in *ODNB*, 38, pp. 332f. The only authority for believing John Milton snr to have been a Christ Church chorister is John Aubrey. Milton did, however, add to his profession of scrivener a very active musical life, including the composition of some twenty anthems, probably for domestic rather than liturgical use; and he ensured that his poet son grew up with a love of music.

Bibliography

The two bibliographies, one of general works and one of works specific to individual choral foundations, contain details of published books referred to in the endnotes. For information about unpublished manuscript and printed sources, pamphlets, articles from journals and periodicals, published music, recorded music and websites, reference should be made to the endnotes.

BIBLIOGRAPHY: GENERAL

The Book of Common Prayer ... According to the Use of the Church of England (1662, and frequently reissued subsequently).

The Choir Schools' Directory (London, periodically issued, 1925–1972).

Common Worship (London, 2000).

Independent Schools Year Book, formerly *Public and Preparatory Schools Year Book* (London, published annually).

New Grove Dictionary of Music and Musicians (ed. Stanley Sadie), 20 vols (London, 2nd edn, 2001). [*NGD* in endnotes.]

Oxford Dictionary of National Biography, 60 vols (Oxford, 2004). [*ODNB* in endnotes.]

Parliamentary Papers: *Report of the Commissioners on Cathedral and Collegiate Churches* (London, 1854).

Parliamentary Papers: *Report of Her Majesty's Commissioners for Enquiring into the Condition of Cathedral Churches in England and Wales* (London, 1882–84).

Alcuin (ed. Levinson, W.), *Alcuinus, Vita Willibrordi* (Hanover and Leipzig, 1919).

Alexandre-Bidon, Daniele and Lett, Didier (trans. Gladding, Jody), *Children in the Middle Ages: Fifth-Fifteenth Centuries* (Notre Dame, Indiana, 1999).

Andrews, Lawrence, *The Education Act, 1918* (London, 1976).

Anglo, Sydney, *Spectacle, Pageantry and Early Tudor Policy* (Oxford, 2nd edn, 1997).

Archbishops' Commission (1948), *Music in Church* (London, 1957).

Archbishops' Commission (1992), *In Tune with Heaven* (London, 1992).

Archbishops' Committee (1922), *Music in Worship* (London, 1922, 4th edn, 1947).

Armytage, W.H.G., *Four Hundred Years of English Education* (Cambridge, 2nd edn, 1970).

Arnold, Ralph, *The Whiston Matter* (London, 1961).

Arnold Forster, F., *Studies in Church Dedications*, 3 vols. (London, 1899).

Ashbee, Andrew, *Lists of Payments to the King's Musick in the Reign of Charles II* (Snodland, 1981).

Ashbee, Andrew, *Records of English Court Music*, 5 vols (Aldershot, 1986–91).

Austern, Linda P., *Music in English Children's Drama in the Later Renaissance* (Philadelphia, Pennsylvania, 1992).

Balthasar, Hans Urs von, *The Glory of the Lord: A Theological Aesthetics*, 7 vols (Edinburgh, 1985–89).

Banks, M.M. (ed.), *An Alphabet of Tales: A Fifteenth-century Translation of Alphabetum Narrationem of Etienne de Besancon* (London, 1904–5).

Barlow, Frank, *The English Church 1008–1066* (London, 2nd edn, 1979).

Barrett, Philip, *Barchester: English Cathedral Life in the Nineteenth Century* (London, 1993).

Baskerville, Geoffrey, *English Monks and the Suppression of the Monasteries* (London, 1937).

Baxter, J.H. and Johnson, C., *Medieval Latin Word-List* (Oxford, 1934).

Becon, Thomas, *The Seconde Parte of the Bokes which Thomas Beacon Hath Made* (London, 1560).

Bede, *Historia Ecclesiastica* (ed. Sherley Price, Leo, as *A History of the English Church and People*) (Harmondsworth, 1955).

Benedict, St (ed. McCann, Justin) *The Rule of St Benedict in Latin and English* (London, 1951).

Berlin, Isaiah, *Historical Inevitability* (Oxford, 1954).

Bishop, E., *Liturgica Historica* (Oxford, 1918).

Boden, A., *Three Choirs: A History of the Festival* (Gloucester, 1992).

Bowers, Roger, *English Church Polyphony* (Variorum Collected Studies Series, Aldershot, 1999).

Bradshaw, H. and Wordsworth, C. (eds), *Lincoln Cathedral Statutes*, 2 vols. (Cambridge, 1897). The texts in these volumes by no means exclusively concern Lincoln.

Brewer, A.H., *Memories of Choirs and Cloisters* (?London, 1931).

Brewer, J.S., Gairdner J. and Brodie, eds, *Letters and Papers (Foreign and Domestic): Henry VIII* (London, 1862–1910).

Brinkley, R.F., *Nathan Field, the Actor-Playwright* (Yale, New Hampshire, and Oxford, 1928).

Brown, David, *Thomas Weelkes* (London, 1969).

Brown, R. (ed.), *Calendar of State Papers (Venetian)*, 38 vols (London, 1869–1947).

Bumpus, John S., *A History of English Cathedral Music, 1549–1889*, 2 vols. (London, 1908; reprinted in facsimile by Gregg International, 1972).

Burney, Charles, *General History of Music* (London, 1776).

Butler, Charles, *The Principles of Musik* (London, 1641).

Byng, John (ed. Bruyn Andrews, C.), *The Torrington Diaries* (London, 1934, reprinted New York and London, 1970).

Chadwick, Owen, *The Victorian Church*, 2 vols (London, 1987).

Chambers, E.K., *The Medieval Stage*, 2 vols (Oxford, 1903).

Chambers, E.K., *The Elizabethan Stage*, 4 vols (London, 1923).

Charlton, Kenneth, *Education in Renaissance England* (London, 1965).

Charlton, Peter, *John Stainer* (Newton Abbot, 1984).

Chaucer, William, *The Canterbury Tales*: ed. Benson, L.D., *The Riverside Chaucer* (Oxford, 3rd edn, 1988); ed. Burrell, A. (London, 1948); ed. Coghill, N. (Harmondsworth, 1951); ed. Skeat, W.W., *The Prioresses Tale* (Oxford, 1916).

Church Music Society, *Choral Foundations in the Church of England* (London, 1924).

Church Music Society, *Forty Years of Cathedral Music, 1898–1938* (London, 1940).

Church Music Society (*The) Present State of Cathedral Music* (London, 1934).

Church Music Society, *Sixty Years of Cathedral Music* (London, 1963).

Clarke, M.L., *Paley: Evidences for the Man* (London, 1974).

Clucas, Humphrey, *Gods and Mortals* (Liskeard, 1983).

Collins Baker, C.H. and Baker, Muriel I., *The Life and Circumstances of James Brydges, First Duke of Chandos* (Oxford, 1949).

Collinson, Patrick, *From Iconoclasm to Iconophobia* (Reading, 1986).

Collinson, Patrick, *English Puritanism* (Historical Association Pamphlet G106) (London, 1983).

Conway Davies, J. (ed.), *Studies Presented to Sir Hilary Jenkinson* (Oxford, 1957).

Cook, G.H., *Medieval Chantries and Chantry Chapels* (London, 2nd edn, 1963).

Cox, J. D. and Kastan, D.S. (eds), *A New History of Early English Drama* (New York, 1997).

Cragg, G. R., *The Church and the Age of Reason* (Harmondsworth, 1960).

Creighton, L., *Life and Letters of Mandell Creighton* (London, 1904).

Cunningham, P., *Extracts from the Accounts of the revels at Court, in the Reigns of Queen Elizabeth and King James I, from the Original Office Books of the Masters and Yeomen* (London, 1842).

Curtis, S.J., *History of Education in Great Britain* (London, 2nd edn, 1950).

Davies, Horton, *Worship and Theology in England*, 6 bks in 3 vols (Grand Rapids, Michigan, and Cambridge, 1996).

Deanesly, Margaret, *History of the Medieval Church* (London, 6th edn, 1950).

Dearnley, Christopher, *English Church Music 1650–1750* (London, 1970).

De Lafontaine, L.C., *The King's Music* (London, 1909, reprint New York, 1973).

De Vogue, Adalbert and Philippi, Charles (ed., Eberle, Luke) *The Rule of the Master: Regula Magistri* (Kalamazoo, Michigan, 1977).

Diack Johnstone, H. and Fiske, Roger (eds), *The Eighteenth Century* (Blackwell History of Music, 4) (Oxford, 1990).

Dibdin, Charles, *The Professional Life of Mr Dibdin Written by Himself* (London, 1803).

Dickens, A.G., *The English Reformation* (London, rev. edn, 1967).

Dix, Dom Gregory, *The Shape of the Liturgy* (Westminster, 2nd edn, 1945).

Doe, Paul, *Tallis* (Oxford, 2nd edn, 1976).

Duchesne, L. (trans. McClure, M.L.), *Christian Worship: Its Origins and Evolution* (London, 1927).

Duffy, Eamon, *The Stripping of the Altars* (New Haven, Connecticut, and London, 1992).

Eberle, Luke, De Vogue, Adalbert and Philippi, Charles (eds), *The Rule of the Master: Regula Magistri* (Kalamazoo, Michigan, 1977).

Edwards, Kathleen, *The English Secular Cathedrals of the Middle Ages* (Manchester, 2nd edn, 1967).

Egeria (ed. Gingras, G.E.), *Egeria: Diary of a Pilgrimage* (New York, 1970).

Ekwall, E., *Oxford Dictionary of English Place-Names* (Oxford, 4th edn, 1960).

Evelyn, John, *Diary* (No edition specified in endnotes.).

Faber, Geoffrey, *Oxford Apostles* (London, 1933, rev. Harmondsworth, 1954).

Fassler, M.E. and Baltzer, R.A., *The Divine Office in the Latin Middle Ages* (Oxford, 2000).

Fellowes, E.H. (rev. Westrup, J.A.), *English Cathedral Music* (London, 1969; pb., 1973).

Fellowes, E.H., *Memoirs of an Amateur Musician* (London, 1946).

(The) First and Second Prayer Books of Edward VI (London, 1910).

Frere, W.H. (ed.): for his editions of Sarum Use documents, see under Bibliography: Individual Foundations: Salisbury.

Frere, W.H. and Douglas, C.E. (ed. Sykes, Norman), *Puritan Manifestoes* (C.H.S., 1954).

Frere, W.H. and Kennedy, W.McC. (eds), *Visitation Articles and Injunctions of the Period of the Reformation*, 3 vols (London, 1910).

Friends of Cathedral Music, *The Past the Present the Future* (London, 1996).

Garmonsway, G.N. (ed.), *The Anglo-Saxon Chronicle* (London, 1960).

Gaventa, B.R., *Mary* (Edinburgh, 1999).

Graef, Hilda, *Mary: A History of Doctrine and Devotion* (London, 1963).

Greenway, D., Holdsworth, C. and Sayers J. (eds.), *Tradition and Change* (Cambridge, 1985).

Hackett, Maria, *A Brief Account of the Cathedral and Collegiate Schools*, privately published (London, 1st edn.,1827, and periodically revised into the 1870s).

Hall, Edward (ed. Whibley, Charles), *Chronicle of the Reign of Henry VIII* (London, 1904).

Hall, Richard and Stocker, David (eds), *Vicars Choral at English Cathedrals* (Oxford, 2005).

Hamilton, W.K., *Cathedral Reform* (London, 1855).

[Hammond, Lieutenant] in Anon. (ed. J. Wickham Legg), *Breife Description* of his 'Northern tour' of 1634 and *Relation of a Short Survey of the Western Counties*, his 'Western tour' of 1635, *Camden Miscellany*, 16 (London, 1936).

Harley, John, *Music in Purcell's London* (London, 1968).

Harley, John, *William Byrd: Gentleman of the Chapel Royal* (Aldershot, 1997).

Harley, John, *Orlando Gibbons* (Aldershot, 1999).

Harpur, John, *The Forms and Orders of Western Liturgy from the Tenth to the Eighteenth Century* (Oxford, 1991).

Harrison, Frank Ll., *Music in Medieval Britain* (2nd edn, London, 1963).

Hawkins, John, *A General History of the Science and Practice of Music*, 5 vols (London, 1776), 2 vols (London, 2nd edn, 1875, repr. 1963).

Hayburn, Robert F., *Papal Legislation on Sacred Music, 95 AFD to 1977 AD* (Collegeville, Masachusetts, 1979).

Hiley, David, *Western Plainchant: A Handbook* (Oxford, 1993).

Hill, Christopher, *Society and Puritanism in Pre-Revolutionary England* (London, 1964).

Hill, David, Parfitt, Hilary and Ash, Elizabeth, *Giving Voice* (Rattlesden, 1995).

Hillebrand, H.N., *The Child Actors*, University of Illinois Studies in Language and Literature, xi, 1 (Urbana, Illinois, 1926; freestanding reprint, New York, 1997).

Hogwood, C. and Luckett, R. (eds), *Music in Eighteenth-Century England* (Cambridge, 1983).

Hooker, Richard (ed. R. Bayne), *On the Laws of Ecclesiastical Polity* (London, 1902).

Howson, J.S. (ed.), *Essays on Cathedrals* (London, 1872).

Hughes, P.E., *Theology of the English Reformers* (London, 1965).

Kalton, Graham, *The Public Schools: a Factual Survey* (London, 1966).

King, Robert, *Henry Purcell* (London, 1994).

Kitton, F.G., *Zechariah Buck, Mus. D., A Centenary Memoir* (London, 1899).

Knowles, Dom David, *The Monastic Order in England, 943–1216* (Cambridge, 1940).

Knowles, Dom David and Hadcock, R.N., *Medieval Religious Houses: England and Wales* (London, 1953).

Lanfranc (ed. Knowles, David), *The Monastic Constitutions of Lanfranc* (London, 1951).

Leach, A.F., *Educational Charters and Documents, 598–1909* (Cambridge, 1911).

Le Goff, J. (trs. Goldhammer, A.), *The Birth of Purgatory* (London, 1984).

Lehmburg, S.E., *Cathedrals under Siege* (Exeter, 1996).

le Huray, Peter, *Music and the Reformation in England (1549–1660)* (Cambridge, 1978).

Leinster-Mackay, Donald, *The Rise of the English Prep School* (London, 1984).

Long, K.R., *The Music of the English Church* (London, 2nd edn, 1991).

Lyly, John (ed. David Bevington), *Endymion* (Manchester, 1996).

Lyly, John (ed. G.K. Hunter), *Galatea and* (ed. David Bevington), *Midas* (Manchester, 2000).

McGee, Timothy J., *The Sound of Medieval Song* (Oxford, 1998).

Mace, Thomas, *Musick's Monument* (1676, facsimile, Paris, 1958).

Malcolm, J.P., *Londinium Redevivum* (London, 1803).

Marcombe, D. and Knighton, C.S., *Close Encounters* (Nottingham, 1991).

'Marprelate, Martin' (ed. William Pierce), *Marprelate Tracts* (London, 1911).

Marston, John (ed. Gair, R.), *Antonio and Mellida* (Manchester, 1991).

Martland, Peter, *Since Records Began* (London, 1997).

'Master, The' (ed.) Eberle, L., de Vogue, A. and Philippi, C., *The Rule of the Master: Regula Magistri* (Kalamazoo, Michigan, 1977).

Mertes, Kate, *The English Noble Household, 1250–1600* (Oxford, 1988).

Migne, J.P.(ed.), *Patrologiae cursus completus, series Latina* (Paris, 1844–64).

Millard, J.E., *Historical Notices of the Office of Choristers* (London, 1848).

Morehen, J. (ed.), *English Choral Practice, 1400–1650* (Cambridge, 1995).

Napier, A.S. (ed.), *The Enlarged Rule of Chrodegang* (London, 1916).

Nicholson, Sydney H., *Peter: The Adventures of a Chorister* (London, 1944, republished, Capella Archives, Malvern, 2002).

Nicholson, Sydney H., *Quires and Places Where They Sing* (London, 1932).

North, Roger (ed. Wilson, John), *Roger North on Music* (London, 1959).

Orme, Nicholas, *Education and Society in Medieval and Renaissance England* (London, 1989).

Orme, Nicholas, *English Schools in the Middle Ages* (London, 1973).

Payne, Ian, *The Provision and Practice of Sacred Music at Cambridge Colleges and Selected Cathedrals, c. 1547–1646* (New York and London, 1993).

Pearce, E.H., *The Sons of the Clergy, 1655–1904* (London, 1904).

Peel, A. (ed.), *The Seconde Parte of a Register*, 2 vols (Cambridge, 1915).

Pepys, Samuel, *Diary* (No edition specified in the endnotes.)

Percy, Thomas (ed.), *The Regulations and Establishments of the Household of Henry Algernon Percy, Fifth Earl of Northumberland* (privately printed, 1770, 1877 and 1905).

Pevsner, N. (rev. Cherry, Bridget) *The Buildings of England: Hertfordshire* (Harmondsworth, 2nd edn, 1977).

Pfaff, Richard, *Liturgical Calendars: Saints and Services in Medieval England* (Aldershot, 1998).

Pierce, William, *Historical Introduction to the Marprelate Tracts* (London, 1908).

Power, Eileen, *Medieval English Nunneries* (Cambridge, 1922).

Powicke, F.M., Johnson, Charles and Harte, W.J. (eds), *Handbook of British Chronology* (London, 1939).

Public Schools Commission, *First Report* (London, 1968).

Quinn, Patricia, *Better than the Sons of Kings* (New York, 1989).

Rainbow, Bernarr, *The Choral Revival in the Anglican Church (1839–1872)* (London, 1970).

Riley, H.T. (ed.), *Gesta Abbatum Sancti Albani*, in *Chronica Monasterii Sancti Albani*, 12 vols (London, 1863–76).

Riley, H.T. (ed.), *Ingulph's History of the Abbey of Croyland* (London, 1854).

Rimbault, E.F., *Two Sermons Preached by the Boy Bishop* (Camden Miscellany, 7) (London, 1875).

Robertson, Anne Walters, *The Service-Books of the Royal Abbey of St. Denis: Images of Ritual and Music in the Middle Ages* (Oxford, 1991).

Routley, Erik *(A) Short History of English Church Music* (London, 1977).

Routley, Erik, *Twentieth-Century Church Music* (London, 1964).

Rowse, A.L., *The England of Elizabeth* (London, 1950).

Russell, J.G., *The Field of the Cloth of Gold* (London, 1969).

Scarisbrick, J.J., *Henry VIII* (London, 1968).

Scholes, Percy, *The Puritans and Music* (Oxford, 1934).

Seton Watson, R.W., *Tudor Studies* (London, 1924).

Shahar, Shulamith, *Childhood in the Middle Ages* (London and New York, 1990).

Shakespeare, William, *Collected Plays* (No edition specified in endnotes.)

Shapiro, Michael, *Children of the Revels* (New York, 1977).

Simon, Eckehard (ed.), *The Theatre of Medieval Europe: New Research in Early Drama* (Cambridge, 1991).

Simon, Joan, *Education and Society in Tudor England* (Cambridge, 1966).

Smoldon, William L., *The Music of the Medieval Church Dramas* (Oxford, 1980).

Snow, Jon, *Shooting History* (London, 2004).

Spink, Ian, *Restoration Cathedral Music, 1660–1714* (Oxford, 1995).

Stanford, C.V., *Pages from an Unwritten Diary* (London, 1914).

Stenton, F.M., *Anglo-Saxon England* (Oxford, 3rd edn. 1971).

Stevens, J., *Music and Poetry in the Early Tudor Court* (Cambridge, 1979).

Stevens, R.J.S. (ed. Argent, Mark), *Recollections of R.J.S. Stevens* (London and Basingstoke, 1992).

Stranks, C.J., *Anglican Devotion* (London, 1961).

Strunk, Oliver, *Source Readings in Music History* (London, 1952).

Swanson, R.N. (ed.), *The Church and Mary* (Studies in Church History, 39) (Woodbridge, 2004).

Swanson, R.N. (ed.), *Continuity and Change in Christian Worship* (Woodbridge, 1999).

Sylvester, D.W., *Educational Documents, 800–1816* (London, 1970).

Symons, Dom Thomas (ed.), *Regularis Concordia* (London, 1953).

Tanner, J. R., *Tudor Constitutional Documents* (Cambridge, 1948).

Temperley, Nicholas, *The Music of the English Parish Church* (Cambridge, 1979).

Thompson, A.H., *Song Schools in the Middle Ages* (London and Oxford, 1942).

Thompson, B. (ed.), *Monasteries and Society in Medieval Britain* (Harlaxton Symposium, 6) (Stamford, 1999).

Torrington, Lord: see Byng, John.

Tuckwell, William, *Reminiscences of Oxford* (London, 1900).

Tusser, Thomas (ed. Payne, W. and Herrtage, S.J.), *Thomas Tusser's Five Hundred Pointes of Good Husbandrie* (London, 1878).

Varley, E.A., *The Last of the Prince Bishops* (Cambridge, 1992).

Walton, Izaak (ed. S.B. Carter), *Walton's Lives* (London, 1951).

Warton, T. (ed. Hazlitt, W.C.), *The History of English Poetry* (London, 1871).

Wathey, Andrew, *Music in the Royal and Noble Households in Late Medieval England* (New York and London, 1989).

Watkins Shaw, H., *Eighteenth-Century Cathedral Music* (Church Music Society Occasional Paper, 21) (Oxford, 1952).

Watkins Shaw, H., *The Succession of Organists of the Chapel Royal and the Cathedrals of England and Wales from c. 1538* (Oxford, 1991).

Watkins Shaw, H., *The Three Choirs Festival* (Worcester and London, 1954).

Wedderspoon, Alex (ed.), *Grow or Die* (London, 1981).

Wesley, S.S., *A Few Words on Cathedral Music* (London, 1849, reprint, 1975).

Westfall, S.R., *Patrons and Performance: Early Tudor Revels* (Oxford, 1990).

Wharton, T.F., *The Critical Fall and Rise of John Marston* (Columbia, South Carolina, 1994).

White, D.J., *Richard Edwards' Damon and Pithias* (New York, 1966).

Wilkes, Roger, *English Cathedrals and Collegiate Churches and Chapels: Their Music, Musicians and Musical Establishments: a select bibliography* (Friends of Cathedral Music, 1968).

Wilkins, D. (ed.), *Concilia* (London, 1737).

Williams, Shirley, *Politics Is for People* (Harmondsworth, 1981).

Wood, Diana (ed.), *The Church and the Arts* (Studies in Church History, 28) (Oxford, 1995).

Wood, Diana (ed.), *The Church and Childhood* (Studies in Church History, 31) (Oxford, 1998).

Wood, Margaret, *The English Medieval House* (London, 1950 and 1983).

Woodfield, Ian, *The Early History of the Viol* (Cambridge, 1984).

Woodfill, W.L., *Musicians in English Society from Elizabeth to Charles I* (Princeton, New Jersey, 1953).

Wood-Legh, K.L., *Perpetual Chantries in Britain* (Cambridge, 1965).

Wordsworth, C. (ed.), *Horae Eboracenses: The Prymer or Hours of the Blessed Virgin Mary* (Surtees Society, 132) (Durham and London, 1920).

Workman, H.B., *John Wyclif*, 2 vols (Oxford, 1926).

Wright, Craig, *Music and Ceremony at Notre Dame of Paris, 500–1550* (Cambridge, 1989).

Wright, Susan (ed.), *Parish, Church and People* (London, 1988).

Wulstan, David, *Tudor Music* (London, 1985).

Wynn Jones, David (ed.), *Music in Eighteenth-Century Britain* (Aldershot, 2000).

Yeats-Edwards, Paul, *English Church Music: a Bibliography* (London, 1975).

Yorke, Barbara, *Wessex in the Early Middle Ages* (Leicester, 1995).

Young, Karl, *The Drama of the Medieval Church*, 2 vols (Oxford, 1933).

BIBLIOGRAPHY: INDIVIDUAL FOUNDATIONS

Bangor

Clarke, M.L., *Bangor Cathedral* (Cardiff, 1969).

Paul, Leslie D., *Music at Bangor Cathedral Church* (Bangor Cathedral Monograph, 1) (Bangor, 1971, 2nd reprint 1975).

Bristol

Collard, J., Ogden D. and Burgess, R., *'Where the Fat Black Canons Dined': A History of Bristol Cathedral School 1140–1992* (Bristol, 1992).

Morgan, E.T., *History of Bristol Cathedral School* (Bristol, 1913).

Cambridge, King's College

Henderson, R.J., *A History of King's College Choir School, Cambridge* (Cambridge, 1981).
Saltmarsh, J., *King's College and its Chapel* (Cambridge, 1969).

Cambridge, St John's College

Guest, George, *A Guest at Cambridge* (Cape Cod, Massachusetts, rev. ed., 1998).
Miller, Edward, *Portrait of a College* (Cambridge, 1961).

Canterbury

Brooks, Nicholas, *The Early History of the Church of Canterbury* (Leicester, 1984).
P. Collinson, N. Ramsay and M. Sparks (eds), *A History of Canterbury Cathedral* (Oxford, 1995).
Deanesly, Margaret, 'The Familia at Christ Church, Canterbury', in *Essays in Medieval History Presented to T.F. Tout* (Manchester, 1925).
Edwards, D.L., *History of the King's School, Canterbury* (London, 1957).
Graham, Rose (ed.), *Registrum Roberti Winchelsey, Cantuariensis archiepiscopi* (Canterbury and York Society, 1946).
The Statutes of the Cathedral and Metropolitical Church of Christ Church, Canterbury (Canterbury, 1926).
Woodruff, C.E. and Danks, W., *Memorials of Canterbury Cathedral* (London, 1912).

Chester

Burne, R.V.H., *Chester Cathedral* (London, 1958).

Chichester

Hobbs, Mary (ed.), *Chichester Cathedral: an Historical Survey* (Chichester, 1994).
Ollerenshaw, Neville, *A History of the Prebendal School* (Chichester, 1984).
(For Brown, D. *Thomas Weelkes*, see Bibliography: General.)

Crowland/Croyland

Riley, H.T. (ed), *Ingulf's History of the Abbey of Croyland* (London, 1854).

Durham

Crosby, Brian, *Come on Choristers!: A History of the Chorister School, Durham* (Durham, 1999).
Crosby, Brian, *Durham Cathedral Choristers and Their Masters* (Durham, 1980).
Fowler, J.T. (ed.), *The Rites of Durham* (Surtees Soc., 107) (London, 1903).
Horseman, A.E., *Dobsons Drie Bobbes* (Durham, 1953).
Stranks, C.J., *This Sumptuous Church* (London, 1973).
(For E.A. Varley's study of Van Mildert see the General Bibliography.)

Edinburgh

Crosfield, Philip, *Songs and Stones: The Story of St Mary's Cathedral, Palmerston Place, Edinburgh* (Edinburgh, 1996).
Townhill, Dennis, *The Imp and the Thistle: The Story of a Life of Music Making* (Edinburgh, 2000).

Ely

Anon., *King's School, Ely: a collection of documents* ... (Cambridge Antiquarian Records Society, 1989).
Evans, S.J.A., *Ely Chapter Ordinances* (Camden Miscellany, 17) (London, 1940).
Evans, S.J.A., 'Ely Almonry Boys and Choristers in the Middle Ages', in Davies, J. Conway (ed.), *Studies Presented to Sir Hilary Jenkinson* (London, 1957), pp. 159 ff.
Ikin, R.G., *Notes on the History of Ely Cathedral Grammar School or the King's School, Ely* (Cambridge, 1931).
Saunders, R.G., *The King's School, Ely, 970–1970* (Ely, 1970).

Eton

Maxwell Lyte, Sir H.G., *A History of Eton College, 1440–1910* (London, 4th edn, 1910).
Mellor, Albert, *Music and Musicians of Eton College* (Windsor, 1929).

Exeter

Hungeston-Randolph, F.C. (ed.), *Register of Walter Bronscombe, Bishop of Exeter* (London, 1889).
(For the Enlarged Rule of Chrodegang, see Napier, R.S. in the General Bibliography.)

Gloucester

Eward, Dorothy, *No Fine but a Glass of Wine* (Wilton, 1985).
Robertson, David, *The King's School, Gloucester* (Chichester, 1974).

Guildford

Carpenter, Simon, *The Beat Is Irrelevant* (Guildford, 1996).

Hereford

Aylmer, Gerald and Tiller, John (eds), *Hereford Cathedral: A History* (London, 2000).
Howard-Jones, Jill, *From Teddy Tail Collars to Itchy Tights* (Logaston Press, 1998).

Leicester

Hamilton Thompson, A., *The History of the Hospital and the New College of the Annunciation of St Mary in the Newalke at Leicester* (Leicester, 1937).

Lincoln

Foster, C.W. and Major, K., *The Registrum Antiquissimum of the Cathedral Church of Lincoln* (Lincoln, 1931).
Kirwan, A.L., *The Music of Lincoln Cathedral* (London, 1973).
Owen, D. (ed.), *A History of Lincoln Minster* (Cambridge, 1994).
Woodward, Reg, *Boy on a Hill* (Lincoln, 1984).
(For *Lincoln Cathedral Statutes* see under Bradshaw, H. and Wordsworth C. in the General Bibliography.)

Liverpool (Metropolitan Cathedral)

McGough, Roger, *Watchwords* (London, 1969).

Llandaff

Anon., *Brief Notes on the Cathedral School, Llandaff* (Landaff, 2001).

London, All Saints', Margaret Street

Forster, W.R., *The Choir School* (All Saints' Booklet Series, 2) (London, 1954).

London, The Chapel Royal

Ashbee, Andrew and Harley, John, *The Cheque Books of the Chapel Royal* (Aldershot, 2000).

Baldwin, David, *The Chapel Royal: Ancient and Modern* (London, 1990).

De Lafontaine, L.C., *The King's Musick* (London, 1909; reprint, New York, 1973).

Rimbault, E.F., *The Old Cheque Book of the Chapel Royal* (reprint, New York, 1996).

London, St Mary of the Angels' Song School

Morse-Boycott, Desmond, *A Golden Legend of the Slums* (London, 1951).

Morse-Boycott, Desmond, *A Pilgrimage of Song* (London, 1972).

Morse-Boycott, Desmond, *A Tapestry of Toil* (London, 1970).

London, St Paul's Cathedral

Frost, William, *Early Recollections of St Paul's Cathedral* (London, 1926).

Gair, Reavley, *The Children of Paul's* (Cambridge, 1982).

Gregory, Robert (ed. Hutton, W.H.), *Autobiography of Robert Gregory* (London, 1912).

Hackett, Maria, *Correspondence, Legal Proceedings and Evidences Respecting the Ancient School Attached to St Paul's Cathedral* (London, 1832, latest edn 1916).

Keene, D., Burns, A. and Saint, A. (eds), *St Paul's: The Cathedral Church of London, 604–2002* (New Haven, Connecticut, and London, 2004).

Matthews, W.R. and Atkins, W.M. (eds.), *A History of St Paul's Cathedral* (London, 1957).

Prestige, G.L., *St Paul's in its Glory (1831–1911)* (London, 1955).

(For *Recollections* of R.J.S. Stevens, see the General Bibliography.)

London, Westminster Abbey

Bridge, J.F., *A Westminster Pilgrim* (London, 1919).

Carpenter, Edward (ed.), *A House of Kings* (London, 1966).

Fellows, E.H., *The Music of Westminster* (London, 1927).

Perkins, Jocelyn, *Westminster Abbey: its Worship and Ornaments* (London, 1952).

Pine, Edward, *The Westminster Abbey Singers* (London, 1953).

Tatton-Brown, T. and Mortimer, R. (eds), *Westminster Abbey: the Lady Chapel of Henry VII* (Woodbridge, 2003).

London, Westminster Cathedral

Doyle, Peter, *Westminster Cathedral, 1895–1995* (London, 1995).

Newark-on-Trent

Brown, Cornelius, *A History of Newark-on-Trent*, 2 vols. (Newark, 1904 and 1907).

Norwich

Boston, J.N.T., *The Musical History of Norwich Cathedral* (Norwich, 1963).
Harries, Richard, Cattermole, P. and Mackintosh, P., *A History of Norwich School* (Norwich, 1991).
Tolhurst, J.B.L., *The Customary of the Cathedral Church of Norwich* (London, 1948).
(For Greatrex, Joan, 'The Almonry School of Norwich Cathedral Priory ...' in Wood, D. (ed.), *The Church and Childhood*, and for the memoir of Zechariah Buck by Kitton, F.G., see the General Bibliography.)

Oxford, Magdalen College

Clark, D.L.L., *Magdalen School: Five Hundred Years On* (Oxford, 1980).
Davis, Virginia, *William Wayneflete: Bishop and Educationalist* (Woodbridge, 1993).
Middleton, R.D., *Magdalen Studies* (London, 1936).
Stanier, R.S., *Magdalen School* (Oxford, 2nd edn, 1958).
[Tuckwell, L.S.], 'A Former Chorister', *Old Magdalen Days, 1831–1911* (Oxford, 1913).
(For William Tuckwell's reminiscences see the General Bibliography.)

Oxford, New College

Buxton, J. and Williams P. (eds), *New College, Oxford, 1379–1979* (Oxford, 1979).
Edmunds, Jonathan, *New College Brats: A History of the Life and Education of the Choristers of New College, Oxford* (Oxford, 1996).
(For William Tuckwell's reminiscences see the General Bibliography.)

Peterborough

Anon., *Peterborough Cathedral Choir* (Peterborough, 1968).
Larrett, W.D., *History of the King's School, Peterborough* (Peterborough, 1966).

Rochester

Cooper, H.G., *The Choristers of Rochester Cathedral (1679–1955)* (Chester, 3rd edn, 1999).
Coulson, L.H. (ed.), *History of the King's School, Rochester* (Rochester, 1989).
Johnson, R., *Rochester Cathedral Choir School: A Short History* (Chester, 1959).

Salisbury

Baxter, Phillip, *Sarum Use* (Salisbury, 1994).
W.H. Frere (ed.), *Antiphonale Sarisburiense* (London, 1901–24).
Frere, W.H. (ed.), *Graduale Sarisburiense* (London, 1894).
Frere W.H. (ed.), *The Sarum Ordinal* (Cambridge, 1898).
Frere, W.H. (ed.), *The Use of Sarum*, 2 vols. (Cambridge, 1898–1901).
Gascoyne, David, *Collected Poems 1988* (Oxford, 1988).
Henderson, W.G. (ed.), *Processionale ad Usum Insignis et Praeclare Eccelsiae Sarum* (Leeds, 1882).
Robertson, Dora, *Sarum Close* (London, 1938).
Ross, Christopher, *The Canons of Salisbury* (Salisbury, 2000).
Sandon, Nick, *The Use of Salisbury* (Antico Church Music, 6 vols, 1989–, continuing).
Smith, Peter L., *900 Years of Song: a Concise History of the Cathedral School, Salisbury* (Salisbury, *c.* 1992).
Stanton, W.K., *A Register of the Choristers' School, Salisbury, 1810–1921* (London, 1921).
Wickham Legg, J. (ed.), *The Sarum Missal Edited from Three Early Manuscripts* (Oxford, 1916, reprint, 1969).
Wordsworth, C., *Ceremonies and Processions of the Cathedral Church of Salisbury* (Cambridge, 1901).
Wordsworth, C. and Macleane, D. (eds.), *Statuta et Consuetudines Ecclesiae Cathedralis Beatae Mariae Virginis Sarisberiensis* (London, 1915).
(For Greenway, Diana, 'The False *Institutio* of St Osmund', see under Greenway, Holdsworth and Sayers in the General Bibliography.)

Southwell

James, W.A., *An Account of the Grammar School and Song Schools of the Collegiate Church of the Blessed Virgin Mary of Southwell* (Southwell, 1927).

Tenbury

Alderson, M.F. and Colles, H.C., *History of St. Michael's College, Tenbury* (London, 1943).
Bland, David, *Ouseley and his Angels: the Life of St.Michael's College, Tenbury and its Founder* (Eton, 2000).
Watkins Shaw, Harold (ed.), *Sir Frederick Ouseley and St Michael's College, Tenbury* (Birmingham, 1988).

Warwick

Leach, A.F., *History of Warwick School* (London, 1906).

Wells

Colchester, L.S., Tudway Quilter, David and Quilter, Alan, *A History of Wells Cathedral School* (Wells, *c.* 1986).

Winchester Cathedral

Bussby, Frederick, *Winchester Cathedral, 1079–1979* (Southampton, 1979).
Kitchin, G.W.(ed.), *The Obedientiary Rolls of St Swithun* (London, 1892).

Winchester, Cathedral and College

Crook, John, *The Pilgrims' School* (Chichester, 2nd ed. 1991).

Winchester College

Hooper, Patricia, *William Whiting* (Southampton, 1978).
Leach, A.F., *A History of Winchester College* (London, 1899).
Rannie, Alan, *The Story of Music at Winchester College, 1394–1969* (Winchester, 1970).

Windsor, St George's Chapel

Russell, Richard (ed.), *Carven Arches; Soaring Vault; Storied Banner* (published privately, 2000–2001).

Russell, Richard, *Headmaster, some reminiscences, 1971–1983* (published privately, *c.* 1984).

Thorndike, Russell, *Children of the Garter* (London, 1937).

Wridgway, Neville, *The Choristers of St. George's Chapel, Windsor Castle* (Windsor, 1980).

Worcester

Craze, Michael, *King's School, Worcester* (Worcester, 1972).

Roslington, Caroline (ed.), *The King's School, Worcester and a History of its Site* (Worcester, 1994).

York

Bass, Bernard and Ingamells, John (eds), *A Candidate for Praise, William Mason, 1725–97* (York, 1973).

Bell, C.C. (ed.), *Us and Our Song School, 627–1927* (York, 1931).

Holtby, Robert, *The Minster School, York: A Retrospect* (York, 1994).

Roden, John, *The Minster School, York: A Centenary History 1903–2004* (York, 2005) – not available for consultation by the author.

(For the *Horae Eboracenses* see under Wordsworth, C. in the General Bibliography.)

Index

Institutions such as abbeys, cathedrals, colleges and schools, also councils, edicts etc., are indexed under their location, e.g. St Paul's Cathedral under London, Council of Nicaea under Nicaea. Written works and compositions are indexed under their author or composer. The various Salisbury liturgical volumes (e.g. the *Processional*) are indexed under Sarum Use.